To My Sister, Trish
for being an inspiration
to us all and a chronicler
of the DC Chapter!
Oct 2004
K

D1616833

Tenleytown, D.C.

Country Village into City Neighborhood

Judith Beck Helm

Tennally Press
Washington, D.C.
1981
Second Edition, 2000

The written materials in this book, as well as the cover, photos, and sketches, are not to be used or reproduced without the consent of the author or the owner of the graphic material, as labeled. All rights reserved, including the right to reproduce this book or portions thereof in any form.

Copyright ©2000 by Judith Beck Helm
Published by Tennally Press
Library of Congress Control Number 00-090721
ISBN: 0-9606986-1-2
Printed in the United States of America by Kutztown Publishing Company

The cover illustration by Lily Spandorf is of the Chappell-McLaughlin house, Nebraska Avenue and Albemarle Street, torn down in 1999.

Title page:
(Photo c/o Gladys Smith Clemons)
The "Tenallytown" trolley, Car Number 1, as seen in the 1890s on Wisconsin Avenue in Tennallytown, heading back down to Georgetown. Hiliary Smith is the conductor on the back; the motorman up front is unidentified.

Contents

THE TENNALLY-LIGHTFOOT HOUSE
(See p. 143)

"THE REST," BUILT EARLY 1800s: 4343 39TH STREET
(See p. 249)

Introduction 2000

This book was originally published in 1981, and 3,000 copies were sold in the first few years. It has been out of print for more than ten years.

There is now a resurgence of interest in the history of the Tenleytown area by its newer residents, most specifically because some of its landmarks are disappearing.

The question is asked, can anything be done about the tearing down of old homes and stores? Can a school, church, library, or home be enlarged, remodeled, or even replaced by something more modern?

It has been the history of Tenleytown, like other urban areas throughout America, that changes can and do take place. Individual property owners have the ability to do what they want, within zoning guidelines.

If, however, an appreciation of the past and of the history of Tenleytown can persuade people to reconsider plans to make physical changes in local properties, then many people will be pleased.

It was not my original intention to foster preservation of historic properties, yet I find I always lament the loss of another house or landmark. It was my intention to preserve the memory of what Tenleytown once was, to document in map, photo, and text what preceded today's life in this neighborhood.

I have not lived in Tenleytown since 1985, but I still love the place. My memories of quiet streets (and subway construction) in the 1970s can be followed by your memories in this new century.

Not one person remains of the residents of the 3800 block of Alton Place who lived there when my family moved in, in 1966. All have died or moved away, as I have. So it's not realistic to think that nothing will change.

Meanwhile, we write what we know and read what others have written. And we cherish the memories.

Judith Beck Helm
Macungie, Pennsylvania
January 1, 2000

"GRASSLAND"
(See p. 26)

Introduction 1981

In the children's classic, The Little House, Virginia Lee Burton tells the story of a little house that was once out in the country, but is gradually encroached upon by streets, developments, stores, high-rise apartments, and even a subway, as the city spreads further outward. That story, told in 1942, is a simple but far-seeing tale of the effects of urbanization. And it has many similarities to the story of Tenleytown, D.C.

Tenleytown used to be out in the "county" part of the District of Columbia, before the city of Washington grew out to meet the boundaries. The people who lived in Tenleytown were farmers, dairymen, storekeepers. But because the village lay on a main route of travel—a route that has been significant since 1755—it grew in numbers and in importance as a stopping place for travelers and tradesmen.

Tenleytown was, until the 20th century, called Tennallytown—or Tenallytown, or Tenley Town, or any number of a variety of spellings. It was called Tennally's Tavern in the 1780s, and Tennallytown after about 1800. It is therefore older than every other neighborhood in the District with the exception of Georgetown.

Tenleytown grew up around the intersection of the Road to Fredericktown and the Road to Great Falls—which today are called Wisconsin Avenue and River Road.

In Tenleytown is the highest point of elevation in the city, 420 feet above sea level. That high point was the site of the largest Civil War fort in Washington, Fort Reno. It was the Civil War that changed the sleepy village into a busy suburb of the nation's capital.

Tenleytown once contained one of the city's substantial neighborhoods of free Negroes after the Civil War—the Fort Reno settlement, as it came to be called.

It was never incorporated as a village, having been included within the boundaries of the District of Columbia in 1791. One hundred years before the writing of this history, "Tennallytown" was the post office for farmers further west than the District border and as far east as Rock Creek.

In the 1890s the streets of the city of Washington were extended north and west beyond the original Boundary Street (Florida Avenue). Soon after, Tenleytown, with its healthful air, attractive scenery, and convenient location on the streetcar line, attracted developers. Streets were cut in and rows of houses were built. New people moved in, in great numbers. Large new schools were built; the churches expanded.

The houses on the main street were transformed into stores. The main street itself came to be called Wisconsin Avenue. Gas stations, apartment houses, then office buildings and a department store changed Tenleytown's appearance from a muddy village into a bustling part of a city.

By the 1950s the Tenleytown name had all but disappeared from maps and from general usage. The more esthetically pleasing name "Friendship"—the name of an original land grant in the area—came into popular use for that area of the city between Cleveland Park and Bethesda.

But the changes continue, and the history of Tenleytown continues. A subway is being built that will bring the name Tenleytown back into general usage, as well as connect the neighborhood even more with city and suburbs.

What makes Tenleytown unique in American villages grown into cities is its location in the city of Washington. The political, social, and economic growth of the nation's capital has been reflected in the changing makeup of the population of Tenleytown. The citizens who own businesses and live in the area also have helped to maintain Tenleytown as a neighborhood of beauty and charm, and have prevented its becoming an area of neglect. But the influx of new people, and the frequent change of occupants, has threatened the "home-town" character of the neighborhood.

*   *   *   *

In describing the development of a town, we document the physical changes as the important, visible demonstrations of growth. But the people—the families, the children, and the business owners—are as important as the landmarks in Tenleytown. They have brought life to the community and have made Tenleytown a special place of historic interest.

The people who remember old Tenleytown are becoming fewer and fewer. Whenever one of the old Tenleytowners dies, we lose another unique source of information and memories.

Much material on family histories was collected, but time and space have made it impossible to include an appendix of brief genealogies of the major Tenleytown families. Researchers of family histories may contact me for whatever materials I may have about their Tenleytown families.

I have chosen to use the spelling "Tennallytown" in discussing the history of the village through the 19th century. After 1900 the spelling "Tenleytown" was more generally used, and I have done likewise. Where other spellings are found in this book, they are either in quotations or are the spellings used in the context.

Judith Beck Helm
Tenleytown, D.C.
September 1, 1981

CHAPPELL-McLAUGHLIN HOUSE, 3901 ALBEMARLE STREET
(See p. 124)

Acknowledgments

I am indebted to my friend Priscilla McNeil, who performed most of the archival research on the earliest history of Tenleytown. The results of her research and discoveries on land grants, deeds, and wills provide the basis for much of the material in my first two chapters. Priscilla McNeil's best sources were the original records preserved in the Hall of Records in Annapolis.

I am very grateful to the staff members of Wisconsin Avenue Baptist, St. Ann's Catholic, Eldbrooke Methodist, and St. Columba's Episcopal Churches, who willingly shared their files, photos, and resources with me in the interest of putting together a local history.

The city archivists were especially helpful and encouraging. At the Columbia Historical Society were Perry Fisher, Robert Truax, and Betsy Miller. At the Washingtoniana Collection, Martin Luther King Memorial Library, Betty Culpeper, Alex Geiger, Roxanna Dean, and their staff members provided access to material and photos. Dorothy Provine at the National Archives led me to the Fort Reno acquisition papers. Jon Reynolds, at the Georgetown University Special Collections, and Robert W. Lyle, curator of the Peabody Room, Georgetown Library, were helpful.

Beginning in 1972, I interviewed in person, on the phone, or by letter over 200 long-time residents of Tenleytown, many of whom have died since. They are too numerous to mention, but I am forever indebted to them for their descriptions and information, insights and memories about life as it was lived in Tenleytown. Most of the material of Chapters IV through VI is based on these interviews.

Photographs and maps came from every possible source—archives and institutions and publications— but very important, from the albums and frames and desk drawers and attics of the families of Tenleytown. I am most grateful to all who entrusted me with their prized pictures, in order to share them with you, the readers.

Mrs. Ruline Baker of Baker Photo has been the diligent caretaker and processor of all these old photos. Special thanks also go to Ann Marie Parenteau, Harold "Doc" Farnham, and Ernie Newhouse for their work on the photographs.

Recent photos in the book are the work of Jerry Yurow, John Russo, Priscilla McNeil, Petra Schultze, and Bob Gerber, all of whom are excellent photographers. The cover drawing by Lily Spandorf and the sketches by Sammie Sellers are much appreciated.

Many thanks go to those who read the manuscript and offered suggestions—Don McNeil, Neil Helm, Barbara Martin, Tish Grant, Perry Fisher, and C. Ray Johnson of Seattle. I am grateful too for the work of the typists—my mother, Marian Beck, Tish Grant, and Clara Young. Bill Hamilton, Anne Thibault, and Ann Nolan were most generous in affording me the use of their word processing system, typewriters, Xerox machines, space, and time.

Others who were helpful with materials include Michael Tames, Donald Barnes, C. Ray Johnson, Walton Shipley, and Jean Pablo. Thanks go also to those writers and publishers who gave me permission to quote from their works.

To Neil and Karl Helm, a special appreciation for their love and encouragement in this historic project, which lasted for so many years.

To Kip Rushin, thanks for giving me a deadline.

J.H.

ROCKVILLE, C.H.

Montrose P.O.

Offutts X Roads

John Creek

Great Falls Potomac

Cold. Deposits

Ohio Branch Canal

Canal

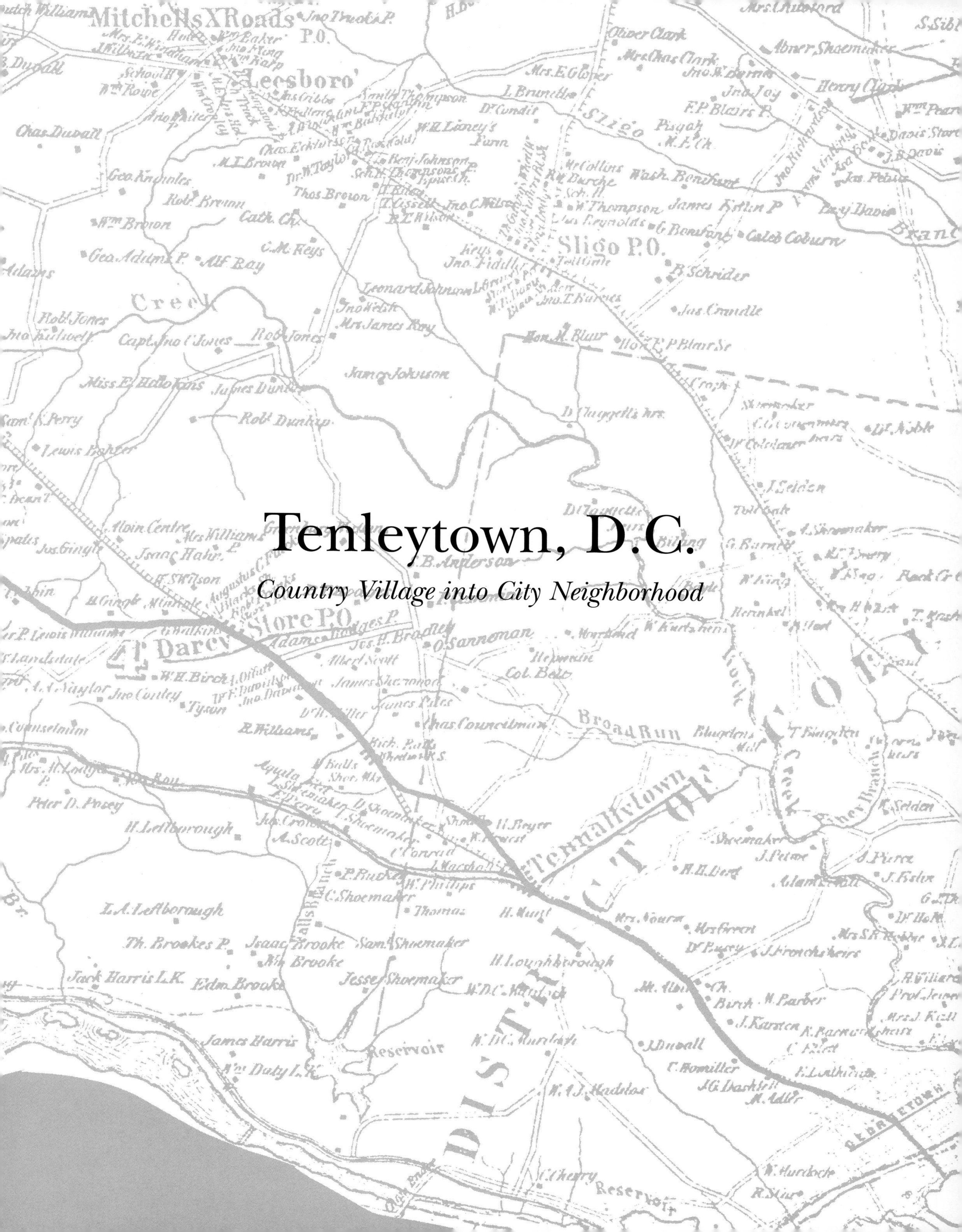

Tenleytown, D.C.

Country Village into City Neighborhood

PATOWMECK REGION MAPPED IN 1670 BY A. HERRMAN

(published London, 1673)

Early map shows eventual site of the District of Columbia at Turkey Buzzard Point on the Patowmeck River where the Eastern Branch enters into it. Rock Creek, also unlabeled, flows into the Patowmeck across from "Anacostien Ile" (today's Roosevelt Island).

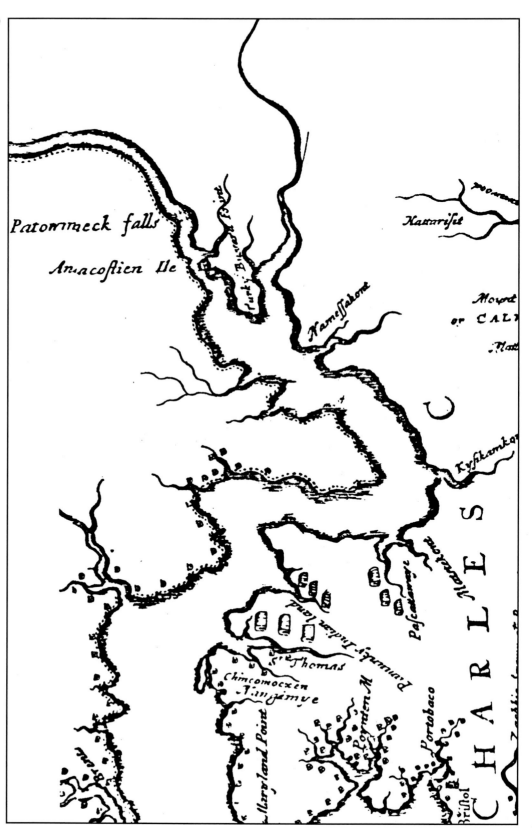

I
THE BEGINNINGS:
BEFORE 1790

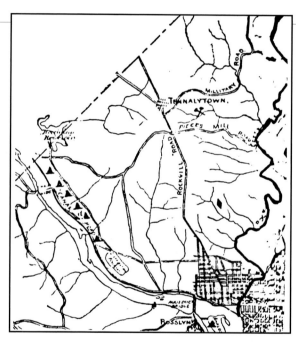

(S.V. Proudfit, "A Collection of Stone Implements From the District of Columbia," <u>Proceedings of the United States National Museum,</u> Vol. 13 (1890): Plate 10, p. 189)

1890 MAP OF WASHINGTON WEST OF ROCK CREEK, SHOWING ANCIENT INDIAN VILLAGE SITES

Traces of Indian stone quarries and "workshops" have been discovered near today's Western Avenue; at many sites along the Potomac Palisades near Chain Bridge and Little Falls; on the promontory near today's Wisconsin Avenue at Edmunds Street, a site that still commands one of the best inland views of the Potomac; around the campus of the American University; near 44th and Chesapeake Sts.; and west of Broad Branch—the Rose Hill quarries. (Sources: Elizabeth Rounds with Neil Judd, <u>Lost Arrows</u>, Cleveland Park Community Library Committee, 1948, and Smithsonian Collection, D.C. Catalog of Artifacts)

Before the first English settlers began exploring the lush and uncultivated land on the north and east banks of the Potomac River in the 1630s, the Piscataway Indians lived there peacefully as hunters, farmers, and fishers. Because of the abundance of animals, the plentiful soapstone, and the fertility of the soil, the Potomac Valley Indians enjoyed prosperity. They were visited by bartering tribesmen from north and south who discovered that sturdy stone implements and vessels were being manufactured from the local soapstone.

The Indian settlements were on the Potomac River, which was their highway for travel and commerce. At the natural harbor now known as Georgetown was a small Indian settlement called Tohoga, which English fur trader Henry Fleete mentioned in the 1632 journal of his travels among the Indians.[1]

The Piscataways farmed, hunted, and quarried stone on both sides of the Rock Creek, which was wide, deep, and navigable by canoe. It was called "Rock Creek" as early as 1687.[2]

Important to the Piscataway Indians was the ready availability of soapstone. The largest of these quarries, later called the Rose Hill quarry, was just east of what came to be Tenleytown. William Henry Holmes called Rose Hill "one of the most interesting native soapstone quarries in the great series extending...from Massachusetts to Georgia.... The spot now the political center of the nation was thus in prehistoric times a chief resort of the native peoples of the region."[3]

Rose Hill was actually two quarries, on either side of what was once Soapstone Creek, just west of Connecticut Avenue at Albemarle Street. The steep south quarry was south of Albemarle. The only remnant of the south hill,

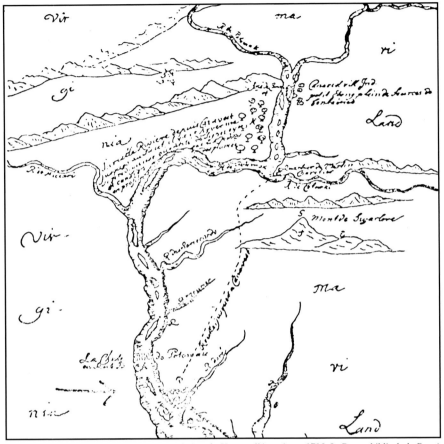

(Baron Christophle DeGraffenried, <u>Relation du Voyage d'Amerique</u>, 1716. In Burgerbibliothek, Bern)

INDIAN TRAIL THAT PRECEDED WISCONSIN AVENUE

Baron Christophle DeGraffenried's 1712 map (in French) indicates he traveled from Col. Beale's (Ninian Beall's) along the dotted line, "Route jusqu'a Canavest" (route to Conoy Indian territory), past "Mont de Sugarlove" (Sugarloaf Mountain) and on northwest. This dotted line is the predecessor to the Road to Frederick, the Rockville Pike, and Wisconsin Avenue.

once 80 feet above the creek, is visible from the alley west of the 4400 block of Connecticut Avenue. Remnants of the north Rose Hill soapstone quarry were excavated years ago for the building of apartment houses on the west side of Connecticut at Albemarle and Appleton Streets.

Although the settlements, gardens, and workshops of the Indians were gradually obliterated, the network of Indian trails established over the years was maintained by the white settlers. These were old and direct walking trails, from the narrowest crossing of a body of water, to the highest vantage points for seeing into the distance, to the sources of soapstone and granite, to the most fertile fields, and even to burying grounds.

One important trail traveled north from the Tohoga community to the highest trails around. It turned right and left to avoid the many springs whose waters formed creeks flowing to either the "Patawomeke," as the river was called, or the big Rock Creek. This is the trail that became the Road to Frederick Town, The Georgetown-Rockville Turnpike, the Tenleytown Road, and Wisconsin Avenue.

This main Indian trail wound through the woods, bending as the lay of the land indicated, avoiding where possible the steepest hills. The resulting trail, on the highest ridge, ran alongside a hill at that time approximately 430 feet above sea level. On this hill, which we now call Fort Reno hill, the Indians could climb one of the sturdy oaks or pines for a view of rolling hills far beyond the "Patawomeke," or, on a clear day, look northward 30 miles to a single mountain that was called by Baron DeGraffenried the Sugarloaf Mountain.

Baron Christophle DeGraffenried, a Swiss nobleman, explored the area north of the upper Potomac on horseback in June 1712. He was attempting to follow a map made by Franz Luis Michel, a Swiss who had explored the Potomac in 1707. Horace Hobbs, Jr., says that DeGraffenried rode westward over the trail that later became the River Road.[4]

DeGraffenried's map does not, however, indicate that he took a western fork of the Indian trail. It shows he did not cross Muddy Branch, which River Road crosses, but he forded Seneca Creek where it was narrow. The Indian trail traveled by DeGraffenried's party was probably the predecessor of today's Wisconsin Avenue and Old Georgetown Road, to Rockville, Gaithersburg, and on to Sugarloaf.

The Indian trails became the white settlers' footpaths and horse paths. Eventually they were widened to accommodate horse-drawn carts and coaches.

The lay of the land had a major influence on the Indians' and white settlers' readiness to settle on the shores of the Potomac River and the Rock Creek. The Rock Creek Valley is along the Fall Line, the border between the Piedmont Plateau on the west and the Atlantic Coastal Plain on the east.

The Piedmont Plateau, extending from the foothills of the Blue Ridge Mountains, is a rolling heavily forested area of rocky ground. The Atlantic Coastal Plain is flatter, closer to sea level, with a softer, sandier soil. Tenleytown is on the last terrace west of the Rock Creek, which was formed by water falling from the rocky Piedmont highlands to softer coastal soil. The many waterfalls along Rock Creek prompted the construction of as many as seven mills during the late 18th and 19th centuries.

The country through which the Indian trail led was more heavily watered than any other part of what is now the District of Columbia. West of the Indian trail, three spring-fed branches became one creek, which led to the Little Falls Branch (first called Powder Mill Run); another led to the Foundry Branch, as it came to be called. Both empty into the Potomac.

The three branches that flowed west of what came to be known by geologists as the Tennallytown Ridge[5] sprang from three main sources, two of them west of the Indian road. The creek that originated east of the road was referred to as "Dogwood Creek." These creeks united near the road to Murdock's Mill, and thus became the Murdock Mill Creek, which served the mill race. Then the creek, which even

today surfaces in the woods from the storm sewer that contains it, flowed west to the Little Falls Branch and on to the Potomac.

The Foundry Branch (formerly known as Deep Branch) has its origins in Tenleytown, too. Beginning northwest of the intersection of two Indian trails (behind today's fire house at Wisconsin and Warren), this branch flowed in a southwesterly direction, all the way to the Potomac,

(Dennis Griffith map, 1794)

The earliest roads (today's Wisconsin Avenue and River Road) were laid out to avoid the creeks and steepest hills.

3

CREEKS AROUND TENNALLYTOWN

(A. Boschke's Topographic Map of the District of Columbia, 1861, from field inspection of 1857-58; Library of Congress)

where Henry Foxall's foundry was later located, near the Three Sisters Islands. The Foundry Branch runs through the Glover-Archbold Park, as this wooded preserve has been called since 1924.

"Throughout this area of woodland within the watershed of the Foundry Branch may be found some of the finest trees in the District of Columbia." Tremendous beech, elm, and oak trees remind one of "the virgin territory on which the early settlers located more than 200 years ago."[6]

East of the Tennallytown Ridge were two tributaries of the Soapstone Creek, which flowed into Broad Branch. The latter still meets Rock Creek above Pierce's Mill.

About where 38th and Warren Streets now intersect was the origin of a creek that flowed northeast. And near the south end of Wilson High School can still be seen, in a heavily overgrown gully, the little stream that flows east (now underground) and meets up with the aforementioned creek. They emerge as the Soapstone Creek (reportedly also called Tinker Run), just east of Connecticut Avenue and south of Albemarle Street.

Soapstone Creek has been well described by Walton Shipley: "This creek was once full of life—minnows and crayfish." Double violets grew in profusion along its banks. The hills on either side were "covered with trees of all kinds, and . . . dogwood, redbud, wild geranium, May apples,

LAND GRANTS IN AND NEAR TENLEYTOWN AND THEIR DATE OF SURVEY

[Arranged chronologically. Numbers correspond to those on map, right.]

1 St. Philip and Jacob [1674]
2 Whitehaven [1689]
3 Rock of Dumbarton [1702]
4 Friendship [1711]
5 The Scotch Ordinary [1715]
6 Fletchall's Chance [1715]
7 Addition to the Rock of Dumbarton [1721]
8 Chevy Chase [1722]
9 Conjuror's Disappointment [1729]
10 Knave's Disappointment [1732], (a resurvey on Salcom)
11 Fellowship Enlarged [1746]
12 Resurvey on New Seat [ca. 1747]
13 Addition to New Seat [ca. 1755]
14 New Seat Lot [1755]
15 Barnaby [1757], a resurvey on part of Labyrinth
16 The Resurvey of Jacob [1762]
17 Azadia [1762]
18 Gizor [1762]
19 Mount Pleasant [1767]
20 Resurvey on Terra Firma [1769]
21 Arell's Folly [1771]
22 Fox [1783], a resurvey on Noise Enough
23 Mount Airy [1783], a resurvey of Resurvey of Earl Percy and Earl Douglas and part of Fletchall's Chance
24 Below Amsterdam [1784]
25 Resurvey on Amsterdam [1789]
26 Mount Airy [1790]
27 Alliance [1791], a resurvey on part of Knave's Disappointment, part of Resurvey on Salop, part of The Addition to the Resurvey on Salop, Addition to the Addition to the Resurvey on Salop, part of Whitehaven, part of St. Philip and Jacob, and part of The Addition to Philip and Jacob
28 Under the Hill [ca. 1792]
29 Pretty Prospects [1793], a resurvey on part of The Rock of Dumbarton, part of Addition to the Rock of Dumbarton, Beall's Lot, and part of The Gift
30 Resurvey on Lucky Discovery [1793], in two separate parts

Researched and compiled by Priscilla McNeil.

Source documents for these land grants are in the Maryland State Archives, Annapolis.

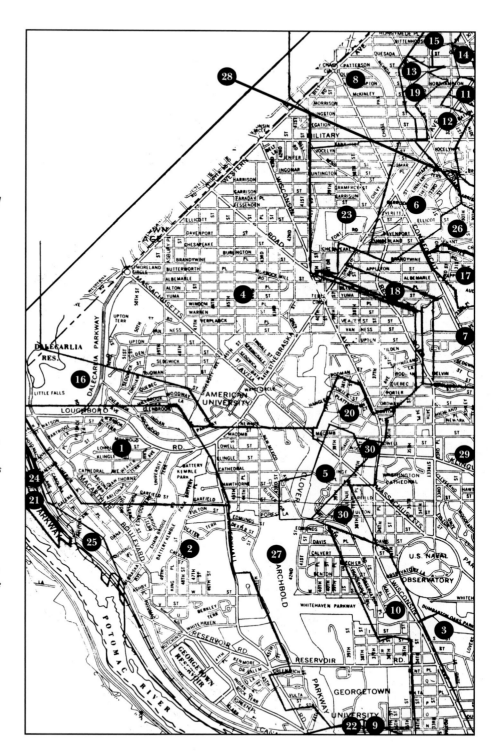

wild roses, honeysuckle, pansy violets, and blue hepaticas" ("the fairest of all flowers growing there").[7]

Another creek flowed east from the main Indian trail (Belt Road) into Broad Branch.

Early Colonists

In 1632 Cecelius Calvert, Lord Baltimore, had received a charter from King Charles I of England for the territory known as Maryland. This territory included today's Delaware, Maryland, and the District of Columbia. Calvert and his heirs were given sole power for granting tracts of land in Maryland to settlers. Each land grant was given a name by its owner.

After the first settlements were made in the Tidewater area, the lands to the north and west were gradually taken up.

In 1696, John Addison of "Oxon Hill" and William Hutchinson received a patent for 759 acres of "White Haven," along the Potomac between Philip Lynes' 400 acres and Robert Mason's 300 acres. Foxhall Road, Chain Bridge Road, and Reservoir Road now run through "White Haven," which was claimed by its owners as early as 1689 (see map). In 1703 Ninian Beall patented 795 acres of "Rock of Dumbarton," mostly west of Rock Creek.[8]

These grants and most of what is Washington were all in what came to be known as "New Scotland Hundred," a "hundred" being an old Roman-Anglo Saxon division of land or civic unit. "New Scotland Hundred" extended along the Potomac River "from the Oxon Branch to the [Great] Falls of the Potomac," which includes the area now called Tenleytown.

As the areas of land became more heavily populated, they were frequently divided. Thus the original Charles County split off (in 1695)

into Charles and Prince George's Counties; Prince George's split off (in 1748) into Prince George's and Frederick Counties; Frederick split off (in 1776) into Frederick, Washington, and Montgomery Counties. So it is that the Tenleytown area was part of four Maryland counties—Charles, Prince George's, Frederick, and Montgomery— before the formation of the District of Columbia in 1791.

The English patentees were, for the most part, educated young men. Most of the Addisons, for example, were educated at Oxford (hence the name "Oxon Hill"). They started from scratch to build homes, roads, institutions, and a new society, and in so doing endured many hardships. But their wealth and the importation of large numbers of indentured servants who could earn their freedom, and Negro slaves who required no wages, allowed the "lords of the manors" to acquire a degree of comfort in the new land much greater than that of their New England predecessors. The importation of fine furnishings, supplies, and skilled builders and craftsmen ensured the continuity of a high standard of British gentility in a very rough frontier land.

The English were in some areas outnumbered by the Scottish and Irish, from the Chesapeake Bay west to the Potomac. Many of the old place names in the Tenleytown area were Scottish, as will be seen.

Addison and Stoddert's "Friendship"

The most important and largest grant of land in the Tenleytown area, and one of the few whose name has remained in use until today, was "Friendship." "Friendship" commemorated the amicable relationship between its two grantees, James A. Stoddert and Colonel Thomas

Addison (son of Colonel John Addison) of "Oxon Hill." The huge 3,124-acre "Friendship" tract was granted by Charles Calvert to Addison and Stoddert in 1713. It extended all the way east of the old Indian trail nearly to George Beall's "Addition to the Rock of Dumbarton" (see map).

The annual rent charged the patentees of "Friendship" was six pounds, five shillings in sterling silver or gold.

By mutual agreement, James Stoddert took ownership of the northern part of "Friendship," generally above what is now Fessenden Street, north into today's Bethesda about as far as Bradley Lane, and west nearly to Kenwood. Thomas Addison's was the southern part, the part that includes Tenleytown, as far south as today's Van Ness Street and Sidwell Friends School, and as far west as Dalecarlia Reservoir. Only the southern part had extensive holdings east of today's Wisconsin Avenue, about as far as Reno Road and Van Ness Street.

It is unlikely that Thomas Addison ever lived on his "Friendship" property. Rather, by the time he acquired "Friendship," Addison was married to his second wife, and was probably living at "Oxon Hill."

Another tract named "Friendship" had been granted in 1715 to Charles Beall and Captain Thomas Fletchall, for 1,368 acres. Confusingly, this "Friendship" was adjacent to the earlier "Friendship" in what is now west Bethesda, from Glen Echo across River Road at Kenwood and up to Wilson Lane. This Captain Thomas Fletchall acquired a great deal of land in the area, including 253 acres called "Fletchall's Chance" west of the Broad Branch, which eventually was part of Tenleytown.

James Stoddert's northern part of "Friendship" was inherited by his sons William, Benjamin, and Thomas Stoddert in 1726. That part of the Stodderts' "Friendship" that was eventually within the District of Columbia north of Fessenden Street (see map) was sold to tobacco merchant George Gordon in 1746. Gordon's 400 acres were acquired by Henry Threlkeld of "Berleith" six years later, and the land was inherited by John Threlkeld in 1781. It is unlikely that any of these owners lived on this land; but they made as many speculative land purchases as they could.

Colonel Thomas Addison's southern part of "Friendship" was, after his death in 1727, inherited by his youngest two sons, Anthony (1200 acres) and Henry (400 acres). These two and their five older brothers and sisters, who grew up at "Giesborough" and "Oxon Hill," also inherited other properties of Thomas Addison's.

The youngest Addison sister, Ann, had married William Murdock and was living at "Perrywood," near Upper Marlboro. William Murdock (1710-1769) was a member of the Maryland House of Burgesses, as it was called at that time, and represented Maryland at the Stamp Act Congress in New York in 1765.

The "Friendship" properties were acquired by the Murdocks in this manner: Ann (Addison) Murdock's unmarried brother, Anthony Addison, was one of the aforementioned heirs of "Friendship." He died and his will was probated in 1753. His real estate (including all of "St. Philip and Jacob," "White Haven," and 1200 acres of "Friendship") was bequeathed to Ann's sons Addison and John Murdock, who were in their early twenties at the time.[9]

The inventory of Anthony Addison's property in Frederick County (which this area was in 1753) at the time of his death lists 20 Negroes, one horse, 31 cattle, and 17 pigs. The 31 head of cattle would have included oxen that the Negro slaves used for field work, planting fields of corn and their own gardens as well as the tobacco crops on the huge "Friendship" tract.

Throughout all these early years of transferring titles from one to another, it is apparent that the local property owners did not build dwellings here for themselves, but preferred to remain on their manors south of the Eastern Branch (Anacostia River). In the early 1700s, however, the expansion of the tobacco crops from southern Maryland northward indicates that resident overseers and slave laborers were established on the land west of the

CHRONOLOGY OF OCCUPATION AND JURISDICTION OF THAT AREA THAT BECAME TENNALLYTOWN, D.C.

Piscataway Indian territory—through the 1690s

Maryland—1634–1791
   Charles County, 1658–1695
   Prince George's County, 1696–1748
   Frederick County, 1748–1776
   Montgomery County, 1776–1791

District of Columbia—1791 through present
   Tennallytown, Washington County, D.C., 1791–1895
   Washington, D.C., 1895–present

Plaque in boulder on west side of Chevy Chase Circle, in front of All Saints Episcopal Church; placed there in 1911 by Society of Colonial Wars in the District of Columbia.

COLONEL JOSEPH BELT
1680 MARYLAND 1761
Patentee of "Cheivy Chace"
Trustee of First Free Schools in Maryland
One of the Founders of Rock Creek Parish
Member of the House of Burgesses
Colonel of Prince George's County Militia
During French and Indian War

MURDOCK'S COUNTRY ESTATE, "FRIENDSHIP"

(1908 photo from the American University Courier, April 1908)

Above: John Murdock built this house at "Friendship" in about 1760. It was located on a knoll south of today's Massachusetts Avenue, where the Chancellor's House stands on the grounds of American University.

Rock Creek. Since most of this heavily forested land had never been cleared by Indians for farming, it was cleared and broken for the first time, laborious acre by laborious acre, and that golden crop, tobacco, was planted. The wood cut down was valuable for building the first slave dwellings and heating them, and for fencing in the livestock.

In 1725 Colonel Joseph Belt, of Anne Arundel County, took possession of a 560-acre tract of land which he named "Cheivy Chace," after a Scottish hunting song, The Ballad of Cheivy Chace. The land lay a bit north of his brother-in-law George Beall's "Addition to the Rock of Dumbarton" and of "Fletchall's Chance," and northeast of "Friendship."

The southwestern corner of "Cheivy Chace" touched the old Indian trail that ambled north along the ridge from the Potomac River (now Belt Road, near Military Road). Belt Road still exists in places northeast of Tenleytown and (as Brookeville Road) runs through today's Chevy Chase.

"Fletchall's Chance," to the east of the old trail, had been patented in

Right: A broader view of the old "Friendship" homestead, as seen in 1897.

(1897 photo from the American University Courier, January 1918)

1715 by Captain Thomas Fletchall. The land between it and "Friendship" lay vacant until 1743, when George Read patented 73 acres of "Earl Percy and Earl Douglas." (Percy and Douglas were the two major combatants in the battle of Cheivy Chace.) And in 1785, William Bayly, Jr., repatented "Earl Percy and Earl Douglas" and a part of "Fletchall's Chance" under the new name of "Mt. Airy." This land, 232 acres, represents the northeast section of what eventually became Tenleytown.

A narrow strip of land called "Gizor," patented by Samuel Beall, Jr., in 1726 also made up part of the eastern side of Tenleytown. And the "Friendship" tract constituted the rest of the village land to the south and west.

John Murdock assumed or bought out his brother Addison Murdock's portion of "Friendship" and, in about 1760, built a frame house for himself on a knoll with a view of the Potomac to the west and south. This was the house called "Friendship" that eventually was acquired by the American University. It was the first substantial country house near the area that became Tenleytown.

John Murdock became deputy surveyor of Frederick County under Governor Horatio Sharpe, and he served with distinction as a colonel in the American Revolution, when he was in his 40s. Murdock divided his time between his home in Georgetown, where he was a commissioner, and his "Friendship" estate, where he was a gentleman farmer.

By 1780, John Murdock had acquired 1,562 acres of "Friendship," 400 acres of "St. Philip and Jacob," and 759 acres of "White Haven"—a total of 2,721 acres. This was one of the largest holdings in what was then

Montgomery County. Murdock was probably married to Elizabeth Belt, a daughter of Joseph Belt—not the original patentee of "Cheivy Chace," but his nephew, who ran a well-known inn in Georgetown. Their son, William Murdock, was born about 1760, around the same time that the house at "Friendship" was built.

In looking at the genealogies of the local families of the 18th and early 19th centuries, we see that the major landowners of Maryland and nearby Virginia had large families, that they all intermarried, and that many remarried after the spouse died at a fairly young age. The Murdocks, Belts, Smiths, Threlkelds, Spriggs, Queens, Gordons, Brookes, Bealls, Addisons, Harrisons, etc., were intermarried with each other and with many other prominent families in Georgetown, southern Maryland, and northern Virginia.

Tobacco Houses at "Rock Creek"

Tobacco was the colonial planters' number one crop; corn was a distant second. The two most prominent tobacco houses in the area were located along the Potomac waterfront. They were run by George Gordon, whose 100 acres he called his "Rock Creek Plantation."

George Gordon's inspection house was where the great quantities of tobacco were separated, weighed, and assessed.

"This warehouse controlled the destinies of farmers for miles around, for tobacco was the general medium of exchange, and the warehouse was thus virtually a bank as well as a storage house."[10]

The location of a tobacco house below the falls of the Potomac was a most felicitous choice. This natural harbor turned out to be the westernmost point in Maryland to which a

ship could sail. It therefore had advantages over Annapolis (chartered 1708) and Baltimore (1729) for exporting tobacco from the inland plantations and importing English goods. Such imports were in even greater demand as the tobacco planters grew wealthier.

The planters had the tobacco carried to the new market along the old Indian trails; in many cases they blazed their own more direct trails. Wheeled vehicles were still rare in those early days, and the narrow, rutted trails would hardly accommodate them. Accordingly, the large wooden hogsheads (casks) of tobacco were rolled right along the road, dragged behind a horse or ox and attached to two wooden shafts, one at either end of the barrel.

The flattened roads made by rolling hogsheads of tobacco came to be called "rolling roads," generally very roundabout so as to avoid steep hills. George Gordon's and George Beall's tobacco inspection houses were likewise called the "rolling houses."[11] The old Indian trail from "Rock Creek Plantation" north became one of the main rolling roads.

The great increase in the tobacco trade in the 1730s and 1740s prompted the building of ship wharves near George Gordon's tobacco inspection house. As the area gradually grew in importance as a center for tobacco and shipping, the land grew in value. Wharves, stores, houses, and inns were built at or near the Potomac, where the Indian town of Tohoga had existed for many years.

A demand arose for the formal establishment of a town, which up until then was called "Rock Creek" or "Rock Creek Landing."[12] And so the Maryland Assembly approved in 1751 the establishment of the town of George Town in the newly formed

(Sketch by Sammie Sellers)

Above: Cask of tobacco being rolled to Georgetown market

The routes traveled by the tobacco farmers came to be called "rolling roads." Wisconsin Avenue was one such "rolling road."

Below: Plaque in boulder on east side of Wisconsin Avenue, north of St. Alban's Church. "This memorial was erected in 1907 by the Society of Colonial Wars in the District of Columbia to mark the road over which on April 14, 1755, a division of the British Army under General Braddock marched on its way to Fort Duquesne."

(Photo by Petra Schultze)

Frederick County. Although it was probably named after King George III of England, it could also have been named in honor of the two Georges whose lands were taken—George Beall and George Gordon.

By the time the segments and streets of George Town were officially laid out, it was close to becoming the largest tobacco port on the east coast, and that meant in all of America. The development of George Town and the gradual removal of the heirs of the original manors from tobacco plantation to bustling seaport marked the beginning of the growth of the colonial towns. The growth of George Town as a commercial center strongly affected the traffic, the market for goods, and the culture of the area that came to be Tenleytown.

Other towns being established at the time were Bladensburg (originally Garrison's Landing), a port on the Eastern Branch, in 1742; Frederick Town, Maryland, in 1745; and Alexandria, Virginia, in 1749. The network of roads linking these towns was an important aspect of colonial society. The old Indian trail north from George Town became the increasingly well-traveled wagon road to Frederick Town. When Frederick County was separated from Prince George's County in 1748, Frederick Town became the county seat.

The wagon road to Frederick Town (today's Wisconsin Avenue) became the first military road in colonial America when General Edward Braddock's troops marched along its narrow trail in 1755. A renowned English general, Braddock had been appointed commander of British forces in America in 1754. He arrived in Alexandria in March 1755 with two regiments of British infantry, each 500 strong. Two hundred Americans were added to the two regiments.

In the mission to recapture Fort Duquesne from the French, one regiment of Braddock's soldiers left Alexandria and marched westward through Winchester toward Fort Cumberland. Soldiers in Colonel Thomas Dunbar's regiment marched north to the Potomac, and were ferried across to George Town. There they picked up nine days' provisions, to last until Frederick Town. It was on Saturday, April 12, that George Town was "treated to its first sight of a British redcoat."[13]

As commemorated by the Society of Colonial Wars plaque (1907) on a boulder in front of the Washington Cathedral, the British Army marched by on Monday, April 14, 1755.

Braddock's Orderly Book[14] does not specifically record that Braddock accompanied this regiment, and some sources indicate that he followed a day or so later.[15] Noma Thompson's sources indicate Braddock did not leave Alexandria until April 19, arriving at Owen's Ordinary on the 20th. In either event, surely the farmers along the north ridge trail hailed the British regiments as they passed during mid-April 1755. Dunbar's troops took three days to walk the 45 miles to Frederick.

George Washington's expedition to Fort Duquesne a year earlier had necessitated the building of new roads in western Virginia and Maryland in order for military equipment to be transported to the Ohio Valley. Braddock's expedition in 1755 similarly required roads wide enough for horse-drawn military vehicles, provision carriers, and guns. The year before, Governor Horatio Sharpe of Maryland had cooperated with the anticipated British expedition by ordering the construction of a 12-foot-wide road from Rock Creek to Wills Creek.[16]

This, of course, included the old Indian trail from the Potomac north toward the new town of Frederick. Today we trace the route from Georgetown up Wisconsin Avenue, veering right at Tenleytown onto Belt Road, back to Wisconsin Avenue just north of the District line, again veering left onto Old Georgetown Road until just south of Rockville.

"While the physical condition of the roads is not specifically recorded, they were adequate to transport [Braddock's] regiments in normal marching time. Accompanying his men were heavy artillery, hundreds of loaded wagons, thousands of horses and mules, together with women and camp followers."[17]

Continuing on present Route 355, the Braddock road went through today's Rockville, Gaithersburg, Clarksburg, Hyattstown, northeast of Sugarloaf Mountain, and on to Frederick. From Frederick we trace Braddock's line of march northwest to Williamsport (then Watkins Ferry), down into (West) Virginia to avoid the highest mountains and back north to (Fort) Cumberland, and on to Pittsburgh (Fort Duquesne).

After Braddock's defeat at Fort Duquesne, the French and Indian Wars continued to demand the involvement of colonial militia until 1758. George Town surveyor Alexander Beall and Samuel Wade Magruder—both from the newly-formed Frederick County—commanded companies sent to the western frontier. Other local men also fought the French and Indians.[18]

As a result of the building of the Braddock Road, as it was called for a time, the way was cleared for northwestward trade and travel that even more benefited George Town and the area above it.

Settlers from Frederick Town who followed the newly-widened road southward to George Town were the first Germans to come to the area, and a large number of them arrived. At the same time, the English, Scottish, Welsh, and Irish immigrants who kept arriving by ship often traveled along the road to Frederick Town and beyond, to the opening Western frontier lands of Maryland, Virginia, Pennsylvania, and Ohio.

By 1770 the Maryland Assembly authorized the establishment of a system of roads and highways throughout the province, "to mark out the most convenient highways and paths."[19]

George Town's inland trade depended on not only the road to Frederick Town, but also "The Main Road" from George Town to Bladensburg; the road to Watts Branch (which became River Road); the road across Rock Creek Ford to Rock Creek Church; and the road across the Potomac River in Fairfax County.[20]

The Frederick Road is often confused with another old north-south route: the Union Turnpike, beginning along 7th Street in the city, which also connected Washington to Rockville, Maryland. After one branch was built to Brookeville, in the 1790s, it was known as the Brookeville Road. The Washington-Rockville turnpike (toll road) was chartered in 1829, preceding today's Georgia Avenue and Veirs Mill Road.[21]

Days of Revolution

The prosperity of the Maryland tobacco farmers, merchants, and other settlers was clouded by England's ever-tighter restrictions on territorial expansion, increased taxes, and navigation laws affecting colonial trade.

In January 1776 the Maryland convention formally resolved to raise an armed force for defense against the British. A battalion from Frederick County had John Murdock as its colonel, Thomas Johns as lieutenant colonel, William Brooke as first major, and William Deakins as a second major.

Other area men whose descendants have taken pride in their forefathers' participation in the American Revolution were Samuel Duvall, General John Burrows, Richard Brooke, Benjamin Stoddert, Joseph Magruder, Charles Jones (of "Clean Drinking Manor"), Zadock Magruder, surveyor Archibald Orme, and others named Hunt, Paine, Hurdle, Barnes, Ray, Riley, Trail, Love, Wise, Moxley, Veatch, Chappell, and West.

An oath of loyalty to Maryland and disavowal of loyalty to Britain was required of every adult male citizen of the province. Any man who did not swear to this oath was not allowed to conduct business and so was effectively ostracized. The Rev. Henry Addison, who had inherited 400 acres of the southern part of "Friendship," was a supporter of Great Britain. Consequently, his land was confiscated and his nephew Colonel John Murdock bought the confiscated land.

The River Road is Built

In 1774, the Maryland Assembly had ordered that major market roads in the province be "improved" (built or rebuilt), including both "the road from Frederick Town leading by Dowdens to George Town"

(which became Wisconsin Avenue) and a "road from the mouth of Watts Branch to George Town aforesaid" (which became River Road). But the necessities of war had delayed the road-building.[22]

There were isolated early homes and plantations to the west of the Indian trail, such as "Milton" and "Springfield."[23] Beginning in 1715, there had been in that area land grants to Scottish and English settlers named Offutt, Beall, Edmonston, Magruder, Wallace, and Evans.[24]

A (Great) Falls Road probably existed in the 1740s, but it ran from the Great Falls of the Potomac north to the community around Lawrence Owen's Ordinary (later known as Rockville). It is likely that a road connecting the Falls Road with the Old Georgetown-Frederick Road was the

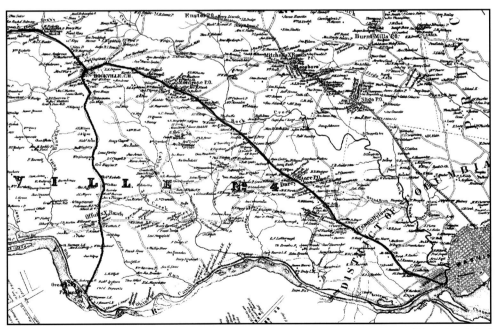

(Martenet & Bond's Map of Montgomery County, Md., in 1865. Reproduced by West Montgomery Citizens Association)

EARLY ROADS IN MONTGOMERY COUNTY

In the 18th century the only road from Georgetown (lower right) to Montgomery Court House (Rockville, upper left) went through Tennallytown and Darcy's Store (Bethesda), along the Old Georgetown Road to Montrose. The Great Falls Road ran from Montgomery Court House south by way of Offutt's Cross Roads (the village of Potomac) to the Great Falls of the Potomac. The Cabin John Road connected the old Georgetown Road with Great Falls Road, and River Road led from Tennallytown through Offutt's Cross Roads to Watts Branch and beyond.

old Cabin John Road, now lost in today's Greentree Road.[25] These early settlers most likely traveled in a north-south direction, along the creeks and trails that led from the main Indian trails to the Potomac River, which was in itself a means of travel.

It was not until about 1779 that Jacob Funk completed the River Road, which paralleled the Potomac. It was also called the Upper Falls Road, the Great Falls Road, and later even the Road to Harper's Ferry.

The Assembly ordered that

"in the middle of the Watts Branch-George Town road, until it intersects the Frederick-George Town road, large posts shall be well set up in sight of and not exceeding 100 yards distance from each other. When the road is finished, no wagon or carriage of burthen with wheels of a less tread than 5 inches, shall pass upon the part of this road that lies to the north of the posts erected, under a penalty of 20s. current money."[26]

The River Road, which intersected the Frederick-George Town Road at the place we call Tenleytown, was thereby to have the lighter vehicles with narrower wheels remain on the south half of the road, so as not to ruin the road for the larger, wider-wheeled wagons.

We know that the "Indian path" or the "Main Road" referred to in early land grants (e.g., "Friendship," 1713) was the present Wisconsin Avenue and Belt Road because we have identified these land grants (e.g., "Cheivy Chace") as touching that road (see map). And the 1780 deed citing 17 acres on "the west side of the main road leading from George Town to Frederick Town" refers to 17 acres that today lie west of Belt Road but east of Wisconsin Avenue.[27]

In 1780, John Murdock leased to real estate dealer William Bayly, Jr., land lying "in the fork of the main road leading from George Town to Frederick Town and the new road cleared by Jacob Funk which runs through Dr. Walter Smith's plantation." It was the River Road that ran through Smith's acres of "Friendship." (Smith and Murdock were brothers-in-law, both married to daughters of Joseph Belt.) This triangle of land in the fork of two roads, rented to Bayly and later sold to John Threlkeld, included the plot that much later became known as Gloria Point.

In 1781, the Montgomery County internal improvements list mentions for the first time "the Road newly cut from the fork near Mr. Joseph Belt's Quarter to Captain John [Cabin John] Run above Mr. James Offutt's Mill." "Joseph Belt's Quarter" refers to 200 acres of "Friendship" that Belt rented from his son-in-law on the east side of the George Town-Frederick Road, the northern part of which was just opposite the beginning of the River Road.

The Jacob Funk who finished the construction of the River Road was the same Jacob Funk who founded and promoted Hamburg, a small German community on the waterfront east of George Town—later called Foggy Bottom. He was also the founder of Funkstown, a rural community on Antietam Creek.

The DAR plaque on River Road near Wisconsin Avenue asserts that George Washington "traveled and inspected" this road, but it does not say when. Washington's journals give no indication of any traveling in this area of the country before 1776.[28] He did, however, travel from George Town to Hagerstown in 1790, and from George Town to Frederick in 1791. Wilhelmus Bogart Bryan concluded that Washington traveled by way of the River Road in 1790, and by the Frederick Road in 1791.[29]

Mrs. Lilly Stone, Montgomery County historian who did the research for the 1932 DAR plaque at River Road and Wisconsin Avenue, mistakenly designated River Road as Braddock's route between today's Tenleytown and Rockville. Actually, River Road did not exist until during the Revolution. It was cut through for wheeled vehicles for the first time in 1779-1780.

Census Taking

The first and only colonial census, conducted in 1776, marked the area between George Town and Hungerford's Tavern (Rockville) as Lower Potomack Hundred. There were about 220 white households counted at that time, comprising 912 persons; 616 blacks' first names only are given. The census included not only the names Murdock, Beall, Belt, Jones, Magruder, Reed, and Smith, but also a couple of Germans—Cokendorfer and Keizer—and other names that continue through Tenleytown's history, such as Collins, Chapple, Hurdle, King, Ray, Riley, and Shoemaker.

In 1783, the first personal property assessment, to raise supplies for the Revolutionary War, was made in Middle Potomack, Lower Potomack, and Georgetown Hundreds. According to this accounting, as reported by assessor Joseph Sprigg Belt, the wealthiest man was Robert Peter of Georgetown (total assets 7,250 pounds English currency).

Second wealthiest was Colonel John Murdock of "Friendship," whose 49 slaves, 17 horses, and 50 cattle were counted in his estate of 6,630 pounds. Other well-to-do landowners listed in the 1783 assessment were John Threlkeld and Colonel Charles Beatty, whose

"HISTORIC" PLAQUE ON RIVER ROAD

(1973 photo by
Judith Helm)

**This road traveled and inspected by
George Washington**

**Tehogee Indian Trail, in 1716.
Tobacco Rolling Road, next.
Wagon Road, in 1748.**

**Widened by order of Governor Sharp,
for march of Braddock's Army, in 1755.**

**George Washington Bi-Centennial 1732-1932
D.A.R. Marker
Erected by Janet Montgomery Chapter, N.S.D.A.R.**

*This plaque erroneously attributes
to River Road those qualities and
historic events that should be
attributed to the Rockville Pike
(Wisconsin Avenue). The River
Road was not constructed as a
road until about 1780, according
to Montgomery County records.*

properties were just north and east of Murdock's "Friendship."

In the first U.S. federal census, in 1790, Montgomery County still included George Town and the area that became Tenleytown. Although there were a few more German families than there had been in 1776— Reintzel and Wetzel, for example—the local names were still mainly English, Scottish, and a few Irish.

Trade with England had been completely curtailed during the nearly ten years' difficulty with the mother country, and British immigrants to Maryland were few. The village of George Town and the surrounding countryside therefore did not prosper or even grow. All energies had been spent on maintenance and support of the patriots.

After the peace with Britain was signed in 1783, however, George Town enjoyed a resurgence of prosperity. Robert Peter's firm dominated the tobacco trade after George Gordon moved to "Woodyard" in Prince George's County.

By 1789, the year it was formally incorporated as a town, George Town boasted a customhouse and was an official port of entry for Maryland. It was still one of the foremost seaports on the eastern seaboard, with eight to ten seagoing vessels, many from Europe, at its wharves on any day. (Forty years later there would be berths for 70 merchants' ships.) Large amounts of corn, seeds, and furs were exported, as well as the enormous stock of tobacco.[30]

The first President of the United States was instrumental in selecting the exact site for the federal city, adjacent to the Port of Georgetown, which he described as the greatest tobacco market in Maryland, "if not in the Union."[31] In 1791 the Maryland Assembly ceded 69 square miles for the capital, including Georgetown and "Tennally's Tavern," and Virginia gave 31—the "100 square miles" or "Ten Miles Square." The plan was to build a brand new city on the Potomac, scheduled to be ready in ten years (by 1800) for the Congress, President, and Judiciary to move in.

Surveyors began to erect boundary markers around the "Ten Miles Square" in 1791. They were placed at one-mile intervals all around the square, beginning at the Alexandria waterfront. Many of the original markers that were placed in 1791 and 1792 along the District Line above the Potomac and west of Rock Creek (the northwest markers) can still be seen today. Each of these has the inscription "Jurisdiction of the United States."[32]

Boundary Stone (BS) 4 is today behind the Dalecarlia Filtration Plant, near MacArthur Boulevard. BS 5 is on parkland above Dalecarlia Reservoir. BS 6 is on the northwest side of Western Avenue between Fessenden and 47th Streets. BS 7 is in the front yard of a house at 5600 Western Avenue, at the corner of Cedar Parkway. The number 3 on this marker designates three miles from the Potomac River. BS 8 is southwest of Pinehurst Circle. And BS 9 is south of Beach Drive, off Daniel Road.

President Washington traveled the Great Road leading from the Federal City to Frederick Town on June 30, 1791—but only a farmer who arose with the roosters could have caught a glimpse of him.

"Thursday; 30th. The business which brot me to Georgetown being finished and the Comrs. instructed with respect to the mode of carrying the plan [for buying property for the federal city] into effect I set off this morning a littel after 4 Oclock in the prosecution of

my journey towards Philadelphia; and being desirous of seeing the nature of the country North of Georgetown, and along the upper road, I resolved to pass through Fredericktown in Maryland and York and Lancaster in Pennsylvania . . . ."[33]

---

1 Henry Fleete, "A Brief Journal of a Voyage made in the Bark Virginia to Virginia and Other Parts of the Continent of America," in J. Thomas Scharf, History of Maryland, Baltimore: 1879

2 Patent for "Salcom," Annapolis Hall of Records

3 William Henry Holmes, "Stone Implements of the Potomac-Chesapeake Tidewater Province," 15th Annual Report of [Smithsonian] Bureau of Ethnology, 1893-94 (1897), p. 15

4 Horace P. Hobbs, Jr., Pioneers of the Potowmack, Ann Arbor: University Microfilms, Inc. 1961 and 1964, p. 113

5 Holmes, op. cit., p. 62

6 Washington, City and Capital, American Guide Series, New York: Hastings House, 1937

7 Walton Shipley, "I Remember," 1973, published in Origins, Washington: 1975

8 Land grants, Hall of Records, Annapolis. All research on original land grants quoted in this chapter was performed by Priscilla McNeil.

9 Will of Anthony Addison, PG County, Box 8, Folder 19, Hall of Records, Annapolis

10 Washington, City and Capital, op. cit., p. 724

11 Bessie Wilmarth Gahn, Washington's Headquarters at Georgetown, Silver Spring: 1940, p. 76

12 Gahn, op. cit., p. 77. Her references: Maryland Archives, Vol. 44 (1745), pp. 44, 45, 218, 611.

13 Hugh T. Taggart, "Old Georgetown," RCHS Vol. 11, 1908

14 "Maj. Gen. Edward Braddock's Orderly Books," Appendix in Will H. Lowdermilk, History of Cumberland, 1878

15 Noma Thompson, Western Gateway to the National Capital, Washington: Stewart Printing Co., 1949, p. 81

16 Maryland Archives, Correspondence of Governor Sharpe, Vol. 1, pp. 77 and 97

17 Lowdermilk, op. cit., p. 114

18 Taggart, op. cit.

19 Maryland State Roads Commission, Chas. T. LeViness, A History of Roadbuilding in Maryland, Baltimore: 1958

20 Taggart, op. cit.

21 J. Thomas Scharf, History of Western Maryland, Vol. 1, Baltimore: 1882, p. 697

22 Acts of Assembly, 1774, Chapter XXI, Maryland Archives

23 Samuel C. Busey, Pictures of the City of Washington in the Past. Washington: Wm. Ballantyne & Sons, 1898, pp. 175-177

24 Eugene and Edythe Clark, The Spirit of Captain John, New York: Carlton Press, Inc., 1970

25 Ibid.

26 Acts of Assembly, op. cit.

27 Montgomery County Deeds, Liber A, pp. 564-565, recorded October 9, 1780

28 John C. Fitzpatrick, editor, George Washington Colonial Traveller 1732-1775. Indianapolis: Bobbs-Merrill Co., 1927

29 Wilhelmus Bogart Bryan, History of the National Capital, Vol. I 1790-1814, New York: The MacMillan Co., 1914, pp. 110-113

30 B. Albertson, Rambling Through Georgetown, 1975

31 J. Bernard Wyckoff, Georgetown's Bicentenary, 1951, p. 14

32 Fred E. Woodward, "A Ramble Along Boundary Stones," RCHS, Vol. 10, 1907, p. 64

33 O.W. Holmes, "Suter's Tavern," RCHS, Vol. 49, 1973-74, citing John C. Fitzpatrick, editor, The Complete Diaries of George Washington, Vol. IV

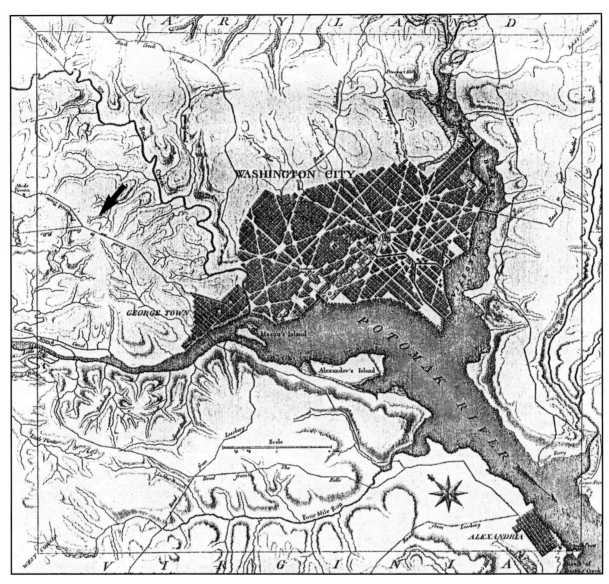

(1815 map drawn by Andrew Ellicott, engraved by Tardieu, Paris. National Archives)

II
The Tennallys and Tennallytown:
1790-1860

Angle of intersection at Tennallytown (upper left of George Town) indicates that the old Road to Frederick Town traveled the route of Brookeville Road. "Mud's Tavern" was popularly known as Valdanier's. "Road to Great Falls" is the River Road.

Tennally's Tavern

By the time George Washington rode through in June 1791, a man named John Tennally was running a popular public tavern on the west side of the Road to Fredericktown, just north of the fork of the new River Road. "John Tennely" had been granted a license in Montgomery County to run an ordinary—a tavern that serves meals—from November 1789 until November 1791.

Tennally was in the spirituous liquors and tobacco business at an earlier date, too. Montgomery County court records show that in 1788, "John Tennoly, John Chapple, and Francis Valdonous" [Valdanier] were fined "for John Tennoly's keeping a publick house." And again in 1789 John Fennely (as it was spelled), Edward C. Veirs, and G. Magruder were fined for "Fennely's keeping a publick house of entertainment." A fine was a fee for a license.

In August 1790 the tavern rates for Montgomery County indicate that beer, cider, wines, rum, and gin were generally available as well as "A Hott diet" and "A Cold diet." Lodging was to include clean sheets. Stablage with hay for horses was provided, but oats or corn were extra; pasturage was optional.[34]

John Tennally's ordinary was probably a small wooden building with a stone or brick chimney. It would have had one public eating room with a large fireplace and a

WILLETTS' SPINNING WHEEL TAVERN

(The Rambler, glass plate, 1915 Columbia Historical Society)

EARLY TAVERN ON RIVER ROAD

The Willetts' old Spinning Wheel Tavern on River Road near Falls Branch, which the Rambler (in The Star, March 14, 1914) reported was used as a tavern during Revolutionary days.

John Tennally's tavern, at the intersection of the Road to Frederick-Town and the River Road, was probably as small and plain as this one.

kitchen with cooking fireplace on the first floor, and one or two dormitory rooms on the second floor. After a bland but solid meal, the traveler would be put up overnight in one of the beds upstairs. If it were crowded, he might share a bed. But guests were not numerous in those early days of bad roads and primitive carriages.

Tennally's tavern was most likely the first business establishment above Georgetown where food and liquors could be bought. Here the local men also gathered to hear the news from travelers, talk politics, and drink.

John Tennally and his mother and two sisters had been listed in the 1776 census still in Prince Georges County, as was his older brother William Tennally and his family. They were not then in the area above George Town, which was in Frederick County by the time of the 1776 census. The census lists the family as follows, with the age of each: John Tennally, 27 (head of household); Joanna, 52 (probably his mother); Elizabeth, 30, and Sarah, 20 (his sisters).

Both John and William Tennally signed, with an X, the Oath of Fidelity and Support of the State of Maryland in 1776. They probably did not serve in the Revolutionary War, for only a George Tennaly is listed in Revolutionary pensioners in Maryland.

The Tennallys came to their new home in Montgomery County in the 1780s, soon after the River Road was cleared.

The intersection came to be called Tennallytown very early. Records of the Prebyterian church in early Maryland[35] indicate that as early as 1786, "the church at Tenally Town was recorded as being without a pastor." As Eugene and Edythe Clark point out, the Rev. James Hunt of Cabin John (who died in 1793) was appointed to preach at Tennaly Town one Sabbath; "but thereafter that church was not heard of again except for two brief supplies by Stephen Balch in 1813" and 1814.[36] Possibly the "church" at Tennallytown was a few families—perhaps the Tennallys and one other family—who requested periodically the services of a clergyman. It was not the church, but the tavern that defined the original community of Tennallytown.

The tavern that John Tennally ran was well known, as is indicated by references to "Tennally's Tavern" in deeds and newspaper notices throughout the 1790s. The May 26, 1790, issue of Times and Patowmack Packet (Georgetown) ran an ad:

"Lost between George Town and Montgomery Court House a dark mixed Surtout-Coat with red lining, yellow metal buttons on each side of the breast. Any person finding the above-mentioned surtout, and leaving it at Mr. John Tennally's tavern or this printing office, shall have Two Dollars Reward."

This item may have been the basis for assuming Tennally's Tavern was in Georgetown.

On September 22, 1790, Nicholas Straney advertised in the Packet: "Eight Dollar Reward. Ran away from subscriber living near Tennelly's Tavern, Montgomery County, an Irish servantman, Named James Harvey . . . ."

The census of 1790 had John Tennerly and Josiah Tennelly living in Montgomery County. In this first U.S. federal census (the 1776 was a colonial census for the province of Maryland), only heads of household were named, so there is less information than the 1776.[37]

In 1791 three surveyors were directed to measure the road from George Town to the Mouth of the Monocacy (River Road), as well as other county roads. In their report, dated the 15th of June, 1791, they referred to "the road at tenerly's tavern then up the road leading from the mouth of Wats Branch to George Town . . . ."

A plat map (see map above) provided by these surveyors is the very first time the name Tennally appears

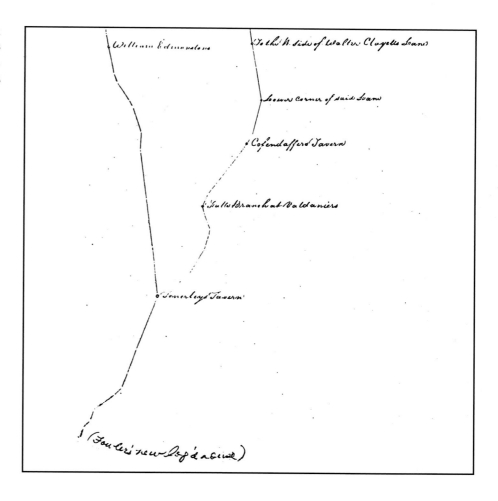

(Montgomery County Courthouse land records, Deed F-6, f195 recorded March 13, 1793, Frederick to Georgetown)

on a map; and as usual, it is misspelled. "Tenerleys Tavern" is indicated as the very point of the fork of two roads: one the old Indian trail, then called the Great Road between George Town and Frederick; and the other the newer Road to Watts Branch.

Records of property transactions from 1793 through 1804[38] indicate that John Tennally's Tavern was on the west side of the road to Frederick Town, just north of the fork of the River Road, and that his sister Sarah Tennally lived in a frame house just across the way, on the east side of the road. John Threlkeld actually owned the land on which Tennally's house and tavern stood; the latter leased it.

The 1793 map shows the 1791 survey of the road "from GeorgeTown to the Mouth of the Monocacy" (River Road), which forks to the west at Tenerleys Tavern. The curving main road that continues in a northwesterly direction is the predecessor to today's Wisconsin Avenue; "Falls Branch at Valdaniers" marked a tavern near today's Oliver Street; "Cofendaffers Tavern" was south of today's Bradley Lane; and the "Lower corner" of Walter Clagett's land marked the fork of today's Old Georgetown Road.

In January 1799 "John Tenalley" published a notice in the Georgetown Centinel of Liberty: "I intend to petition the next General Assembly of Maryland to discharge me from debts due the State which I am unable to pay." No explanation was offered for Tennally's indebtedness.

Apparently John Tennally was not living by the time of the 1800 census. Sarah Tennally (misspelled Fennely) was named the head of household (over 45); also in the household were one male under 45 and two females.

How John Tennally lived and how he died are shown to us by tales handed down by later residents of Tenleytown.

Mary Ann Lightfoot Britt (1834-1918), who lived her whole life in what was called the Tenley House, was interviewed in 1891 by George Simmons, who wrote "Roadside Sketches" for the Star:

"Mr. Tenley was of English birth, but came here from Charles County, Md . . . . He was a blacksmith by trade, and located his shop and residence on the site now occupied by Mr. [and Mrs.] William Britt . . . . He was never married, but two maiden sisters, Sarah and Elizabeth, kept house for him. Their remains now rest in the back end of Mr. Britt's lot. John died suddenly at a public ball given in the town.

"A close intimacy existed between the Tenleys and Mrs. Britt's family, the Lightfoots, and the latter has in her possession some relics of the former which she highly prizes. Among them is an old clothes brush that must be more than 100 years old . . . . She also has a small leather box in which Tenley used to store his lucre,

but as he was never in very opulent circumstances it is not probable that the capacity of the box was ever overtasked.

"Neighborhood gossip says that Mr. Tenley was a man of quiet, retiring disposition, but that he was not averse to participating in an occasional frolic." [39]

Mrs. Britt was sure that John Tennally was a blacksmith. She makes no mention of his ever having owned a tavern that was a landmark in these parts. Possibly the popularity of the Anti-Saloon League in her day, as well as her religious convictions (she was a member of the Tennallytown Baptist Church) helped her to ignore Tennally's vocation as a seller of liquor and beer. Perhaps she did not know he ran a tavern.

The story of John Tennally's dying at "a public ball given in the town" also provokes questions. Which town? George Town is more likely to have held a public dance; did Tennallytown at this early time host public dances? And to expire at an occasion such as is suggested—surely that was a remarkable event!

In 1915 the Rambler, J. Harry Shannon, published another interview with Mrs. Britt, who was then 81, and her sister Barbara Lightfoot, who was 79; this added a little more to the story of the Tenleys, as they insisted the name was spelled.

According to the sisters, the half-acre property the Tenleys bought was on the east side of the main road. The house in which the Tenleys lived, they said, was next to the Lightfoot house. The Tenleys were poor people:

"There were no other houses near here when the Tenleys built their small frame house. At last a few other families moved here; a store and a blacksmith shop were opened

and the hamlet came to be called Tenleytown." [40]

This version says that a blacksmith shop was opened—but not that Tenley was the blacksmith. Records show that Jacob Colclazer owned a blacksmith establishment at the fork before 1818, having bought the three and a half acres formerly owned by John Threlkeld. [41]

The Lightfoot family, as well as earlier writers, have insisted that Tenley was the only correct spelling of the name—but the records disagree. The 1776 census gives us John Tennally; the 1790 census, John Tennerly; the 1799 news item, John Tenalley; and in the 1822 will of his sister, she marks her "X" over Sarah Tennalley.

The "X"es are important in the brothers' 1776 Oath of Fidelity and in Sarah's 1822 will. The Tennally family was, no doubt, illiterate, and those contemporaries who could write spelled the name the way they heard it pronounced—always with three syllables. The great variety of spellings reflects the variety of pronunciations and accents of the speakers and the imagination of the hearers.

Although John Tennally was no longer in the list of tavern-keepers by 1800, the fork in the road where he did business has carried his name for nearly two centuries after his death. And, as LeRoy O. King, Jr., believes, the name Tennallytown could just as well have come from Miss Sarah Tennally. [42]

It was she who bought the half-acre on the east side of the road; she also lived in the area over 30 years, whereas her brother John lived here only about 13 years.

The Murdocks

The Tennallys came to this new fork in the Great Road a few short years before the death of Colonel

John Murdock of "Friendship." No doubt the Tennallys got to know the Colonel, for although the latter was wealthy and the former were not, they were neighbors in a very sparsely populated district.

Another near neighbor was Joseph Belt, a nephew of the original owner of "Cheivy Chace." This Joseph Belt and his wife Esther Smith paid "one ear of Indian Corn" a year to rent a 200-acre plantation on the east side of the Frederick Road from Col. John Murdock, who may have been their son-in-law.

It is very possible that John Murdock had built a log or frame house on the "Belt plantation." There must have been a house standing when Murdock "out of love and affection" leased these 200 acres in 1780 to the Belts.[43] There was no mention of a brick house in Murdock's 1783 property assessment; but the brick house known as "The Rest," which still stands today, was later built on this same plantation.

Colonel John Murdock of "Friendship" died August 3, 1790, in his 58th year. As the next day's obituary stated,

"he was descended from an ancient and respectable Family in this State; his Genius far superior to the common Level—his Mind was great and comprehensive; these Qualifications procured him the most honourable Appointments previous to the Revolution.—In the Cause of the Liberties of his Country, he acted the PATRIOT, STATESMAN, and SOLDIER."[44]

The inventory of Colonel Murdock's property made after his death counts among his possessions 48 Negroes, 26 head of cattle, 56 hogs, 23 horses, 7,000 pounds of hay, and a large number of farm utensils and household furnishings. He was

"Roadside Sketches," The Star, August 15, 1891)

The Sarah Tennally house, inherited by Sarah Robey in 1822. The addition on the south (right) side was made about 1840 by Daniel Lightfoot, Sarah Robey's husband. John Tennally may have lived here, but his tavern was on the other side of the road. The Tennally-Lightfoot house, as it came to be known, was torn down in the late 1950s to make room for Hechinger's lumberyard.

one of the wealthiest men in the area.

John Murdock had only one legitimate child—Captain William Murdock, who had married Jane Contee Harrison in 1783. In 1790 there were three young grandchildren, Addison, Kitty, and Eliza Murdock. Colonel John Murdock's will arranged for the trustees of his estate to provide for and to maintain his son William and William's family, including educating the grandchildren; but only the grandson, Addison, was to inherit any land. The granddaughters were to receive money.

William died at a very young age, just the year after his father died. Young Addison Murdock inherited a large amount of his grandfather's "Friendship" when he turned 21. But, like his father before him, he also died young, in his late 20s.

(Some confusion exists over the activities of John and William Murdock of "Friendship" because they had a contemporary named William Murdock [1748-1825] who was a partner with Uriah Forrest and Benjamin Stoddert in a successful Georgetown-to-London import-export business.)

Before his death, Colonel John Murdock deeded to Dorothy Barber and her young son John 141 acres of "White Haven," which included a number of existing dwellings. John Threlkeld was appointed trustee to administer this estate for her as long as she remained single.[45] To Dorothy, John, and his two sisters Elizabeth and Mary, Colonel Murdock bequeathed two Negroes "and their increase." Later deeds indicate that John Barber was referred to as "alias John Murdock"[46]—an indication that he was an illegitimate son by Dorothy Barber; possibly his two sisters were likewise children of the Colonel. Dorothy Barber later (by 1815) married a Mr. McPherson, 25 years after the Colonel died. By then her children were grown.

Other Early Settlers

After the establishment of the nation's capital and the setting of the boundaries of the District of Columbia, the few owners of the large tracts around Tenleytown had no trouble finding buyers for their land.

Isaac Pierce, beginning in 1794, bought property that eventually amounted to over 2,000 acres east and west of Rock Creek. Pierce built a sawmill, a stone house, a spring-house, and several barns, and refurbished a grain mill on the creek. The winding lane leading east from the Georgetown-Frederick Road was laid out eventually as Pierce's Mill Road.

Dr. John Weems, member of a prominent Prince George's County family, had begun buying property northeast of the Tennallys in 1795. The previous owner, William Bayly, Jr., had named the property "Mt. Airy," but Dr. Weems called it "Weemsborough" or "Weemsburgh." Dr. Weems' country home was built on not only the highest hill in Tenleytown, but also the highest land in the District of Columbia, now called Fort Reno.

John Chapple (great-grandfather of the late Tenleytown doctor John Chappell) had purchased a good but hilly part of "Fletchall's Chance" (see map) west of the Broad Branch, in 1780. The road leading down to the branch and to Broad Branch Road (and later, up to Grant Road) was called Chappell Road. It is now 36th Street north of Fessenden. The Chappell family kept that property for a century.

What President Adams Saw

The President's Mansion was almost completed when President John Adams first visited his new residence. On May 27, 1800, the President had left the old capital, Philadelphia, and started the trip to the new capital, Washington, by way of Lancaster, York, Frederick, and Montgomery Court House. Hugh T. Taggart wrote that "the President arrived at the boundary line of the District on Tuesday, June 3, and he was there met by a large number of citizens on horseback and escorted to the Union Tavern" [in Georgetown].[47]

As the President's carriage passed along the dusty road that afternoon in early summer, the first occupant of the new President's House saw some of the forests, farms, and fields in the Washington county, as the area outside the city boundary was called. Much land had been cleared for farming and pasture. Trees had been felled by the thousands for use as fuel in the cold winters.

After having passed first "Cookendoffer's" and then Valdanier's taverns, President Adams' carriage crossed from Maryland into the District of Columbia. He and his escort did not have to descend and then ascend a long hill up to the village of Tennallytown, as later travelers did and still do. The route taken in 1800 was a little more to the east—a level stretch of road, over the old Indian trail, which later was connected to and called the Brookeville Road, and even later the Belt Road. On his left the President could see the Belt, Weems, and Bayly properties and on his right, Threlkeld and Murdock land.

Upon arriving at the high point that was called Tennallytown, the President had his first long view in the new District of Columbia: to the east, the Rock Creek valley and the wooded hillsides beyond; to the south, the hills above Georgetown; and to the west, the Potomac valley and the Virginia hills, perhaps even to the Blue Ridge.

Tennally's tavern was on the President's right, just before he passed the Upper Falls (River) Road junction. It is likely that by May 1800 John Tennally had died and Sarah Tennally or Theophilus Robey was operating Tennally's tavern. Opposite, on the left, was Sarah Tennally's two-story frame house.

About a third of a mile after Tennally's, on the left side, was what had been Joseph Belt's plantation. It was later the site of the large brick house known as "The Rest."

The Murdock house was not visible from the Frederick Road. It was almost a mile to the west, on what is now the campus of the American University. A caretaker probably occupied the house in 1800.

Further down the road, President Adams passed the entrance road to "Rosedale," Uriah Forrest's family home, built in 1794—the only structure existing in the neighborhood of Tennallytown in 1800 that still is standing today. (A few days after his arrival in Washington, the President supposedly dined at General Forrest's).[48]

All along this road, the President passed the slower moving wagons heavily laden with produce for Georgetown and Washington markets.

When the President's carriage left the high land, it descended a steep hill from what later came to be known as Tunlaw Heights or Mount Alto. At this point John Adams saw for the first time the Potomac River, the "old" town of Georgetown, and the "new" town of Washington, where he spent the last months of his term of office.

Early Roads, Stagecoaches

In 1797 the first Georgetown-to-Frederick stagecoach line passed right by Tennally's tavern. It ran only once a week each way at first, leaving Frederick every Thursday morning and arriving at Georgetown Friday morning. It left Georgetown again the same day and reached Frederick late Saturday afternoon. The overnight stopping place would have been at Owens' or Dowden's Ordinary, halfway along the route.[49]

By the summer of 1800, the stagecoach, which by then was carrying the mail, started at 4 a.m. and ran through the same day. The trip was made twice a week each way, and the passenger fare was $3.00, or 6¢ a mile.

Competing lines soon sprang up, which indicates there was a good demand for transportation between Georgetown and Frederick. New stopping places were Adam Robb's Fountain Inn (Montgomery Court House) for breakfast, and Scholl's Tavern (near Clarksburg) for dinner. There was also Valdanier's old stone tavern north of the District line, as well as Tennally's tavern.

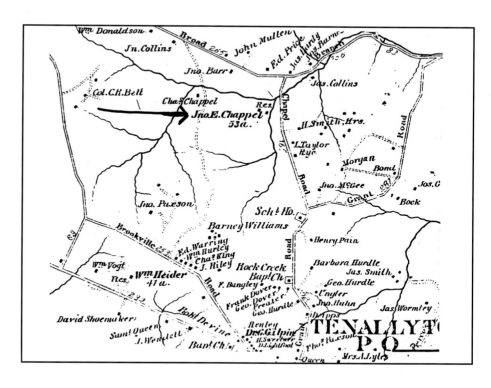

(G.M. Hopkins, Part of Second District, District of Columbia, Washington: Library of Congress, 1878)

1878 map shows the land of John Chappel (Chapple) still in the family a century after he bought it—northeast of Tennallytown, near Broad Branch and "Chapel" Roads.

The community of Hungerford's Tavern, the seat of Montgomery County since 1777, had become Montgomery Court House after construction of a courthouse in 1779. In 1801 the Maryland legislature renamed the village Rockville, after the nearby Rock Creek.[50] Despite the new name, most area residents continued to refer to the county seat as Montgomery Court House, even as late as 1814.

Tales told by stagecoach riders between Georgetown and Frederick show they traveled always in fear of capsizing when careening down a steep hill or crossing a creek; and their worst fears often came true. Robberies were reported—whether by fellow travelers or "highwaymen" is not clear.

Stagecoaches frequently broke down, and passengers had to wait while an axle was repaired, or make other arrangements. Delays were consequently routine; schedules were inconvenient; one had to arise early

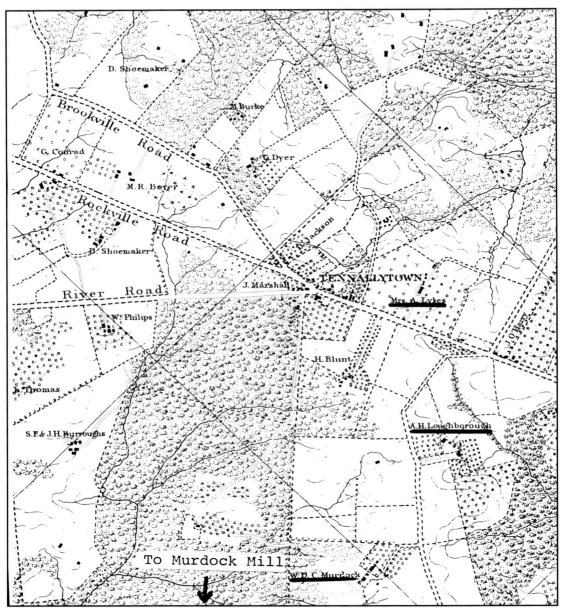

(A. Boschke's Topographic Map of the District of Columbia, 1861, from field inspection of 1857-58. Library of Congress)

Sarah Love's home, "The Rest," is indicated on this map as "Mrs. A. Lyles," and Nathan Loughborough's "Grassland" is then owned by his son, A.H. Loughborough. Note the turnings of the Loughborough Road.

to board the departing stage at 4 a.m. And the interior of the vehicle was never of great comfort, unheated in winter and suffocating in summer.

Henry Winemiller tried to reassure prospective riders of the reliability of his stagecoach between Frederick Town and George Town:

"Ladies and gentlemen disposed to take passage in the

above conveyance may confidently rely on being accommodated with a good stage and horses, and also provided with a careful and excellent driver."[51]

By 1800 three main routes of travel ran in and out of Washington. One route went from Washington northeast via Bladensburg to Baltimore and beyond to the cities of

Philadelphia, New York, and Boston; another, going south from Georgetown to Alexandria, paralleled a ferry route between the two cities on the Potomac. The third road went north from Georgetown through Tennallytown to Montgomery Court House, Frederick, and points northward and westward.

These three routes had enjoyed a fair amount of travel ever since 1751, when Georgetown was established as a shipping and commercial center. And now that the capital of the United States was growing up adjacent to Georgetown, these routes became heavily traveled, and new, connecting roads grew in number.

Early Estates

In 1801 Mrs. Sarah Love was living on 100 acres of Belt's plantation, "to the north of [Pierce's] Mill road and to the east side of the main road leading from Georgetown to the [Montgomery] Court House." Mrs. Love, the widow of Samuel Love, resided on the property (now 39th and Windom) which her brother, Charles C. Jones, had bought for her.[52] It was Jones, of "Clean Drinking Manor," who built the brick house, "The Rest," for his sister. The millstone in front of "the Rest" is supposed to have come from Jones's Mill, which ran until 1848.[53]

"The Rest" is "of English brick," which describes the dimensions and kind of brick used. George Alfred Townsend[54] says that colonial houses were built of brick made locally, not of imported brick, though many insist otherwise. The term "English brick" actually refers to a brick (from any kiln) that is larger and thicker than Dutch brick, for example.[55] Brick used in this area of Maryland was usually a dark red color.

"The Rest" does, however, have hinges, doorknobs, and other fix-

(Sketch by Judith Helm)

"The Rest" as it probably looked when it was built for Sarah Love in the early 1800s. Still standing at 4343 39th Street.

tures that may well have been imported from England.

Nathan Loughborough, acting comptroller of the U.S. Treasury for many years, acquired about 250 acres of Murdock's "Friendship" property, beginning in 1804.[56] He built a large brick house and stone barn for his family of eight children. This estate, which Loughborough named "Grassland," was southwest of Tennallytown on an old road.

The Loughborough Road, as it came to be called, was first an Indian trail to the Potomac. In early times called the Falls Road or the Little Falls Road, it traveled southwest from the main Indian trail, through Murdock's "Friendship" and down a steep hill to the Potomac ferry near Little Falls. When it came to be called Loughborough Road, it left the Frederick Road opposite its connection with Pierce's Mill Road, passed by Loughborough's estate as well as Murdock's, and connected eventually with the Tunlaw Road, the Ridge Road (now Foxhall Road), Chain Bridge Road, and the Canal Road, to the Little Falls (see page 196). The first log bridge below the Little Falls was built in 1797, and it

"GRASSLAND," NATHAN LOUGHBOROUGH'S ESTATE

(Sketch from Lizzie A. Tompkins, "Some Washington Homes," unsourced periodical at CHS)

Above: "Grassland," built by Nathan Loughborough in the early 1800s. After it was built, the Old Road to Little Falls was called Loughborough Road, and later Nebraska Avenue. "Grassland" was torn down about 1955 for construction of NBC studios.

Left: Note that Loughborough mansion had access roads to both the Rockville Turnpike on the east and Loughborough Road on the west.

(copy of a survey March 1866 by Templeman and Shipman; drawn by Priscilla McNeil) was replaced by the first "chain" bridge in about 1810.

The upper part of Lough-borough Road is what is now Nebraska Avenue. The lower part is still called Loughborough Road and continues down to MacArthur Boulevard.

"Grassland" stood until about 1955 behind the buildings of the Naval Security Station northeast of Ward Circle.

In 1808 Nathan Loughborough also acquired a farm which he called Milton, or Melton. It was further out in the Maryland country—on the south side of River Road, about two miles west of Tennallytown. This country house was in the northern part of the original "Friendship." Loughborough added a large stone central portion and small balancing wing to the Dutch style house in 1847, according to Gertrude S. Bradley.[57] This Loughborough house stands today at 5312 Allendale Road, Bethesda, almost two blocks south of River Road.

The National Road

In 1806 Congress had authorized the completion of the Great National Road (also called the National Pike, the Cumberland Road, and the National Old Trail Road). It was to be constructed from Cumberland, Md., westward to St. Louis, Mo. The road that already existed from Georgetown through Tennallytown and north to Montgomery Court House was a southeastern link to the National Pike. (U.S. Route 40 from Baltimore to Frederick, which was completed in 1825, is the main eastern section of the National Pike.)

The existing road followed what is now Wisconsin Avenue to Belt Road, then back to present-day Wisconsin Avenue at a point just north of today's District line, to "Five

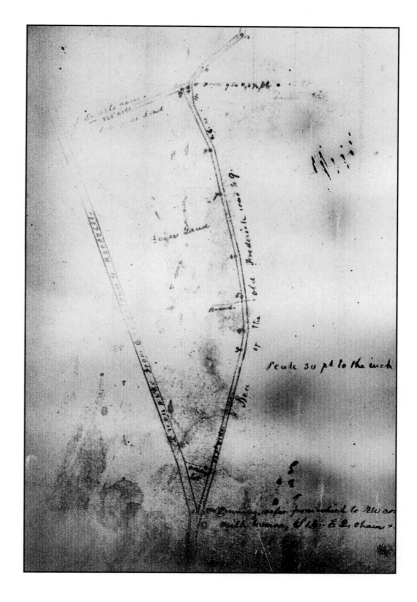

(map c/o Michael Spevak)

L. Carberry's 1847 survey of the new "Turnpike from Georgetown to Rockville (left) and the "Bed of the old Frederick road to G." (right). Today they are called Wisconsin Avenue (left) and Belt Road (right), with the link at the top known as Belt Lane, just south of the District line.

Points, where it veered to the left on the Old Road (later called Old Georgetown Road), and northward through Rockville."[58] A Madonna of the Trail statue on Wisconsin Avenue at Montgomery Lane, Bethesda, was dedicated in 1929 by the Old Trails Association to honor those pioneer women who traveled this road west.

The new National Road was instrumental in opening up the western frontier to settlers; brightly painted Conestoga wagons frequently lumbered through Tennallytown.

But the traffic between Frederick-town and Georgetown was primarily farm wagons loaded with produce and tobacco bound for the Georgetown market or the port, and returning home with fish, flour ground at the mills, and imported and bartered processed goods.

In the early 1800s, only two roads converged at Tennallytown: the River Road and what we now call the Belt Road, or Brookeville Road (see 1815 Ellicott map, page 16). The new section of the road to Fredericktown had not then been built.

The Second Tennallytown Inn

In 1805 Addison Murdock sold ten acres of "Friendship" on the southwest corner of the intersection of the Fredericktown Road and the River Road. The buyer was Henry Riszner, who built a large place of business. Riszner (also spelled Reisner, Reizner, Risener, and Rizener) sold whiskey, brandy, and other spirits; also pork, veal, and lamb, according to his account books.[59]

Riszner's establishment, a tavern and general store combined, probably replaced Tennally's tavern as the stagecoach stop. Like other Maryland inns, the Tennallytown Inn would have charged $1.75 to a wagoner for a bed overnight, grain and hay for up to six horses, a meal for himself, and "all the whiskey he could drink."[60]

The First Military Encampment, 1814

The few villagers of Tenleytown were surprised suddenly to discover themselves host to frightened Washingtonians and about 800 American soldiers one hot evening in 1814. A British regiment, under Major General Robert Ross, had been plundering in the Chesapeake Bay area and finally proceeded by horse and by foot to attack the city of Washington.

The unfortunate skirmish called the Battle of Bladensburg, on Wednesday, August 24, 1814, resulted in a scattering of the untrained American troops, under the hapless leadership of General William H. Winder. The British soldiers marched into Washington after their Bladensburg victory, vandalized and set fire to the Capitol building and the President's House, and terrorized the residents who remained in the city that summer night.

Earlier in the day, the Frederick Road had become crowded with Washington residents who had heard about the British invasion and who had fled their homes in terror. The local farmers and Tennallytowners began to take these refugees into their homes, and the country roads were crowded with city carriages. Henry Riszner's Tennallytown Inn was filled to overflowing.

The Battle of Bladensburg had ended about 4 p.m., and the appearance of the anxious and disordered troops in the early evening added fuel to the rumors that the British would eventually come even to Tennallytown.

Part of the retreating American troops marched beyond "the Heights of Georgetown" and camped north of Tennallytown that night. General Winder's written defense of his movements indicated he decided that

"it was wise and proper to retire through Georgetown, and take post in the rear of it, on the heights, to collect my force. I accordingly pursued this course, and halted at Tenleytown, two miles from Georgetown, on the Frederick road . . . .

"After waiting in this position until I supposed I collected all the force that could be gathered, I proceeded about five miles further on the river road, which leads a little wide to the left of Montgomery Court House, and in the morning gave orders for the whole to assemble at Montgomery Court House."[61]

General Winder's account is corroborated by that of Colonel William D. Beall, who commanded nearly 800 American men:

"I received an order to march through Georgetown to the heights above it, but we reached TenlyTown; and from thence, about 12 o'clock at night, were ordered to move on the river road, no point designated; the next day we arrived at Montgomery court house; the next we encamped at Gaither's heights, thence to Ellicott's Mills, thence to the two mile stone toward Baltimore."[62]

An 1899 newspaper story[63] suggests that one reason the troops went no further than Tennallytown that night was that the tollgate was "locked" and that such an obstacle made the retreating forces stop long enough to reconsider their cowardly flight, and to rally. This achievement of "martial glory" was attributed to either the inattention or the stubbornness of the Tennallytown toll-gate-keeper.

Besides the unlikelihood that 800 soldiers traveling north on the Frederick Road could have been unwillingly stopped by one gatekeeper or even one tollgate, there is a more convincing argument against the story. The fact of the matter is, there was no tollgate in 1814. The first one appeared in Tennallytown in 1829.

The diary of Mrs. William Thornton, a friend and neighbor of Dolley Madison, gives us a feeling for that very hot day, August 24, 1814, when Mrs. Thornton and her party decided to abandon their Washington house and flee to their farm in Montgomery County:

"We saw our retreating army come up the avenue—we then hastened away, and were escorted out of town by our Defeated troops, General Washington's picture, and a cart load of goods from the president's house in Company . . . . When we got to the upper part of GeorgeTn — we met Mr. Richards who advised us not to proceed up the road, as it was crowded with troops etc. and that there was a rumour that the British were to head them that way & give them Battle.

"Dr. T. [her husband] having gone round by Mr. Peter's we did not know what step to take but decided to go to Mr. Peter's and wait till we could send for him—I sent off [servant] John on one of the carriage horses and he did not overtake him till he got to TennelyTown he supposing we were before him—We staid all night at Mrs. Peter's . . . and there witnessed the conflagration of our poor and undefended and devoted city."[64]

The President's wife also escaped the burning capital by way of the Frederick Road and Tennallytown. As Margaret Bayard Smith relates,[65] Dolley Madison later told her ("she could scarcely speak without tears" at the memory of it) that she had "retreated with the flying army" about four o'clock in the afternoon and had slept that first ter-rifying night under guard in a tent in the encampment. Tennallytown was the site of the encampment, as indicated by General Winder.

The high ground of Tennallytown made it possible for residents and refugees to see the clouds of black smoke that began to rise from federal buildings in Washington city. Mrs. Madison, protected by an armed escort, viewed the horrible sight of the burning of the capital.

After the sun went down, a strong wind came up and dark clouds rolled over the city. A summer thunderstorm of near hurricane force added to the intense drama of the day. The prolonged downpour helped the feeble fire fighting apparatus in the city to drown the fires that had been started by the British. The thunder and lightning sent all but the soldiers indoors in Tennallytown.

On Thursday morning, Mrs. Madison told Mrs. Smith, she had escaped across the Potomac River into Virginia. Other stories say Mrs. Madison stayed in "the inn at Tennallytown" with friends. Another old Tennally tavern may have still been in existence, run by Sarah Tennally or perhaps the Robeys, the Willetts, or Anastasia Dial.

Anastasia Dial, also known as Ann Stacy Doyle, advertised for sale in 1818 "one of the best stands for a tavern . . . on which is a good dwelling house, cook house, stables, waggon yard, a good well of water . . . ." Her land was adjacent to the Tennally house on the east side of the road.[66] But by 1814, the new three-story inn had also been built on the west side of the road by Henry Riszner. There is inadequate evidence, however, that Mrs. Madison stayed at an inn in Tennallytown.

Decline of Tobacco Trade

The prosperity and growth of Georgetown had been expected to continue after the Revolution. But tobacco production was cut back in the 1790s, primarily because tobacco growers discovered that the crop had removed all nourishment from the soil. Secondarily, the British market was now hostile to American imports.

By the end of the 18th century, the total value of Georgetown exports, primarily tobacco, had greatly declined from what it had been at its height. Even though the waterfront was still quite busy and new residents and businesses were sprouting up every day in nearby Washington, the decline in tobacco trade was very real.

Many of the largest real estate speculators had suffered losses in their land sales to the government and to individuals, which had its effect on the Georgetown economy. And the growth of Washington as a city meant the decline of Georgetown as the center of commerce.

A double blow to the future of Georgetown as a port came about by 1816. The larger new steamships could not navigate the Upper Potomac.

The accumulation of silt in the Georgetown harbor had been speeded up by the building of a causeway to Analostan Island (today's Theodore Roosevelt Island). This raised the bottom of the Potomac River markedly and nearly closed lower Rock Creek to all but flat-bottom boats and canoes.

The Georgetown waterfront never recovered from this decline in shipping. Gradually, fewer and fewer ships could navigate the Potomac beyond the Eastern Branch. Georgetown's heyday as a shipping

"THE VINEYARD"

(Gift of John A. Saul, Washingtoniana Collection, Martin Luther King Memorial Library)

John Adlum, the "father of American winemaking," lived in this once-beautiful house south-east of Tennallytown. The house had fallen into disrepair by 1906, the year this picture was taken, when the land was acquired for the Bureau of Standards.

"SPRINGLAND"

(1981 photo by Petra Schultze)

Built about 1840 by H. Hatch Dent and his wife Anna Maria Adlum, this house stands today at 3550 Tilden Street. The current owner is Bardyl Tirana.

port was over by the mid-19th century.

The economic ups and downs of Georgetown had a direct effect on the prosperity of Tennallytowners. The decline in the tobacco market and production meant a decline in the prosperity of the Tennallytown area tobacco farmers. Real estate speculators around Tennallytown sold off parcels of land in desperate attempts to forestall bankruptcy.

The large Conestoga wagons by-passed Tennallytown as they carried new settlers to the Ohio Valley and beyond. As the Maryland lands were bought up and the economy worsened, fewer new arrivals chose to settle within the District of Columbia or in lower Montgomery County. Some unsuccessful farmers in this area picked up and moved west, seeking a better life.

In 1810 John Counselman had acquired 450 acres on both sides of the Maryland-D.C. line, and east of the proposed new section of the Road to Frederick Town. Samuel Shoemaker had bought 102 acres on both sides of the city line, west of the new Frederick Road and extending to River Road, in 1819, from Clement Smith. These two acquisitions in the northern part of "Friendship," which had been held by John Threlkeld, changed the land from uncultivated woodlands to active farmlands.

The 1820 census of Washington County, which then included Tennallytown, listed the county population at 2,729. Almost half the people in the county were black, mostly slaves. There were 1,512 whites, 1,049 colored slaves, and 168 free colored persons.[67] This population included the entire rural area of the District from the Potomac to the Eastern Branch and down to Oxon Run. Tennallytown and its surrounding country, especially toward the Potomac, had a large percentage of the total Washington County population. The 1830 census, ten years later, listed, for the Tennallytown area only, 451 white households, eight slave families, and three free Negro families.

* * * *

One of the early estate owners was horticulturist John Adlum, who obtained over 200 acres, mostly of the "Addition to Rock of Dumbarton" and "Gizor" tracts, from John Heugh and James Dunlop. Adlum built his home, "The Vineyard," on this site on Pierce's Mill Road, prior to 1820.[68] He successfully cultivated 22 varieties of grapes for winemaking, the most popular of which was the Catawba grape. He was not successful, however, in persuading the government to support a horticulture experimental station on public ground.[69]

While Major John Adlum was living at "The Vineyard," he wrote the earliest book on the cultivation of the vine in America (1823), and was henceforth known as the father of American wine. In addition to corresponding with other grape growers, including Thomas Jefferson, Adlum bottled his own wine for sale to local markets.[70]

Adlum died in 1836. His frame house stood until the early years of the 20th century, when the land around it was purchased for the National Bureau of Standards.

Anna Maria Adlum, the Major's younger daughter, married H. Hatch Dent, of Port Tobacco. They purchased from Charles Nourse of "The Highlands" property adjacent to her father's "Vineyard." Their own brick house, built about 1840, and surrounded by 50 acres of farmland, was named "Springland." Dent changed the course of Pierce's Mill Road to run closer to his home. "Springland" still stands today, in well preserved condition, at 3550 Tilden Street.

Joseph Nourse, the Register of the U.S. Treasury, bought about 100 acres of "Friendship" and 30 acres of "Pretty Prospects" for his son, Major Charles Nourse. Charles took ten years to build the Georgian stone house, "The Highlands," beginning in 1817. His father, who also acquired parts of other tracts, "Gizor," "Mt. Airy," and "Friendship," was the owner of a home named "Mt. Alban," later the site of the Cathedral.[71]

Charles J. Nourse and his wife Rebecca Morris, of Philadelphia, had 18 children, 11 of whom survived. The first seven were born before the Nourses moved into the house in 1827. As the years passed, the house was expanded to accommodate the growing family.

Anthony Morris of Philadelphia, at one time Madison's envoy to England, was the father of Mrs. Nourse. When he came to live with the family in Tennallytown, he renewed his long-time friendship with Dolley Madison, who was living in Washington. The Nourses were pleased to exchange letters and visits with the President's widow, who had been to Tennallytown before on one very memorable evening in 1814.[72]

"The Highlands" was built entirely of stone from a local quarry, under the direction and design of Charles Nourse. Since the Nourse property then extended east nearly to Rock Creek, the quarry may have been on this property. Many of the substantial homes built at that time and in this vicinity were of local stone or brick.

"The Highlands" still stands at 3825 Wisconsin Avenue, now the administration building of the Sidwell Friends School. It is listed in Landmarks of the National Capital.[73]

In 1830 English writer Frances Trollope described the area above Georgetown:

"The country rises into a beautiful line of hills behind Washington, which form a sort of undulating terrace on to Georgetown; this terrace is almost entirely occupied by a succession of gentlemen's seats."

Mrs. Trollope was sharply critical, however, of the neighboring farmers whose "cottages" she visited:

"The class of people the most completely unlike any existing in England, are those who, farming their own freehold estates, and often possessing several slaves, yet live with as few of the refinements and I think I may say, with as few of the comforts of life, as the very poorest English peasant."[74]

One of the reasons for this poor quality of life observed among the farmers was the decline of the productivity of the farms. Even as early as 1790, the farmers had begun to emigrate to the more fertile lands in the West and South.

Farmland in this area and lower Montgomery County was fast being denuded and exhausted. The tobacco fields were wearing out from excessive planting without fertilizer; fences were broken and not repaired; and the fine old homesteads of some of the early rich planters lay in neglect.[75]

Many plantation owners, convinced of the injustice of slavery, set

("The Rambler," glass plate, 1918, Columbia Historical Society)

"The Highlands," built 1817-27 by Charles and Rebecca Nourse. They reared 11 children in this house, which was built of stone from a quarry to the east. The house is now occupied by Sidwell Friends School, 3825 Wisconsin Avenue. Notice block at front driveway for dismounting from horses and carriages.

free their slaves, but discovered they could then not afford as many farm workers as they were used to employing. Sons left home because of the increasing poverty of the land. By 1840 the population of Montgomery County had dropped to 15,456, four thousand less than it had been ten years earlier.

"The land would no longer yield an increase, and they made no attempt at renovating and improving the soil, and Montgomery lands became a synonym for poverty. The lands bordering the Rockville and Georgetown Turnpike, the then only paved road in the County, were with the exception of Robert Dick's and one or two other farms, but a succession of uninclosed old fields."[76]

On the west side of the Georgetown-Fredericktown Road, just south of Tennallytown, were parts of "Friendship" and "Terra Firma" acquired in the early 1800s by members of the French family of Prince George's County and Georgetown. Mrs. George (Arianna) French, a Georgetown widow with four children, inherited this prominent site in Tennallytown. Samuel Busey[77] says that a brick house on the west side of the Rockville Road was owned by "a member of the Peter family" and was named "Eden Bower." Arianna French, who was a sister of Mrs. Robert Peter of Georgetown, supposedly named "Eden Bower" after a house in a novel popular at that time.[78]

In 1809 Addison Murdock's widow had married Charles French,[79] one of Arianna's sons, and so brought to the marriage a large part of the "Friendship" tract, as well as the "Terra Firma" property east and south of it. In 1810 Charles French paid $1,750 for $110\frac{1}{2}$ acres of Murdock's land "near Tenely Town," by order of the chancery court.[80]

His brother George French (Jr.) and wife Peggy Weems also lived at "Eden Bower" after their marriage in 1807. Their sister Elizabeth was the widow of Dr. John Weems of Georgetown, who owned the highest land in Tennallytown.

The French family sold "Eden Bower" to Clement Smith, whose relatives were intermarried with the same prominent southern Maryland families. Clement and his brother Walter Smith were prosperous merchants and landowners. At one time the brothers were owners or part owners of twelve ships that exported goods from Georgetown's harbor.

The Turnpike Is Built

In 1805 the Maryland Assembly had passed "An Act to incorporate a company to make a turnpike road from the District Line . . . to Fredericktown." The necessary funds for building up the road were to be raised by subscription, and the subscribers would be repaid by the collection of tolls. In 1809 the D.C. commissioners declared the busy road leading from Georgetown to Tennallytown "a public highway."[81] And in 1813 the state of Maryland and even President Madison approved construction of a new turnpike.

The fact is that a well-traveled road already existed, but it was unpaved. "Construction of the road" meant widening and eventually macadamizing, by which layers of stone or crushed rock were compressed onto the roadbed. The old Frederick-Georgetown Road was in the process of being macadamized from 1817 to 1823.

The stagecoach lines northwest to Frederick became of greater importance with the opening of the National Road to Wheeling in 1818. It carried the "Great Western Mail" from Washington to Ohio.[82]

In 1818 a Georgetown newspaper carried a notice of election of officers of a Frederick Turnpike Company, interested in "making a road" from the District line to Rockville and beyond.[83] In 1819 John Threlkeld had granted a right-of-way through his land to the Washington Turnpike Co. to build a new turnpike between Tennallytown and the District line. But it was not until the 1820s that the new road was begun.

According to an 1825 writer, "The Rockville Road, from the District, has been opened and formed for three miles, thus connecting the whole line between the two places. The travel on this road is very considerable."[84] (This was north of the District line.)

Milestones were erected along the turnpike, as attested to by the 1820s records of the Bethesda Presbyterian Church, which was established "near the sixth milestone of the Georgetown to Frederick Turnpike."[85] The first milestone above Georgetown would have been at Woodley Road; the second, south of River Road at Tennallytown; the third, south of the District line, near Belt Lane; the fourth, near Cookendoffer's tavern, south of Bradley Lane; and the fifth, above the Old Georgetown Road fork to the west.

An 1828 letter from D.C. postmaster Thomas Munroe[86] to the honorable George Corbin Washington explained why it took 22 hours for a letter to travel from Fredericktown to Georgetown: The road between Frederick and Rockville was so bad it had to be driven during the day, so the route from Rockville to Georgetown had to be traveled during the night. And that was slow moving too, in the days of rutted roads, horses, and no headlights or streetlights.

In 1829 Nathan Loughborough wrote from "Grassland" to inform the Senate Commission on Roads and Canals that the Washington Turnpike Company, formed by him and others from Georgetown and Rockville, was responsible for building "an excellent road" (it was not yet finished) from Georgetown to Rockville, at a cost of $46,000. They therefore hoped to regain their expenditure by selling stock in the company as well as by collecting tolls.[87]

Although it was supposedly under construction in 1829, the new, more direct section of the Rockville Turnpike from Tennallytown to the District line was not completed until around 1840, and does not appear on a map until the publication in 1861 of A. Boschke's Topographic Map of D.C., based on field inspection of 1857-58.

Tollgates first appeared on the new turnpike in 1829[88]—one near the hilltop intersection in Tennallytown, one in Bethesda (Darcy's Store), and another near Garrett Park (south of Montrose). The toll collectors were directed "to stop any person or persons riding, leading, or driving any horses, cattle, hogs, sheep, sulky, chair, chaise, phaeton, coach, etc. from passing until [the tolls] have been paid."

Tolls collected along the pike were 12¢ for a score of cattle; 6¢ for a score of sheep; 4¢ for one horse and rider; 6¢ for horse and sulky; and 12¢ for a four-wheel coach with two horses.[89] Wider rim wagons paid less, for they kept the road surface nicely rolled and flattened. Local residents were exempt from paying a toll, and of course the tollkeeper knew who everyone was for miles around.

The Tennallytown tollhouse, a white frame building eventually covered with ivy,[90] was near the point between the Rockville and River Roads. It may even have been Tennally's old tavern.

The land on which the tollhouse was situated was acquired by James O'Reilly in 1826, just before the toll gate was installed. O'Reillys were probably the toll-keepers until 1851, when Isaac Marshall bought the acreage at the point. Marshall owned it until his death after the Civil War, but he rented to a series of men who performed the duties of tollgate-keeper.

The keeper collected tolls only from those traveling on the Rockville Road. At this busy intersection the stagecoaches also changed horses. By 1840 this triangle of land was bisected by the new extension of the Rockville Pike.

From 1824 to 1836 the Washington-Frederick stagecoach route enjoyed its most active and lucrative years. But after the opening of the railroad lines (to Baltimore in 1835, for example), the stages declined in business, especially when the mail business was also carried by rail. The Frederick stage continued to operate once a day until 1870, when the Metropolitan Branch of the B&O Railroad from Washington to Point of Rocks, Maryland, was completed.

A regular schedule of mail routes and deliveries in Tennallytown was first recorded in 1844. The route ran from Washington to Georgetown to Tennallytown to Rockville to Middle Brook Mills to Clarksburg to Hyattstown to Urbana to Frederick—a total of 42 miles. This mail route was traveled three times a week in two-horse coaches.

After the name of Montgomery Court House was changed to Rockville, residents referred to the road as the Rockville Turnpike as

(Sketch by Sammie Sellers)

Early stagecoaches had tough going on unpaved roads.

often as the Road to Frederick Town. And as the village of Tennallytown grew, people in Georgetown and Washington came to refer to the lower road as the Tennallytown Road.

It was not until the new section was completed in the 1840s that the old section came to be called Brookeville Road, because it passed through "Cheivy Chace" and connected with the Road to Brookeville (later Georgia Avenue). After the Civil War it was also called Belt Road, because it ran along and through the Belt family's property.

The stagecoach was not the only vehicle on the Rockville turnpike, of course. The farmers of Montgomery County used the pike and the River Road to carry their farm products to markets in Georgetown or Washington, and to bring home provisions. Farm wagons were pulled by mules, horses, or occasionally even oxen. The farm "traffic" was heaviest, however, on Friday nights and early Saturday mornings, coming to town, and Saturday evenings going back home.

"DUNBLANE"

(1973 photo by Jerry Yurow)

The effect of an improved road into the countryside was not only speedier travel time for all; it was also a stimulation for new people to purchase land further out into the rural area.

In 1841 German immigrant William Heider bought 41 acres of land between the old Frederick Road (Brookeville Road) and the new section of the Frederick Road. Heider was the forerunner of a substantial influx of German immigrants after the German Revolution of 1848. Many of these Germans, forced to flee their homeland because of their political beliefs, became tenant farmers of Maryland landowners. Heider was fortunate enough to acquire a large tract of well-placed and well-watered farmland on the north side of Tennallytown.

After 1845, as Peruvian guano was introduced as fertilizer in the area, prosperity slowly returned, with an increased demand for grain as the population increased.

"Old buildings were renovated and repaired, while new buildings and handsome residences . . . took the place of the old tumble-down, moss-covered and worm-eaten cottage of the past . . . . The fields teemed with bountiful harvests. The decade from 1850 to 1860 was one of universal prosperity to the people of the county. Towns and villages sprang up, stores were established at crossroads . . . ."[91]

"Dunblane"

In 1818 Clement Smith had also bought, probably for speculation, 55 "unimproved" acres of "Friendship" from the estate of Charles French. Smith may have built a house on this Tennallytown Road property, for when it was sold after his death in 1839, the land was "improved." Smith, who was president of the Farmers and Merchants Bank of Georgetown, also built a large brick house in Georgetown, later known as Bodisco house.

John Mason, Jr., and his wife Catherine Macomb were the purchasers in 1839 of the Tennallytown property of Clement Smith; they probably also bought it for speculation, but used it as a country retreat and lived in Georgetown. It was a large house, originally stone but now stuccoed, with a glass cupola on its hipped roof. Its severe, unadorned exterior now contrasts with an ornate double door.

In 1852 the Masons turned the property over to Thomas and Sallie Lyles Marshall (daughter of Arianna Lyles of "The Rest") for $5 compensation. When his wife died three years later, Marshall sold the house and 63 acres to Harry Woodward Blunt. Blunt was a descendant of John "of Dunblane" Magruder of Prince George's County, whose house at Forestville (Upper Marlboro), built in 1715, was named "Dunblane."[92]

And so Blunt may have been the one to name this house "Dunblane."

"Dunblane" (or "Dumblane"), probably built prior to 1855. This mansion was named after another "Dunblane," near Upper Marlboro, by one of John "of Dunblane" Magruder's descendants.

This house in Tennallytown has been occupied by the Dunblane School since 1905.

(Georgetown University, Special Collections)

Teachers of Loyola at Georgetown Villa, 1862. The Villa was bought by the McLeans 30 years later.

But Clement Smith was also related to John "of Dunblane" Magruder. In any case, the house has been called "Dunblane" (or "Dumblane") for at least 125 years.

The last survivor of the Tennally family died in 1822, at age 66. Sarah Tennally, surviving sister of John and Elizabeth, willed her house and property in Tennallytown to Sarah Elizabeth Tennally Robey, a young woman who had lived with her for many years. Sarah Robey was born next door or in that house, and was named for Sarah and Elizabeth Tennally. The story is that Sarah Robey, though not related to the Tennally sisters, lived with them after her father, saloon-keeper Theophilus Robey, died and the rest of her family decided to move to Ohio.[93]

In the early 1830s Sarah Robey married Daniel Lightfoot, and raised four children in the old Tennally home. Lightfoot built an addition onto the south side of the house, in about 1840. The initials DL and the date of the addition were written on a cornice near the eaves. Although this addition doubled the size of the house, it was still a modest frame house; but it had nearly five acres of land behind it.

The Tennally-Lightfoot house, as it was called, remained a landmark in the center of Tennallytown until it was torn down in the 1950s.

The Jesuits' College Villa

In the 1840s an English sugar planter from Barbados, Colonel Richard Parris Pile, acquired from Clement Smith's estate two portions of "Terra Firma." But in 1845 the colonel mortgaged the properties, and eventually put them up for sale.[94]

In 1847 the Georgetown College, in conjunction with the Jesuit Province, bought Colonel Pile's 63 acres on the Road to Fredericktown, including house and farm. The country house and land were used for a place of recreation and a retreat house by Jesuit priests, brothers, and scholasticates (students) from Georgetown College and Woodstock Seminary near Baltimore.

The estate was called the "Georgetown Villa" or "College Villa." The gardens were beautifully landscaped and laid out for meditative strolls.[95]

In his article on the old Georgetown Villa, Father W.C. Repetti says,

"Many [Jesuits] no doubt cherish pleasant recollections of the happy vacation days which they passed amid the rugged but picturesque scenery in which, before the hand of improvement began to level the hills and fill up the valleys, the quiet villa reposed like a beautiful gem in a brilliant setting."

First Churches

Religious groups organized informally in the early days of the

First Tennallytown Methodist Church, built about 1840 at corner of River and Murdock Mill Roads; rebuilt after the Civil War.

(1862 sketch from History of 9th and 10th Regiments, Rhode Island Volunteers)

St. Alban's Episcopal Church, established 1854, served Tennallytown until an Episcopal mission (St. Columba's) was built on Murdock Mill Road in 1875.

(1896 photo, The Story of St. Albans Parish)

village. Since Revolutionary days the Dumbarton Avenue Methodist Church (West Georgetown) had served Protestants in the area west of Rock Creek. In the 1830s Methodists in the area met for Sabbath school classes in homes—most frequently in the home of Philip L. Brooke on Loughborough Road.

In 1840 the first church was built in Tennallytown—the Mt. Zion Methodist Episcopal Church, usually called the Tenleytown Church, and in 1899 renamed Eldbrooke

Methodist. The little schoolhouse-church was located on the northwest corner of the River Road and the Murdock Mill Road, "about 100 yards" from the intersection with the Rockville Road.[96]

According to a 1903 interview with John H. Harry, the schoolmaster at the Tenleytown Methodist school in the 1840s was James Bell.[97] By 1855 the Tenleytown Sabbath School was flourishing, with 12 teachers, 60 "scholars," and 100 volumes in the library.

As mentioned earlier, references to a Presbyterian church "at Tennally Town" exist from the 1780s and 1790.[98] The Bethesda Presbyterian Church, built on the Frederick Town Road in 1820, took its name from a Biblical place of healing. Eventually the surrounding community adopted the name Bethesda from the church.

In September 1847 the Sharon Presbyterian Church was organized "in Tenleytown," with Aquila Eld as ruling elder. The congregation shared a minister, The Rev. Randolph A. Smith, with the Bethesda Presbyterian Church. But in 1849 the Sharon Church at Tenleytown had only six members; by April 1850 the church was closed because of "peculiar circumstances," unexplained by the records.[99] It is likely that the few Presbyterian families in the area were not enough to support a separate church. Where services were held is not indicated by the records.

At "Mt. Alban," the Nourse property a mile and a half south of Tennallytown, an Episcopal parish was begun in 1847 and a church begun in 1851. Until a mission was established in Tennallytown in 1875, the St. Alban's Church, as it came to be called, served Episcopalians in the entire area north of Georgetown. First vestry members of St. Alban's parish included Charles and James Nourse, William D.C. Murdock, Thomas Marshall, Robert C. Jones, and Thomas A. Brooke, all of whom lived near Tennallytown.

"Some of the early statistics of St. Albans Parish are surprising when one considers the difficult working conditions of the period, the scattered population of the neighborhood, and the lack of easy communication; the fact that few of those living within the parish limits were Church people."[100]

Nonetheless, there were 13 baptisms in 1854.

One of the first vestrymen of St. Alban's was William D. C. Murdock, the only son of Addison Murdock and the great-grandson of Colonel John Murdock of "Friendship." William had married Louisa Burnett at Christ Church, Georgetown, and they had two daughters.

Since St. Alban's was the closest church to Tennallytown that had a regular clergyman, a great number of baptisms, marriages, and funerals were performed there for Tennallytown residents of all religious backgrounds.

Records of St. Alban's as early as 1855 mention burials at a "St. Albans cemetery." This was apparently in Tennallytown, adjacent to the Methodist burying ground on Murdock Mill Road. The Episcopal mission church which became St. Columba's was also adjacent to this cemetery.

Local Roman Catholics worshipped in Georgetown's Holy Trinity Church from 1792 until 1867, when a Tennallytown mission (later St. Ann's) was first organized.

First Schools

During the early years of the 19th century there was little or no provision for school children in the Tennallytown area. Most likely the children of the earliest landowners were tutored at home. Later they attended schools in Georgetown, where the Lancastrian private school and the West End public school were begun prior to 1812.[101]

In 1818 a quarter of an acre had been sold by John Chappell and his wife to George French, William Mackennie, John Adlum, and Isaac Pierce, for the sum of one dollar, that "they should erect and build ... thereon, a house, to the use and purpose of a school house for the benefit of the neighborhood, and for a place of public worship for all denominations of Christians."[102]

This site for a school and chapel was down along Broad Branch Road, not far from Chappell's residence (see map on page 23). Although no documentation has been found that worship services were held at that place, it is possible that the Protestants of this area met there until the first little Methodist church was built in 1840. It is also likely that this was the site of the first school for the children of the Tennallytown area, and that John Chappell became the schoolmaster.

Young John E. Chappell came to Tennallytown from Waterford, Virginia, in 1845, having inherited 53 acres of his grandfather's estate west of Broad Branch Road. Chappell, whose main occupation was farming, conducted a private school on Grant Road (the "new-cut" road) "for the instruction of young men" during the winter months. After the close of the Civil War, he was instrumental in establishing public schools in the county, and was one of the first public school trustees.[103]

Miss Rosa Nourse, daughter of Charles Nourse of "The Highlands," started a small school in the 1830s across from "Mt. Alban," her grandparents' property and later the site of the Episcopal chapel and the cathedral. For 30 years Miss Nourse taught the children of her neighborhood—until after the Civil War, when public schools were opened nearby.[104]

Private schools were maintained also for free blacks in Georgetown and Washington. It is estimated that by 1860 there were more than 1200 free colored children in schools, all of them private.[105] It is unlikely that the black children in the "county" received any formal schooling before 1860.

In 1856 an attempt was made to establish free public schools in Washington County for all, white and colored.

"Congress provided for the approval of the proposition by a majority of all the white taxpayers, without distinction of sex, then residing in the territory affected. The proposition was rejected by a large majority. They did not enthuse very much over popular education if they had to pay for it."[106]

Abolition

The anti-slavery and abolitionist movements were active in the 1830s and 1840s. Washington was by then already a mecca for free blacks. In 1830 there were 6,152 free Negroes counted in D.C. as well as 6,119 slaves. By 1840, the balance had changed: 8,361 free and 4,694 slave Negroes. In 1860, there were 11,131 free Negroes and only 3,185 slaves.[107]

The free blacks had most likely been willingly liberated (manumitted) by their masters or had purchased their freedom at some time. There were many free blacks in the District prior to emancipation. They held a variety of occupations besides laborer—some were messengers, many were hack drivers, and not a few had their own businesses and bought and sold property. The Wormleys, whose Tennallytown connections are discussed in Chapter IV, were the best known and most prosperous Negroes in the District in the 19th century.

Other landowners in the area retained a number of slaves until emancipation. The 1855-1864 tax assessment shows that Arianna Lyles, at "The Rest," owned 18 slaves; Thomas Marshall, her son-in-law across the road at "Dunblane," had 34 slaves, which he transferred to H.W. Blunt in 1856.[108]

William D. C. Murdock kept 10 slaves, and his uncle Benjamin Hodges, 11. John H. King, who had 43 acres along the road near Tennallytown, owned four slaves, and Giles Dyer, whose 72 acres were at the highest point in the city, owned five. Charles R. Belt still had nine slaves on his 175 acres of "Cheivy Chace" in 1859.

Many free blacks owned small properties in Tennallytown prior to emancipation. Isaac Marshall and Aquila Eld (white) sold land along Brookeville Road to four members of the Williams family (colored) in the 1850s. Arianna Lyles sold an acre to James Smith, a "free colored man," in 1852.

The records of Holy Trinity Catholic Church, Georgetown, include the baptisms and marriages of many slave and free colored persons who lived in the county—for example, the slaves of Nathan Loughborough.

Before cemeteries were in general use, and even after, the dead were buried in family graveyards, and slaves were buried in the graveyards of the families they belonged to. The Pierce Shoemaker, Murdock, Lyles, Thomas Marshall, Belt, Loughborough, and Dyer estates all had slaves as well as family burying grounds.

It is reported that the "underground railroad"—the system of secretly transporting blacks from the South to Canada—was especially active in Washington County of the District. Two of the large old houses in the area, the Lyles-Magruder house ("The Rest"), east of the Frederick Road, and the Loughborough House ("Milton"), south of River Road in Maryland, were reputed to have had underground tunnels or secret cellars for hiding runaway slaves.

The Lyles house (4343 39th Street today) does have a bricked-up archway in an eastern wall of its basement; however, it is just as likely that it was an old fireplace as a tunnel entrance. "The Rest" had been acquired in 1835 by Mrs. Arianna Jones Bruce Lyles. Mrs. Lyles, however, owned 32 slaves in 1840 and still had 18 slaves in the years before the Civil War.[109] Five of these she sold on her own, and the other 13 were freed by federal decree in 1862, when she was reimbursed $3,679.20 for them, according to the Star's Rambler. Mrs. Lyles was no abolitionist, nor did she participate in the underground railroad.

"MILTON"

("The Rambler," glass plate, 1914)

The other Loughborough house, "Milton," nearly two miles west of Tennallytown, off River Road. The house still stands at 5312 Allendale Road, in Green Acres (Bethesda).

The Loughboroughs' country house, "Milton," was known to have an underground tunnel. But the authors of <u>Washington, City and Capital</u> report that one of Loughborough's heirs had the underground passage cut to connect the kitchen in one wing with the dining room in the other wing. Furthermore, members of the Loughborough family were known to be Southern sympathizers and owners of a large number of slaves. It is therefore extremely unlikely that their master would participate in the "underground railroad" by hiding runaways in his cellar.

For all the abolitionists in the area, these landowners' way of life was guaranteed only by the continuation of the institution of slavery.

Origins of Grant Road

Much of the old country lane known as Grant Road is still visible today. Like many others, it was first referred to as the "New Cut Road." It came to be a major thoroughfare linking the Frederick Road and therefore the Tennallytown residents with the rest of the county to the east. New-Cut Road meandered down across the Broad Branch and beyond, to where it connected at Rock Creek with the Milkhouse (Rock Creek) Ford Road.[110]

This in turn led up to the Brightwood neighborhood to the east and over toward the Brookeville and Frederick roads to the northwest.

During the Civil War, Grant Road, as this road was renamed, became an important link in the military roads connecting the forts that constituted the defenses of Washington. It is apparent from old maps that it also linked up with the Murdock Mill Road to the west. Probably the road was named after Ulysses S. Grant. It was not on any line separating land "grants," as some have thought, nor was it "granted" for public use by the landowners.

The Third Tennallytown Inn

In 1815, the year after it had seen the passing of American troops after the Battle of Bladensburg, Henry Riszner's tavern and 10 acres had been purchased by James Gannon, in partnership with Jonathan Buckman and William Cunningham. Gannon ran the inn until his death in 1833, when his

THE THIRD TENNALLYTOWN INN

(Sketch by Judith Helm)

heirs advertised for sale by auction "a valuable Tavern and premises, situated in Tenallytown." The highest bidder was Gottfried Conradt, who was already occupying Gannon's tavern.

Conradt, a German immigrant whose name he Americanized to Godfrey Conrad, ran the inn through the 1850s, when he built a new hotel and tavern on the site. This new three-story building became the third Tennallytown Inn, also known in those early days as Conrad's Tavern. It stood on the west side of the road until the 1930s (when it was torn down and replaced by the Sears, Roebuck store).

Remembering back to the antebellum days in Tennallytown, a Washington newspaper writer recalled when the first Tennallytown grocery store

"bought in a new stock of whisky and tobacco, crochet needles, chewing gum, dry goods, worsted, pork, horse-feed and molasses, everything in and out of hades, for subsistence of Tennallytown. It was then the only store for miles, and there was nothing like sitting around on molasses kegs o' cold nights smoking Tennallytown tobacco—that's famous to this day down along the Horse Bazar (sic)—and drinking rye to warm, and watching tobacco spit sizzle on that red-hot stove, and smelling burning leather of a dozen farmers' boots—gee—that made a fellow live!"[111]

Probably this was Conrad's Tennallytown hotel that was the center of social activity. Charles and Joshua Pierce and Isaiah Shoemaker also had general stores in the area at that time.

Built in the 1850s by Godfrey Conrad. This building stood until 1938 on the west side of the Road to Rockville (Wisconsin Avenue). It was replaced by Sears, Roebuck.

Another journalist described in 1903 the Tennallytown country store, where

"anything from a codfish to a coffin, from a bed to a button, was for sale. As for the whiskey, the old inhabitants say it was beyond reproach; and to this day they smack their lips at recollection of its good qualities."[112]

Although Tennallytown was not on any body of water, and it had no special industry, it was at the intersection of two major roads, and three or four minor roads led to it. It was at

41

an unusually healthful and scenic elevation. Its soil was fertile, the land well watered, and stone and gravel were plentiful. It was remote from the city, but the stagecoaches and the farmers stopping in the village kept the residents well informed. And so the community grew in popularity as a stopping place and as a permanent residence.

According to George Simmons, visiting Englishman Charles Dickens once visited the Tennallytown neighborhood and

> "likened its landscape to parts of north of England, and he was wont to declare that there was 'nothing finer in all England' than the scenes presented from the vicinity of Tenleytown, on what is now known as Reno hill."[113]

Dickens may have been referring to the heights above Georgetown, but we must appreciate Simmons' enthusiasm for the views from Reno hill.

Not only was the country life in Tennallytown a peaceful one; but the people in the county part of D.C. were politically southern in orientation. Slavery was generally taken for granted in Tennallytown in the middle of the 19th century, and many residents had secessionist leanings.

And so it came as a shock to the Tennallytowners when their sleepy little southern village became host to thousands of Union soldiers defending the capital during the War Between the States.

---

[34] Minute Book, Montgomery County Records, August 1790, 15614

[35] Minutes of the Presbytery of Baltimore, 1786-1822 (Library of Congress)

[36] Clark, op. cit., pp. 56-57

[37] 1790 census, Washington, Government Printing Office 1907

[38] Tennally's tavern is mentioned in a 1793 delineation of the boundaries of "Friendship"; an October 1794 proceeding of the Chancery Court involving William Murdock's widow; a 1795 land transfer from William Bayly to John Threlkeld; an August 1795 sale by John Weems to Sarah Tennally; and an 1804 record of sale by Anastasia Dial. All are found in the Hall of Records, Annapolis, or the D.C. Recorder of Deeds.

[39] George Simmons, "Roadside Sketches," The Sunday Star, August 8, 1891

[40] The Rambler, J. Harry Shannon, The Sunday Star, January 3, 1915

[41] Deed of gift of Jacob Colclazer recorded 28 December 1818, D.C. Recorder of Deeds, Liber AT, pp. 236-237

[42] LeRoy O. King, Jr., 100 Years of Capital Traction. Dallas: Taylor Publishing Co., 1972, p. 39

[43] Montgomery County Deeds, Liber A, pp. 538-539, recorded 8 August 1780

[44] The Times and Patowmac Packet, George Town, August 4, 1790

[45] Montgomery County Deeds, Liber D, ff 387-388, recorded July 23, 1790

[46] D.C. Deed Liber A.I. #34, pp. 502-503, recorded 9 September 1815 ("John Murdock alias John Barber"; "Dolly Barber and her son called John Murdock by Col. John Murdock"). D.C. Deed Liber WB #77-52 recorded March 24, 1840 ("John Addison Barber alias Murdock").

[47] Hugh T. Taggart, "The Presidential Journey in 1800," RCHS, Vol. 3, 1900. Frederick Gutheim, The Potomac (New York: Holt, Reinhart & Winston, 1949, pp. 5-9) also describes Adams' arrival in the capital.

[48] Bryan, A History of the National Capital, op. cit.

[49] Oliver W. Holmes, "Stagecoach Days in the District of Columbia," RCHS, Vol. 50, 1948-50

[50] T.H.S. Boyd, History of Montgomery County, 1879, reprinted Baltimore: Regional Publishing Co., 1968, p. 52

[51] Advertisement in The Centinel of Liberty and George Town Advertiser, April 25, 1797

[52] Thomas Beall of George's Account Book (1802-1811) of the Estate of John Murdock, p. 116, December 6, 1804; N. Lufborough paid 1,000 pounds for 73 1/2 acres of Murdock's land. (Library of Congress, Manuscript Division)

[53] 1902 newspaper article, "Old Colonial Manor," unsourced. Mr. Chris Tenley, in a letter dated November 20, 1974, says the Tenleys were said to be related to both the Weems and the Jones families.

[54] George Alfred Townsend, "Houses of Bricks Imported from England," RCHS, Vol. 8, 1904

[55] Washington, City and Capital, op. cit., p. 431

[56] Thomas Beall of George's Account Book, op. cit.

[57] Gertrude S. Bradley, Bethesda Not So Old, Gaithersburg: Franklin Press, p. 84

[58] Doree Germaine Holman, Old Bethesda, 1956.

[59] Addison Murdock's account at Henry Riszner's 1805-07, National Archives RG 21, Chancery Docket 1 #79

[60] Thomas B. Searight, The Old Pike: An Illustrated Narrative of the National Road, 1894. Reprinted by Greentree Press, 1971.

[61] William H. Marine, The British Invasion of Maryland, 1812-15. Hatboro, Pa.: Tradition Press, 1965

[62] Michael I. Weller, "Comm. Joshua Barney: The Hero of the Battle of Bladensburg," RCHS, Vol. 14, 1911, p. 174

[63] "A Real Little Thrums," The Washington Post, February 12, 1899. "Thrums" was J.M. Barrie's name for the Scottish weaving town of Kirriemuir. Janet Dunbar writes that it was an undistinguished little town, once described by Robert Louis

Stevenson as a haphazard group of houses, "squeezed round that square like chickens clustering round a hen." (Janet Dunbar, J. M. Barrie: The Man Behind The Image, Boston: Houghton Mifflin Co., 1970)

[64] "Diary of Mrs. Wm. Thornton," August 1814, RCHS, Vol. 19, 1916 (original in MS division, Library of Congress)

[65] Margaret Bayard Smith, The First Forty Years of Washington Society, ed. by Gaillard Hunt. New York: Frederick Ungar Publ. Co., 1965 (originally published 1906). pp. 110-111

[66] National Messenger, Georgetown, March 4, 1818

[67] "The Sessford Annals," RCHS, Vol. 11, 1908

[68] Grace D. Peter and Joyce D. Southwick, Cleveland Park, Washington, 1958, p. 41

[69] Bessie Wilmarth Gahn, "Major Adlum of Rock Creek," RCHS, Vol. 39, 1938, p. 133

[70] John Saul, "Nurseries in the District of Columbia," RCHS, Vol. 10, 1906, pp. 39-47

[71] Peter, Cleveland Park, op. cit., pp. 39-40

[72] Maria Catherine Nourse Lyle, James Nourse and His Descendants, 1897 (DAR Library)

[73] Downtown Urban Renewal Landmarks, National Capital Planning Commission, 1970

[74] Frances Trollope, Domestic Manners of the Americans, edited by Donald Smalley, republished New York: Alfred A. Knopf, 1949

[75] Boyd, History of Montgomery County, op. cit., p. 107

[76] Ibid.

[77] Busey, Pictures of the City of Washington in the Past, op. cit.

[78] Column by Mrs. Bathon, Washington Times-Herald, May 15, 1938

[79] D.C. Recorder of Deeds Liber AF 31, pp. 171-176, recorded 15 September 1813

[80] Thomas Beall of George's Account Book, op. cit., p. 144, July 14, 1810

[81] George A. Townsend, Washington, Outside and Inside. Hartford: Jas. Betts & Co. 1873, p. 566. Townsend says the turnpike company between Georgetown and Fredericktown was incorporated in 1812.

[82] Holmes, "Stagecoach Days in the District of Columbia," RCHS, op. cit.

[83] National Messenger, Georgetown, 4 March 1818

[84] "The Sessford Annals," RCHS, op. cit.

[85] Clark, The Spirit of Captain John, op. cit., p. 103

[86] Vertical files, Washingtoniana Collection, Martin Luther King Memorial Library

[87] Vertical files, Washingtoniana Collection, Martin Luther King Memorial Library

[88] Holman, Old Bethesda, op. cit.

[89] Maryland State Roads Commission, A History of Road Building in Maryland, op. cit., p. 26

[90] "A Real Little Thrums," op. cit.

[91] Boyd, History of Montgomery County, 1879

[92] The Rambler, The Star, April 2, 1916

[93] Mamie Lightfoot Bradford, interview with Priscilla McNeil, March 26, 1972; and Rock Creek Church (St. Paul's Parish) Index to Register 1711-1845

[94] W.C. Repetti, S.J., "Georgetown University and McLean Gardens," Woodstock Letters, Vol. 84, No. 1, 1955 (Georgetown University Archives)

[95] Father Francis A. Barnum, S.J., "The Old Georgetown Villa," 1955. Unpublished MS in Georgetown University Archives, Friendship-Villa Property file

[96] "Laying of a cornerstone of a new Catholic Church at Tennallytown," Georgetown News [1868], Georgetown University Archives, Tenleytown file

[97] James G. Holland, "A Unique Trip from Tenleytown," Washington Times, July 19, 1903.

[98] Minutes of the Presbytery of Baltimore, 1786-1822, op. cit.

[99] Minutes of the Presbytery of the District of Columbia, 1823-1858 (Library of Congress)

[100] Mary B. Wilson, editor, The Story of St. Albans Parish 1854-1929. Washington: St. Albans Parish, 1929

[101] John Clagett Proctor, "Joseph Lancaster and the Lancaster Schools," RCHS, Vol. 25, 1923

[102] D.C. Recorder of Deeds, Washington County records, Deed Liber AS-43, p. 282, recorded October 31, 1818

[103] Unsourced newspaper obituary of John E. Chappell (September 1907)

[104] Grace D. Peter, "Unpublished Letters of Dolly Madison to Anthony Morris Relating to the Nourse Family of the Highlands," RCHS, Vol. 44-45, 1944

[105] Washington, City and Capital, op. cit., p. 70

[106] Proctor, op. cit.; and William Hazaiah Williams, The Negro in the District of Columbia During Reconstruction, unpublished MA thesis, 1924, Howard University, Moorland-Springarn Library

[107] Washington, City and Capital, op. cit., p. 71

[108] Tax Assessment of Washington County, 1855-1864, made by Charles R. Belt and Henry Haw, National Archives

[109] 1840 Census and Tax Assessment of Washington County, 1855-1864, National Archives

[110] "It is a well authenticated fact that U.S. soldiers crossed the upper Potomac and marched along Old Milkhouse Road to Bladensburg, where a Battle was fought with the British in 1814." Louis P. Shoemaker, "Historic Rock Creek," RCHS, Vol. 12, 1908-09, p. 50. [Remains of the Rock Creek Ford Road, as it was also called, are still visible on the east side of 32nd Street between Quesada and Rittenhouse and east of the Park going up to Brightwood.]

[111] "A Real Little Thrums," op. cit.

[112] James G. Holland, op. cit.

[113] George Simmons, "Roadside Sketches: Picturesque Regions North of Georgetown: Tenleytown and Bethesda," The Star, August 15, 1891.

III

THE WAR BETWEEN THE STATES COMES TO TENNALLYTOWN:

1861-1865

"Then through the dust and mud we marched,

till the fourth night settled down,

as we built our fires, and pitched our tents,

on the hills near Tennallytown."[14]

The election of Abraham Lincoln meant the arrival in 1861 of a new and controversial President, about whom the Tennallytowners were divided. Some were fiercely anti-slavery and pro-Lincoln; others were the reverse; and still others disliked both slavery and "Honest Abe."

The residents of Tennallytown may not even have heard about Fort Sumter until days after the soldiers from the Confederate states fired on that Union fort. But because of Tennallytown's strategic location at a northern entrance to the nation's capital, the subsequent events profoundly affected Tennallytown life—not only for the next four years, but also for all time. Very quickly after April 1861, Tennallytown was "at war."

Although the village was within the District of Columbia, by reason of its distance from the capital city it was considered by many to be a Maryland town. With relief, Tennallytowners learned that Maryland, though a slave state, decided not to secede from the Union. It was bad enough having Virginia, just two miles as the crow flies from Tennallytown, join the Confederacy.

Early in the war, the Federals feared that the Confederates would try to attack Washington from the north (and, in fact, that is what happened in 1864). And so they set up a total of 26 forts and nearly as many supporting artillery batteries in an effort to block all northern approaches to the city. Another 29 forts and eight batteries were eventually constructed in northern Virginia to defend the capital.

(E.B. Thompson negative, gift of Frank B. Cook, editor, Mayflower's Log, 1945; Washingtoniana Collection, Martin Luther King Memorial Library)

"CAMP TENNELLY"

Sketch by Oregon Wilson of Camp Tennelly, camp of the 10th Pennsylvania Regiment, October 1861. This view is probably looking south from the top of Fort Pennsylvania (Fort Reno), as across Chesapeake Street and Wilson High School grounds.

Union engineers, under Major John G. Barnard, selected the highest point in Washington, in the northeast part of Tennallytown, for a fort in early August 1861, and began building in great haste.

On September 10, 1861, only five months into the war, President Lincoln attended a presentation of colors to Pennsylvania troops by Governor Curtin (of Pennsylvania) "at Tennallytown," followed by a review of General George McCall's division.[115]

The fort had already been constructed, adjacent to Brookeville Road. The site was originally called Fort Pennsylvania, since the 119th Pennsylvania Volunteers built the fort.[116] As will be described later, the name was changed in 1863 to Fort Reno; it has been called that ever since.

In the winter of 1861-62, the 55th New York regiment quartered "at Tennallytown" were mostly French Algerian "Zouaves," led by Colonel Regis de Trobriand.[117] Their encampment was actually at Fort Gaines,[118] near the old Murdock house (American University grounds), one mile southwest of Fort Pennsylvania.

When Massachusetts Avenue was much later extended west of Nebraska Avenue, it cut right through the elevation on which Fort Gaines was located. The Fort Gaines location actually was closer to Tennallytown than to any other place, and so it is understandable that it should have been so designated, though this confused it with Fort Pennsylvania.

The New York 55th "Zouaves," in their red jackets, stockings, and caps,

The Washington Star of January 9, 1862, reports that President and Mrs. Lincoln and party attended a celebration with "the French regiment" near Tennallytown. And apparently the French cuisine served at Fort Gaines was far better than any other camp food. Unlike the usual regimental mess, the Frenchmen of the 55th New York

"knew something about cooking, and their officers' mess, at least, was famous. President Lincoln dined with them... and told the officers afterward that if their men could fight as well as they could cook, the regiment would do very well indeed. They had given him, he added, the best meal he had had in Washington."[120]

Locating Fort Pennsylvania on the highest hill in the District of Columbia was a natural and good choice. Not only did its elevation of more than 420 feet above sea level command a wide view of the countryside to the north and west; but from that site one could also oversee travel on three roads into the capital: the River Road, the new Fredericktown Road, and the old Brookeville Road. The thickly wooded countryside served to camouflage approaching troops, but the dust of

shaved heads, and long swords, must have provided a fascinating sight. Colonel Elmer Ellsworth formed many Zouave units in the area, bringing an element of romance, danger, style, and even humor into the tedium of soldiering.[119]

FORT PENNSYLVANIA

This sketch of Fort Pennsylvania (Fort Reno) looks west, over the Brookeville Road and Rockville Pike to the mountains of Virginia beyond. The Dyer family farmhouse, to the north of the fort, was used as headquarters until the advanced battery was built years later. The house is seen at the far right in this sketch.

(Spicer, History of the 9th and 10th Regiments, Rhode Island Volunteers, 1892, p. 225)

FORT PENNSYLVANIA AND ENCAMPMENT AT TENNALLYTOWN, NEAR WASHINGTON D.C.

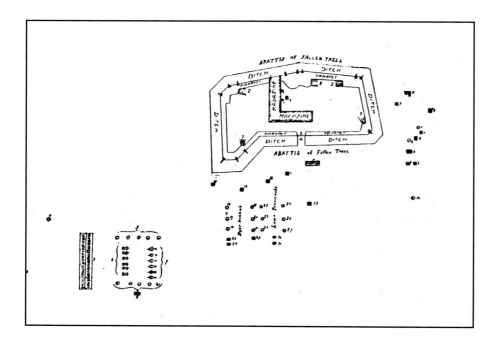

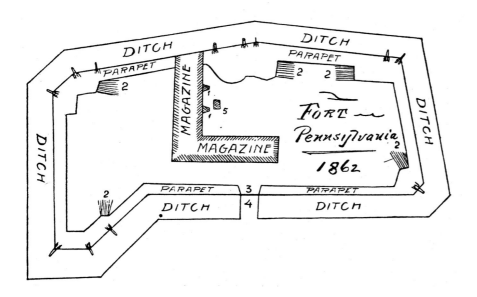

(both sketches from History of 9th and 10th Regiments, Rhode Island Volunteers)

The extended part of the fort outline extends to the east, so the northern end of the fort is to the right in both drawings.

many marching men could be spotted from afar.

Other centrally located forts such as Fort Stevens, commanding the Brightwood Road, and Fort Lincoln, overlooking the Baltimore Turnpike and the new B&O Railroad, were also quickly constructed in the early days of the war and were later improved and strengthened. In fact, Fort Reno was eventually the largest fort (917 yards perimeter) between the Potomac River and the Eastern Branch.

Other major fortifications close to Tennallytown included Fort Sumner (originally comprising Forts Davis, Kirby, and Cross) on the Glen Echo Heights; Forts Simmons and Mansfield, on Shoemaker property just over the District line in Maryland; Battery Kemble, east of Chain Bridge Road and overlooking the Potomac; Battery Vermont, southeast of Dalecarlia (Sibley Hospital site); Fort Gaines, near the Murdock House, "Friendship" (west of Ward Circle now); Fort Bayard, about 330 feet elevation, at the District Line, now Western Avenue and River Road; and, to the east, Fort DeRussy near the Milkhouse Ford Road, northeast of Daniels Road (Oregon Avenue) and the present Military Road.

The main signal training camp of the Union army was located at the high point south of what is now Wisconsin and Massachusetts Avenues; a signal tower was erected, and the camp was called Red Hill. [The Mount Alto Veterans Hospital was constructed there in later years, and most recently it is the site of the new Russian Embassy Compound.]

According to the Rambler's account in the Star,[121] the land that was possessed by the federal army for the fort in Tennallytown was owned by brothers Giles and Miles Dyer. The Dyers had purchased this very desirable farmhouse and acreage

(Mathew Brady photo c/o American University Archives)

The dashing French (and American) Zouaves, posing by one of their cannon at Fort Gaines, just north of Murdock's "Friendship" house. Fort Gaines was cut down years later for the extension of Massachusetts Avenue west of Ward Circle and adjacent to the American University.

from Isaac Marshall, who in turn had bought it from Dr. John Weems. The Weems family burial plot was on the hill (close to what later became the Fort Reno water pumping station) and was in Giles Dyer's garden. The Weems tombstones were standing before the Civil War, but construction of the fort destroyed all traces of the graveyard.

It was customary for the armed forces to take possession of private lands because of "military necessity," with little or no compensation paid to the owners or occupants. The exigencies of war frequently made it necessary for citizens to turn over their lands, buildings, and even houses to the troops.

In addition to clearing the sites for the forts, the planners deemed it necessary to clear all the land in front of the line of defense of trees and brush.

"The trees were cut about three feet from the ground, and all made to fall with the branches toward the enemy.... [This] added greatly to the desolate looks of this war-afflicted vicinity."[122]

The soldiers cleared of timber all the land for two miles north and west of Tennallytown in the autumn of 1861.[123]

William D.C. Murdock complained twelve years later of the $7,000 in damages he received from the government at that time. He declared that his land had been cleared in 1861 of lumber that he valued at $70,000.

At the same time that the land was being cleared, a military road was constructed to link the forts around the city. Civil War maps show that this road ran from Fort Sumner in

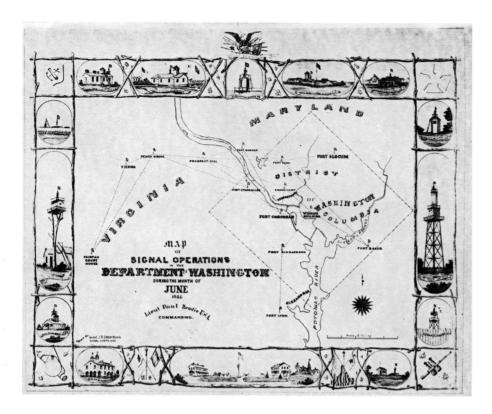

(U.S. Signal Corps photo, No. 111-BA-2107, Brady Collection, National Archives)

The Fort Reno signal tower is photographed in the center of the right margin. The Red Hill signal camp above Georgetown is pictured in the center of the bottom margin.

Maryland (at Sangamore Road, near Glen Echo Heights) eastward, passing just north of the Dalecarlia Reservoir and traveling to Tennallytown by a "new military road" that later came to be called Murdock's Mill Road. (Most traces of this road west of Murdock Mill had vanished by 1893.)

Maps indicate that this military road and the new-cut road that became Grant Road were linked together south of the inn (Conrad's Tavern) in Tennallytown. The military road continued east and northeast, south of Fort DeRussy, toward Fort Stevens, on the 7th Street Road (Georgia Avenue). [The Military Road by which we cross Rock Creek Park today is a good distance north of the military road constructed in 1862 to link the new forts.]

Grant Road itself had been called the New-Cut Road until the war, when it became part of the new military road. It was renamed Grant Road most likely after Ulysses S. Grant became commander of the

Army of the Potomac and inspected the defenses of Washington in March 1864.[124]

B.D. Carpenter's 1870 map calls it Grant Road. Tax assessments of the 1870s, however, continue to refer to Arianna Lyles' property as "near Military Road," so it was not yet well known as Grant Road.

At the close of the Secession War, as he called it, poet Walt Whitman wrote of the military roads around the city:

"A great recreation, the past three years, has been in taking long walks out from Washington, five, seven, perhaps ten miles and back, generally with my friend Peter Doyle, who is as fond of it as I am. Fine moonlight nights, over the perfect military roads, hard and smooth—or Sundays—we had these delightful walks never to be forgotten. The roads connecting Washington and the numerous forts around the city, made one useful result, at any rate, out of the war."[125]

The then-new military road was used initially to transport material to construct the new forts and the many batteries that were built between them. As the forts were manned by large numbers of troops, the army wagons, pulled by mules and heavily loaded with food, ammunition, and other supplies, rumbled back and forth between the camps.[126]

"A few barns and hungry looking houses straggle along a lean and hungry looking street. A tavern and blacksmith's shop confront each other, and are flanked by the post office. In the rear of the latter and at the entrance of our camp, stands the village church, never, from appearances, a very notable structure, but now, alas! sadly dilapidated, and converted to other uses than originally intended."

Such was the graphic description provided by young William Hale, a Rhode Island volunteer, in a letter home June 3, 1862. He was describing his first impressions of Tennallytown—"and if you know where that is, your knowledge of geography is more extensive than mine was a week ago . . . ."[127]

Another Rhode Island recruit noted that the village had two blacksmith shops, a hotel, and a tollgate in addition to the post office and church. Harry's blacksmith shop faced the inn; another blacksmith, probably Morrow, was on the New Military (Grant) Road.

The post office was in the fork at the top of the hill. John O. Harry manned the post office but, as it turned out, the volume of the soldiers' mail soon overwhelmed him. Corporal Pabodie of Company H wrote in 1862,

> "We have our letters directed to us at Washington now, instead of at Tennallytown as at first. It appears that the village postmaster had been in the habit of receiving only one or two letters per day previous to our arrival, and when he begun to get upwards of a thousand, he didn't know 'what on airth to do with them.' They say he's been in the hospital ever since."[128]

Perhaps it <u>was</u> the overload of mail that led to the collapse of postmaster John O. Harry. He died in 1864, and his son Billy took over as postmaster for the next five years.

The Rhode Island regiment set up camp along River Road, behind the Mt. Zion Methodist Church. That church was variously used as a guard house, quartermaster's store house, hospital, and mess hall. After

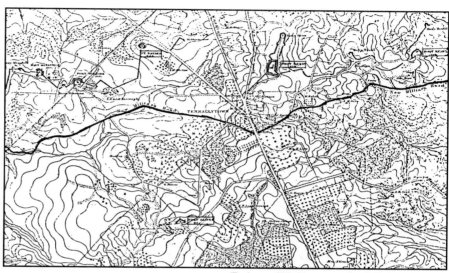

(Environs of Washington, undated, National Archives)

the takeover by the rough New York troops, the Methodists had been forced to resume worshipping in each other's homes. The New Yorkers had posted a hand-made sign over the door to the church, "New York Eating house."[129]

Before the Rhode Island Volunteers arrived, the "Anderson Zouaves" had used the meetinghouse as a guardhouse,

> "and tore out the pulpit, and destroyed the Sabbath School library. Quartermaster-Sgt. Lysander Flagg learning about it, sent to the Methodist Sabbath School in Pawtucket [R.I.] and the Baptist Sabbath School in Central Falls, and informed them of the facts, and they immediately sent a large collection of their books to the little Sunday School of Tennallytown. The books we presented last Sabbath. Both teachers and scholars were greatly pleased with this remembrance from the children of the New England schools."[130]

R.W. Chappell of the 9th Rhode Island Volunteers passed on a local story (unconfirmed) that

TENNALLYTOWN DURING THE CIVIL WAR

This map shows the New Military Road running south of Fort Bayard, into Tennallytown, and east of Fort Reno on towards Brightwood and Fort Stevens. After the Civil War the western part of the New Military Road became known as Murdock Mill Road, and the eastern part became Grant Road.

(Both drawings from <u>History of 9th and 10th Regiments, Rhode Island Volunteers</u>)

Two sketches of the Rhode Islanders' Camp Frieze, showing the Methodist Church, which faced River Road. The enclosed Methodist Cemetery is visible behind the church in both drawings, but the Murdock Mill Road (then the new Military Road) is not visible behind the cemetery.

"the old meeting house at Tennallytown was the last building in which John Brown preached on his way to Harper's Ferry in October 1859, where in an effort to free the slaves he lost his life, 'but his soul is still marching on.' "[131]

Another source, however, indicates that John Brown rented a farm near Harper's Ferry in July 1859 and stayed in that area until the attack on October 16.[132]

The Rhode Island Volunteers' camp along River Road was used as back-up support for the soldiers at Fort Pennsylvania, as it was still called. Camp Frieze (named in honor of the quartermaster general of Rhode Island) was located behind the Methodist Church. It was a clean, well-ordered camp in which its New England builders took pride. Lt. DeWolf of Company D, June 3, 1862:

"The elevation of our camp is considerable, for it appears to be downhill for 3 miles in every direction, the air is deliciously pure, water good and plentiful."

Captain A.C. Greene, Company G, June 5th:

"The country is very rich and fertile, but owing to the cold dry spring, vegetation is rather backward."

H.T. Chace, Company D:

"Last Sunday evening we all enjoyed very much. Several of us sat in the tent-door, enjoying the scene. The air was still, the moon bright, the sky blue, the great trees threw a soft shade, a choir near us furnished sweet music, while we discoursed of home and heavenly themes."

While days were spent in building fortifications, digging wells and dams, battalion drilling, and artillery practice with 12-pound "Napoleon" guns, the young soldiers had time for trips to the nearby creeks or the Potomac to bathe (a real luxury), and occasionally got passes to go into Washington.

There were the usual discomforts of military life, including ill-fitting uniforms and boots, bad food, rain, and wood ticks. H.T. Chace wrote, "Some of the boys call one tent the 'Smithsonian Institute,' on account of the variety of bugs and insects it contains."

Heavy rains and mud complicated life for the troops. Next came a terrible heat wave and then sickness. "The day (June 9) was the warmest we have had yet, the thermometer being at camp that noon 104 degrees." July 3rd, 1862, found the temperature again nearly to 100 degrees.

On August 1, fever broke out in Rhode Island's Company D, stationed at Fort DeRussy; 20 men were sick at one time. Subsequently, the fever moved to Fort Pennsylvania, where 33 patients were stricken. While the temperature outside registered anywhere from 100 to 130 degrees in the sun, Pvt. Mathew Meggett died of typhoid fever "in the hospital at Fort Pennsylvania."

From the beginning of the War Between the States, "frightened, destitute, and helpless" blacks had flocked to the Union forts, looking for protection as well as for shelter and food.[133] Those blacks who sought such protection were called "contraband" by the thwarted slaveholders.

The District of Columbia forts were especially attractive to escaped slaves and freedmen. Fort Reno, one of the largest forts around Washington but further from the city than most, attracted a good number of blacks. In return for housing and food, the blacks served the soldiers as laborers, cooks, black-

smiths, grooms for the horses, seamstresses, etc.

The Rhode Island Volunteers enjoyed the attention of "the contrabands," who washed clothes, shined boots, foraged for food, washed dishes—all for the few pennies the soldiers paid them.

Chace, Company D:

"Our mess has engaged a prepossessing young contraband who boasts the name of Abraham Douglass, to do the singing and wash the dishes, for the modest salary of two dollars and a half per month . . . . Last evening he sang for us 'De Gospel Ship's a Sailin'. . . .' "

Another writer:

"We do not lack for amusements. Two evenings we have been entertained by a Negro fiddler, with dancing by both Negro men and women."

And the soldiers' own band boasted at one time two violins, guitar, banjo, tambourine, triangle and bones, "accompanied by a dozen manly voices . . . an occasional interlude during which the Negro fieldhands from the neighboring farms indulge in a regular Virginia 'hoedown' with 'walk around' and 'double shuffle' embellishments."

On January 1, 1863, Abraham Lincoln's Emancipation Proclamation went into effect. This declared all slaves in the secessionist states to be "forever free." Slavery in the District of Columbia, however, had been declared out of existence in 1862, and slave owners were compensated for the loss of their slaves. In 1860, there were already 11,000 free Negroes in D.C. and only 3,000 slave Negroes.

One resident, a black man called Uncle George (probably George Dover), recalled in an 1899 interview "how a mess o' soljers, breast to breast, was lined down from Fort

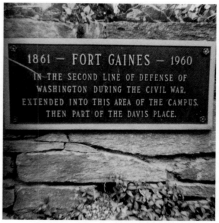

(1973 photo by Priscilla McNeil)

Plaque at Fort Gaines

Little Abe.

(Sketch of "Little Abe" from History of 9th and 10th Regiments, Rhode Island Volunteers)

"A PREPOSSESSING YOUNG CONTRABAND WHO BOASTS THE NAME OF ABRAHAM DOUGLASS . . . ."

Reno cl'ar to de batteries by de 'Piscopal Church, an' dey was like a blue cloud risin'."[134] The basic blue uniforms, if decorated with blue, denoted infantry; yellow decoration was worn by the cavalry; and red, by the artillerymen.

Over the years thousands of troops were stationed in and around Tennallytown. Some were local defense militias, such as the Tenleytown Rifles; most were from elsewhere in the Union, or even Southerners sympathetic to the North. Because the majority of the Tennallytown folk were Southern in their origins, and favored slavery, the Northern troops who descended into their midst were initially unwelcome.

We do have some record of what the visiting soldiers, at least the Rhode Island Volunteers, thought of Tennallytown and its inhabitants. A few war-time residents also passed on to their children and grandchildren mementoes of the days of occupation.

Mrs. Rebecca French Harry, a young mother when the war broke out, was one of those who offered hospitality and care to the Pennsylvania soldiers who first came to Camp Tennally, as it was also called. A book of memories, called "The Token Album," has been passed down in the Harry family. In it are sincere but flowery tributes from four or five members of the 32nd Regiment of Pennsylvania Volunteers, one who modestly calls himself "Sam, the Soldier," and another, Richard B. Nixon.

Lieutenant John Stanton of Philadelphia wrote the most eloquent testimony to the goodness of the "one who takes pleasure in acts of kindness," and composed this poem:

To Mrs. Harry

Through vale and wood I've travelled far
To obey my country's call to war,
But ne'er have I such greeting met
As woman, in kindness gave
To one, who, stranger yet
Could no return, save gratitude,
Boundless as the ocean wave,
Give, to one whose every thought
Was with deeds of kindness fraught.

Lieut. John Stanton

No doubt the local residents grew quite fond of many of the young volunteers, and were pleased to demonstrate their "Maryland hospitality" to the Yankees.

Two of the most hospitable of the local gentry were Mr. and Mrs. Samuel F. Burrows of River Road. The young couple were in their 30s when they rebuilt a farmhouse on their land on the south side of River Road. Their front yard was about where River Road Presbyterian Church is today, near 45th and Fessenden.

Samuel and Harriet Burrows and their first four children had been in their newly rebuilt farmhouse only three years when they found themselves between two large Union camps. Fort Pennsylvania (Reno) and the camps around it were to their east, at Tennallytown, and the new Fort Bayard was right next to them on the west, where River Road crosses over into Maryland. In fact, 50 acres of Burrows' land were used for Fort Bayard's barracks and parade grounds. Mr. Burrows sold milk, vegetables, and even cattle regularly to the quartermaster.

Mrs. Burrows, the former Harriet America Shekell of Georgetown, had her fifth baby, Lelia, in 1861, and her sixth in 1864. But she and her husband exerted effort on behalf of the lonely soldiers, many of them still in their teens and away from home for the first time. Her hospitality to the soldiers was documented in notes preserved by the family, e.g., from one sergeant who "was hungary for something besides soldiers food."

A testimonial from 75 members of Company M, 9th New York Volunteer Artillery (22nd N.Y. Heavy Artillery Battery) expressed their "thanks for the many kindnesses and hospitalities we have received from Mr. Samuel [Burrows] and wife near Fort Bayard—since our first arrival at that place (January 4, 1863) and removal to Fort Simmons [May 4] . . . and which they were always willing and ready to bestow."[135]

Rhode Island regimental historian William A. Spicer, whose camp was on River Road above the Burrows farm, wrote that their rations had been "of such a uniformly bad quality since we arrived in Washington, that some of us have been out to a neighboring farmhouse to get a good square meal for 25 cents! And didn't it go good?"[136]

H.T. Chace of Company D described camp food:

"They gave us rations of salt meat and pork . . . which would almost motion to us when to come to dinner. We have eaten so much salt pork of late that we are inclined to speak in grunts, prick up our ears, and perform other animal demonstrations."

Another soldier complained he had some hard-tack that was marked "B.C."

Harriet Burrows' father, Richard R. Shekell, was a prominent Mason in Georgetown, and no doubt was instrumental in finding Masonic members among the young men stationed in and around Tennallytown. A Tennallytown lodge had not yet been formed; but records indicate that a Masonic group from Fort Reno met regularly at the home of Jonathan Buckman on Grant Road.[137]

Many years after the war was over, and few traces of those active forts remained, soldiers continued to write to Mr. and Mrs. Burrows and other Tennallytown folk who had befriended them in the difficult days when they were stationed in the area.

*   *   *   *

The Army of the Potomac was visible constantly over the four years of the war, marching north and south along the Rockville Pike, New Military Road, and River Road. The rhythm of marching troops and the rumble of wheeled artillery soon became unremarkable occurrences.

As hospitable as local landowners tried to be to the defending army, and no matter how much a commanding officer might have tried not to offend the local population in a neighborhood such as Tennallytown, some rude and unsupervised soldiers were the perpetrators of acts of vandalism.

The St. Alban's Episcopal congregation, organized in 1854, was host to many soldiers from Fort Gaines and Fort Reno who worshipped with them. One disorder during the war, however, was reported as follows:

"One morning it was found that the altar was pushed forward toward the church rail. It was learned that some rough soldiers bent on plunder thought the church silver was hidden under the altar. They

were arrested and put under guard and there was no further disturbance."[138]

The intruders were apparently Union soldiers, supposedly defending the area in which they were plundering.

The St. Alban's historian also records that there were many incendiary fires in the neighborhood—whether by Union or Confederate troops is not clear. As a result, one member of the vestry kept a key to the church always with him so that "he might ring the bell in case of a fire close enough to threaten the property."

Besides appropriating wood and other materials for fuel and construction, the soldiers also often displayed a contempt for Tennallytowners' property and privacy. The Rhode Island history gives many examples of takeovers of houses, wheelwright shops, barns, and sheds for temporary or long-term use. The more the owners protested, it seems, the more aggressive the soldiers became.

Foraging for food was a common activity. Potatoes from the local gardens, fruit from Mrs. Lyles' orchards, milk from cows, chickens and eggs from Burrows' henhouses—all of these were fair game for the soldiers.

"Foraging is procuring necessary subsistence by buying when you can't steal it, or stealing when you can't buy it, or stealing, per se, whether you can buy it or not. The last is the favorite mode in this section."[139]

The noise of weapons practice may have become an everyday sound, but locals never got used to it. "The almost hourly belching forth of their numerous weapons of destruction gives ample assurance that they are well manned and ready for action." "July 24 target practice—our

shots fell very near our target, nearly a mile distant." Many Tennallytowners fervently believed they had more to fear from the Union army than from the Confederates.

The Pennsylvania, New York, Vermont, and Rhode Island Volunteers who were stationed at Tennallytown over the years of the war had their share of harassment from the locals, especially in the early days of the war. It was said that the real supporters of Southern secession ("Secesh," they were called) left their homes in the District of Columbia and "retreated to a safer locality further down in Dixie."[140] In some cases the abandoned farms were cared for by one or two slaves.

But some Southern sympathizers, confident that the Union would be overturned, stayed and fought their little battles at home. Captain A.C. Greene, Company G of the Rhode Island 10th, wrote home June 5, 1862,

"One of the pickets [guards] of the New York 69th Regt., which is encamped near us, was shot while on duty Friday evening last. The scoundrel who committed the deed was arrested and sent to Washington on Saturday. He was a desperate looking fellow, and made his boast that he had shot six Union soldiers before . . . ."

On a Sunday afternoon tramp to bathe in Rock Creek, the soldiers "kept well together, as the neighborhood was considered unfriendly." One mail messenger, who was once confronted after stealing apples from an orchard, a few days later, riding in the same locality, heard a musket shot whistle close to his ear. "The matter was investigated by the major, but nothing ever came of it."

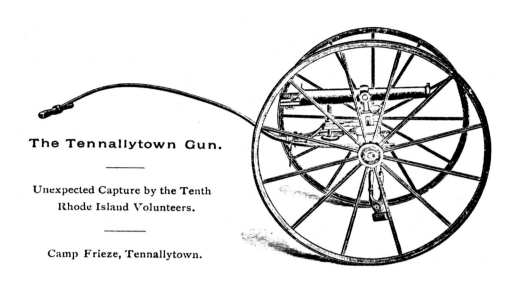

The Tennallytown Gun.

Unexpected Capture by the Tenth
Rhode Island Volunteers.

Camp Frieze, Tennallytown.

(Sketch from <u>History of 9th and 10th Regiments,</u>
<u>Rhode Island Volunteers</u>)

*This small cannon was seized
from a Tennallytown resident
with Southern sympathies, by
members of the 10th Rhode
Island Volunteers.*

*It was later turned over to the
museum of the Rhode Island
Historical Society.*

On June 18, 1862, Rhode Island
Company B was sent out on a special
secret search mission: a rebel cannon was reportedly

"concealed in the barn of a
well-known Southern sympathizer, and it was considered
not improbable that he might
turn it some dark night on our
sleeping regiments at Camp
Frieze [River Road] . . . . Visions
of a 32, if not a 42-pounder
rose before us . . . . And lo, what
a disappointment! Instead
of a mighty 42-pounder, a
Stonewall Jackson, we beheld a
small field howitzer about two
feet long, such as is used in the
field by infantry. It was rifled,
and carried a ball weighing a
pound, about a mile.

"But such as it was, it was
mounted on its carriage and
trailed back to camp by Co. B.,
who thus earned the honor of
capturing the <u>only</u> rebel cannon taken by the Tenth
Regiment Rhode Island
Volunteers."

[The "Tennallytown Gun" (see
sketch) was subsequently placed in
the museum of the Rhode Island
Historical Society.][141]

Among the many state regiments stationed at Fort Gaines and
Fort Pennsylvania in and around
Tennallytown were the 63rd Indiana;
the 55th, 59th, and 69th New York
Volunteers, including the French
Zouaves regiment; the 62nd and 71st
New York; the 11th and 17th
Regulars; the 9th and 10th Rhode
Island Volunteers; and the 93rd,
98th, 102nd, and 119th Regiments of
Pennsylvania Volunteers.

The Pennsylvania 98th, the
majority of whom were of German
origin, came to Fort Pennsylvania in
October 1861. "A school for officers
was established, which was in session
one hour nightly, and the non-commissioned officers received instruction in artillery drill at Fort
Pennsylvania . . . ." The 98th departed in March 1862 for the Virginia
campaign.[142]

September of 1862 brought
Union veterans of the Virginia campaign into Tennallytown to await
orders to Antietam Creek, Md.,
where Robert E. Lee's troops
engaged them in a bloody battle.

One soldier who later rose to
national prominence was stationed
briefly in Tennallytown in
September 1862. Oliver Wendell
Holmes, Jr., wrote to his mother on
September 5 that the 20th
[Massachusetts] Regiment was "at
TenAlleyTown (near GeorgeT.)
ready to march in any direction
we're wanted." This regiment had
undergone long marches through
Virginia, from the James River to
Newport News, and from Aquia
Creek northward until it finally
encamped with "the rest of the
Second Corps at Tennallytown, Md.,
(sic) on Sept. 4."[143]

This frequent mispronunciation, and the consequent misperception of Tennallytown—as a town of ten alleys—were probably the best reasons for using the spelling Tenleytown.

Between September 5 and 17 the Second Corps advanced to a point near Antietam Creek. The terrible battle of Antietam, in which 22,000 died, occurred on the 17th and 18th of September, 1862. Young Oliver Wendell Holmes was injured.

As the battles raged in nearby Virginia and Maryland, the wounded were transported to new hospitals that had been set up in the District of Columbia. By the end of December 1862, there were an estimated 14,000 sick and wounded soldiers in the hospitals in Washington, Georgetown, and Alexandria.[144]

Military doctors established a post hospital called Camp Ohio near Tennallytown.[145] Its exact site might well have been the Jesuits' "Georgetown Villa" (now McLean Gardens). Emma Moore, who was born in 1859, later recalled to friends that her nurse told her, as they strolled through the beautiful grounds of Georgetown Villa, that during the Civil War the house was used as a hospital and that military tents were pitched on the grounds.[146]

According to one Jesuit history, the College Villa, Tenleytown, was occupied from January to April 1862 by Brigadier General John J. Peck and his staff.[147] Peck's Brigade, of Smith's Division, Keyes Corps, was the designation of the Union volunteers at Tennallytown. General Samuel P. Sturgis, who followed Peck as commander of the fortifications around the city, also maintained his headquarters at the College Villa, as correspondence from the General indicates.[148] On June 8, 1862, Sturgis moved to the War Department office and Captain Henry R. Mighels assumed duty at the College Villa.

Camp Ohio was also used as a military prison in early 1863. National Archives records show that its 18 prisoners at that time included one sergeant, two corporals, and 15 privates—but whether they were of the Union or the Confederate army is not clear.[149]

The little Tennallytown Methodist Church at River Road was also taken over for hospital use, and subsequently destroyed. Minutes of the Methodist West Georgetown circuit meeting of July 8, 1862, show the Sabbath school "at Tenlytown has suffered for want of a place to hold its meetings." The minutes of January 7, 1863, reported "the [Sabbath] school at TennallyTown as suspended, in consequence of the destruction of the church by the army."

In April of that year a committee was appointed to "superintend the erection of a room at Tenlytown for Sabbath School & other purposes." In July 1863, the quarterly minutes say, "the school at Tenlytown has been reorganized after a long season of unavoidable suspence."[150]

Obviously the site of the Methodist church and school near the juncture of the River Road, the Frederick Road, and the new military road (Murdock Mill Road), was a good one on which to erect rifle pits and "breastworks." Up until a few years ago, one could still detect parts of these defenses behind the newest Eldbrooke Methodist Church. Such fortifications were erected in an uneven line on either side of all the major forts and batteries. The Methodist congregation built a second church in 1866, after the war was over and the occupation ended.

Land had been set aside in 1855 for a cemetery behind the Methodist Church. A deed shows that William D.C. Murdock and his wife, heirs to much of the property west of the turnpike, sold one half acre for

cemetery use to the trustees of the church for $50.

Some overzealous but short-sighted soldiers carried off tombstones from the cemetery behind the church for use in the construction of ovens. The Lightfoot family was said to have covered over the Tennally family gravestones, which lay flat in their backyard, to prevent their being stolen by the soldiers.[151]

Lt. DeWolf of Company D described his guard duty alongside the Methodist cemetery:

"Over the low paling, in a grass grown corner of the enclosure, half a dozen headstones, yellow and streaked with rain, are visible. Round about the resting place where 'the rude forefathers of the hamlet sleep,' has been heard the bustle of great camps, the tread of armies for more than a year, yet they slumber on. Their march is over . . . ."[152]

Mrs. John Jerome Lightfoot, Jr., said in a 1928 interview that the Tennally house had been an officers' headquarters during the "armed encampment" of 1861.[153] The house had only three bedrooms, however, and the Daniel Lightfoots had four grown children who presumably all lived at home. Mamie Lightfoot Bradford, in a 1974 interview, said that during the Civil War the Lightfoots only "took in a few boarders. They gave food to the soldiers all around." One detachment, said Mrs. Bradford, was camped "over near where the church and school is now on Wisconsin"—south of St. Ann's.

The Tennallytown Inn, owned by Godfrey Conrad's heirs, was also occupied during the Civil War as a hospital and provided offices for General Samuel Sturgis in May 1862, prior to or in addition to the College Villa.

In 1861 Godfrey Conrad had been buried in the Methodist

(Photo from Washingtoniana Collection, Martin Luther King Memorial Library)

MAJOR GENERAL
JESSE LEE RENO

The Late General Reno, as photographed by Mathew Brady. From Harper's Weekly, October 4, 1862. Fort Pennsylvania was renamed Fort Reno in his honor. Years later, the town of Reno, Nevada, was also named after Jesse Lee Reno.

The officers had gone into the hotel to pay their respects to Gen. Saml. P. Sturgis, to whose brigade we had been assigned.

"The rain poured, some of the men broke ranks and tried shelter under the veranda. Gen. Robbins stalked across the street with measured dignity, and whilst the rain formed rivulets down his back exclaimed, 'For God's sake, sergeant, keep the men in line, this is Gen. Sturgis' headquarters." [155]

The name of the fort at Tennallytown was changed from Fort Pennsylvania to Fort Reno in 1863, after the death of Major General Jesse Lee Reno at the Battle of South Mountain, Maryland, September 14, 1862. Not only was the fort renamed in his memory, but the settlers (mostly blacks) who came to the site after the war also called it Reno; and a lovely, winding residential road that connected the fort area with Cleveland Park to the south was named Reno Road.

Jesse Lee Reno was born in Wheeling, (then) Virginia, on June 20, 1823, and was graduated from the U.S. Military Academy in 1846. He was a captain when the Civil War broke out, but was commissioned brigadier-general of volunteers with Burnside's Expeditionary Corps and major general of volunteers with the 9th Army Corps. He had fought at Roanoke Island, New Berne, Camden, Manassas, and Chantilly, and was placed in command of the 9th Corps on September 3, 1862, eleven days before his death. [156] Reno is buried at Oak Hill Cemetery, Georgetown.

Fort Reno, Oklahoma, and Fort Reno, Wyoming, were named after Major General Jesse Lee Reno, as was Reno, Nevada. That new town's name was chosen by Civil War veterans who had served with Jesse Reno in Mexico. [157]

Cemetery, just north of the tavern. His daughter Mary and her husband, John C. Howard, continued to run the business during the Civil War, for an 1866 will referred to it as the "Howard house" as well as "Conrad's Old Tavern at TennalyTown." The large number of beds and other furnishings in the appraisal of Conrad's estate confirms that he offered overnight lodging. [154]

On the morning of May 30, 1862, when the Rhode Island Volunteers were marched through Georgetown to the village of Tennallytown, they had ended their march at the Tennallytown Inn.

"After the hot, two-hours march, the regt. halted, the right resting near the village hotel. Suddenly the black clouds which had been gathering, were rent . . . we were soaked through and through.

After Fort Pennsylvania, or Fort Reno, was originally built, it was deemed too small for its functions, was not sturdily protected, and did not have the best view of the land to the north. So it was enlarged and strengthened (see diagram). An advanced battery was constructed about 300 yards north from the highest ridge, across what is now Fessenden Street and along 39th Street. This advanced Battery Reno had eight 12-pounder guns and a magazine; a covered walkway connected it to the main fort to the south. A double line of rifle trenches was added to strengthen the position.[158]

Lines of rifle pits extended from west of the Methodist church north of what is now Gloria Point, and east across Brookeville Road to the south side of the fort. A less intense line of rifle pits extended east to Battery Russell, now near the north corner of Connecticut and Fessenden, to Fort Kearney (about 30th and Garrison Streets) and to Battery Terrell, now the site of the Peruvian Embassy to the northeast of that intersection. The latter two overlook the Broad Branch.

As for Fort Reno itself, at its time of greatest development there were six barracks, seven kitchens, one commissary storehouse, four officers' quarters, and one adjutant's office—these were on the west side of the fort property, towards Brookeville (Belt) Road. The central part consisted of a mess hall, a storehouse, quartermaster's storehouse, adjutant general's office, two hospitals, a cook house, a dispensary, surgeon's quarters, and stable.

The east side of the fort, going towards Grant Road, had six stables and four other buildings (see diagram). These were the buildings as of 1864; they did not include the guns and ammunition storage area in the fort itself, or the rows of tents

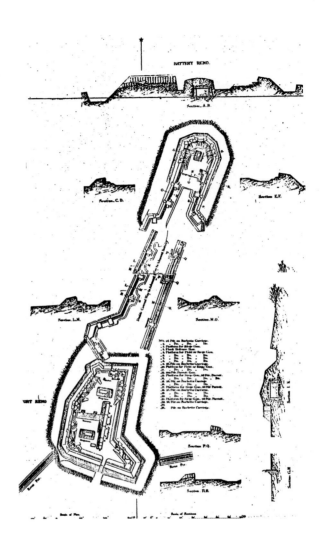

(from Barnard's <u>Defenses of Washington</u>, Plate 21)

Detailed drawing of the original Fort Reno and the extended Battery Reno, showing rifle pits, magazines, gun emplacements, etc.

that stretched behind the fort, down River Road to Fort Bayard, and elsewhere on empty fields around Tennallytown.

Fort Reno, eventually the largest and strongest fort defending the capital, mounted a dozen heavy guns—three Parrott siege guns and nine 24-pounder barbette guns.

Fort Gaines, next to the Murdock house, was mounted by four 32-lb. barbette guns, and Fort DeRussy, near Rock Creek, had seven smaller cannon.

A steady strength of three thousand men of the First Brigade made Fort Reno the stronghold of the capital's northern defenses.[159]

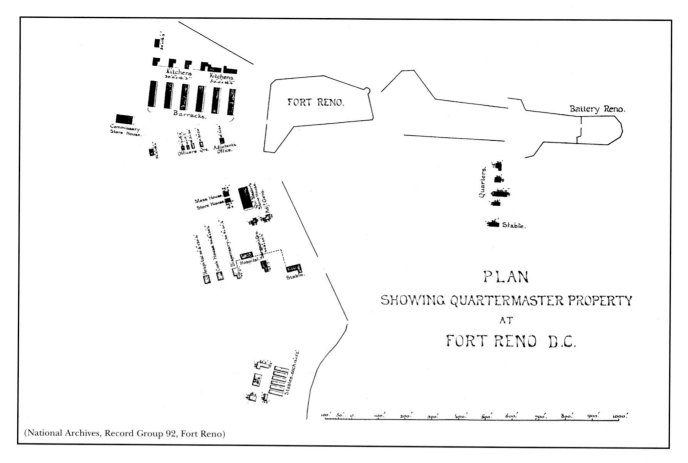

(National Archives, Record Group 92, Fort Reno)

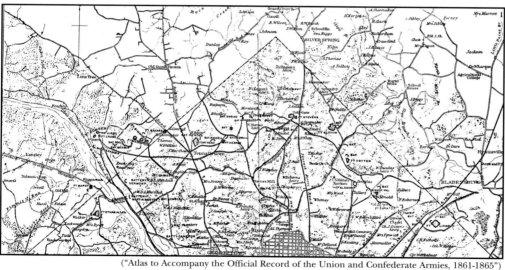

("Atlas to Accompany the Official Record of the Union and Confederate Armies, 1861-1865")

Approaches to the capital from Maryland are indicated on this Civil War map. Fort Stevens was located on the 7th Street Road to Silver Spring (now Georgia Avenue). That road and the Rockville Road (Wisconsin Avenue) were the only two north-south routes into the District of Columbia.

A great number of local militia companies had been organized during the years of the war, most for only a few months at a time. Part of the D.C. militia, the first that had been mustered into service in April 1861, was called the Tenleytown Rifles. Commanded by Captain Harry W. Blount (Blunt), who lived at "Dunblane," the 64 members of the local militia were uniformed and equipped with long-range rifles that they kept with them.

Most members of the Tenley-town Rifles were required to spend nights in local armory tents, but all were permitted to attend to their usual occupations during the day—always within call. Their purpose was strictly to support troops defending the District, not to be moved to another site.[160]

The fighting actually did get close to the city of Washington on a hot Sunday, July 10, 1864. Following the battle at the Monocacy River, near Frederick, on July 9, part of the Confederate forces under General Jubal Early approached Washington by way of Rockville. At Hagerstown and Rockville the Rebels had forcibly taken great sums of money, as well as food, clothing, and horses from the frightened residents.

General Early then led troops southward the ten miles toward Fort Stevens, and General John McCausland's army came down the Rockville Pike toward Fort Reno. Early probably had no real expectation of actually capturing the capital, but was retaliating after the siege of Fredericksburg. As Margaret Leech said, Early intended to plunder as much of Washington as he could, in order to weaken the already unsteady confidence of the Union.[161]

Late Sunday afternoon, Union Major General Christopher C. Augur received this urgent message:

> Washington Road,
> Two miles from Rockville,
> July 10, 1864 - 4 p.m.

General: I have taken position and formed. My rear guard is fighting the enemy near Rockville. I have been joined by a squadron Eighth Illinois Cavalry and expect to be engaged in a few moments. I would respectfully suggest that the forts in the vicinity of Tennallytown be strongly guarded as the enemy's column is a mile long.

> Very respectfully,
> Your obedient servant,
> Wm. H. Fry,
> Major, Commanding[162]

Before noon on Monday morning, July 11, the lookouts from the signal tower at Fort Reno saw first

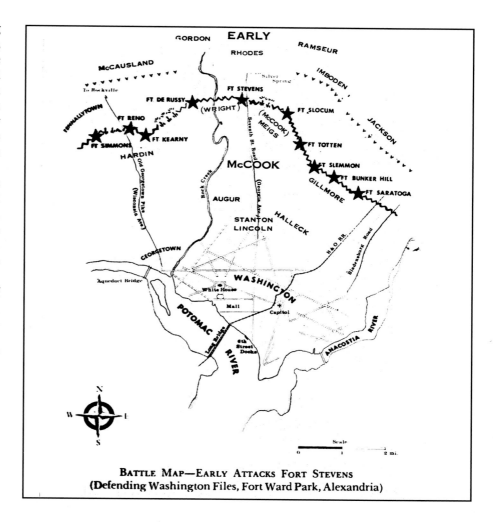

BATTLE MAP—EARLY ATTACKS FORT STEVENS
(Defending Washington Files, Fort Ward Park, Alexandria)

clouds of dust and then Confederate army wagons moving toward the city. President Lincoln, who was visiting the fortifications at Tennallytown, ordered his driver to take him directly downtown, where he conferred with General Henry Halleck.[163]

After three years of occupation, Fort Reno was at that moment undermanned, and a call went out for reinforcements for the 9th New York Artillery, encamped at Tennallytown. Civilians as well as veteran reserves responded to the call; additional local men were quickly drafted.[164]

McCausland's cavalry pressed on toward Tennallytown, drawing fire and engaging occasional defenders

JUBAL EARLY'S PLAN OF ATTACK, JULY 1864

(map from Symbol, Sword, and Shield: Defending Washington during the Civil War; by Benjamin Franklin Cooling, Hamden, Conn: Archon Books, 1975)

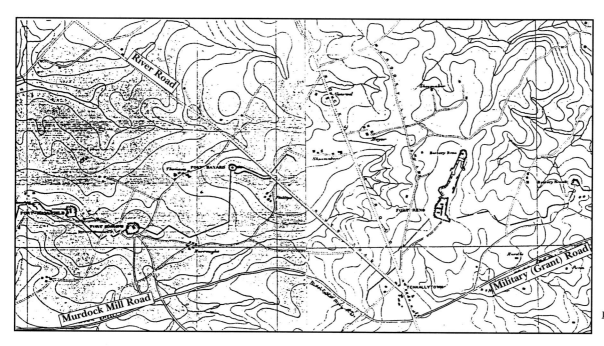

(Map from Barnard's
Defenses of Washington,
plates 8 and 9)

Civil War era map shows military installations, topography of the land and creeks, roads, and names of local landowners. The Phillips farm on River Road, adjacent to Fort Bayard, came under the ownership of Samuel and Harriet Burrows. Other names are Shoemaker, Boyer, Conrad, Hurdle, Buckner (Buckman), and Paine (Payne).

on horseback. At first the Georgetown Pike's emptiness encouraged McCausland. But as he approached Fort Reno, the shells bursting nearby and his field glasses told him that the fortifications near the Georgetown Pike were much too strong for attack.[165]

In the words of General Early:

"On the right was Rock Creek, running through a deep ravine which had been rendered impassable by the felling of the timber on each side, and beyond were the works on the Georgetown Pike [Fort Reno] which had been reported to be the strongest of all."[166]

The existence of signal towers at Forts Reno and Stevens also cautioned the Confederates that their movements could not go unnoticed.

While Early's troops moved south on the Georgetown Pike and 7th Street Road, the desperate commanders of the Washington defenses hurried to organize their veterans, many of whom were sick, ill-equipped, and of little use. A compa-

ny of reservists was called upon to perform most of the active fighting, with a National Guard detachment and other invalids as back-up. Three companies of equally "useless stragglers" had been sent to Tennallytown.[167]

Meanwhile, the roads into the District were filling up with desperate Maryland farmers who had hurriedly gathered up their families, hitched their fastest horses to the family wagon, and raced toward the city. Rumors flew that the advancing Confederates were frighteningly close, that they were stealing livestock and household goods, and even setting fire to some of the farmhouses and barns. The refugees shouted to everyone they passed that the country was swarming with Rebs.[168] The pro-Secessionists smiled smugly, hoping that the tide of war had turned.

Even the Tennallytown residents, fearing an attack on Fort Reno, were packing up their valuables on carts, and heading down into the city. Herds of cattle were driven to the city's slaughterhouse pens by the anxious farmers.

One reported incident in Bethesda demonstrated the power of the 100-pounder Parrott rifle. It seems that Confederate troops occupied the Bohrer house and farm, which were located where the tower section of the Naval Hospital is now, off Rockville Pike. One shell fired from Fort Reno, three and a half miles to the south, "burst in the field between the house and the pike." Four Confederates were killed from the shelling, and were buried on the land.[169]

Jubal Early perceived that Fort Stevens was poorly defended and ordered the attack on that fort for midday Monday. As Major General Horatio Wright's 6th Corps of the Army of the Potomac arrived by boat at the Washington docks, skirmishes continued in front of Fort Stevens. Wright's veterans gradually replaced the reservists, volunteers, and government clerks who had bravely defended the 7th Street Pike fortifications. The blaze of battle continued through the twilight hours.

As night fell, the noise of battle died down; both sides tried to rest in anticipation of a renewed fight in the morning. But with the dawn came the realization that Jubal Early's rebel forces had no chance of piercing the shield around the capital city. And so Early made plans to withdraw; but he decided to wait until cover of darkness Tuesday night.[170]

All day Tuesday, Wright's 6th Corps troops made a concerted assault on Early's infantry; by dusk the Rebels were in retreat. At Fort Reno, the Union troops kept McCausland's cavalry busy all day. Wednesday morning, all was quiet again.[171]

The cost of the battle for the Federals was a little more than 250 men. The Confederates, however, lost about 2,000 in their unsuccessful fight to gain Washington.[172]

And so it was that the strong position of the fort at Tennallytown did, in fact, help prevent a dreaded Confederate invasion of the capital. The three years of training and equipping and preparing Fort Reno, one of the defenses of Washington, culminated in the battle of July 1864.[173] Such was the sole experience of military action at Fort Reno during the Civil War.

During the fighting of July 10-12, 1864, small detachments of soldiers from Forts Reno and Stevens had advanced into the countryside north of the city to fend off the invaders. A few Confederates were taken prisoner and brought back into camps, where they were held until transfer to a central prison. A 1903 newspaper reporter says Mr. John H. Harry told him of citizens of Tennallytown "in war's grim period feeding Confederate soldiers that had been taken prisoner . . . ."[174] Perhaps the Union soldiers neglected to feed the Rebs, and the local residents were more merciful.

In early April 1865, after Robert E. Lee's army had surrendered at Appomattox, Va., the city of Washington was in an uproar of celebration over the ending of the war.

"The chain of forts around the city, and batteries of field artillery between, made a ring of cannons . . . which were fired in rotation for several hours. The line of cannon salutes . . . always proceeded in the same direction, so that it went round and round the circuit 20 to 30 miles."[175]

One week later, the city was in mourning for the assassinated President, Abraham Lincoln.

*   *   *   *

After the close of the war, the forts that had defended Washington so well were slowly dismantled and abandoned. All the army hospitals had closed or were closing, as the sick and wounded veterans returned to their homes. One last Grand Review of the troops was held in Washington at the end of May, and soldiers from all over the states came to Washington for the occasion. Once again the local citizens, who had been put upon by occupying troops for nearly four years, made their homes and lands available to the visiting troops—but this time it was a special occasion, an expression of gratitude that the long, cruel war was over.

One force left evidence that it camped—at least briefly during the Grand Review—along the Soapstone Creek east of Connecticut Avenue. A huge beech tree, now gone, bore the incription of "W.T. Holt, Co. C, 53rd Indiana volunteers, June 5, 1865." This area is in the valley behind the former Dumbarton College of the Holy Cross, now the Howard University Law School.

Other trees in the Soapstone Valley bore inscriptions of 1861, 1862, and 1863—but we cannot determine from this evidence how many, if any, troops camped there.[176]

Over the years, young and then older veterans of the occupation at Fort Reno came back with their families to visit Tennallytown and see where the forts and camps had been. In 1890 some of the veterans held a reunion at Fort Reno. By this time the Bangerter family's dairy cows were grazing over the fort property at the top of the hill. Lillian Bangerter, who had been born in 1874 and was then a lovely girl of 16, was named Daughter of the Regiment by the veterans.[177]

Most of the fort could still be seen as late as 1892, 27 years later. A

VIEW WEST FROM FORT RENO

(from Senate Report No. 166, The Improvement of the Park System of D.C., 1902; Washingtoniana Collection, Martin Luther King Memorial Library)

Although the property was returned to the Dyer family, the last remains of Fort Reno were not removed until about 1900, when the land was being prepared for a reservoir. This 1902 view looks west from Reno, beyond the Brookeville (Belt) Road in the middle distance and the Rockville Pike in the further distance. "Fence is limit of present public ownership."

guide published in that year [178] indicates that the emplacement for the 100-pound Parrott rifle was still visible, as well as a short section of rifle trenches back of the Negro schoolhouse on Grant Road. The guide also states that the fort and battery at the north end were soon to be entirely graded down. This anticipated the development of a water reservoir on this site.

The city and county of Washington resumed once again their peacetime functions and pleasures. But the war had brought so much devastation of lands and buildings; thousands of new people to be housed, employed, fed, educated, and churched; and such a great quantity of new construction

of roads and forts that the face of the District of Columbia was changed drastically. The little villages in the county, including Tennallytown, were no longer isolated and small in population.

[114] Reunion poem by Mrs. B.F. Pabodie, wife of Corporal B.F. Pabodie, Company H, 10th Regiment, in William A. Spicer, History of the Ninth and Tenth Regiments, Rhode Island Volunteers (Providence: Snow & Farnham, 1892)

[115] Earl Schenck Miers, editor in chief, Lincoln Day by Day: A Chronology, Vol. III, 1861-65. Washington: Lincoln Sesquicentennial Commission, 1960

[116] Office of Military History, Reference Branch, Fort Reno file

[117] Bruce Catton, Mr. Lincoln's Army. Garden City: Doubleday & Co. Inc., 1951, p. 74. Catton was quoting from Trobriand's Four Years with the Army of the Potomac, Boston 1889, translated by George K. Dauchy.

[118] Fort Gaines was named after Brigadier General Edmund Pendleton Gaines, veteran of the War of 1812

[119] Margaret Leech, Reveille in Washington, 1860-1865. New York: Grosset & Dunlap, 1941

[120] Catton, Mr. Lincoln's Army, op. cit., p. 184

[121] J. Harry Shannon, "The Rambler," The Sunday Star, January 3, 1915, op. cit.

[122] Benjamin Franklin Cooling, Symbol, Sword & Shield: Defending Washington During the Civil War. Hamden, Connecticut: Archon Books, 1975, p. 87

[123] J.G. Barnard, A Report on the Defenses of Washington. Washington: Government Printing Office, 1871

[124] Bruce Catton, Grant Takes Command. Boston: Little, Brown & Co., 1968

[125] The Works of Walt Whitman—Vol. II, The Collected Prose. New York: Funk & Wagnalls, 1948

[126] Zack Spratt, "Rock Creek's Bridges," RCHS, 1953-56

[127] This and most of the succeeding quotes are from Spicer, History of the Ninth and Tenth Regiments, Rhode Island Volunteers, op. cit. A large amount of material for this chapter was acquired from the Spicer book, which is to be found in the National Archives.

[128] Spicer, op. cit.

[129] Grover G. Burrows, unpublished manuscript, "Mrs. Harriet America Burrows 1828-1923"

[130] Spicer, op. cit., p. 276

[131] Spicer, op. cit.

[132] Harold R. Manakee, Maryland in the Civil War. Baltimore: Maryland Historical Society, 1961

[133] Gladys Marie Fry, "The Activities of the Freedmen's Aid Societies in the District of Columbia, 1860-1870" MA thesis, Howard University, 1954

[134] "A Real Little Thrums," op. cit.

[135] Burrows, "Mrs. Harriet America Burrows, 1828-1923," op. cit.

[136] Spicer, op. cit.

[137] D.C. Masonic records, Columbia Historical Society

[138] Wilson, The Story of St. Albans Parish, 1854-1929, op. cit.

[139] Spicer, op. cit.

[140] Spicer, op. cit.

[141] Spicer, op. cit.

[142] Samuel P. Bates, History of Pennsylvania Volunteers, 1861-65, Vol. III. Harrisburg: B. Singerly, State Printer, 1870

[143] Mark DeWolfe Howe, editor, Touched with Fire: Civil War Letters and Diary of Oliver Wendell Holmes, Jr. Cambridge: Harvard University Press, 1946

[144] Harvey W. Crew, Centennial History of the City of Washington, D.C. Dayton: The United Brethren Publishing House, 1892

[145] Marcus Benjamin, editor, Washington During Wartime, 36th Annual Encampment of the Grand Army of the Republic, 1902

[146] Interview with Mrs. Susan Cockrell, May 22, 1975, by the author

[147] Barnum, "The Old Georgetown Villa," op. cit.

[148] Spicer, op. cit.

[149] National Archives RG 105, Camp Ohio, D.C., Guard Reports, in Vol. 406/1056 DW

[150] Early records of the West Georgetown Methodist Circuit, at Eldbrooke United Methodist Church

[151] Theodore D. Gatchel, Rambling Through Washington. Washington: printed by The Washington Journal, 1932

[152] Spicer, op. cit.

[153] "May D. Lightfoot Recalls Olden Days," Top Notch (newspaper), November 1928

[154] Inventory of the goods, chattels, and personal estate of Godfrey Conrad, November 23, 1861 (D.C.); National Archives, RG 21, from Adm. 4421 Old Series

[155] Spicer, op. cit.

[156] Francis Trevelyan Miller, editor in chief, The Photographic History of the Civil War, 1911, Vol. 10, reprinted New York: T. Yoseloff, 1957; p. 208

[157] Bruce Grant, American Forts Yesterday and Today. New York: E.P. Dutton & Co., 1965, and Nevada: The American Guide Series. Portland: Binfords & Mort, 1957

[158] Barnard, Defenses of Washington, op. cit.

[159] Voluntary Organizations, Office of Adjutant General, National Archives RG 94, as noted by Mary Mitchell, Divided Town (Barre, Mass.: Barre Publishers, 1968), p. 89

[160] Vertical files, Civil War, Washingtoniana Collection, Martin Luther King Memorial Library

[161] Leech, op. cit., p. 345-346

[162] War of the Rebellion: A Compilation of the Official Records of the Union and Confederate Armies. Washington, Government Printing Office, 1880-1901, Series I, Vol. 37, Pt. 2, pp. 166-167

[163] Leech, op. cit., p. 338

[164] Ibid., p. 336

[165] Frank Vandiver, Jubal's Raid. New York: McGraw-Hill, 1960

[166] Lt. Gen. Jubal Early, A Memoir of the Last Year of the War for Independence in the Confederate States of America. Lynchburg: Chas. W. Button, 1867

[167] Leech, op. cit., p. 337

[168] Ibid.

[169] Holman, Old Bethesda, op. cit., p. 44

[170] Vandiver, op. cit.

[171] A detailed account of the battles of July 1864 is to be found in Appendix A of <u>A Report on the Defenses of Washington</u>, by Brevet Major General Barnard, op. cit. General Barnard had command of Washington fortifications beginning in July 1862.

[172] Vandiver, op. cit.

[173] Leech, op. cit., p. 344

[174] Holland, 1903, op. cit.

[175] John M. Longyear's reminiscences, "Georgetown [University] During the Civil War," <u>Georgetown Today</u>, March 1975

[176] Interviews with and unpublished writings of Walton Shipley; and Maude C. Lukens, "Rock Creek Trees, a Civil War Story," <u>American Motorist</u>, January 1931

[177] Interview with Eda Schrader Offutt, November 13, 1974, by the author

[178] <u>Guide to and Maps of the National Capital and Vicinity, Including the Fortifications</u>. Engineering Platoon of the Engineer Corps, D.C. National Guard, 1892

PLAT MAP OF PLANNED FORT RENO SUBDIVISION, 1869

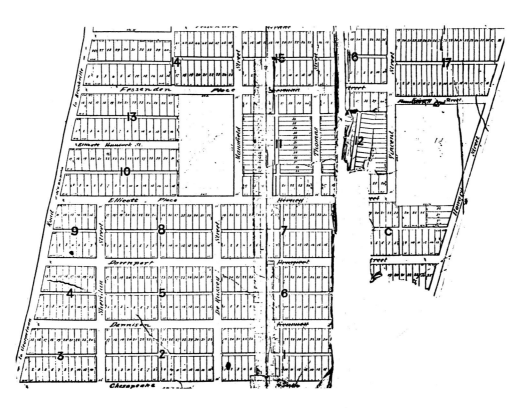

(Subdivision of Reno, The Estate of the late Giles Dyer, National Archives, RG 351, Gov. Shepherd, No. 1, p. 61)

Fort Reno Subdivision extended from Brookeville (Belt) Road on the west, to Fessenden Street on the north, Howard Road on the east, and Chesapeake Street on the south. Note open spaces for planned reservoir and school. 1869 was the year Fritz Bangerter bought up many lots for use as pasture. Note old and new street names on map.

IV

THE GROWING VILLAGE:

1865-1899

After the Civil War, Washington was recognized as the seat of government and power; and the establishment of new departments prompted an influx of new employees by the thousands—as well as tradesmen and small businessmen to serve these new residents. Most government employees still lived in Washington city, that is, south of Boundary Avenue.

Before the war, the population of Washington had been 75,000; twenty years later, it had more than doubled, to 178,000. The number of federal employees grew as the government's functions multiplied. Professionals, clerks, technicians, and unskilled laborers found ready employment in the post-war capital.

Tennallytown's population growth reflected that of the city and the government. The gardeners, butchers, and poultrymen; the carpenters, painters, and stonemasons; the tradesmen and merchants; and the heavy construction contractors—all these newcomers found they could make a good living in either the city or the Tennallytown area. The still-rural atmosphere of Tennallytown was the ideal place to raise their families. And how the village began to grow!

Fort Reno Subdivided

During the Civil War, the freed blacks had come in such large numbers to the Northern forts that the Union soldiers had had to turn to the government for help. In 1865, just before the close of the war, the government established the Bureau of Refugees, Freedmen, and Abandoned Lands, better known as the Freedmen's Bureau. The Bureau helped blacks find housing, employment, and supplies, offered them legal and medical aid, and established schools. It also kept marriage and other vital records.

At Fort Reno and other D.C. forts, the properties reverted to the owners who had held them prior to their being claimed for military use. Fort Reno was retained by the Army as late as January 1866, and many freed blacks continued to live there. Eventually it was returned to its previous owner, Giles Dyer, whose heirs sold the land in 1869 to two real estate men, Newall Onion and Alexander Butts. The latter subdivided the land into 21 sections of about two acres each. There were many building lots to a section (see maps).

At this time the land became formally for sale or for rent, at minimal prices. The black squatters were, for the most part, able to make $5 down payments to buy the lands on which they had already built little one- or two-room houses. Rudolph Warren recalls that his grandfather, who had driven a cow all the way from Richmond to D.C., bought a lot at Fort Reno for $25.

Not all of the property of Fort Reno was sold by Giles Dyer's heirs to blacks. Mary Ellen and Adelle French, Charles Barr, Frederick Bangerter, Isaac Marshall, and Barbara Lightfoot were whites who bought Reno land.

In 1873, eight years after the Civil War had ended, George A. Townsend described the general appearance of the old forts of the District of Columbia:

"All the forts around the city are dismantled, the guns taken out of them, the land resigned to its owners. Needy Negro squatters living around the forts have built themselves shanties of the officers' quarters, pulled out the abatis [wooden defenses] for firewood . . . . The woods, cut down to give the guns sweep, are overgrown with shrubs and bushes. Nature is unrestingly making war with War.

"The strolls out to the old forts are seedily picturesque. Freedmen, who exist by selling old horse-

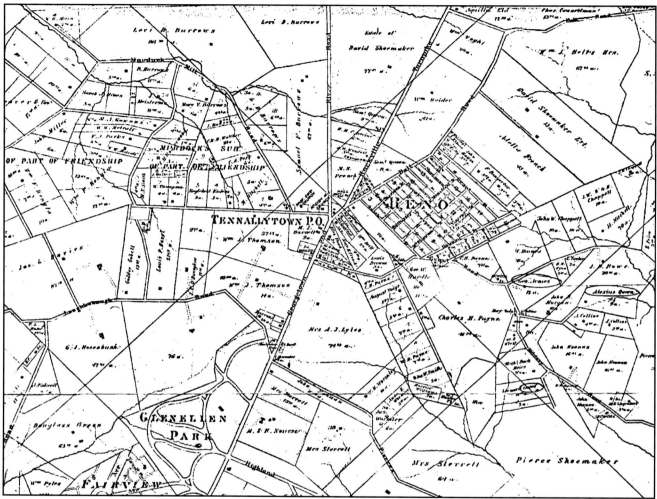

(G.M. Hopkins Real Estate Atlas, 1887)

*Map of Tennallytown in 1887
indicates Reno section is
extensive.*

shoes and iron spikes, live with their squatter families where, of old, the Army sutler kept the canteen; but the grass is growing its parallels nearer and nearer the magazines."[179]

The first houses at Fort Reno were, as Townsend wrote, shanties built by the freed slaves of leftover wood. But as they were able to work steadily, the blacks learned skills in construction work, in which most of them found employment. And their houses reflected these skills.

Remains of the Civil War defenses were still visible at Fort Reno until construction began on the reservoir about 1900.

Blacks who grew up at Fort Reno recall that their parents and grandparents came to Tennallytown as freed slaves from nearby Montgomery County, Maryland, or from Virginia—Louisa County, Madison County, Loudoun County. Many came first to other black communities in the area—along Broad Branch Road in Chevy Chase, D.C., or along River Road across the District line.

Tennallytown's appeal for the blacks included the availability of cleared land; a growing number of families, farms, and businesses that would employ them; a school; and, eventually, three churches.

The black population of Fort Reno grew steadily and rapidly. An 1894 Hopkins map indicates about 60 houses on the fort, some occupied by white families. A Metropolitan Police Department census of 1892 counted 520 whites and 211 blacks in all of Tennallytown.[180] Five years later, the totals were 758 whites and 369 blacks—just about one-third of the local population being black, as in the rest of the District of Columbia.[181]

The area bounded by Belt Road, Fessenden Street (first called Flint Street and Grant Street), Howard Road, and Chesapeake Street (South Street) was listed in city directories from 1872 to 1906 as Reno City. The residents, however, rarely used the word "city"—it was always Fort Reno, the Fort, Reno, or just Tennallytown.

Streets were cut through as early as the 1880s, and the Fort Reno area was, from then on, approximately three squares (blocks) east-west, and five squares (blocks) north-south. The streets were originally named for Union generals—Sheridan, DeRussy, Howard, Grant, Thomas, Kearney, and Birney. Most street names were later changed to conform to an alphabetical system.

Most Tennallytown blacks lived at Fort Reno; they had a separate school; they had separate churches; and almost all of them worked as laborers and domestics for white people.

Old Tennallytowners, black and white, remember the situation at Fort Reno as a generally good one. They affirm that the blacks and whites got along well, that the children played together, that there was a feeling of good will among the people of Tennallytown. A very real interdependence existed.

It would not be accurate to describe the Fort Reno area as a ghetto or even as an enclave, for two reasons—there were many whites

FORT RENO HOUSES

(1936 photos c/o National Park Service)

Top: 3909 Emery Place, owned by Harriet G. Taylor.

Bottom: 3957 Emery Place, owned by Robert H. Thomas

SEMI-DETACHED HOUSES, FORT RENO

(1936 National Park Service photos)

Top: 4017-19 Dennison Place, occupied by Snowdens, owned by Sue K. Harrison in 1920s

Bottom: Address and owners unknown.

who also lived on the Fort, and some streets were very attractive, with homes whose appearances were not at all different from those in the surrounding village. On many old maps, however, as well as in the minds of many residents, Reno was considered a village separate from Tennallytown.

Compared with those who lived in the city of Washington, the blacks of Tennallytown were well off. Physically, they lived at the highest elevation in the District, and so enjoyed summer breezes blowing through the Virginia pines; many had acres for gardens and livestock; and there was open space for the children to play in. The residents were not neglected, because the neighbors, black and white, knew and cared about one another. Most of the families on the Fort were related to other families there, were members of a local church congregation, and shared a very real feeling of community.

Miss Mary Thomas, who was born at Fort Reno in 1894, recalls that some people called it "the quiet spot."

"When I was young, we didn't have bad boys or girls. The police were on horseback in those days—and if a child got in trouble, they came up and talked to the parents. Everybody was like one big family, black and white together. There was no hatred. It was the quiet spot. It was beautiful—so congenial. If anything happened, it happened to all of us."[182]

Despite the memories of happy times, there were some bad times for Fort Reno blacks. There was discrimination, there was segregation in all institutions, there was racism, there were ugly incidents. White Tennallytown residents, like most of the county folk, were Southern in orientation and tradition. Many of them had not overnight become Yankees or abolitionists. And their children, in turn, often carried on the family points of view in those matters.

A large amount of the Fort Reno acreage was purchased, parcel after parcel, by Frederick (Fritz) Bangerter, beginning in 1869. Bangerter, a young Swiss immigrant, brought his German bride Christiana to live in a "fort house" before building his own substantial farmhouse.

The land was not considered valuable, not even for its recent historic importance. In 1869, Bangerter bought six lots from Giles Dyer's widow—all for only $50—and two lots nearby from Richard and India Dorsey for $140. (Sixty-five years later, the Bangerter heirs sold the land for 20 to 25 times as much as Fritz Bangerter had paid for it.)[183]

Bangerter used much of his acreage for the grazing of the cattle for his "Swiss Dairy," which supplied milk in the city. But he also acquired houses or had houses built on his land and rented to many black families. In 1893, for example, John Hurdle built three houses for Bangerter, at a cost of $600 each.

After her husband's death of typhoid fever in 1894, Bangerter's widow and son Fred, Jr., continued the dairy, until about 1915. Thus it was not uncommon after the turn of the century to see cattle grazing on the south side of the reservoir tower.

Farmers and Germans

In 1841 William Heider had bought farmland on the Rockville Pike in Tennallytown from Godfrey Conrad; but Heider had maintained a residence in Georgetown throughout the Civil War.[184] In 1871 he, his wife, and four young children moved

(1890 photo c/o Eda Schrader Offutt)

(1890 photo c/o Wm. F. Heider)

Top: BANGERTER HOMESTEAD, FORT RENO

Bottom: WILLIAM HEIDER'S FARMHOUSE, TENNALLYTOWN
German immigrant William D. Heider built this farmhouse about 1860, on 41 acres. Photo shows Heider, his wife, and one daughter on the porch, and sons Will and Fred standing with hunting dogs. Bill Paxton is on horse to left. House stood at 4200 Harrison Street, N.W.

71

to the farm, since by then there was a school, two churches, and a store or two—the few amenities that made the area more attractive to families. The Heiders' move was typical of a trend toward Tennallytown after the Civil War.

Farming was still the best way of making a living in the area. The Heiders and other farming families worked hard to make their war-torn fields productive again. Their vegetables were taken to city markets. About 30 Tennallytown heads of household called themselves farmers in the 1880 census; another 20 called themselves gardeners—and some of them had very extensive gardens.

George A. Townsend, writing in 1873, painted a mixed picture of farming in the area:

"The regions back of Washington City in Maryland . . . are susceptible of improvement by being cultivated in small patches, and the cheap prices of land ought to compensate settlers for the general sterility. Before Washington City grew to be a market, land anywhere in Montgomery county could be bought for from $3 to $5 an acre. At present the land near Rockville is held at from $12 to $50, and the gravel hills near Washington bring even $500.

"Hay is the best crop the Maryland county farmers make. Good poultry is raised all through this region and finds a market here . . . . The vicious system of agriculture practiced here for 100 years has so exhausted the land that it must be fed, as one said, with 'guano and phosphates, just as pigs are fed.' "[185]

Boyd, in his 1879 History of Montgomery County, spoke more positively about the situation of the county:

"As the location of Washington seems to be on ground prepared for a site of the seat of Government of a great Nation, so Montgomery Co. seems prepared to furnish supplies of all kinds for the inhabitants of such a city: Milk, Butter, Poultry, Hay, Fruit and Vegetables, in fact, everything which will not stand long carriage."[186]

Although Tennallytown was no longer part of Montgomery County, its agricultural assets were identical to the county that adjoined it.

Townsend also wrote that "this county needs the German farmer, with his practical knowledge, economy, and persistence." And the German farmers flocked to the Tennallytown area: besides William Heider, there came August and William Voigt, Frederick and Otto Sonnemann, John H. Wendel, Charles H.M. Walther, John Schumann, Charles Wehrle, Traugott Rosenbusch, and George Stadtler. There were the dairymen Engelbert Enders (from Baden, Germany) and Frederick Bangerter (from Switzerland).

Other German immigrants in the area were butchers—Huhn, Kengla, Goebel, and Hoemiller. Widower Bernard Scherer, a Swiss, was the restaurant keeper at the Tennallytown Inn. He was followed by Germans Ernst Loeffler and William Achterkirchen. Charles Volkman was the first tailor and Henry Schweitzer was the first shoemaker in the village.

The Irish, the Italians, and the Stone Business

A few Irish immigrants and their offspring also populated Tennallytown, as they did in greater numbers in Georgetown, Swampoodle (near today's Union Station), and Anacostia. The local Irish, however, were less farmers than they were skilled tradesmen—such as wheelwrights Francis Morrow and Robert Devine, blacksmiths Morris Fitzgerald and Mike Ryan, and stonecutter John Mullin. Other Irish immigrant workingmen in Tennallytown in 1880 were John Callahan, William Canning, William Cunningham, James Fagan, and Michael Slattery.

The end of the century brought a large number of Italian families to Tennallytown; they all lived near Wisconsin Avenue and Brandywine Street. Louis and Frank Perna had come to Tennallytown from Calabria, southern Italy, in the late 1880s. They were the sons and grandsons of stonemasons in Italy. Frank Perna—or Frenchy, as he was called—first worked as a stonemason on the Glen Echo Amusement Park buildings, and married a local woman, Alice Dean. The two Perna brothers prospered as stone contractors, and acquired a good bit of property in Tennallytown. Many local houses were built in part or completely by the Pernas.

The Perna brothers were eventually contractors for a great many D.C. bridges, churches, schools, residences, and commercial buildings; three of Louis Perna's local projects were at Georgetown University, St. Alban's Church, and St. Columba's Church. Four red limestone row houses in the 4100 block of Chesapeake Street were built by the Pernas around 1910, and still stand in very good condition. Frank Perna built for his family a 13-room grey-blue stone house on Brandywine Street above River Road.

The Pernas acquired their stone mainly from the Stoneyhurst rock quarries on River Road near Seven Locks Road, toward Potomac. Occasionally stone was used from a quarry east of Connecticut Avenue between Newark and Ordway Streets; from a small quarry on the Piney Branch; or from the Virginia side of the Potomac River, near Chain Bridge. Sandstone was also obtained from Seneca.

Ben Porto, the Pernas' nephew, is a Tennallytown stonemason whose son Joe still runs the Tri-State stone quarry off River Road. The Portos had a large stone house on Chesapeake Street, now torn down. The Segreti brothers and Anthony Pellegrino, a Perna brother-in-law, were also Tennallytown stonemasons; Pellegrino's concrete block house still stands in the 4600 block of 41st Street.

Mary Curry, a graduate student at American University in 1974, wrote a paper on Tennallytown's stonemasons and stone buildings. It was her thesis that stone resources in the area had meaning for settlement of Tennallytown and eventually provided a theme for community identity, in its stone buildings and in its ethnic (Italian) identity.[187]

Other Italian families in Tennallytown were the Errigos and Bredices, who were shoemakers (see Chapter V).

Blacksmiths and Stagecoaches

Horses were the sole means of transportation—besides feet—until the electric streetcar (1890) and then the first automobile (about 1899) arrived in Tennallytown. Owners took care that their horses were healthy and well shod, and the blacksmith was an essential member of the community.

The first blacksmith in Tennallytown might have been John Tennally himself, in the 1790s, or Jacob Colclazer, 20 years later. John O. Harry was the village blacksmith, as well as Tennallytown's first postmaster, probably as early as 1830. A Civil War map shows a "b.s. shop,"

BLACKSMITHS

(1890 photo c/o Morris Fitzgerald, Jr.)

Above: Morris Fitzgerald's shop was located at the intersection of the Pike and Pierce's Mill Road. The blacksmith is on the right and his assistant, Mike Ryan, is on the left. The shop stood where Leeds Liquor is today, in the 4200 block of Wisconsin Avenue.

Below: 1860s map indicates a blacksmith (B.S.) shop at intersection of the Frederick-Washington Pike and Grant Road.

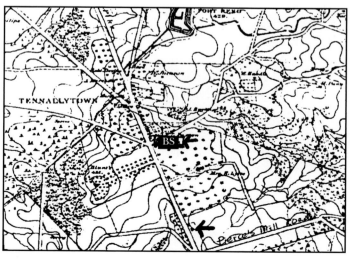

(Environs of Washington, undated; National Archives)

VICTORIAN HOMES WISCONSIN AVENUE

(1910 photo c/o Hattie Burrows Porter)

(1942 photo c/o Ray Johnson)

Top: 4620 Wisconsin, built by John Cannon, occupied by Henry Burrows family when this photo was taken. Note Baptist Church to right. Now a vacant lot.

Bottom: "Victorian House," 4624 Wisconsin, also built by Cannon, still standing; occupied by James Walter Riley family. Note Baptist Church to the left.

probably Robert Morris's, at the intersection of the New Military Road (Grant Road) and the Rockville Road.[188]

John Duvall was a local blacksmith and wheelwright before, during, and after the Civil War. Before his death in 1881, Duvall had shops on either side of the Rockville Road above its intersection with Pierce's Mill Road, south of Tennallytown. His last blacksmith shop was taken over by Samuel Duvall, who later moved up next to the Tennallytown Inn.

Wallace Ricketts was a blacksmith at Fort Reno, and the Morrow brothers had a shop down on Broad Branch Road.

Morris Fitzgerald took over Duvall's shop on the east side of the Tennallytown road in 1890 (see photo) and eventually acquired as a good customer John R. McLean, the wealthy newspaper publisher who had bought the old College Villa. Fitzgerald later moved to the west side of the road when Van Ness Street was to be cut in.

Writer Norman Underwood provides us with his memory of one of the blacksmith establishments on Wisconsin Avenue, which had

"a hitching post on the front and a large entrance door with a space on one side for tying two animals, racks for holding sheet iron, oblong pieces of wrought iron for making the shoes, racks for tools and nails. On the other two sides were two smoked windows, an open stone hearth, with a large bellows pointing into it, a half barrel of water to cool the hot iron, and finally a large anvil mounted on a sawed-off trunk of a tree."[189]

The only postwar public transportation was still the horse-drawn stagecoach, probably run by the local livery stable owners. Tennallytown, like all rural villages, was still quiet. Horsepower had not yet been replaced by motorpower. The roads, rutted by wagon wheels, were infamously muddy in the winter and spring rainy seasons and dusty in the summer dry season. River Road remained a narrow two-lane road with tall trees arching overhead. Cows, pigs, and chickens wandered out into the dirt lanes.

According to Ed Riley, "Uncle Tommy" Paxton of Grant Road used to drive the stage from Tennallytown to Georgetown. Mr. Riley's mother would pay 25¢ each way to go shopping in Georgetown on Saturdays—but the children saved the fare by trotting alongside!

Tom Paxton, who married successively two of Officer Eli Riley's sisters, was always a very popular figure. He died in 1908 at the age of 78. But he is remembered by many as sitting on his sunny front porch on Grant Road all day long, his long white beard lying on his chest as he dozed.

"There is one period in Tennallytown's history which deserves a chapter all to itself; that is the 'stage chapter,' when Tennallytown really got her own stage all by herself, with her own horses, her own driver, and went all the way down High street and carried only Tennallytown passengers. It was another Deadwood, and it did its work nobly until those bucking bronchos, mad Texas steer buzzing boxes of cars took her place, and still are taking it, save when the little Tennallytown kids wave a red flag at 'em to see 'em charge off the track."[190]

The View from the Carriage

Back in 1868, a local writer said that carpenter Joseph W. Harry "has erected about half the buildings in Tennallytown, and their neat

WISCONSIN AVENUE HOUSES

(1919 photo c/o Doris Connor Tansill)

(1942 photo c/o Ray Johnson)

Top: Connor and Webb families pose across the street from Wendel's houses, 4717 Wisconsin (now Amberger and Wohlfarth) and 4713 (now Ellen Kaye Flowers).

Bottom: 4839, 4837, and 4835 Wisconsin Avenue as seen in the 1940s.

TENNALLYTOWN ARCHITECTURE OF THE 1890s

(1974 photographs by John Russo)

Houses on 41st Street between Davenport and Ellicott.

appearance and beauty of design stamps him as a master mechanic."[191] Builders John L. Cannon, beginning in 1892, and Fred Parks and Web Chappell, later, constructed quite a few houses along both sides of the Rockville Road, north of the intersection with River Road.

The land on both sides of the pike was owned by Samuel Queen and his daughters, John H. Wendel and his son and daughter, and Mary Ellen French. David Shoemaker and his heirs retained the land further north to the District line, from the Pike to River Road.

Samuel Queen's family home was on the west side of the pike where Ellicott Street intersects Wisconsin today. After Queen died in 1885, his three surviving daughters built handsome Victorian houses for their families on the west side of Wisconsin Avenue, on either side of the Baptist Church, in the early 1890s. The northernmost one, 4626 Wisconsin Avenue, was built by John Cannon for Louisa Queen Johnson and her husband.

Further downhill in that same block, Samuel O. Wendel built a row of six houses. Two are still standing, and four were torn down where Volvo of Washington is now located, at 4800 Wisconsin. Across the street and further south, Wendel built four or five more houses, which came to be known as "Wendel's Row." These houses in the 4700 block were rented out at the rate of $8 a month in the 1890s, and were very popular and convenient homes.

Before the days of apartments, young couples and growing families rented houses much more frequently. Families moved from house to house, from year to year—most likely in the spring. A house might have had only one owner for years, according to the Recorder of Deeds or tax records; but a long series of families might have occupied the house during those years.

Most of these old houses on Wisconsin Avenue, as well as some houses along River Road, and on 41st Street near Davenport, are still some of the oldest houses in Tennallytown. They bear testimony to their good construction as well as to their good fortune at not having been torn down.

Tennallytown was in no way an exclusive residential community, and so its heterogeneous quality was always part of its character.

The population steadily increased in the Tennallytown area during the 35 years after the Civil War. The 1868 Georgetown writer estimated that "the population of Tennallytown is about 500" and "at present there is some demand for building lots."[192] The 1880 census covered nearly 200 households north of Tunlaw Road and west of Broad Branch Road, about 50 of these black or mulatto. Many were tenants, and so were not listed as property owners on maps.

That the area was becoming very popular was noted in 1885 by a writer in The Star:

"One of the pleasantest drives in this vicinity is out over the road from Georgetown to Tenleytown and by the winding country roads through the beautiful scenery of Rock Creek Valley to Brightwood.... Any pleasant evening, carriage after carriage may be seen rolling along these roads, the occupants enjoying the fresh, cool air and the picturesque views which come in sight at every turn.

"The beauty of the scenery and the healthfulness of the locality are not a recent discovery, as any one can see who glances at the fine old houses

(1973 photo by Judith Helm)

(1973 photo by Judith Helm)

Top: Stone House 4528 Fessenden

Middle Right: Alexander St. John house, 4200 block Wisconsin. During the 1940s it was Mrs. Lois Dickens' millinery shop.

Bottom Left: Carl Johnson in front of his grandfather Samuel Queen's house, west side of Wisconsin at Ellicott.

(1918 photo c/o Mamie R. Davis)

GRANT ROAD HOUSES

(both photos from National Park Service, 1936)

Top: Probably built in the 1880s, these houses stood on the north side of Grant Road, around the corner from Wisconsin Avenue.

Bottom: Tom Paxton gets the credit for having built these three houses on Grant Road, which still stand in the 1980s, a century after they were built. Stonemason W. Thyson Burrows added stone touches to 4426, his house at the left.

which may be seen along the road, surrounded with fine lawns and forest trees. In fact, as soon as Washington was located, these sites were taken up by people, in some cases of wealth, who preferred a residence in the country to one in the city."[193]

A few of these "fine old houses," surrounded by many acres, had been in the area for generations. Murdock's "Friendship," however, was decaying for want of good care. William D. C. Murdock, born in 1806 at "Friendship," had moved closer to Georgetown in 1833, when he married. His mother, Mrs. Mariamne French, had died in 1849. After the Civil War, Murdock lost all of his "Friendship" property as a result of poor business dealings. When he died in 1886 at age 80, the old homestead was occupied by James L. Davis.[194]

Other old homesteads in the area that had been maintained for generations were Loughborough's "Grassland"; the College Villa, rented by a variety of tenants after the Jesuits left; Nourse's "Highlands"; John Adlum's "Vineyard," later replaced by the Bureau of Standards; Dent's "Springland" next to it, inherited by the Sterretts; "Dunblane"; and "The Rest," which Arianna Lyles left to her granddaughters upon her death in 1888.

New houses of grand design were fewer after the Civil War. One exception was the three-story stone house south of River Road, between the Burrows' farmhouse and Fort Bayard. (Its current address is 4528 Fessenden.) One story goes that a General North, who was stationed during the war at Fort Bayard, subsequently bought the land from Samuel F. Burrows and built the house for his family.[195] It was later known as the Seiler or Bonsal house, and American University President and Mrs. Hurst Anderson also lived there at one time.

The newer country houses were frame; some had stone foundations. Most were quite handsome, with two stories, two parlors, sizable front porches and, as Victorian styles came into vogue, turrets and bay windows.

But despite the substantial homes in Tennallytown, it was characterized by many as an unremarkable collection of working-class or rural dwellings. Our 1899 journalist portrayed it accurately:

"Tennallytown is very apt to be dismissed by average Washingtonians with shoulder shrugs or turned up noses as a whitewashed shanty, somewhere above Georgetown, hanging in space, maybe, for all they know or care. And they don't know in the least that, barring Scotch dialect, it is as genuine a little Thrums, as quaint and gossipy a beehive, as ever grew up out of county soil.

"The village itself, from a mere wrist stump jutting out of the dust of a county road, has become a whole hand, which holds in its palm a real town hall, a church, a school house, and 'stores,' and forks out its fingers far down along other roads, which hold more churches still. The thumb has long since run away with itself down Grant road, and taken too many knuckles and twists for proper proportions, and is grabbed on by more than its share of houses . . . .

"Mostly folks just yawn, 'What a good-for-nothing looking place this is; so countrified, don't you know. Queer to run across it just so near the city. What do the people do who live here?' Well, they are the losers, not Tennallytown.

4500 BLOCK OF GRANT ROAD

(1974 photo by John Russo)

(1940s photo c/o Clara Poore Broderick)

Top: These houses (except for the brick one) were built before 1900, when Grant Road was a busy thoroughfare to Chevy Chase.

Bottom: William F. Poore house, built circa 1894 in the 4500 block of Grant Road. Today the address is 3831 Albemarle Street.

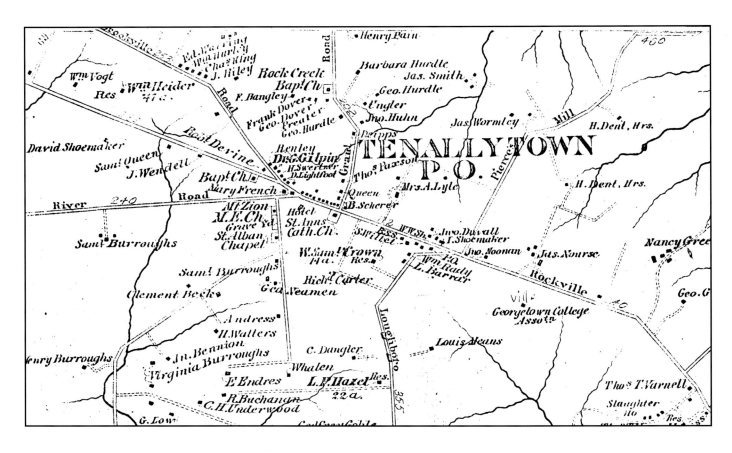

(G.M. Hopkins, 1878, Part of Second District, District of Columbia)

"It is at early dawn of summer that Tennallytown is seen at its best, looking down from the eyrie of 'Gloria Point,' where the old toll-gate stood, for then bunches of trees hide the plain-fashioned, ugly houses and they seem to nestle warm against each other like a quiet, white, cozy corner in a vast stretch of green with the roofs of cities and the pale blue circle of mountains seeming far beyond."[196]

As George Simmons had written in his "Roadside Sketches" in 1891, "For far-reaching views and natural beauty, the region of country penetrated by Wisconsin Avenue can hardly be excelled anywhere."[197]

The post-war arrivals were not as prosperous as the first settlers had been 100 years earlier. Most Tennallytowners were lower middle class or working class people; some would have been classified as poor, and very few would have been called well off.

Farmers, blacksmiths and wheelwrights, carpenters, painters and construction laborers, skilled tradesmen, merchants, policemen, streetcar motormen, and meat, poultry, and grocery men more and more made up the male population of Tennallytown. Even after the arrival of the streetcar, very few men, in the latter days of the 19th century, were employed by the government or, for that matter, worked in Washington or Georgetown.

Married women worked full-time caring for their own families, and some took in additional sewing or washing or worked for the few wealthy families. Unmarried women and widows who could not find work in the village were more likely to work in the city.

By the 1880s a few stores were supplying the people directly in Tennallytown. James and Susan Willett, whose family also ran an old tavern on River Road, opened a grocery store and lived above it, north of the Lightfoot family house. Charles B. Pierce and his brother ran a general store and stable next to the Inn; Jack Lenhart eventually took over Pierce's store, which had a front porch and hitching rail.

Jack Lenhart and Isaac Shoemaker (the elder) were later dealers "in fine groceries and feed" on the east side of the Tennallytown-Rockville Road. Frank Burrows took over their frame building and the business, then rebuilt a red brick building in 1900. George W. Burdette ran a general grocery and feed store across from the Inn.

One of the new frame stores was that of John J. O'Day and his wife, Rebecca, at the northeast corner of Grant Road and what came to be called Wisconsin—the oldest Tennallytown store that is still standing. Mr. O'Day also served as postmaster at that site.

As Lerone Walther recalled, "When we were youngsters, Tenleytown was considered from O'Days' to Lightfoots'. There were just two grocery stores, a post office, and a real estate office."

*   *   *   *

The 1888 Dickson's Directory gives us an idea of some of the Tennallytown blacks' occupations.[198] It lists Thornton Lewis as being a grocer at "Reno City." Black laborers at Fort Reno are named in that directory, as well as a plasterer, a blacksmith, and a teamster. A few black farmers were listed in the Fort area in the

OLDEST HOUSES IN AMERICAN UNIVERSITY PARK

(1974 photo by John Russo)

(1981 photo by Judith Helm)

Top: Norman Underwood's summer home, built in or before 1870. It still stands at 4308 - 46th Street. The side that faces 46th Street used to be the back porch of the house.

Bottom: Engelbert Enders' farmhouse, now 4330 Yuma Street.

1891 SKETCH BY GEORGE SIMMONS

TENLEYTOWN STREET.

(George Simmons' "Roadside Sketches," The Evening Star, August 1891)

Wisconsin Avenue looking south from the point at River Road. The Tennallytown Hotel is off to the right, but one store, blacksmith shop, and the Tenley School are visible on the right, and a row of houses and stores, on the left.

1880 census, and three young Johnson boys were "cowherds"— probably for dairyman Fritz Bangerter.

Resin and Janie (Ginny) Addison lived not on Fort Reno, but on Murdock land, off Murdock Mill Road, near where Yuma Street was cut through. Resin Addison, who was born in Maryland in 1830,[199] may have been a Murdock slave. He worked his own land and that of his neighbors.

Ginny Addison, who outlived her husband by about 30 years, worked as a domestic for neighboring women and had her own milk cows. When she was young she would gather blackberries and "poke salad" (pokeweed) and sell them at the market at 21st and K Streets in the city. "Aunt Ginny," as everyone called her, was 90 years old and blind when she died about 1925. Her old brown

house had burned once in the 1890s and was rebuilt; it finally burned down many years later, before the land was cleared for new American University Park development houses.

There were other black families (Coats, Parks, and Smith) who lived near Murdock Mill Road. Until the 1920s there were blacks living just north of the newly-cut Massachusetts Avenue.

Many of the black women "did day work" for people in Friendship Heights, Bethesda, Chevy Chase, and Cleveland Park, as well as in Tennallytown. Some worked as domestics in downtown hotels; a few took in laundry in their homes.

At one time or another most of the black men did construction work for the District government or for local builders. Some acquired teams of horses that they hired out for construction or road work.

Black laborers were used in road construction, which before the days of heavy machinery meant working with horses in digging, tarring, and sanding new roads and widening the old ones. The growing suburban area of Tennallytown provided many opportunities for such labor before and after 1900.

Some black men worked as gardeners for individual families, at the local country clubs, or on the McLean estate. Local businesses and schools employed many black men, some of whom worked for the same businesses, families, or institutions for 50 years. A few became guards or chauffeurs.

The early blacks at Fort Reno were not "white collar" workers. But as the younger generations were educated—first at Reno School, then at downtown high schools, such as Armstrong, and some at Howard University or Miner Teachers College—many became teachers and government employees.

One of the wealthiest and best-known black families in Washington[200]—but ironically not personally known by most Tennallytown blacks—was that of James Wormley, who owned country houses on Pierce Mill Road during the 1870s and 1880s. The Wormley grandchildren attended schools in Washington.

James Wormley was born free in Washington and worked for years as a steward at a white men's club. After the Civil War he opened the well-known Wormley House hotel at the southwest corner of 15th and H, which catered to both blacks and whites, but was mostly patronized by the wealthiest and most influential people—Senators, Congressmen, and businessmen.

James and his son William bought land along the northeast line of Pierce Mill road, northwest of where Van Ness Street now crosses Reno Road and enters the old

THE MURDOCK MILL

(George Simmons' "Roadside Sketches," The Evening Star, August 1891)

The Murdock Mill, located on Dogwood Brook, northeast of the Dalecarlia Reservoir. Murdock Mill Road led from Tennallytown to the mill.

Bureau of Standards property. There were three good-sized houses on the Wormley tracts, and one of them was said to be used as a country house frequented by Washington celebrities, and especially by owners of race horses.[201] (See photo of Wormley-Lancaster house, page 144.)

The 1880 Census indicates that William Wormley, age 38 (and labeled mulatto by the census-taker), his wife and their eight children lived with two servants on the Pierce Mill Road property. A brother, Garret Wormley, a "confectioner," also lived there with his wife, six children, and two servants.

In 1886 William Wormley advertised in The Star:

"Country real estate: FOR SALE—I have one or two of the prettiest and most complete

83

country homes in the District, just in the rear of the President's home [Cleveland Park] on the Pierce Mill road. Will sell one or both; large houses on both places, 10 and 11 rooms each, with pantry, bath-rooms, latrobes, hot and cold water supply; fruits of all kind, and good stables . . . ."[202]

The Murdock Mill

Many local farmers took their grain to be milled at the Murdock Mill (often misspelled Murdoch), the closest mill west of Tennallytown. It was located on the stream that still empties into the Potomac at Little Falls, above Loughborough Road.

Norman Underwood described the Murdock Mill as he remembered it in the 1880s: One reached it by walking or driving a cart down Murdock Mill Road (now visible also as parts of Butterworth Place) past the Methodist graveyard, the wooden Episcopal church, an apple orchard, and the lane to Enders' dairy farm. After paralleling and crossing Murdock Creek, named Dogwood Brook by some, the road led to the mill with its wooden water wheel on the creek. Wheat, and sometimes oats, were taken to be ground there. Norman Underwood remembered the miller always being covered with flour.[203]

The Murdock Mill did not operate after the dam was washed out by the flood of 1889. It had always had strong competition from the Pierce Mill and other mills on Rock Creek and in Montgomery County. But the miller, an elderly Englishman named Charles Poole, continued to live for a few more years at the Murdock Mill.[204] The mill was, on one map, labeled the Barton Grist Mill; but the name Murdock Mill was always used by the people in the area. The mill itself was northeast of what is now Dalecarlia Reservoir (see also photo, p. 133).

Riley Slaughterhouse

Andrew J. Riley and his wife Sarah lived near the Heiders, on Brookeville (Belt) Road. Their sons, Andrew Jr. and Joseph, and later, Walter, Frank, and Sam, went into the meat business, buying a slaughterhouse built by the Kenglas. It was located east of the Brookeville Road and south of today's Chesapeake Street, near where the radio antenna towers are now.

James (Bud) Riley recalled that when he was about 13 (1908) he was hired by his uncles who ran the slaughterhouse. Bud's job was to intercept farmers who were driving their animals down the pike toward the Georgetown "abattoirs," and to offer to buy their calves, lambs, etc., from them. Cattle owners would bypass the Riley establishment only in hopes of getting better prices from the Georgetown slaughterhouses.

Riley's slaughterhouse was approached by a long dirt lane that led up to the unpainted frame building, which was built upon a concrete slab. A windmill pumped water into the slaughterhouse. Animal pens were behind the building to the south and east, where Broadcast House and Wilson High School stand today. Cattle, older and younger calves, and lambs were separated in the pens; Lindner's pasture next door was also used when necessary. Some killing and butchering was done outside in the early days: Bud Riley remembered a "blood pit" where the high school is now.

Inside was a large open space, a cold building with a cement floor. A big round hole in the floor was under a ring of sharp iron hooks that hung down from the high ceiling. Sides of beef and lamb hung on these hooks, and were lowered by wheels to a cold storage compartment below. The butchered meat ("home dressed") was carried at three or four in the morning to the old Center Market in Washington. Sometimes two loads a day would be trucked in.

By 1922 Frank Riley had closed down the old slaughterhouse on Chesapeake Street, and, for about five years, he ran a much smaller operation out of what had been a small stable behind the Riley family's home at 4807 41st Street. As recently as 1974 the garage-type building, now painted white, had "T.T. [TenleyTown] Garage" painted on it. It still stands on Belt Road.

Other local farmers butchered meat in small or large quantities from time to time; but the Riley slaughterhouse was the only such operation in Tennallytown.

In 1880 there were nearly 20 men in Tenleytown who called themselves butchers—working either at the Riley slaughterhouse, the Kengla or Hoemiller slaughterhouses closer to Georgetown, or in the Georgetown or Washington city markets.

Postmasters

Tennallytown remained a stopping place on the Washington-to-Rockville post route at least through 1885. It was for a long time the first post office north of Georgetown, and the next (1871) was at Darcy's Store, called Bethesda. In 1883 a post office was opened at "St. Alban's."

The first Tennallytown postmaster, in 1846, had been John O. Harry, who ran a blacksmith shop just south of where Tennally's tavern had been located. Harry's smithy became the gathering place for those awaiting the mail delivery from Washington or from Frederick. Harry retained his appointment as postmaster for 18 years, through the busy years of the Civil War and the occupation by

Union troops. When he died in 1864, his son William O. (Billy) Harry served as postmaster of Tennallytown. After that the position of postmaster changed hands frequently, as can be seen by the list of appointments."[205]

Wm. Travis Beach	19 November 1869
Thomas F. Ward	1 June 1870
W. Harry	2 May 1871
John H. Wendell	5 May 1871
Isaiah Shoemaker	20 February 1873
Perry Sherwood	2 January 1878
Charles H. Duvall	26 August 1878
Emma A. Duvall	7 March 1881
John L. Brunett	20 May 1882
Emma A. Duvall	31 May 1882
Wm. M. Buckman	21 December 1883
John J. O'Day	17 July 1886

Isaiah Shoemaker, Charles Duvall, and John O'Day were grocers as well as postmasters. Emma Duvall, the only postmistress, probably received her appointment after the death of her husband.

Records are sparse after 1894, but John O'Day and his wife most likely maintained the post office until about 1901, when Mr. and Mrs. Andrew Burga took over the duties.

The Tollgate and Gloria Point

The tollgate that was opened at Tennallytown on the turnpike in 1829 was in or adjacent to John Tennally's old tavern, on the west side of the newly-cut section of the pike.

An 1870 deed by which Isaac Marshall contributed land for a Baptist church says that the church site was "190 yards north of the present tollgate at Tennallytown on the turnpike road." The 110-year-old church building that still stands at 4620 Wisconsin Avenue is exactly 190 yards north of the northern point of the corner of Wisconsin Avenue and River Road.

TWO VIEWS OF THE HOUSE AT GLORIA POINT

(Photo c/o Myra Burrows Entwisle)

(Photo c/o Allan Robey)

The tollgate itself was a piece of timber that stretched across the Rockville Turnpike, just north of the River Road intersection. The gate was swung to the side by the toll-keeper when he was satisfied that the toll had been paid.

The Tennallytown tollgate keeper often served as postmaster. In 1868 William Harry's post office was located "in the fork of the Rockville and River Roads."[206]

Top: Shoveling snow off streetcar tracks on Wisconsin Avenue. Top left in background is Mrs. Alice Hunt's house, Gloria Point, at the River Road turnoff. At the right in this photo are houses and the Police Substation-Tenleytown, which was built 1904.

Bottom: The large house at Gloria Point, taken from in front of Eldbrooke Methodist Church. The Tenley Sunoco gas station is located on the site today.

In 1869 William Travis Beach was postmaster, and it is said that he also served for a time as tollgate keeper. Irishman Robert M. Devine was keeper of the tollgate in the 1870s. He lived across the pike, at the beginning of the Brookeville Road.

In 1873 Isaac Marshall died, and his 30 acres on both sides of the new pike—parts of "Friendship" and "Mt. Airy"—were inherited by his wife's nieces, the French sisters. Adelle and Mary Ellen French were unmarried; their sister Rebecca had married John Henry Harry. And so these parcels of land came to be owned by the Frenches and the Harrys.

An 1878 Hopkins map shows a good-sized house at the point of land between River Road and the pike. The house is literally out in the intersection, and another large house is behind it, owned by Mary French. Carpenter's 1881 map calls a building at the point "toll gate" and the house and land behind it that of M. and A. French.[207]

The tolls were collected for the Rockville turnpike at least until 1887. By 1893 the tollhouse was torn down, when the District of Columbia began taking responsibility for this county road. The tollgate frame itself was not removed until about 1900.

The large white frame house, close to the point, faced south; this had been the home of Isaac Marshall, and later of Mary Ellen French. The Charles Volkman family rented the house in 1885.[208]

In 1892, Mary Ellen French sold nearly eight and a half acres of her "Friendship" and "Mt. Airy" property to the pastor of St. Ann's parish, Father John M. Barry. Two 1892 building permits for houses on the "Tenaylatown Road" are in "Berry's Subdivision, near old toll gate."

Father Barry sold the large house on the point in September 1893 to Governor and Mrs. Alexander C. Hunt. Governor Hunt had been appointed territorial governor of Colorado in 1867, for a one-year term, after an unsuccessful try for the House of Representatives. Alice Underwood Hunt was his second wife.

Governor Hunt had led a long and varied life as a wealthy speculator, judge, Indian fighter, and a founder of Denver. He was appointed territorial governor of Colorado by President Jackson (1867) but was not reconfirmed the following year, for he had been accused of dishonest dealings. A railroad builder in Colorado and Texas, Hunt also had a hand in founding Salida, Hoosier Pass, and Colorado Springs. He had three children by his first wife, who died in 1881. In 1891, Hunt suffered a paralytic stroke, the same year he married Alice Underwood and Gloria was born.[209]

An extensive Victorian-style renovation was performed on the old house at that high point—a 400-ft. elevation—where River Road meets the Rockville Pike. The River Road was being widened, which placed the house closer to the street. The renovated house and the prominent site on which it stood were renamed Gloria Point for Mrs. Hunt's mother and her daughter, Gloria John Hunt. Some oldtimers remember a sign in the front garden that read "Gloria Point."

The Governor did not live long at Gloria Point; he died May 14, 1894, not long after they had moved in. It was at this house that "Jack the Slasher" was apprehended in March 1894, as will be described later in this chapter.

The big house at Gloria Point, painted a dark red, came to be used as a rooming house. In the summer, people would escape the heat of the city by spending a few days at a country house in an elevated location such as Tennallytown. Mrs. Hunt also rented out rooms to many who were employed locally. Although the Governor was at one time a very wealthy man, Mrs. Hunt's considerable ingenuity was necessary for her to maintain Gloria and herself in comfort.

Tennallytown Inn

The three-story Tennallytown Inn had been rebuilt in the late 1850s on the west side of the pike just south of the River Road turnoff.[210] It served as an overnight stopping place for horse and coach travelers, especially farmers and merchants going to or coming from Georgetown and Washington. Meals were served in the ground-floor public room, which doubled as a saloon. Farmers could put up their horses overnight in livery stables just north of the Inn.

The tavern property had been sold by Godfrey Conrad's heirs in 1865 to Joseph N. Fearson, a Georgetown banker and real estate operator. Fearson died in 1867, and the Tennallytown Inn and 10 acres were inherited by Mary Julia Barrett, probably Fearson's daughter. Bernard Scherer was for 20 years the restaurant and hotel keeper at the Inn, although it was owned by Fearson and Barrett.

John H. Harry, the blacksmith who lived in the Harry homestead across the street, was employed as a bartender at the inn for a short time. John Bernard Harry, his son, later liked to recall the story of the man in Georgetown who asked the way to Tennallytown. He was told to "keep going" out the Rockville Road "until you hear a lady on a second floor porch hollerin' for Willie!"—then the stranger would know he was in Tennallytown![211] According to this story, Mrs. Mary Scherer, wife of the proprietor, was always looking for her son, Willie.

The hotel property was acquired by Charles B. and Calista Pierce, who in turn sold it to Christian B. Heurich, wealthy Washington brewer, in 1889 (with 9.41 acres surrounding).

The adjacent building that housed Lenhart's store and the first Masonic Hall, on the west side of the pike, was bought by Heurich, too. He also eventually acquired the old Loughborough-Whitney estate, "Grassland," and properties along the pike (Wisconsin Avenue) north of the McLean estate. Christian Heurich continued to purchase Tennallytown properties over the years. He died in 1945 at the age of 102.

After Bernard Scherer left, Ernst Loeffler was hired by Heurich in 1894 to run the restaurant and barroom. In his application for a barroom license, Heurich wrote that [the petitioner has] "spent hundreds of dollars in improving it and has been very careful in letting it to a responsible man [Loeffler], who will perform his contract with him and carry on the business that it may be a credit to the neighborhood, thereby enhancing the value of the property."[212] The value of the Tennallytown Inn to the neighborhood was often hotly debated, for drunkenness was a problem for many Tennallytown men, of high and low station.

Church Building

The little Tennallytown Methodist Episcopal Church (Mt. Zion, it was called then) had been totally destroyed by the occupying Union army, and was rebuilt in 1863 on the same site—River Road at Murdock Mill Road. The congregation renamed itself Eldbrooke Methodist Church in 1899, after Aquila Eld and Philip L. Brooke. A large, new frame building was also built.

CHRISTIAN HEURICH'S INN

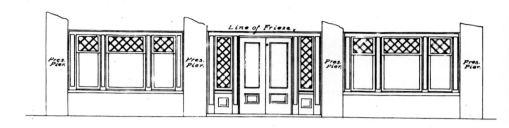

~ELEVATION~

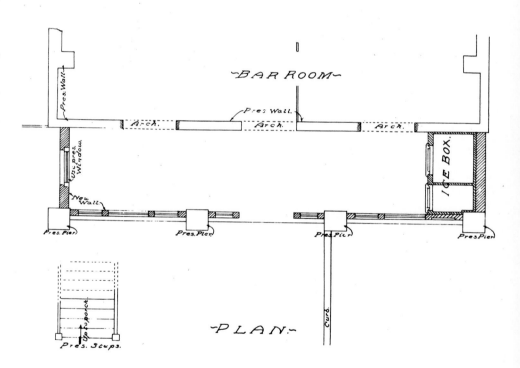

~PLANS·FOR·REMODELLING~
~TENALLYTOWN·INN·FOR~
~MR. CHR. HEURICH~

(National Archives, RG 351, D.C. Building Permits, 1877-1949; permit 1412—April 1, 1904)

87

THE TENNALLYTOWN METHODIST CHURCH

(Postcard photos c/o Ellen Wright)

Exterior and interior views of Mt. Zion Methodist Episcopal Church, located at the intersection of River Road and Murdock Mill Road. This was the church that was rebuilt in 1863, after the first church had been destroyed by occupying Union troops.

The growing population brought on a surge of church development and construction. Some churches were organized by the expressed desire of the would-be parishioners. Others, however, were established by the church bodies as missions to an area that apparently needed a Christian influence. As Dr. Samuel Busey wrote,

"It is true that east of the now [1895] prosperous village of Tenleytown there was a region of country bordering on Rock Creek [Broad Branch Road] known as 'Louse Neck,' inhabited by a thriftless and besotted class, who trudged on foot to town every Saturday and back again, with jug in hand, 'to raise Cain' in drunken saturnalia of crime; but it was too far distant to disturb the peace and tranquillity of the neighborhood of Christian friends.

"After the establishment of the parish of St. Ann, named after the hostess of Rosedale, and through the good offices of the Jesuit father, that region of ignorance, laziness, and debauchery submitted to the influence of Christian civilization."[213]

The St. Ann's Roman Catholic parish was organized in 1866, and the first wooden chapel was erected a year later, on the west side of the pike, just north of the Grant Road intersection. The part of Murdock Mill Road that had once run through this property and connected with Grant Road was by then obliterated. Mrs. Mary Julia Barrett, owner of the Tennallytown Inn, made available a lot at the southeast corner of her 10-acre tract, opposite Grant Road, for construction of this first Catholic chapel in Tennallytown.[214] [This gift had an ironic twist many years later, when the District government ruled that a saloon had to be a certain distance away from schools and churches, thus forcing the Tennallytown Inn to lose its liquor license.]

"That little Jesuit chapel! How that is heart and sinew of Tennallytown! It was built years ago and was always washed out looking on the outside, a tiny frame all steeple with a big black cedar at the front. But inside it was warm colored and bright, with confessionals red-curtained off the communion rail and a deep blue background throwing the tiny altar in relief and spangled with stars. The body of the little church still remains, but it has a rear addition and its long steeple snapped off in the last big storm we had which also took the cedar . . . .

"There's many a story belonging here. There was a father here once, not very long ago, whose face beamed such peace and good will that he found his way into every heart, so that the gentleness and the charity of good Father Barry is yet spoken of as yesterday and he is brought very near the great Bishop of Les Miserables."[215]

St. Ann's first school was started in 1870, but not until 1890, under Father John M. Barry, was there a separate two-story school building, south of the first church. The old school had a girls' entrance on the south side and a boys' entrance on the north side. Attendance at St. Ann's school declined, however, as the Tenley School grew in reputation. In 1896 the parochial school was temporarily discontinued.[216] A three-story stone and brick rectory was also constructed in 1892.

ST. ANN'S ROMAN CATHOLIC CHURCH, TENNALLYTOWN

(Photo c/o estate of Marjorie Scholl)

(Photo c/o Clara Poore Broderick)

Top: St. Ann's first chapel was erected in 1867 on the west side of Wisconsin Avenue (then the Rockville Pike) at Grant Road. By the time this photo was taken, it had been converted into an annex for the Tenley School, the brick building seen to the right. A straw-hatted gentleman, four ladies, and a nun are waiting for the morning streetcar.

Bottom: Miss Maggie Callahan (rear left) and Mrs. Stadtler (rear right) with students at St. Ann's School, circa 1890. Note pinafores on young girls, short pants on young boys.

TWO BAPTIST CHURCHES IN TENNALLYTOWN

(1942 photos by Ray Johnson)

*Top: Rock Creek Baptist Church
(colored) at Fort Reno, on the
corner of Nebraska Avenue and
Chesapeake Street. Organized
1872; razed 1950s.*

*Bottom: Mount Tabor Baptist
Church (white), later named the
Wisconsin Avenue Baptist
Church; organized in 1880. This
building still stands at 4620
Wisconsin Avenue.*

The Rock Creek Baptist Church for "colored people" was organized at Fort Reno in 1872;[217] the congregation first met in the Grant Road School, then built a church at the corner of Chesapeake and Howard (now Chesapeake and Nebraska). This was the first black congregation in Tennallytown.

The second church for blacks was the Mount Asbury Methodist Episcopal Church, established by 1888 on Belt Road near Fessenden. Its name was later changed to St. Mark's.[218] The hurricane of 1896 tore the roof off St. Mark's, and permission was granted by the District to rebuild the little church at Fort Reno. Four years later it was completed.

The Episcopal parish of St. Alban's on the Tennallytown Road above Georgetown had been in existence since 1855. After the war,

> "the most populous section of the parish was in and near Tennallytown; and at that time there were certain elements in the Tennallytown settlement that presented a challenging need for missionary work . . . . Consequently in 1874 the church made its first effort to establish a mission."[219]

The Episcopal mission in Tennallytown (later called St. Columba's) consisted of a small frame chapel built in 1875, just beyond the Methodist cemetery. The chapel was built next to a large oak tree on Murdock Mill Road, which still stands in front of the present church at 42nd and Albemarle Streets.

An "Episcopal mission for colored persons," called St. George's, was later established at Fort Reno in 1899 as an outgrowth of the Tennallytown Episcopal Church.

The Mount Tabor Baptist Church (white) was organized in

1880. Also later known as the Tennallytown Baptist Church and the Wisconsin Avenue Baptist Church, the congregation worshipped in a frame structure on the west side of the pike; the building is still standing at 4620 Wisconsin Avenue. Mount Tabor began with 19 members, and a year later the membership was 37. Not until the arrival of Pastor George W. McCullough in the 1890s, however, did the struggling congregation count as many as 60 persons in its membership.

This made three black churches and four white churches in Tennallytown before the turn of the century.

(Natl. Archives photo, NCPC records)

TWO CHURCHES AT FORT RENO

(Photo from St. Alban's Chronicle, 1902)

Above: St. George's Episcopal Mission (colored) at Fort Reno was first in this row house (center); later a frame chapel was built.

Left: Mt. Asbury Methodist Episcopal Church (colored) on Belt Road. Later called St. Mark's AME Church.

(Photo from St. Alban's Chronicle, Vol. IV, No. 7, 1909)

Above: St. Columba's first church, built 1875 on Murdock Mill Road (now 42nd and Albemarle Streets). It was first called St. Alban's Chapel, for it was a mission of St. Alban's Episcopal Church, and the St. Alban's burying ground was to the right. This cemetery was later merged with the Methodist Cemetery beyond.

Right: Coast and Geodetic Survey map.

Engraved by Evans and Bartle, 1893.

Schools

In 1864 Congress provided Washington County children with one- or two-room frame school buildings; two of these were on Grant Road.[220] The white children's school, built near today's Reno Road and Ellicott Street, near the present Murch School, was on the north side of Grant Road, high up on a hill. That school was under the supervision of John E. Chappell and Miss Carrie Ferris.

As of 1874, there was one school on Ridge Road (Foxhall Road) to accommodate all the black children who lived in Washington County's 1st District, north and west of Georgetown and west of the Rockville turnpike.

There was also, at that time, a school down on Grant Road, near Broad Branch, taught by a Mr. Shippen and French C. Lugenbeel, a white man and member of Tennallytown Methodist, who was appointed in 1871; this school accommodated all the black children who lived in the 2nd District, east of the Rockville turnpike, all the way to the 7th Street Road (Georgia Avenue). Many children from the Broad Branch Road settlement, as well as from Reno, attended that school.

The red brick Tenley Elementary School was built in 1882 and doubled in size in 1896, when the front addition was put on. It was located on the west side of Wisconsin Avenue (Rockville Pike) where St. Ann's school addition now stands. When painted white, it was used as a school building by St. Ann's. The school was torn down about 1970.

THE TENLEY SCHOOL OVER THE YEARS

(1920s photo from estate of Marjorie Scholl)

1942 photo by Ray Johnson

1966 photo by Carol Sanbower

(photo c/o Mr. and Mrs. Wiley Buchanan, from John M. Lynham)

The Dumblane Oak tree was the site of this gathering of the Chevy Chase Hunt, formerly the Dumblane Hunt. Clarence Moore, Master of Fox Hounds, is in the foreground, and Gist Blair (of Blair House) is on the right. Date of photo is about 1900.

A small school is shown on 1887 and 1894 maps, on a half-acre lot where Grant/Old Military Road (now Davenport) crosses Linnean, a little west of Broad Branch Road. The black children first went to school in this building near Broad Branch, then moved up to the Grant Road School when it was vacated in 1882.[221]

The black students continued to attend the frame school on Grant Road until 1903, when the Jesse Lee Reno School was built on Howard Road.

The white children attended the public school on Grant Road from 1864 until 1882. In that year the new red brick Tenley School was built on the Pike to accommodate the growing number of children in the area. The white student population grew so fast that the size of the school was doubled by an addition in 1896. In 1890, when new schoolmaster

William B. Ireland arrived, the enrollment was 88; by 1903, there were 350 children in grades one through eight.[222]

The Dumblane Hunt

The rolling terrain of rural Tennallytown was especially appealing to those horsemen and horsewomen who enjoyed "the chase." Fox hunting had been organized in the District in the 1830s but had lapsed during the Civil War.

In 1885, a sportsman named Samuel S. Howland imported what was probably the first pack of English hounds to this vicinity. Howland, brother-in-law of wealthy horseman August Belmont, organized with these hunting dogs the Dumblane Hunt in Tennallytown.[223] The club was located at "Dumblane," formerly the stately country home of John Mason, Jr., Thomas Marshall, Harry Woodward Blunt, and others.

The fashionable Dumblane Hunt "cut a wide swath in the social and sporting life of the period, many of the hunts ending at "Grassland,'"[224] Nathan Loughborough's brick house nearby. "Grassland," the 76-acre estate on Loughborough Road, had been occupied by Louis D. Means after the Civil War, and in 1885 by the newly-appointed Secretary of the Navy William C. Whitney. Whitney and his wife were subscribers to the Dumblane Hunt.

After William Whitney moved his family to New York City in 1891, he amassed a $40 million fortune in rails and oil. Although his wife died after a hunting accident, his sons and especially his grandsons, cousins John Hay Whitney and Cornelius Vanderbilt Whitney, carried on the sporting tradition of owning stables and champion horses—in a manner much more lavish than had been their fathers' country life when they were boys at "Grassland."[225]

Acting as kennelman and whip to the English hounds was Bob Curran, oldest of 11 children born to Mary Devine and Joseph Curran of Tennallytown. After the Dumblane Hunt moved in about 1897 from Tennallytown to Chevy Chase, Bob Curran was huntsman there for years, eventually becoming the official Master of Fox Hounds at the Chevy Chase Club—one of the best known social clubs in America.

Old Mike Callahan recalled the old days:

"Shure, I remember the Dumblane and the Chevy Chase Hunts. The Chevy Chase often galloped over my farm and the adjoining lands of the Cummings family, and to the north of us in the country beyond Clean Drinking Manor on Jones Mill Road. Aye, and there was Clarence Moore always with a bill for a lad

opening a gate, and the gentlemen in their silk hats and red coats, and the ladies, God bless 'em, with their little huntin' derbies and veils and riding habits, and Bob Curran racing along, whoopin' and a cappin' his hounds for'ard. Ah! it was wild, rare music to make your blood tingle."[226]

Mary Chappell Robey remembered seeing people "riding to hounds" in the fields between Murdock Mill Road and River Road. Mrs. Robey's parents (Addison Elsworth Chappell and Lydia Lee Sherwood) had held their wedding reception at the Dumblane Club in 1889. "Dumblane" was sold to Anastasia Patten[227] and was rented to a variety of persons before it became a school in the 20th century.

Not far from the clubhouse stood the Dumblane Oak, estimated at the time to be between 250 and 400 years old. The old oak tree still stands next to Wiley Buchanan's home on Nebraska Avenue, appropriately named "UnderOak" by builder Scott Welker.

After the Dumblane Hunt moved to Chevy Chase, the Loughborough estate, "Grassland," was called The Country Club, with a polo field and a golf course. It was purchased by Christian Heurich, who continued to run it as The Country Club after the turn of the century.

Cleveland Park Development

The 1880s brought a surge in the development of the suburban land north of Georgetown and west of Rock Creek. In addition to those who lived there year-round, many Washington families built summer homes on their "country" property.

President Grover Cleveland, shortly before his marriage to

Frances Folsom, bought in 1886 a 15-room stone house off the Tennallytown Road and a little north of Woodley Road. (The house is no longer standing; it occupied a site at what is now 36th and Newark Streets.) As soon as the President of the United States bought his summer home there, the neighborhood increased in status and value. And it eventually came to be known as Cleveland Park.

The Star reported,

"It is in this paradise of suburban homes that the President . . . has selected his country residence, and the people who drive out along Tennellytown Road may see the two-story stone house with its old-fashioned hip roof, nestled among the old forest trees where the Woodley Lane intersects with Tennellytown Road."[228]

As wealthy Washingtonians during Cleveland's first administration (1885-1889) traveled more frequently on the Tennallytown Road—to the suburban home of Secretary Whitney at "Grassland," to the Dumblane Hunt club which adjoined it at Tennallytown, or just to go for a drive in the country—they became more aware of the attractiveness of the area and the desirability of owning a home there, in summer or year-round.

Woodley Road and Highland Avenue became alternate but bumpy routes to take between the Tennallytown Road and the city. Those who wished to take a less hazardous route went down the Pike from Tennallytown and through Georgetown. The extension of Massachusetts Avenue west from Boundary (Florida) Avenue to the Tennallytown Road was completed about 1890.

(Photo c/o Gladys Smith Clemons)

The "Tennallytown" trolley, Car Number 1, as seen in the 1890s on Wisconsin Avenue in Tennallytown, heading back down to Georgetown. Hiliary Smith is the conductor on the back; the motorman up front is unidentified.

The Tennallytown Streetcars

The real estate boom of the 1880s began before the extension of the streetcar line from Georgetown through Tennallytown and Bethesda all the way to Rockville, and before the construction of Connecticut Avenue and its streetcar line all the way through the new suburb of Chevy Chase. But the new transportation greatly enhanced the desirability and value of all properties served by it.

Horse-drawn omnibuses had been introduced in Washington in 1860, and horse-drawn cars on tracks came in 1862, to aid the efficiency of transportation in the capital during the Civil War. The lines extended from the Navy Yard to Georgetown.

Although LeRoy O. King, Jr., makes no mention of it in his streetcar history, it is affirmed by many that a horse-car line was first extended to Tennallytown in about 1888, and that the horses were changed at the livery stable at the top of the hill in Tennallytown.

The first electric streetcars had arrived in D.C. in 1888. But it was not until April 1890 that the Georgetown and Tennallytown Railway Co. completed the new electric line from 32nd and M, Georgetown, up High Street, as Wisconsin Avenue in Georgetown was called, through the village of Tennallytown and on to the District line.[229]

William Henry Voigt, of Wisconsin Avenue, encouraged General Richard C. Drum to extend his Georgetown and Tennallytown line through Friendship Heights, the area developed at the District-Maryland line.

An extension to Alta Vista—by way of the Old Georgetown Road—was authorized in 1890; the trolleys made four round trips a day, from the carbarn above Georgetown to Alta Vista and back. [Another route, from Willard Avenue and Wisconsin to Glen Echo and Cabin John, began operation in 1891.] Eventually the streetcar line was extended to Rockville.

Construction of the streetcar line in Tennallytown required the leveling off of the highest point on Tennallytown Road, where the tollgate had been, just north of River Road. Going downhill from the point used to be much steeper in both directions, and the crest was higher than the present 400' altitude.

The first carbarn and powerhouse for the Tennallytown line was located on the east side of High Street above Georgetown, just above the Industrial Home School. It was opposite the point where Tunlaw Road (now Calvert Street) met the Tennallytown Road. And it was near this point where High Street became Tennallytown Road, later Wisconsin Avenue.

The tracks were originally built on the east side of the pike—not in the center—from Georgetown to Tennallytown. Then at the top of the hill, at the River Road intersection, the tracks curved over to the west side of the road, continuing downgrade and across a stone bridge over the creek at Fessenden, then gradually upgrade to Friendship Heights. North of the District line, the tracks were again on the east side of the road to Alta Vista. By 1900 the line was continued cross-country to Rockville.

A board sidewalk was built on the east side of the street in Tennallytown. The sidewalk was so close to the streetcar tracks, however,

(Photo c/o Gladys Smith Clemons)

(1909 photo c/o LeRoy O. King)

Top: Conductors and motormen of the Tennallytown streetcar line. Note also presence of police officer, local businessman, and one kitten.

Bottom: Tennallytown car barn on lower Wisconsin Avenue, east side, near where Calvert Street was later cut in.

that as Lerone Walther insisted, you "had to turn sideways when the trolley went by." When it was heading south on a parallel track, the trolley was not quite so close to the sidewalk.

Many Tennallytowners worked as motormen or conductors on the local streetcar lines for years, among them George W. Burdette, Harry and Charlie Dean, Ollie Weaver, Hiliary Smith, George Stadtler, Nick Stephens, Will Christian, and Henry and William Voigt.

The residents of Tennallytown were deservedly proud of their new white and blue electric cars, and the novelty of riding them never really wore off. Children were fascinated with the interiors and idolized the uniformed motormen. The young women were especially interested in the young motormen, who were certainly more knowledgeable about Georgetown and the rest of the outside world than the "local boys."

And the Tennallytown men admired the new cars for their efficiency—but delighted in retelling the stories of derailments. Some insisted that derailed cars had traveled all the way to the Potomac, and missed by inches crashing into the water.[230]

More important than the excitement of the new railway line was its lasting impact on Tennallytown. For the first time its residents could go to Washington city to work, attend school, shop, or visit, any time of the day, without encumbrance of horse and cart. And the extension of the streetcar line was simultaneously favorable to the expansion of home building in the area.

The new trolley line meant the closing of the distance between Washington city and Tennallytown. Within five years, Congress acted to include the county of Washington, which included Tennallytown, and

the town of Georgetown into Washington city.

Connecticut Avenue Extended to Chevy Chase

About 1886 Congressman Francis G. Newlands of Nevada conceived the idea of extending Connecticut Avenue northward through Washington County and building an ideal suburb at its terminus. Until then, the intervening land east of the Tennallytown Road and west of the 14th Street Road had remained rural, with only a very few country lanes. The Rock Creek area was not set aside as a park until 1890; it was then farms and woodlands.

The story goes that in 1889 Newlands visited the home of Major George A. Armes, whose estate "Fairfield" was located on Grant Road, three-fourths of a mile east of the Tennallytown Road. From the top floor of Armes' home, Newlands surveyed the land to the south, west, and north, and, with the encouragement of Major Armes, determined the route that Connecticut Avenue extended should take.

In fact, Newlands originally planned Connecticut Avenue to meet the Road to Rockville north of the District line, and wanted his new suburb there. But when he and his brokers began trying to buy up the land on which the road would travel, they ran into obstacles. So it was decided that the Connecticut Avenue extension would parallel the Road to Rockville, and not intersect it.[231]

The Chevy Chase Land Company was incorporated as purchaser of the farm land. The land that was bought extended from what is now Connecticut Avenue and Calvert Street about three and a quarter miles northwest to the District line and about two miles due north into Maryland; 304 acres of

the original "Cheivy Chace" tract were bought from the Bradley family.

According to George Armes' journal, he bought 47 acres from the Payne family of Grant Road in 1890, for $500 per acre, for the Chevy Chase Land Company.[232] Other local lands were acquired—including parts of the Shoemaker, Noonan, Ryan, Gates, and French tracts—under the supervision of Edward J. Stellwagen. This acquisition of property for the extension of Connecticut Avenue was unblushingly hailed as "the most notable transaction that has ever been known in the history of surburban property."[233]

In order to construct the Connecticut Avenue extension and provide streetcar service to Chevy Chase, it was necessary first to grade the land and build bridges; then to build a power plant, at Chevy Chase Lake; and finally, to lay the tracks for the streetcars.

Chevy Chase Lake was a family entertainment spot built by the Chevy Chase Land Company. It was located on Coquelin Run, east of Connecticut Avenue and south of today's B&O Railroad line. The man-made lake was the end of the line for the Chevy Chase streetcars.

The difficulty of the work of road-building was described by Edward Hillyer of the Chevy Chase Land Company, in his memoirs:

"The grading of Connecticut Avenue was through rolling terrain. The hills had to be cut down by pick and shovel and the valleys filled by horse-drawn or mule-drawn carts. A good illustration of that operation was the cutting down of what was known as Soapstone Hill on the west side of the Avenue at Albemarle Street, and the earth had to be carted across the Avenue and filled in where the Ice Center Shopping

LOOKING WEST OVER CHEVY CHASE CIRCLE

Chevy Chase Circle, Chevy Chase, Md.

(1911 postcard photo c/o Harriet Beane Kerins)
(Photo by Minnie Brooks)

Center is today, a fill of 40 or 50 feet. In some places a train of small dumping cars with a donkey engine carried the dirt on very narrow gauge rails."[234]

At the time the two streetcar extensions were being built—one on the Tennallytown Road and another on Connecticut Avenue—horse-drawn streetcars were giving way to cable and electric cars. Overhead wires were permitted in "the county," but south of Boundary Avenue the trolleys ran over a newly developed underground third rail.

By 1892 the Rock Creek Railway was completed all the length of Connecticut Avenue from Calvert Street to Chevy Chase Lake. By 1895 it had become the Capital Traction Company.

Newlands decided that his first residential subdivision should be on the Maryland side of the District line. The D.C. side was not developed until 1907. Because this tract had been named "Cheivy Chace" when Joseph Belt acquired it in 1720, and since it was a euphonious and aristocratic-sounding name, Newlands readily adopted Chevy Chase as the name of his ideal suburban community.

The community was designed to attract the wealthy and "genteel" elite of Washington to buy its gracefully beautiful homes. His grand scheme was phenomenally successful, for the time was ripe for the development of just such a residential area—for those who could afford to escape, with their large families, from the ills of the city to a country suburb with all the Victorian amenities.

THE WILLOWS

(photo c/o Karl Treubig)

The Willows Hotel and Restaurant was located on the east side of Wisconsin Avenue, just south of today's Western Avenue. Karl and Mamie Voigt Heurich ran this popular establishment, a three-story Victorian delight.

Newlands provided the amenities, and much more. Besides the all-important streets and transportation system, his Chevy Chase Land Company developed the sewage system; it provided land in 1898 for the Chevy Chase School in the District, although most of the 25 students came from Maryland; it built the Chevy Chase Inn; and it built Chevy Chase Lake, a most idyllic entertainment area.[235]

The Willows

From the Gay Nineties through the Roaring Twenties, the Willows Hotel and Restaurant held forth south of the junction of the Tennallytown and Glen Echo streetcar lines—now the southeast corner of Wisconsin and Western Avenues. The large, rambling, frame hotel, three stories high and surrounded by lovely willow trees, was built by William Henry Voigt. For many years it was run by Voigt's daughter Mamie and her husband Karl Heurich, a nephew of Christian Heurich.[236]

Though in later days the Willows had a questionable reputation, initially it was a very nice place. Patrons drank and dined in the big lighted "beer garden," and danced on the cool verandas when the city was sweltering on a summer night. Couples and families would spend a weekend at this "country" resort. Local residents remember Alice Roosevelt and her friends coming out to the Willows in horse-drawn carriages.

Stafford Hawken recalls that the Willows had a German band, and that people "sat outside on benches (under the willows) and drank beer" and listened to the band.[237] The beer was 5¢—or 15¢ for the best Heurich brew. The bar (no children permitted) was run by Karl Heurich, and the kitchen was under the direction of his wife Mamie.

An 1894 guidebook says of the Willows,

"An hour upon its verandas after a refreshing ride in the open [trolley] cars is very enjoyable. The cars pass over some very high ground before reaching the Willows, where the air is always cool."[238]

Major George Armes

Major George A. Armes, one of the Chevy Chase Land Company developers, was a controversial but well known character around Tennallytown—an opportunistic and successful promoter of local real estate who made a fortune in the late 1880s and early 1890s. He bought a large frame house on Grant Road from William E. Ellison in 1886. It was located where Connecticut Avenue and Ellicott Street were later cut through.

In 1890, Armes built on an addition to give the house 25 rooms for his family of nine children. The house and 12 acres, part of the old land grant "Fletchall's Chance," were known as "Fairfield." In 1897, after his wife and children had left him, Armes added another 25 rooms onto "Fairfield" and tried to run it as a hotel.[239] He wanted "Fairfield" to be a showplace, but bad luck and poor management kept it from happening.

Armes acquired land up and down the proposed Connecticut Avenue corridor, as well as on Albemarle Street, Howard Street, and Chappell Lane, where he built houses, about 1890. He had a half interest in part of the Wormley tract on Pierce Mill Road.

Armes also acquired many acres south of Grant Road and east of the Rockville Pike between the Lyles-Magruder and Curran homes, laid out public streets at his own expense, and named it Armesley Park—hoping to start another Cleveland Park type development. He sold to Charles C. Glover that portion of the proposed development that faced on the Tennallytown Road. But it was not until 1918, after the death of George Armes, that builders Harry and Sam Kite were able to develop Armesleigh Park, as they spelled it.

A familiar event during the years Major Armes lived at "Fairfield" was to see him driving one of his beautiful horses at a break-neck gallop down the roads and across the fields of Tennallytown. Often he would be yelling and shooting his revolvers—one in each hand—into the air. "We thought he was a wonderful character!" said Norman Underwood. A cavalry officer during the Civil War, Armes was a member of the Dumblane Hunt. He owned many beautiful horses.

Major Armes finally abandoned "Fairfield" in 1912. He died in New Jersey in 1916, with his third wife at his bedside.

"FAIRFIELD" AND GEORGE ARMES

(Photos c/o Edith Claude Jarvis)

Major George Armes' 24-room house, "Fairfield," which he tried to promote as a hotel. It was located on the west side of Connecticut Avenue, where Grant Road intersected it (now the top of the hill at Ellicott Street and Connecticut).

1881: TENNALLYTOWN EAST OF THE PIKE

(B.D. Carpenter's Map of the Real Estate in the County of Washington: Sections 6, 7, 8, 10; copied by Priscilla McNeil)

Municipal Concerns

After the Civil War three distinct governments existed within the District of Columbia—the City of Washington, Georgetown, and the County of Washington. "The latter was administered by the Levy Court, whose members, appointed by Congress, could levy taxes, pass local ordinances, make building regulations, issue liquor licenses, and appoint trustees to supervise public schools in the county." In 1865 the only villages in the county were Tennallytown-Reno and Uniontown (Anacostia); all else was farms and estates.[240]

Neither Tennallytown nor Uniontown had ever been incorporated into a self-governing entity, as Georgetown had.

For 30 years this situation continued, with the county and Georgetown being dealt with apart from "the city." By 1895 the city's Boundary Street no longer defined the outer limits of Washington; in that year Congress acted to merge the city, the county, and Georgetown into one municipality, called Washington, District of Columbia. From then on the city eagerly grew into its new boundaries.

The city reorganization did not immediately improve municipal services, communications, or order, however. In the words of Charles C. Lancaster, first president of the Northwest Suburban Citizens Association, this newly-developing area in 1898 had

"neither water mains nor service sewers. We had no telephones or electric light. We had practically no graded, macadamized streets, and our suburban roads were ancient and almost impassable at certain seasons of the year. Modern homes with sanitary conveniences were rare and conspicuous by their absence."[241]

Although the city had its first telephone in 1878, none was installed in Tennallytown until the 1890s. Electric lights were used in D.C. as early as 1881 and street lights in the city in 1882. But these modern conveniences did not replace gas lights in the suburban neighborhoods until the late '90s. And one can imagine the amazement of the residents when street lights on the Tennallytown Road were first turned on—what had been a black country road was lit up by a string of lights that stretched south along the "pike" as far as the eye could see.

In 1905, when the new Immaculata School was completed and electrically lighted at night for the first time, streetcars and automobiles stopped for their occupants to see the amazing sight on top of Mount Marian, as the Immaculata hill was called.[242]

Rebuilding the Road to Rockville

An 1899 reporter wrote that the main street of Tennallytown

"buzzes and rumbles from morning till night with bang-up blue electric cars, rough-beamed hay wagons, and market wagons, whose canvas tops are tied around like rolly-polys crammed full of fruits and vegetables going in to feed Washington."[243]

The Rockville Pike had been renamed Wisconsin Avenue by 1891. A newspaper column of that year[244] says that 32nd (High) Street in Georgetown became Wisconsin Avenue at the outskirts of Georgetown; and Wisconsin Avenue became Rockville Road at the District line.

In December 1893 property owners along Wisconsin Avenue, as it was referred to in their document, deeded to the D.C. Commissioners strips of land along the road for it to be widened to 65 feet. But, oddly enough, the name Wisconsin Avenue was not officially registered in the D.C. Surveyor's office until July 8, 1905; and old-timers continued to call it the Tennallytown Road or the Rockville Pike.

In the 1890s, after municipal reorganizations and the cessation of toll collecting, the "most extensive piece of road-construction undertaken in

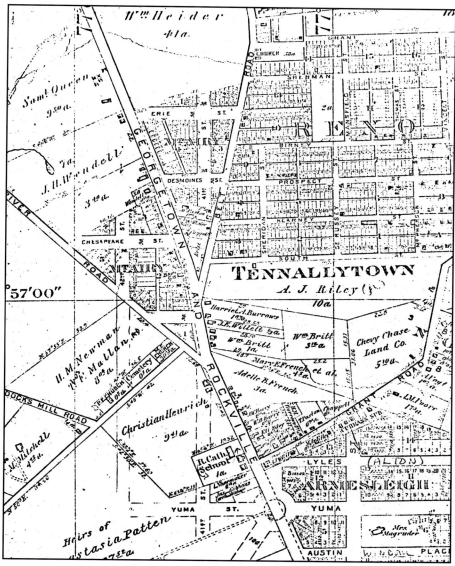

G.M. HOPKINS PLAT MAP OF 1894

this state [Maryland] for a number of years" was the rebuilding of the old turnpike road between Georgetown and Rockville—again.

"No road in the county was more in need of improvement both on account of its condition and of its importance as the direct route from Rockville to Washington. It has long been known as one of the worst pieces of main highway in the state. The old foundation stones, many two or three feet

FIRST POLICE SUBSTATION – TENNALLYTOWN

(Pre-1904 photo c/o
Dorothy Riley Federline)

(Photo c/o Edward N. Riley)

Top: Eli Riley (left) and another policeman (possibly William Easley) in front of the first Sub-T station, on the west side of Wisconsin Avenue below River Road (Sears location today).

Bottom: Retired policeman Eli Riley and his wife, the former Agnes Brooke, watching the horse traffic from the front porch of their house at 4509 Wisconsin Avenue.

in size, formed the surface of the roadway proper which was but little used.

"At the sides a rough single-track dirt road had been worn sometimes 5 to 10 feet below the level of the old road-bed.... As a result where there should have been a well-travelled road and much improved suburban property there was but little travel and land values below those of other neighborhoods no farther removed from Washington."[245]

The Rockville Pike was so muddy during the winter and the spring thaws that it sometimes kept the

farmers from going to market, church, school, and social gatherings. It was the farmers who urged the rebuilding of the road.[246] Although the original intent was to pave the road surface 20 feet wide, available funds permitted only a 16-foot macadam road, flanked on either side by a 12-foot dirt road.[247]

The First Police and Jack the Slasher

Eli Riley came to Tennallytown in 1888 as the first mounted policeman assigned specifically to the area. Since 1861, the officers of the Georgetown police precinct (Number 3, then Number 7) had had responsibility for the entire area west of Rock Creek and north of the Potomac, including Tennallytown, to the District line and a little beyond.

Eli Riley's first Substation-Tennallytown ("Sub-T") was a small frame building not much more than four feet by four feet, with windows on three sides. Heated in winter by a coal-oil stove, this first Sub-T was located on the west side of the pike, north of the Inn, and close to the intersection with River Road. A telephone was installed in this "sentry box," allowing the police to call Headquarters and allowing citizens to call them—but few citizens had phones.

Sgt. William Easley was the second mounted policeman assigned to Sub-T. Officer James Law, also a contemporary of Easley's, came from Ohio to Tennallytown and lived in "Widowsville." McGill Grove came in 1898, but was later transferred to the 8th Precinct.

Officers Easley and Law gained citywide fame as the apprehenders of the daring burglar known as "Jack the Slasher." As John Clagett Proctor retold the story, the winter of 1893-94 was the time of "one of the biggest scares the entire city of Washington ever had." From Fort Myer, Virginia, to Takoma Park, Maryland, homes had been burglarized by someone who stole very little, preferring instead to slash clothing, drapes, and furniture with a knife. No person had been attacked, but the residents of Washington were nonetheless terrified.

"Every householder before retiring locked or bolted every door in the house and put a chair under the doorknob as well . . . . But no burglar as daring as this one could remain unapprehended for long, and so [on March 19, 1894] he was caught entering a house at Tenleytown. A big sigh of relief went up all over town, and everybody breathed more easily."[248]

The Evening Star reported as follows:

"George Taylor, alias Jones, arrested yesterday at Tenleytown while engaged in burglarizing the home of Judge [Governor] Hunt, at the intersection of Rockville and River Roads, is alleged to be 'Jack the Slasher.' Evidence of various kinds points to him as being that much-hunted-for person. In his pockets were found the tools that the slasher must have used in his singular work of destruction—razors and sharp knives—and all were stuffed with small pieces of cloth and dress goods, mementoes of his little trips.

"If he is 'Jack the Slasher,' though, he will probably never be sent to prison. An insane asylum will be his future home, for Taylor is undoubtedly a crazy man—a person not of a violent manner, but one whose brain does not control his actions in conjunction with his conscience.

"When he was discovered by milkman Charles Wise sawing the slats on the blinds of the Hunt home he did not attempt to get away, but remained there until the arrival of the officers. He did not seem to realize that he was being arrested when officers Easley and Law took hold of him."[249]

George "Jack the Slasher" Taylor was sentenced to 30 years in Albany (N.Y.) Federal Penitentiary, not to an insane asylum. It was Proctor's impression that the man died a few years later in the penitentiary.

Along with George Taylor, 20 to 30 other persons were arrested on suspicion of burglary, and a large collection of knives and other weapons taken from them was placed in a museum at police headquarters. The 1894 history of the District of Columbia Police included a humorous 14-verse poem on Jack the Slasher, by far the number one police story of the year. Some of the verses are given here:

The bedstead's on the mantel piece,
   The clock is on the floor,
The cooking-stove is on the roof,
   The bolt's slid in the door.

The cat's in the 'lasses jug,
   The dog's tail's in a loop,
The milk's in sister's slipper,
   The household's in the soup.

"Police! police!" the father cried,
   "Come save the bathroom splasher;
Too late, too late, it's cut in shreds
   By doughty Jack the Slasher."

He fitted on my undershirt,
   He smoked my cigarettes,
He used my well-worn tooth-brush,
   He gave notes for my debts.

He rang the door-bell loud and well,
   He turned on all the gas,
He sat down on the door-step,
   He saw the police pass.

"Police! police!" the father cried,
   "Come catch the naughty dasher;
I cannot stand the impudence
   Of horrid Jack the Slasher."

Jack went into the neighbor house,
   He heard an awful snore,
He didn't stop at anything,
   He even slammed the door.

The tired sleeper lay out-stretched,
   His features drawn and pale,
The coat nearby was closely trimmed
   With knife-slits down the tail.

The sleeper, in his peaceful dream,
   Heard no distressful call,
And cared less how prolonged & sad
   Was his neighbor's mighty bawl.

Smiles were Jack's while others wept,
   As he hastily withdrew.
So soundly the M.P. slept
   Not even said "Adieu."[250]

In the tongue-in-cheek report on the activities of the Tennallytown officers in 1899, the Washington Post writer insisted there were 15 policemen assigned to keep law and order in the village:

"Too many strangers come in [to the corner grocery store] for the loafing nowadays and too much police is about, though for a fact the police keep their eyes glued mostly on pig stys. They had orders from headquarters to take care of Tennallytown pigs because not long ago a fellow swore all of his pigs were stolen, one after one, seven nights in succession, and when the pigs were gone they stole the pig sty, and that they had to carry away stone by stone for a month and a day. Then two more men stole a church in broad daylight, and another came along and stole the ground it was built on.

"But this was before the fifteen came out. Now law and order exists in Tennallytown as in no other town in the universe. Even the saloons have melted away and life is no longer worth the living. The last fight took place two weeks ago."[251]

*   *   *   *

Dr. George E. Gilpin was the Tennallytown "allopathic" doctor after the Civil War. His home and office were at the intersection of River Road and Rockville Pike, on the east side, north of Lightfoots and opposite the tollgate. Many local babies were named after this doctor who delivered them. Dr. Gilpin was still here in 1885, although by then John W. Chappell had also begun to practice.

One Big Family

Tennallytown was always characterized as "one great big family." Everybody knew everyone else, and most were virtually related. People were closer to their own family, their relatives, and their neighbors in those days. It was an isolated country town, and the people were therefore interdependent. Families cared for each other's children as a matter of course.

Front and back doors were never locked, and neighbors and their children knew they were welcome in each other's kitchens or on their porches. As Ray Johnson says, "We had so many relatives on both sides it seems there was company all the time."

Tennallytowners sat on their front porches on summer evenings or Sunday afternoons and chatted with or waved to everyone who passed. Nearly every porch had a swing and rocking chair. Before the days of the playroom, den, or family room, the porch served the purpose of a place for children to play and for adults to entertain; it was also a perch for observation of the neighborhood.

The 1899 reporter gave a very friendly, albeit humorous, report on the village and its residents:

"To the people who live in and never care to go beyond it, there is no place outside of heaven just as good . . . . In spring, when the white and flimsy fences are brushed pink with a mist of peach blossoms or grown green with a climb of honeysuckle, people who drive by in fine carriages say, "Why, this is a picturesque little village, isn't it? What is its name? Tennallytown? Oh, yes, we've heard of it somewhere; how do you spell it?' "

He went on to explain that

"Tennallytown has no exact beginning. It rallies and straggles along anywhere from Georgetown Heights to Cleveland Park, stirs up at Loughborough road till past Fort Reno; then gets lost in West Chevy Chase, Glen Echo Junction, and Bethesda. But to the people who do know, Tennallytown is a town all right.

"Of late years, the . . .'town proper' has been increasing tremendously by addition of two brand-new fancy and dry goods stores, three brand-new grocery stores, an altogether brand-new drug store, a brand-new lawyer's office, a brand-new addition to the schoolhouse, a brand-new mail carrier, a hundred brand-new frame houses, and fifteen brand-new policemen, mounted and patrol."[252]

The village of Tennallytown had passed from stagecoach and tollgate days, through the Civil War, and finally to electric cars and the quickly encroaching suburbs of Washington; and its days as the isolated village of Tennallytown were numbered.

The "Tennallytown" spelling was also no longer the standard spelling. More and more one saw "Tenleytown" after the turn of the century—until it came to be the standard; and it standardized the pronunciation, too. "The Tenley area" has also been used more often in this century. We will, however, use the "Tenleytown" spelling in the remainder of this book.

[179] Townsend, Washington, Outside and Inside, op. cit., p. 640

[180] Roderick S. French, "Chevy Chase Village in the Context of the National Suburban Movement, 1870-1900," RCHS, Vol. 49, 1973-74

[181] 1890 Census, District of Columbia: of 230,000 population, nearly 76,000 were Negroes.

[182] Interview with Mary Thomas, July 9, 1974, by the author

[183] Description, title search, and property documents provided by Mrs. Eda Offutt

[184] Singleton Masonic Lodge biography of Frederick J. Heider, 1948

[185] Townsend, op. cit.

[186] Boyd, History of Montgomery County, op. cit., p. 82

[187] Mary E. Curry, "Tenleytown: Community Identity and Continuity Through the Quarry and Stone Building Business," American University, 1974

[188] Civil War Map, Environs of Washington, 1860s, National Archives

[189] Norman Underwood, "Some Memories of Old Tenleytown, the Rockville Pike (now Wisconsin) Going Into Georgetown and Having a Branch Going Into Washington, D.C." Unpublished manuscript, 1972

[190] "A Real Little Thrums," op. cit.

[191] "Laying of a cornerstone of a new Catholic Church at Tennallytown,"

Georgetown News [1868], Georgetown University Archives, Tenleytown file

[192] Ibid.

[193] The Star, 1885, unsourced article

[194] Obituary of W.D.C. Murdock, The Star, July 24, 1886

[195] Interview with Alvin Parks, May 10, 1976, by the author

[196] "A Real Little Thrums," op. cit.

[197] George Simmons, "Roadside Sketches," The Star, August 15, 1891

[198] Dickson's National Capital Directory, 1888

[199] 1880 Census, Washington County, D.C.

[200] Constance M. Green, Washington, Village and Capital 1800-1878, Vol. I, Princeton University Press, 1962

[201] Letter from Alexander W. Heron to Walton E. Shipley, June 16, 1974; and Mayflower's Log, 1928 (Washingtoniana Collection, Martin Luther King Memorial Library, Vertical file—Houses)

[202] The Star, July 22, 1886

[203] Norman Underwood, interview August 29, 1972, by the author

[204] George Simmons, "Roadside Sketches: Up Near Tenleytown," The Star, August 8, 1891

[205] Record of Appointments of Postmasters, D.C. Post Office Records, National Archives

[206] "Laying of a cornerstone of a new Catholic Church at Tennallytown," op. cit.

[207] Benjamin D. Carpenter, Map of the Real Estate in the County of Washington, D.C., Outside of the Cities of Washington and Georgetown, 1881

[208] Interview with Lulu Volkman Williams, July 1974, by the author

[209] Clippings in a vertical file labeled "Alexander Hunt," at the Colorado Historical Society, Denver

[210] "Chancery Sale of a Very Valuable Tavern and Garden Farm at Tennallytown, D.C." The Evening Star, July 7, 1865

[211] Interview with John Bernard Harry, April 11, 1972, by the author

[212] Milton Rubincam, "Christian Heurich and His Mansion," RCHS, 1960-62, pp. 180-181

[213] Dr. Samuel C. Busey, Personal Reminiscences and Recollections. Philadelphia: Dornan, printer, 1895

[214] Saint Ann's Church, Centennial Book. Hackensack: Custombook, Inc. 1969, p. 4

[215] "A Real Little Thrums," op. cit.

[216] Saint Ann's Church, op. cit., p. 6

[217] Boyd's Directory, 1905, Churches

[218] Ibid.

[219] Mary B. Wilson, The Story of St. Albans Parish, 1854-1919, 1929

[220] Robert L. Haycock, "60 Years of Public Schools of the Dist. of Col., 1885 to 1945," RCHS, Vol. 48-49 (1946-47)

[221] C.B. Smith, "Historical Sketch of County Schools," First Report of the Board of Trustees of Public Schools of D.C. 1874-5. Washington: McGill & Witherow, 1876

[222] "Tenleytown: A Seven-Hilled Citadel of Health," Washington Times, May 26, 1903

[223] Samuel J. Henry, The Old Days with Horse and Hound, Being the Story of the Chevy Chase Hunt, 1916; John A. Lynham, The Chevy Chase Club—A History, 1958; and interview with John Lynham, November 18, 1974, by the author

[224] Henry, op. cit., and Lynham, op. cit.

[225] Dixon Wecter, The Saga of American Society: A Record of Social Aspiration 1607-1937. New York: Scribner's Sons, 1937

[226] Henry, op. cit.

[227] G.M. Hopkins, Plat Map of Washington, 1894

[228] John Clagett Proctor, "Tales of Tenleytown," Sunday Star, January 18, 1948

[229] King, 100 Years of Capital Traction, op. cit.

[230] "A Real Little Thrums," op. cit.

[231] Albert W. Atwood, Francis G. Newlands: A Builder of the Nation. The Newlands Co., 1969

[232] George Armes, Ups and Downs of an Army Officer, published privately in Washington, 1900

[233] "Washington in 1890," The Star, January 1, 1891. See also French, "Chevy Chase Village," op. cit.

[234] Edward L. Hillyer's unpublished memoirs, quoted in Atwood, op. cit.

[235] Edith Claude Jarvis, "Old Chevy Chase Village," in Montgomery County Story, November 1969; and interview with Mrs. Jarvis, October 9, 1974, by Priscilla McNeil and the author

[236] Interview with Louise Voigt Eiker, June 10, 1975, by the author

[237] Interview with Dr. Stafford Hawken, March 13, 1975, by the author

[238] The Night Side of Washington: An Illustrated Guide Book, 1894 (Columbia Historical Society)

[239] Armes, op. cit.

[240] James H. Whyte, The Uncivil War: Washington During the Reconstruction, 1865-78. New York: Twayne Publishers, 1958, p. 18

[241] Christie Rinehart, "Friendship Citizens Pitched In to End 'Good Old Days,' " The Star, March 15, 1955

[242] Early record books of Immaculata Seminary

[243] "A Real Little Thrums," op. cit.

[244] George Simmons, "Roadside Sketches," The Star, August 15, 1891

[245] Maryland Geological Survey. Baltimore: Johns Hopkins Press, 1899, Vol. III, p. 242

[246] A History of Road Building in Maryland, op. cit., p. 41

[247] Maryland Geological Survey, op. cit.

[248] John Clagett Proctor, Washington and Environs, written for The Washington Sunday Star, 1928-1949; pp. 335-336

[249] The Evening Star, March 20, 1894

[250] Richard Sylvester, District of Columbia Police. Washington: Gibson Brothers, 1894

[251] "A Real Little Thrums," op. cit.

[252] "A Real Little Thrums," op. cit.

THE WALTHER FAMILY AND FRIENDS, 1915

(Photo c/o Mary Frances Brown)

V

PEACEFUL DAYS:
1900-1914

Charles Herman Marion Walther (seated front), his wife Sophronia (to his right), and his 15 children and their families are pictured in front of the family home on Murdock Mill Road, about 1915. Dr. John W. Chappell is the elderly gentleman middle right; his wife Ida is the third woman to his right.

In the early days of the 20th century, the interests of the 1,000 or more citizens of Tenleytown (as we will spell it from now on) still centered around family, church, and village. The family was, emphatically, the important social unit in the early 1900s. Almost everyone, even if unmarried, lived with his or her family. Married children built houses adjacent to those of their parents. Ailing parents were brought into their children's homes and cared for until their death.

Most Tenleytown men married Tenleytown women, often quite a bit younger than themselves. Since there was so much intermarriage among the families, any two families you might name would usually be related, at least by marriage. Marriage of second cousins was not unknown.

The Burrows surname (pronounced Burruhs or Burris) was owned by the greatest number of Tenleytowners. All of the Burrowses (and Burroughses too) were apparently not related to each other, but because the Burrows name was most often heard, it was remarked that the name of Tenleytown should have been changed to Burrowstown. The Tennallys had, after all, left no direct heirs to carry the name into the 20th century.

Other most common names in Tenleytown were Riley, Robey, Hurdle, Harry, Poore, Shoemaker, Chappell, Paxton, Queen, Perna, and Walther. There was hardly a white person in the village who was not in some way related to one or more of these 12 families.

Few Tenleytown children attended school beyond the 8th grade. Most went to work, instead, for their parents or for a local farmer or businessman. Tenleytown girls who finished high school went to work in the city stores or offices if they were not needed at home—at least until they married. Some studied to be teachers and returned to teach at the Tenley School. Women who did not marry were flatteringly called "unclaimed treasures."

An 1899 newspaper article described the courting habits of the local boys:

"Uncle George says for the life of him he can't find out when the Tennallytown boys do their courting. They let the young ladies, dressed all in their Sunday clothes, go a-walking up and down the plank walk of summer evenings, and they gather in a bunch on the store porch and blush when the girls pass, or say it's a fine day . . . . 'Yet dey does git married,' says Uncle George. That, however, is because, like in Thrums, the girls have to do the managing."[253]

Many women died young in childbirth or in complications resulting from childbirth. In this event, an aunt or grandmother would care for the children until the widower would eventually take a second wife—sometimes his wife's younger sister. And he and the second wife would, more likely than not, have a "second family" of half-brothers and half-sisters to the original children.

If a husband died and the widow did not remarry, she might support herself by dressmaking or even by continuing her husband's business, if he ran a store. The oldest sons would run the farm.

Divorce was a very rare thing in Tenleytown, although separation was an occasional occurrence.

Being populated mostly by people of English, German, Irish, and Italian descent, Tenleytown had the usual Protestant-Catholic biases that existed in small-town America. But there were marriages between Protestants and Catholics.

A good number of people also attended more than one church. They may have been elders in the Baptist church, but they attended the Methodist church when the preacher there was more appealing. As one woman said, "My father was Episcopalian. I went with him to St. Columba's. My mother was Presbyterian, but there was at that time no Presbyterian church in the neighborhood, so she taught Sunday School at Eldbrooke Methodist." Such separate family arrangements were not unusual; what was unusual was to be affiliated with no church.

Although the post-1900 families in Tenleytown were smaller than the previous generation, many families produced six to eight children who survived to adulthood. To have nine or ten children sired by one father was not unknown. The largest family in Tenleytown was that of C.H.M. Walther, of Murdock Mill Road. Walther had 14 children by his first wife (only six of whom lived to maturity) and nine by his second wife.

The first block of Grant Road, with its many houses close together, was known as the "Incubator Avenue" of Tenleytown. With the average household on that street having six children, one can imagine what it was like when there were 64 children living, playing, and fighting on the block!

In 1905 Tenleytown boasted of two doctors, a pharmacist, and three lawyers; a few new residents were in real estate or insurance. The landed gentry of the old days was fast disappearing, however; the large property holdings were divided among heirs or sold off. Except for a few new well-to-do neighbors, such as George Armes, Charles Lancaster, Scott Welker, S. Hazen Bond, or the phenomenally rich John R. McLean, Tenleytown was a working-class town.

Among some critics, Tenleytown had a questionable reputation. There were those who considered some poor families very "low class." There were boys who managed to get into trouble. There were a couple of women, it was said, who would "go with any man." Some people expressed fears of fights in the saloon and fights in the school. They pointed to men who drank, gambled, and were "scoundrels." About once a year there would be a shooting or a stabbing in Tenleytown.

Such aspersions cast on the reputation of Tenleytown and whispers about "tough people" were, however, spoken only by outsiders. Those who had grown up in Tenleytown knew very well about the "bad" people in town. But since they were their own neighbors, fellow parishioners, customers, and, much of the time, relatives, they accepted them as part of the local color. Also, recognizing that such people were a minority of the population, Tenleytowners continued to take pride in their historic town and its fine occupants.

Another large family was the Queens. Elexious Queen, a gardener, had married Altha Paxton at Holy Trinity Catholic Church, Georgetown, in 1831. They and their eight children lived in a farmhouse near Broad Branch Road (now near Linnean and Fessenden). Elexious died in his 80s in 1885.

When she celebrated her 100th birthday in 1907, shortly before her death, Altha Queen boasted of eight children, 59 grandchildren, 132 great-grandchildren, and (at that time) five great-great-grandchildren. The younger generations were also prolific, and countless descendants of the Queens grew up in Tenleytown—many named Burrows, Donaldson, Riley, Johnson, Skinner, Rye, Barnes, and Harry, as well as Queen.

Making Do

A motorman on the streetcar line supported his wife and seven children on $2.25 a day. "But," his daughter recalled, "we never went without. Pork chops were two pounds for 25¢, round steak was 15¢ a pound, sugar was 5-6¢ a pound. When a 4-cent loaf of bread went to 5 cents, we thought it was awful!" Members of such families did not neglect, however, to make up baskets for the poor at Thanksgiving and Christmas.

"We couldn't buy ready-made clothes then—mothers had to make all the clothes. Dad bought material in Georgetown, always dark colors—black, dark blue, brown, or grey. My sister's wedding dress was grey. We kids wore homemade bloomers with elastic at the waist and legs."[254]

Even during national depressions there was never severe poverty among the people of Tenleytown or Fort Reno, for the government continued to employ workers and these in turn continued to buy products and services from Tenleytowners. Any needs that a family did have were taken care of by relatives and neighbors, black and white, who shared their food and second-hand clothing.

Most families had large gardens; some had orchards. Hattie Burrows Porter, who grew up on Wisconsin Avenue at Windom, recalled that, like most families,

"We grew and canned all our own vegetables and fruits. We had pigs for pork, chickens for poultry and eggs, cows for milk and milk products. We had our own smokehouse, well, and root cellar—for potatoes and canned food."[255]

(Photo c/o Althia Harry McCathran)

ALTHA QUEEN AT AGE 98

Mrs. Queen posed for this photo in 1905 with a daughter-in-law, daughter, and granddaughters and grandson and a neighbor.

The women generally tended the gardens and did the canning. Many remember the large garden of "Wheelbarrow Mary" Wehrle of Brookeville Road, who worked in her garden daily in long sleeves, long skirt, and broadbrimmed hat. She carried her produce to the local grocers in a wheelbarrow.

Most residents had a horse, hogs, chickens, and a cow or two for their own use, even into the 1920s. The livestock were kept in the backyard coops and stables—or grazed in adjacent fields. Mame Colburn recalled,

"We had rabbits. Chickens were walking around everywhere. Cows grazed in a field where Wisconsin Avenue Baptist Church is now; my Mom milked one called Rose. Our horse we kept behind the house."

TOWN AND COUNTRY SIDE BY SIDE

(Photo by Petra Schultze)   (Photo c/o Hattie Burrows Porter)

Left: 1981 photo of first semi-detached brick houses in Tenleytown, 3900 block Windom; built 1911.

Right: Mrs. Samuel R. Burrows (Della Houser) poses with the Burrows' cow in this pre-World War I photo. The historic Lyles-Magruder-Cross house is to the right (39th and Windom), and the new brick row houses on Windom appear to the left. The Joseph Curran house is visible in the left distance.

Dairies

A walk in any direction from Tenleytown would take you to a dairy farm. Fred Bangerter's cows and horses grazed around the reservoir at Fort Reno. The dairy farm of Ed Pyles extended from Grant Road to Connecticut Avenue. Englebert and Francis Enders owned a large herd of dairy cattle off Murdock Mill Road, south of Robeyville.

James Beach had a dairy farm right near Enders', behind Achterkirchen's. The Fred and Samuel Burrows families had dairy and beef cattle south of River Road, and did their own slaughtering. Sonnemans and Saunderses owned dairy farms west of Wisconsin and Ellicott. A 1910 advertisement for the Sanitary Dairy Farm, Tennallytown, D.C. (James M. Saunders, Prop.), reads, "Get your milk from tuberculine tested cows only."

The Wise family of Tenleytown owned and rented pasture land where the American University was under construction, near Loughborough/Nebraska and Ridge/Foxhall Roads. But their larger pastures were on either side of the District line in Chevy Chase (north of today's Pinehurst Circle)—and so they called their business the Chevy Chase Dairy.

The Poores on Chappell Lane, east of Fort Reno, milked goats as well as cattle. Other Reno families kept goats at one time or another, using them also to pull wagons.

The Voigts of Grant Road kept cows and bulls, as well as mules and horses, in their fields north of 38th and Albemarle. Their X-shaped country fences usually succeeded in keeping the neighborhood children out of the pasture, as well as containing the animals.

Poultrymen

Many Tenleytown residents ran poultry or vegetable stands in the downtown markets, or owned their own grocery stores. The 1905 Boyd's City Directory lists three Burrows men with poultry and game businesses at the Riggs Market, 14th and P— George F. Burrows, of Grant Road; Henry Burrows, of Wisconsin Avenue; and his son, Samuel R. Burrows, of Wisconsin and Windom. Their chickens were raised in Tenleytown and taken fresh-killed daily to the market. Samuel O. Wendel of Tenleytown also had a poultry stand at the Center Market, 7th and Pennsylvania Avenue.

(Photo c/o Hattie Burrows Porter)

Gardeners

Truck farming or gardening was the livelihood of many area residents. The land of William Shoemaker, a truck farmer, extended west of Wisconsin Avenue to River Road, from Fessenden almost to today's Harrison Street.

The Heiders, on their large acreage between Wisconsin Avenue and Belt Road, grew celery, turnips, parsley, "oyster plant" (salsify), and horseradish, which they carried to the Western Market, 21st and K. As Bill Heider recalled, "we watered our celery in the spring area where Fessenden is now." The swampy area around Belt Road and Fessenden was called "Frogtown."

William Henry Voigt bought Conrad's old property, north of Heider's, and brought his family out to live on it in 1888, when the youngest of his six children was nine. Voigt and his family grew produce that they sold at the Georgetown market.

The well-watered fields around Tenleytown were an unusually fine source of edible mushrooms. City people came to pick Tenleytown mushrooms from around oak trees after a rain. The fields west of the Bureau of Standards blossomed with mushrooms then; so did the fields beyond Robeyville.

The ground was fertile and the climate favorable for fruit trees as

Henry T. Burrows (father) and Samuel R. Burrows (son) of Tenleytown at their Riggs Market poultry stand. The Burrows poultry business continued into the 1970s in Georgetown.

113

BURROWS' MARKET, LATER A LIQUOR STORE

(photo by John Russo, 1974)

(Photo by Jerry Yurow, 1974)

Top: Frank Burrows built this brick store in 1900 at what is now Wisconsin Avenue and Albemarle Street. Shoemaker and Lenhart had a grocery business there, and then Mostows, who turned it into a liquor store. It was torn down in 1977 for Metro subway construction.

Bottom: Detail of the front of the Burrows - Mostow store. The second story contained a large apartment.

well. The Lyles-Magruder house, at what is now 39th and Windom, was surrounded by fruit trees planted before the Civil War. This property, occupied by the Cross family after 1910, was marked by apple orchards along the east side of Wisconsin Avenue from Pierce Mill Road to Grant Road. Pecan, peach, quince, and cherry trees and an arbor of white and blue grapes also flourished on the Magruder land.

Wherever you walked were springs and branches. The Walthers had a "front branch" and a "back branch" that meandered across their property off Murdock Mill Road. Many creeks east of Wisconsin fed into the Soapstone Creek. Large shade trees and violets growing in profusion along the banks made the clear creeks even more beautiful. Whenever gypsies came to town, they camped alongside one of the creeks.

Tenleytown Stores

"Tenleytown is a historic town. But it does not . . . live in the past and sleep in memories. The Tenleytown of today is a lively, busy village of nearly a thousand inhabitants, who are wide awake and contributing toward making theirs a model town.... Tenleytown, as are few other suburbs, is sufficient unto itself.... [There are] four prosperous grocery stores, a butcher shop...seldom to be found in neighboring suburbs; a dry goods and notions store,...and a yard where is sold flour, feed, coal, lumber, oil, and paints."[256]

The four grocery stores mentioned in this 1903 article included John and Helen Norris's small country store in a pebbledash house on Wisconsin Avenue north of Pierce Mill Road—it served "Widowsville" residents until about World War I. Another was William Franklin

"Frank" Burrows' grocery and meat market, in the new red brick building in the center of Tenleytown, with a large apartment above it. It is said that because Mr. Burrows "gave too much credit," he could not make a profit; he subsequently was much more fortunate in the wholesale meat business.

The Willetts' small store, selling fresh baked goods, was on the east side of Wisconsin where Brandywine Street was to be cut through. And John J. Sheaffer's market stood at 4654 Wisconsin. Mr. Sheaffer did not have his own garden, but went to the Center Market to fetch groceries home in his cart. All four of these grocers lived above or next door to their stores.

The sole butcher shop in Tenleytown was owned by J. Clarence "Dick" Burrows, brother of Frank. Dick Burrows first located on Belt Road (the Belt Road Market); then he remodeled the Good Templars Hall at 41st and Chesapeake into a store and home. About 1917 he moved down to Wisconsin Avenue into the first floor of the Masonic Temple, after Doc Scholl had moved out.

The first drygoods and notions store, selling fabric and sewing supplies, was "The Tenley" at 4509 Wisconsin—in the frame home of Herbert and Gene Riley and her parents, Dennis and Harriet Houser. The house-store combination was the same house in which John Bernard Harry was born in 1867 and later the site of Dr. Parton's pharmacy. It was torn down when Albemarle Street was cut through.

The feed store was that of John J. O'Day at the northeast corner of Grant Road and Wisconsin Avenue. Mr. O'Day and his wife sold not only flour, hay, grain, mixed feed, coal, lumber, kerosene, oil, and paints— but also hardware, implements, provisions, general merchandise, and,

TWO TENLEYTOWN GROCERY STORES

(1942 photo by Ray Johnson)

(Photo c/o National Park Service)

Top: John Sheaffer's store at 4654 Wisconsin Avenue.

Bottom: The Belt Road Market, between Ellicott and Donaldson Place. Burrows, Melton, and "Pop" Richards ran the store at one time and another. Torn down in the 1930s.

115

THE TENLEY

(Photo c/o Dorothy Riley Federline)

Eugenia and Herbert Riley pose proudly in front of their newly redone dry goods store, The Tenley. It was on the east side of Wisconsin, where Albemarle was later cut through. Eugenia's mother, Harriet Burroughs Houser, and her daughter, Dorothy Riley, are also in this picture, which was taken about 1910. Dr. George Parton later had his drugstore in this building, and his family lived upstairs.

eventually, groceries, bread, and milk. The frame building had a round porch at the corner—three steps led up to the porch, where a large red box stored the fresh bread. This store was run by the O'Days until about 1915. The building, now stuccoed, still stands at Wisconsin Avenue and Grant Road.

Other general and grocery stores that opened early in the 1900s included that of Abraham and Rose Mostow, who sold groceries and feed in a frame building at 4601 Wisconsin, near Brandywine, before moving down to take over Frank Burrows' business years later. This second store was their better known store, and Mostow eventually turned it into a liquor store after Prohibition was ended. "A.D. 1900" was visible on the second story.

The Meltons sold food out of their own garden at the Belt Road Market, near Ellicott, which they acquired from Dick Burrows.

In 1912 the Gormans took over Perskin's store on Grant Road between Brandywine and Chesapeake Streets. The Gormans, who sold clothes and beer as well as groceries, remained at this site for 40 years.

Grocery and supply stores made home deliveries by horse and wagon upon request to outlying residents—east to Rock Creek, north to Friendship Heights and Bethesda, and west past American University Park. Local stores generally ran "on tick;" that is, the grocer kept a tab of what was owed, and the regular customer paid his bill at regular intervals.

Many residents also went to the in-town markets (e.g., O Street, K Street) on Saturdays, carrying groceries home on the Wisconsin Avenue or Connecticut Avenue streetcars.

Black businessmen in Tenleytown included the Lewis family, who had a flower shop on the west side of Wisconsin near Pierce Mill Road, and Mr. and Mrs. Jeffrey Smith, whose general store was near the corner of Davenport Street and Howard Road. There was a barber shop for Negroes at the north corner of Belt Road (now 41st Street) and Wisconsin in the early 1900s.

The Village Blacksmiths

Blacksmiths continued to do a good business in horseshoeing, as well as in general iron work, wheelwrighting, and wagon building and repairs—until the internal combustion engine automobiles began to take over.

The best located blacksmith in Tenleytown was Samuel Duvall, whose shop was on the west side of Wisconsin Avenue, north of the Tenley School and south of Achterkirchen's saloon. To get to the shop customers had to ride their horse up a steep bank, an inclined alley-way of clay and stone, for the smithy stood much further back from the street than the saloon and the other buildings there.

George Gilpin Duvall took over the business from his father, but gave it up about 1916. Adam "Rip" Heinrich and his assistant, George "Coxey" Wells, located themselves at the Wisconsin Avenue site until 1925, when the cutting through of Albemarle Street to the west forced their removal.

Heinrich and Wells moved to a blacksmith shop on Belt Road north of Fessenden, run for years by Thomas and William Bowling. Their business had changed to the building of wooden truck bodies—horses were becoming fewer in number. Heinrich eventually moved to Potomac and remained a traveling blacksmith through the '30s. Wells died in 1940.

Next to Bowling's smithy on Brookeville Road was William Hurley, wheelwright. James W. Hurdle was a wagon maker who lived on Albemarle Street.

Morris Fitzgerald kept his blacksmith and wagon and carriage building business (see Chapter IV) north of the intersection of Pierce Mill Road and Loughborough Road until nearly 1930. An office building at 4226 Wisconsin is on the site of the second Fitzgerald blacksmith shop.

Other Tenleytown men who worked as blacksmiths were J. Thomas Finney, George Stadtler, James E. Harry, William L. Warren, John Morrow, Edward Parks, George Martin, and a Mr. Utterback.

The public livery stables were owned by Hilleary Burrows, whose first wife was Minnie Duvall, daughter of the blacksmith. The stables were situated on the north side of Achterkirchen's, closer to River and Murdock Mill Roads. Police and post-office horses were kept in that stable, which was a holdover from the days when stagecoach horses were changed at that elevated intersection.

Maryland children drove horse-drawn buggies into school, and country people drove as far as Tenleytown to catch the streetcar; the livery stable served as a sort of "parking lot" for these people, too. A watering trough for horses was in front of the livery stable entrance.

Others in Tenleytown, such as August and Henry Voigt of Grant Road, owned so many horses and mules that they did their own horseshoeing. Henry Voigt eventually took over the stables from Hilleary Burrows. Contractor August Voigt rented out his animals and the heavy wagons and machines used in road-building—long before the days of dump trucks. Every evening the hired men would drive the horse- or mule-drawn wagons back to Albemarle Street.

William Lindner of Grant Road (who married one of the Voigt daughters) and William R. Skinner of Fessenden Street also owned large number of horses and earthmoving scoops that were used for excavation and construction work. The Spencer Harry family of Howard Road—Bit and Little Bit Harry—were in the excavating business. A number of black men on Fort Reno also had horse teams they rented out for such work.

Shop Owners

A Chinese hand laundry was an early landmark, on the southeast corner of Wisconsin Avenue and Grant Road, opposite St. Ann's. Quang Lee—or Yung Lee, as it was sometimes listed—rented the downstairs corner of what had been a large frame house built by Andrew J. Riley, Jr., and occupied for a time by Father Joseph Mallon of St. Ann's. The coming of the Chinese laundry brought a new luxury to the neighborhood—having one's shirt collars and cuffs washed, starched, and ironed for about 2 1/2 cents each. (Men's pleated shirts were 15¢ and ladies' "waists" were 25¢.)

The "Chinaman" was, however, taunted mercilessly by the neighborhood children, to whom a foreigner was someone to make fun of, no matter what his age or occupation. Although his English was very poor, Mr. Lee knew he was being made fun of when the children sang "Ching, Ching Chinaman"—and he would bring out a rusty pistol to run them off.

Another trick to harass the Chinese launderer was to tie a long string to the handle of his front screen door and, after walking across Wisconsin Avenue, to open the door by pulling on the string, and let it bang shut. So Mr. Lee had to leave his ironing every time the front door opened and closed. This will also give us an idea of how little traffic passed along the Avenue at that time!

A series of other families occupied the rest of the 11-room house adjacent to the Chinese laundry. The shop was taken over before World War I by the Burdette daughters,

(Photo c/o Edna Lester Johnson)

Father Thomas Smyth leads a May Day procession between St. Ann's School (at left) and the church (at right). In middle background is the Chinese laundry; the Lester family occupied the upstairs when this photo was taken, about 1915. On the left, across the street, is O'Day's general store, a frame structure that has since been stuccoed and remodeled, but still stands. Grant Road is the narrow street between O'Day's and the Chinese laundry.

who ran a general store there until 1925. Park Lee moved the Chinese laundry to 41st Street below Chesapeake about that time. The Goulds opened a variety store in what had been the Chinese laundry and the Burdettes' store across from St. Ann's.

William A. Trigger was the earliest barber in Tenleytown. He had one good leg and one wooden leg. Trigger and his wife Estelle lived two doors south of the old police station on Wisconsin Avenue. Like most small businessmen, he had his barber shop in the front of his house.

Eventually the general and feed stores were replaced by the specialty stores—grocery stores, hardware stores, dry goods shops. Willett's grocery store was replaced by Simpson's Hardware. Frank Poch also opened a hardware store on Wisconsin Avenue; his son Bernard Poch moved Poch's Hardware to Potomac in 1958.

Pharmacists

The first pharmacist in Tenleytown was "Doc" Charles A. Becker, who opened a drugstore in the 1880s, next door to Houser's dry-goods store. Doc Becker moved on to Georgetown, however, and Andrew Burga opened a drugstore—which incorporated the Tenleytown post office—in the early 1900s. Mrs. Burga acted as postmistress, and Mr. Burga was the first letter carrier.

Dr. George P. Parton came to the area in 1905. His 1909 advertisement in the Masonic program read "Kill the Catarrh Germ Before It Kills You." Dr. Parton's first drugstore was in the frame building where Herbert and Eugenia Riley had "The Tenley" general store and post office. Dr. Parton not only cooked a lot of medicinal herbs in the family kitchen, but also made ice cream in the basement to use at his soda fountain. He sold root beer, sarsaparilla, or bromo seltzer (for 5¢) and tobacco—Cinco cigars, Early Bird and Snaps chewing tobacco, and Sweet Caporal cigarets.

Dr. Parton's second place of business was on the ground floor of the Masonic Temple, built in 1909 on the east side of Wisconsin Avenue.

When Dr. Parton moved away in 1912, Dr. Robert W. Scholl moved into the Masonic building—he had been in business with Dr. Morgan at Wisconsin Avenue and Macomb Street.

In a few years (after 1915) the O'Days, proprietors of the general store on the corner of Wisconsin and Grant Road, gave up their business. Eventually Dr. Scholl bought the O'Day property, putting a stucco finish over the frame store. Dr. Scholl, who was well liked, had a name that was remembered by everyone; but he was no relation to the one who made the famous foot powder.

Scholl's Pharmacy later featured a soda fountain and metal tables and chairs; by the time World War I came along, soldiers stationed nearby were dropping in for lunch. In about 1922, Doc Scholl retired; he died in 1928.

Ice and Ice Cream

Before the days of electric refrigerators, a 50-pound supply of ice had to be delivered every other day to every house that had an ice box. Frederick Voigt, who lived west of Wisconsin Avenue and Jenifer Street, got his ice from Georgetown and delivered it to Tenleytown homes early in the morning.

Another icehouse in Tenleytown was found behind the Masonic Temple—down an alley to the place where the horse-drawn delivery trucks were loaded with ice each morning.

J. Bernard Harry was part owner of the Tenley Baking and Ice Corporation; it was later bought by the American Ice Company.

The bakery business was in front of the ice house. It also continued the ice cream parlor in the frame building that Dr. Parton had vacated. In 1914 the board of Eldbrooke Methodist thanked the Tenley Baking & Ice Manufacturing Co. for closing its store Sundays.

Public Scales

In 1903 the public scales in Tenleytown were opened just north of Achterkirchen's saloon and south of Murdock Mill Road.

"From the prosperous farms surrounding Tenleytown loads of country produce are brought in for weighing. Hay and corn are raised in abundance and the public scales which have been installed in Tenleytown by the District government will soon be busy."[257]

The scales opened July 1, 1903, and were to be operated by the individuals making the highest bid. Fifty cents per wagon was charged for weighing.

TENLEYTOWN'S MAIN STREET, CIRCA 1920

(Photos c/o estate of Marjorie Scholl)

Top: Scholl's Pharmacy (remodeled O'Day's store) was at the corner of Wisconsin and Grant Road. It and the house next to it still stand, but the rest of the houses have been torn down. The Masonic Temple was rebuilt in 1926.

Bottom: Dr. Robert W. Scholl, at 4425 Wisconsin.

POLICEMEN ON HORSEBACK

(Photos c/o Mrs. James L. Giles, Jr.)

Top: Lt. Giles' horse steps onto public scales. In the background is Gloria Point, and the beginning of River Road is to the left.

Bottom: Four of the Tenleytown mounted policemen in front of the Sub-T building, under construction in 1904. Note wooden sidewalk and streetcar tracks. This sub-station, on the east side of Wisconsin Avenue, later became the Tenley Library.

Achterkirchen's daughter recalled that there was a fence on the north side of her father's place:

"It ran up to the weighing station, maybe 100 feet or more. It was a wooden fence, where they tied police horses. Inside the fence were three beautiful linden trees. The weighing station and stables and a tenant house to the north probably occupied three acres. The ground around our place included seven acres when we had it."[258]

Police Substation

In 1905 the little square box known as the Substation-Tenleytown, or Sub-T, was replaced by a $4,000 stucco building across the street at 4539 Wisconsin Avenue, just south of the Tennally-Lightfoot house, and facing the beginning of River Road. The building had a station desk, offices, and jail cells. A horse-drawn Black Maria came to transport any prisoners downtown. Sub-T was a part of the 7th Precinct, whose headquarters was in Georgetown.

Officers Eli Riley, William Easley, and John Law had been joined by Hiliary M. Smith, another large man whose presence on horseback was most imposing. Mr. Smith, who had worked on the Tenleytown streetcars before he joined the Metropolitan Police, remained for nearly 30 years at Sub-T.

Although the substation had a telephone, very few residents did—so they always had to run to get the police. Much of the policemen's work, it seems, was picking up drunks and breaking up gambling games. Actually, Eli Riley did not usually put the drunks in jail on Saturday nights—he would call his sons to take the revelers to their own homes in Tenleytown or Fort Reno.

Police officers were required to respond to complaints about public gambling—usually registered by the wives of the participants, or by residents who spotted such goings-on. But it was not unusual for the officers to send a boy down to the woods to break up the game before the police got there.

Favorite places for such games included "French's Woods" behind Dr. Chappell's; the woods north of McLean's (called "the jungle"); the woods southeast of Wisconsin and Pierce Mill Road; under the pines behind Achterkirchen's; or under a beech tree where Yuma and Reno now intersect.

Favorite times for the dice games were Saturday (after payday) or Sunday mornings and afternoons. Sometimes there would be as many as 100 men playing crap games down in the woods near McLean's. The young boys could play if they had money—but mostly they were look-outs for the police. Stafford Hawken remembers they would yell, "I.S.B.B.!"—for "I Spy Brass Buttons!"—and the men would scatter before the leisurely-paced officers on horseback would come trotting through. Very rarely was anyone arrested for gambling.

Officer Eli Riley retired before 1908, and new mounted policemen such as Minor Furr, R.M. Canady, James L. Giles, and J.G. Walsh came to Tenleytown. Other officers who became well known in the neighborhood were John Maher, George W. Neale, and Karl Scherer.

George Cornwell and Lt. John L. McLucas were especially remembered for their big, beautiful horses. No doubt every boy around wanted to be a "horse cop" when he grew up. Easley and Law were considered the "best horsemen you ever saw."

In 1912, James L. Giles was assigned as head of the Tenleytown

subdistrict. Lt. Giles proved to be a much respected and admired police officer. He married Nettie Nicholson of Brooke Farm, Chevy Chase, and they lived with their two children on upper Chesapeake Street in a Victorian house build by his brother, Tom Giles. Jim Giles later moved his family to 38th and Harrison Street when that area was developed.

Jim Giles was a very handsome, tall, and popular man who continued

(Photos c/o Mrs. James L. Giles, Jr.)

Top: Lt. James L. Giles headed the Tenleytown police sub-station from 1912 until his death in 1925.

Bottom: Lt. Giles and his daughter Carolyn pose on the front porch of their home at 4015 Chesapeake Street, about 1902. The house, built by his brother Tom Giles, was torn down for the redevelopment of Fort Reno Park in the 1930s.

121

ENGINE NO. 20

(Photo c/o Jack Gerhart, Friendship Fire Association)

The two-story Tenley fire station, on Wisconsin Avenue at Warren Street, was built in 1903. The one-story addition came in 1913. This photo appears in 100 Years of Glory, a history of the D.C. Fire Department.

the practice of maintaining close and friendly relations between the police and the residents and business owners. He was Worshipful Master of the Singleton Masonic Lodge and Worthy Patron of the Eastern Star, and thereby a good friend to many local men and women. Lt. Giles died in 1925, at the age of 55, of a heart attack.[259]

Throughout these years, Tenleytown remained generally free of crime, which can certainly be attributed to the fact that the families all knew one another. It was not until after the growth and development of the '20s and '30s that one saw more strangers than friends on the streets of Tenleytown.

Fire Department

Before Tenleytown acquired its own fire station, the Georgetown firemen responded to calls out Tenleytown way—and their horses

had a difficult time pulling the apparatus up the steep hills of Wisconsin Avenue. For years, Tenleytown citizens complained about the inadequacy of fire fighting facilities in their area.

In 1903, the D.C. Fire Department built the fire station that still stands on the west side of Wisconsin Avenue, just north of Warren Street: a two-story building of light yellow brick, with a red tiled roof. The first fire company was called Chemical Company 3; in 1907 it was redesignated Engine Company 20.

The first hook-and-ladder, hose cart, and pumper engine were horse-drawn for many years. The horses' harnesses were hung in the firehouse overhead and to the side, and on the ringing of a fire alarm, the harnesses were released to fall onto the horses.

Anna Poore Stevens remembers Mr. Warren at the reins of the "steamer" fire engine, which was pulled by four horses. "I remember him coming around the corner [at Wisconsin and Grant Road] yelling 'Gippee! Gippee!' to his horses—they always hit O'Day's steps and knocked them into the street!"

Truck Company No. 12 was organized on the same site in 1913. At that time a one-story extension was added on the north side of the firehouse, with "an extra-wide door to handle the unwieldy electric-powered aerial truck with which [No.] 12 went into service."[260]

In the days before fireproofing and good firefighting service, many frame barns, stables, other outbuildings, and houses burned to the ground—including many flimsily-built structures at Fort Reno. Individual houses on Murdock Mill Road (Ginny Addison's), Chesapeake Street (Elsworth Chappell's), and Grant Road (Will Voigt's) burned down completely. The eastern section of the Magruder-Cross house (39th and Windom) was never rebuilt after it burned. A large barn on that property also was destroyed by fire.

Before there were firehouses in the suburbs, Tenleytown firemen were called on to put out fires in Friendship Heights, Bethesda, and Chevy Chase. Horses were not replaced by motor engines until the '20s.

Ghosts and Superstitions

Some people believed that the Tenleytown firehouse was haunted—that a pale face would often appear at the second-story window when the firemen were out on a call.

Superstitious practices prevailed in those days before there was a scientific answer for every phenomenon. The Dale sisters of Loughborough Road were well known in the area for being spiritualists. Florence "Toncie" Dale regularly held seances, and her sister Margaret consulted Ouija boards as seriously as people consult their doctors. The local children found many occasions to tease the Dale sisters by reporting strange occurrences and pretending to seek an answer from the spirits.

Death had many superstitions about it. "Signs" such as the unusual noises or restlessness of animals were inevitably pointed out to the children upon the death of a relative or neighbor.

Suicides and Death

There was a high incidence of suicide in these early days—and not only among adults; but these deaths, by gas, hanging, or gun, were almost exclusively among males. The high expectations of family and society for males of any age had a good deal to do with these tragic deaths. The perceived inability to escape shame in a small community, fear of parents or authorities, or ignorance of laws and opportunities prompted many desperate Tenleytown men to suicide. Insanity was attributed as the cause of most suicides.

The most remembered suicides were those of a gardener and subsequently of two of his sons; a young boy who hanged himself from a tree south of Alton Place; a man whose body was found eight months later in a field in Virginia; and a young white father whose wife gave birth to a child with Negro features.

In the aftermath of a suicide the grieving family often left the area in order to escape the curiosity of their neighbors.

Accidents caused a relatively greater number of injuries and deaths 70 years ago—mostly because of the lack of safety precautions. There were drownings in the Potomac, and shot-gun accidents, and traffic accidents, and construction and industrial and household accidents—just as there are today.

As was mentioned earlier, a large number of women died in childbirth or in complications after childbirth. Listening to family histories, we hear again and again the sad stories of the deaths of young women. Ray Johnson writes about the effects of the death of his own mother, Louisa Queen Johnson:

"Forrest was born in February, so he was only ten months at Christmas of 1906. Our mother was never real well after his birth. In the spring of 1907 sister Lula left school to help with the housework and although I was in school until the end of the term, we never returned to school again.

"In June of 1907, we lost our wonderful mother, so our home life was never again the same . . . . In January 1908 our father decided to go to Seattle—our Aunt and her three children had already gone . . . . In February we were ready to leave. The last thing sister Lula and I did was to visit the [Methodist] cemetery to bid our mother farewell."[261]

Fathers also died younger in those days than they do now; but most led lives so vigorous that they kept strong and in good health.

An early orphanage in the Tenleytown area was the Children's Country Home, located by 1905 close to Rock Creek Park near where Grant Road crosses Broad Branch Road. It had earlier (1894) been located in the old Adlum house near Pierce Mill Road and Connecticut Avenue. It is probable that some at this Home were children of Tenleytown mothers who had died young.

(Alexander Yowell photo c/o Dr. Mary Frances Brown)

Dr. John W. Chappell built this house on Grant Road in about 1890. It still stands today at 3901 Albemarle Street, at the corner of Nebraska Avenue. In this photo, taken after 1894, Dr. Chappell stands with his wife and son, Sidney, and their neighbor Mrs. Otto Sonneman (nee Clara Walther), and one of her sons. The man by Dr. Chappell's buggy is unidentified.

"Tennallytown Sickness"

As written in John Daly's history of Blessed Sacrament parish, Washington in 1910 was "a lovely but hazardous place to live. Typhoid fever was rampant on the banks of the Potomac. There was merely the beginning of a health department. Consequently, only the strong survived in this period . . . ."[262]

Tuberculosis was contracted by many in the early days of this century—most frequently by young women. The most popular cure was to find a better climate—especially in the Adirondack Mountains. For those who could not afford to travel, there were houses that rented rooms to TB patients. Dr. Anthony Ray of Tenleytown visited such houses located north of the Bureau of Standards. Having tuberculosis was considered a terrible thing, and news of its contraction was given in a quiet voice. Some young people in Tenleytown died of tuberculosis.

Quarantines were strictly enforced by the Health Department for communicable diseases. All members of the family would be confined to the house for the duration of the illness of one member. One woman recalls that during her quarantine for scarlet fever, their black serving woman was prevented from returning to her own home until the quarantine was lifted.

Whooping cough, measles, and diphtheria were common illnesses in the early days of the century, and the quarantine notices were posted on the front doors of the Tenleytown houses.

A Washington journalist, later describing with humor the local pride citizens had even in their illnesses, noted that Tenleytown's ills

"are better than the ills of other towns. Even the children brag on them at school, and decorate the ominous signs on their doorposts with cedar and holly, so as to show that it is real, honest, sure, cross-your-heart Tennallytown sickness what it has 'stead of another kind what ain't half so good."[263]

Dr. John Chappell

After the death of Dr. George E. Gilpin, the first Tenleytown physician, there were two doctors in Tenleytown—Dr. John W. Chappell and Dr. Anthony M. Ray.

Dr. John W. Chappell (1855-1938) was a member of a large, old and well known family in the area. He was one of six children of John E. and Sarah Paxton Chappell, and had grown up on the Chappell land west of Broad Branch Road (near where Nebraska Avenue and Connecticut Avenue now intersect).

His father, John E. Chappell, taught in the first school in Tenleytown, and young John at first followed in his footsteps, teaching at the "new" Tenley School on Wisconsin Avenue.

But in 1881, when he was 26, John W. Chappell obtained an M.D. degree from The Columbian College (George Washington University), and began practicing medicine, in addition to teaching school. Eventually he gave up teaching and confined himself to the practice of medicine.

John W. Chappell married Ida Mary Adamson in 1881; they had two children, Clara and Sidney. About 1890, the doctor built for his family a large white frame box of a home in Tenleytown, on Grant Road, one block east of the Rockville Road. It is still standing at 3901 Albemarle. Patients entered his medical offices, in the west side of this house, by the large front double doors. Some emergency surgical procedures were performed in his patients' homes or in the doctor's office. A few drops of ether were required to put the patient to sleep.

Dr. Chappell was considered a very good doctor. For 14 years a member of the D.C. Medical Association Committee of Public Health, he was very knowledgeable about the latest discoveries in the use of pharmaceuticals and antitoxins, and early advocated the use of injections to prevent disease. He kept a well stocked pharmacy in his office and gave pills and medicines to his patients.

Dr. Chappell also delivered babies and set broken bones; but it was known that he preferred the more scientific aspects of the medical practice. He was not abounding in "bedside manner," and was considered quite pompous and humorless by many. He was often patronizing and authoritative. He was quoted as saying, for example, that cabbage was "fit for only pigs and women to eat." Dr. Chappell did not have Negro patients.

Always vigorous and energetic, John W. Chappell enjoyed telling how he had walked downtown to classes at the Columbian College each day. He was an active member of the Eldbrooke Methodist Church and was generally unsympathetic to patients who consumed alcohol to excess.

Dr. Chappell was remembered by many as a handsome, erect, elderly man with a great shock of white hair and a white mustache—making his rounds in the new Ford automobile which finally replaced his horse-drawn buggy. He died in 1938, in his 83rd year, and was buried in the Methodist cemetery in Tenleytown.[264]

Dr. Anthony Ray

Anthony M. Ray was, much more than Dr. Chappell, the well-loved doctor of the "little people." A rotund bachelor, he had his offices on Wisconsin Avenue—at first just south of the police station, and later in a frame house near Wisconsin and

Davenport, where his widowed mother lived with him for many years.

Anthony Moreland Ray (1866-1930) was the oldest of nine children of Alfred and Eleanor Ray of Forest Glen, northeast of Chevy Chase. The Rays are a Maryland family of many generations. One of Dr. Ray's brothers, Preston, became well known as an attorney and politician in Montgomery County.

Dr. Ray studied medicine at the University of Virginia and opened his practice in Tenleytown in the 1890s. His popularity as an obstetrician was attested to by the large number of children—girls as well as boys—who were given the name of Ray as a first or middle name in honor of the doctor who delivered them. Children warmed up to the jolly Dr. Ray, and trusted him to treat their cuts and broken bones. As Margaret Walmsley said, you could even take your doll to Dr. Ray.

At first Dr. Ray drove a horse and buggy, then eventually he acquired a Model T Ford. He is remembered riding around Tenleytown in his noisy car, always wearing a black "campaign" hat. Dr. Ray used to allow young Stafford Hawken to ride around with him in the Ford as he completed his rounds. That Hawken also became a doctor he attributed to the early influence of Dr. Ray.

Dr. Hawken recalled seeing a sign in the trolley barn at Wisconsin and Jenifer to the effect of "Watch Out for Dr. Ray's Driveway"—because the good doctor never slowed down for vehicles or streetcars when he was going into or coming out of his driveway!

Dr. Ray treated the poor people of Tenleytown, and with respect. He was the family doctor for most black families at Fort Reno, and was appreciated for his cheerful gentleness and willingness to sit and talk with any family, of high or low station.

DR. ANTHONY MORELAND RAY (1866-1930)

(Photo c/o Edith Ray Saul)

A large number of people called themselves friends of Dr. Ray. William Tyler Page, who lived in nearby Friendship Heights, said that Dr. Ray was one of the most delightful companions and interesting talkers he had ever known, and was often amazed to find him so conversant with current events of the world.[265]

He showed wit and humor in a debate on politics or economics, as well as in casual banter with a child.

In his active participation with the Singleton Masonic Lodge, the Junior Order of Mechanics, St. Columba's Church, Sons of the American Revolution, and the D.C. Medical Society, Dr. Ray won many friends and admirers.

Anthony M. Ray retired from his practice in the late 1920s for reasons of poor health. He died March 14, 1930, at the age of 63, at the Ray family home in Boyds, Maryland, near Germantown. Funeral services were held at St. Columba's in Tenleytown, and he was interred in Rock Creek Cemetery.

Aside from a few doctors who resided in the Chevy Chase or Tenleytown area but had their offices elsewhere, Drs. Chappell and Ray were the only general practitioners around for a span of over 30 years. For a short time, Dr. Edward T. Jones, of Freedmen's Hospital, lived on Davenport Street in the 1920s. But he did not set up a practice in the Reno area.

Harry Brooke Riley, D.D.S., son of policeman Eli Riley, had an office in Tenleytown but soon moved his dentistry practice to Georgetown.

Sometimes a doctor did not arrive in time for the birth of a baby—and a midwife would handle the delivery. The two most popular midwives in Tenleytown were Harriet Burroughs Houser and Cora Graves, a black woman from Fort Reno. They often assisted a doctor or delivered the baby alone. Unfortunately, the midwives did not as a matter of course issue birth certificates.

The Sisters of Bon Secours established a convent on Yuma Street in 1905. Members of the order often served as nurses for local families in need.[266]

Despite the medical care available locally, or perhaps because of it, very few people used the facilities of the Georgetown College Hospital for emergencies, surgery, childbirth, or treatment of disease. A large number of people in Tenleytown died because of ignorance that their wounds or sickness could be successfully treated if diagnosed correctly.

Injuries that were not treated correctly caused other crippling conditions or chronic disability throughout the life of the patient. Today's residents would be surprised by the number of people in turn-of-the-century Tenleytown who were lame, disfigured, blind, or deaf.

The 1908 Report of the President's Homes Commission included a medical inspection of the children in the public schools. Out of 145 children tested at the Reno School, one was crippled, five were mouth breathers, nine had defective vision, three had defective hearing, and 29 had had toothache in the past year.

Much worse, however, was the report from the Tenley School (which at 273 enrollment was not quite twice as large as Reno): 28 anemic, three crippled, one deformed, six ill-nourished, 15 mouth breathers, five strabismus (cross-eyed or wall-eyed), eight undersized, 16 defective vision, four defective hearing, and 73 had suffered toothache in the previous year.[267]

Funerals and Cemeteries

Because people knew their neighbors, everyone turned out for a funeral. The family often had black-edged cards printed, giving the name of the deceased, dates of birth and death, and a prayer or Scriptural quotation.

The Tenleytown Methodist Cemetery was located behind Eldbrooke Methodist Church, and the Episcopal cemetery (confusingly called St. Albans) was next to St. Columba's Episcopal Church. A 1905 city directory also lists "Christian" and "Green Vale" cemeteries "near Tennallytown"; and the Belt, Chappell, and Shoemaker families had private burying grounds large enough to be listed in that directory.

The blacks of Tenleytown had their own cemetery, located on a hill west of where Fessenden Street and Reno Road intersect today. Perhaps this was the "Christian" cemetery mentioned above. The cemetery was reached by going north to the end of Howard Street or of Chappell Lane, which ran parallel to it; the cemetery was on the northeast slope of a hill there.

Many called it Moses Cemetery, for it was maintained by the Moses Lodge of Tenleytown (The Brothers and Sisters of Moses), a black fraternal organization that had a meeting hall on Dennison Street. Others thought it was the Rock Creek Baptist Cemetery—but, in fact, the church did not own the burying ground.

The hill on which the cemetery lay, known as "Graveyard Hill," was adjacent to "Barney's Hill"—Barney Williams' sloping property northeast of Fort Reno; and a creek ran along the bottom of both hills. The best sledding in winter was to be found on these hills—a good long run down toward Connecticut Avenue, before Reno Road or even Fessenden Street was cut through.

When Reno Road was extended south through this cemetery in about 1920, most of the coffins were reinterred at a cemetery at the black settlement off River Road, west of the Little Falls Creek and the railroad tracks. That River Road cemetery, across from today's Macedonian Baptist Church, was also eventually removed, this time to Route 28 west of Rockville toward Poolesville.

Undertakers, who provided embalming, coffin, and livery service, were called from Georgetown, Washington city, or Rockville; only Will Moten of Broad Branch Road was a black undertaker for Fort Reno. There was no white undertaker in Tenleytown in the early days of the 20th century. Visiting the family of the deceased was done at home, and funeral services were held at home or at church.

Tenleytown's Methodist Cemetery was used by people from the surrounding countryside. Palisades strongman John "Bull" Frizell, as related by Harold Gray, was interred at Tenleytown in 1879. A hard drinker who had miraculously survived a Chain Bridge collapse 25 years earlier, Frizell was attended by his friends in a "three-day vigil at his tomb to make sure he wasn't kidding."[268]

Singleton Masonic Lodge

In 1901 a group of 35 Tenleytown men who were members of the Free and Accepted Order of Masons (F.A.A.M) met at the Good Templars Hall on Belt Road and petitioned to organize a lodge in the local area.[269]

The new lodge, named after William R. Singleton, then recently deceased Grand Secretary of the Grand Lodge of D.C., was formally opened April 2, 1901. It was No. 30 Lodge in the District, and met for years in the Tenleytown Hall, upstairs over Lenhart's (Magruder's) store, south of Achterkirchen's.

That same year, when the membership was 75, a lot owned by Eli Riley on the east side of Wisconsin Avenue was purchased in order to erect a Masonic Temple. This property had belonged to the Harry family years earlier. The cornerstone was

THE MASONS

(Photo from <u>History of Freemasonry in DC</u>, 1911)

(Photo c/o Lelia Poore Spandou)

Top: The William R. Singleton Masonic Lodge, organized in 1901, built this lodge building in 1909. It was completely remodeled and a third story added in 1926; it still stands at 4441 Wisconsin Avenue.

Bottom: 1909 Masonic officers. Standing, L to R: Henry Gerhardt, Jr.; Edward N. Riley, George Welker, Elmer S. Robey. Seated, L to R: Fred W. Parks, James H. Robey, Worshipful Master; and John H. Larrabee.

not laid until November 1908, however.

The first meeting was held in the new Temple August 5, 1909, under the leadership of Worshipful Master James Harvey Robey, whose family had built the structure. The post office and Scholl's drugstore were soon housed in the first floor of this brick Masonic building.

A three-day housewarming celebration took place in February 1909. The printed program indicates that on Monday evening, February 22, a variety of musical selections was presented: a piano solo by Professor Henry Miles, a blind piano teacher, and a song "I Used to be Afraid to Go Home in the Dark, But Now I'm Afraid to Go Home At All," sung by Mrs. Grace Reiss. Perhaps more uplifting were speeches by Professor Ben Murch ("The Mason As a Citizen") and Maryland politician Preston B. Ray, younger brother of Dr. Anthony Ray.

Tuesday evening featured musical numbers by the Industrial Home School Band, violin and vocal solos, and a lecture, no doubt well attended, on "Courtship and Marriage" by the Rev. Dr. R.F. Clarkson.

Wednesday evening brought a piano solo by Miss Clara Chappell; a comedy act, "The Monkey Man" by Mr. H.C. Gould; a recitation "She Would Be a Mason" by Miss Maday Solyom; and—before the moving picture feature presentation—the Tenleytown Glue Club singing "Owed to Tenleytown" (to the tune of "O Christmas Tree").

I

Oh! Tenleytown, Oh! Tenleytown,
How pleasant are thy suburbs;
There's Washington, a village near,
And old Georgetown, without a peer.
Oh! Tenleytown, Oh! Tenleytown,
How pleasant are thy suburbs.

II

Oh! Tenleytown, Oh! Tenleytown,
How lovely are thy ladies;
They have a soul-alluring smile,
Like Cleopatra of the Nile.
Oh! Tenleytown, Oh! Tenleytown,
How lovely are thy ladies.

III

Oh! Tenleytown, Oh! Tenleytown,
How skillful are thy doctors;
There's Doctor R. and Doctor C.,
And handsome Doctor Harry B.
Oh! Tenleytown, Oh! Tenleytown,
How skillful are thy doctors.

IV

Oh! Tenleytown, Oh! Tenleytown,
How honest are thy lawyers;
There's S. McH. and Howard G.
Just down the street there's Albert E.
Oh! Tenleytown, Oh! Tenleytown,
How honest are thy lawyers.

V

Oh! Tenleytown, Oh! Tenleytown,
How gallant thy policemen;
Their faces always wreathed in smiles,
To prove it, look at Sergeant Giles.
Oh! Tenleytown, Oh! Tenleytown,
How gallant thy policemen.

VI

Oh! Tenleytown, Oh! Tenleytown,
How quiet are thy babies;
They never cry, they never squall,
Nobody ever heard one bawl.
Oh! Tenleytown, Oh! Tenleytown,
How quiet are thy babies.[270]

The words were by "Cy, poet laureate of Bethesda" (Cyrus Eli Perry). In Verse III, reference is made to Doctors Ray and Chappell and Dentist Harry B. Riley; in Verse IV, to lawyers Samuel McComas Hawken, Howard Gott, and Albert E. Shoemaker.

Obviously the Singleton Lodge was very important to the social community of "Tenley," as it had begun to be called; its members were also the Protestant leaders in the civic and religious life of the area. The lodge had especially strong ties to Eldbrooke Church, and several Methodist ministers served as lodge chaplains.

The list of early past masters of Singleton Lodge No. 30 is a list of community leaders in Tenleytown whose families were here prior to the building boom of the 1920s—e.g., Shoemaker, Wendel, Robey, Bowling, Heider, Smith, Parks, Riley, Walther, Ray, Chappell, Giles, Hurley.

Many Masons and their wives also became active in the Order of the Eastern Star (Friendship Chapter No. 17), which had its heyday in the '20s, '30s, and '40s.

Social and Leisure Activities

Other popular social and fraternal organizations included the Daughters of America (a patriotic and religious organization that met in churches); the Junior Order of United American Mechanics (Reno Council 46, which originally met in the hall over Lenhart's store); and the International Order of Good Templars (Silver Star Lodge No. 20), a temperance society that had met at least since 1880 in its meeting hall on Brookeville Road.

The Anti-Saloon League, led by Friendship Heights attorney Albert E. Shoemaker, also held its meetings in the Good Templars Hall. Entrance to the hall was from Brookeville Road. Inside was a raised platform in the center, with chairs all around. Shoemaker's son Mark remembered the hall as a big building with stores on the lower side, facing Wisconsin Avenue:

"When I was about six [1904] I attended meetings with my parents. All the men were in full regalia—with tassels on their hats, etc. Hot air heat came up from grills on the floor. When the men spat their chewing tobacco into the grills—boy, did it stink!"

It was a popular belief that the Good Templars Hall had served during the Civil War as housing for soldiers. In fact, it was quite close to the grounds of Fort Reno. Dick Burrows later converted this building into a store and living quarters.

Some of the German men in Georgetown and Tenleytown—including the Voigts and Fritz Wehrle—formed a small club called Die Guten Bruder (the Good Brothers). They met in the hall above Stohlman's confectionery store in Georgetown (now transported to the Smithsonian Museum).

On Decoration Day, May 30, everything was closed and there were parades and a ceremony at the local cemetery. The children picked flowers to place on all the graves, not only on those of Civil War and Spanish-American War dead.

Churches played a large part in the social as well as the religious lives of the residents. St. Ann's had sponsored jousting events in the 1890s, and later held occasional lawn parties at the Magruder-Cross house. The church's May Day celebrations included a May Queen, parades, dances, athletic contests, and concerts.

In 1902 members of St. Ann's parish began construction of a new stone church and made available

ST. ANN'S CHURCH

(Photo c/o estate of Marjorie Scholl)

(Photo c/o Donna Burrows Rose)

Top: Another view of a May Day procession (compare earlier photo), showing St. Ann's Church on the left and the school on the right; taken from across Wisconsin Avenue. The Convent of Bon Secours is also visible in the background.

Bottom: The second St. Ann's Church, this stone structure was finished in 1903. To the left is the priests' rectory; to the right, the old frame school has been torn down in this 1930s photo, and the old Tenley School, acquired by St. Ann's, is visible.

their old frame church building to the District for use as an annex to the Tenley School. The large hall on the second floor of St. Ann's School, next door to the old church, was used for services and for public meetings, concerts, and dances.

The Episcopal church had a sewing guild in the new parish house (which was finished in 1900) after school one day a week, to teach girls how to crochet and sew. The St. Columba's choir became especially popular when William Tyler Page took over as choir director. And after choir practice, Mr. Page just might

treat all the singers to ice cream from Scholl's drugstore.

Eldbrooke Methodist occasionally held vesper services on warm Sunday evenings on a bank of the Dalecarlia Reservoir—to take advantage of the fact that many people went for long walks on Sunday afternoons, and often ended up near the old Murdock Mill or the abandoned gold mine near the Dalecarlia Reservoir. [The Methodist church officers took a stand in 1911 opposing Sunday baseball in the vicinity of Tenleytown.]

With the black families, Sundays were traditionally given over to church. Mary Thomas recalled, "We attended Rock Creek Baptist in the morning—9 a.m. Sunday School and 11 a.m. church. Then we also attended the St. Alban's Mission Chapel [St. George's Episcopal] in the afternoon at 2 p.m."

Clara Poore Broderick recalls that "blacks from all over came Sunday afternoons and stayed 'til 9 or 10 in the evening"—and her family would listen to the gospel singing coming from the Rock Creek Baptist Church at Grant Road and Howard Street.

Many families owned a piano, and playing and singing were sources of entertainment on Sundays or in the evenings. Children took lessons from Professor Henry Miles, the blind piano teacher, who came around to the houses of the pupils. He was led from the streetcar to the home of his first student, and from there to each of his pupils.

Sunday Walks

Families and groups of young friends went walking after Sunday dinner—to pick flowers, to sing songs, to visit cousins and friends. Everyone would walk for miles—all the way to Conduit Road, to Georgetown, to Rock Creek Park, or to the Zoo—and think nothing of it.

But the favorite walk for Tenleytowners was to the ruins of the old Murdock Mill. In the old days, one went from River Road and Wisconsin west on Murdock Mill Road all the way past the last house. A sharp left turn before 46th Street led across Massachusetts Avenue, and then there was a downhill walk of about two blocks to the old abandoned mill.

The Rambler, writing in the Star, described the approach to Murdock Mill:

"Crossing Massachusetts Avenue, the mill road becomes rougher, narrower and crookeder than it has since you left Tenleytown. Nobody uses it except the colored family living in a house near the mill, and few teams have passed that way since the mill ceased to grind . . . . Nearby is the shell of a small house. This probably was the miller's home. In the bow-like formation around the mill stands another which has the appearance of once having been a store. A colored family dwell there."[271]

Today, you continue to the end of Yuma Street beyond Massachusetts Avenue into very deep woods until you find the creek itself and remains of the cement mill race alongside it. The Dalecarlia Parkway south of Westmoreland Circle comes closer to the mill site than any other street. A careful search will turn up some stone foundations of the mill.

Swimming Holes

The Dalecarlia Reservoir was a favorite place for swimming by local boys; but whenever the superintendent, Mr. Halloran, saw boys swimming in the reservoir, he would jump into his row boat and go after them— somehow he never caught them. Occasionally the boys would catch

TWO EPISCOPAL CHURCHES

(1922 photo c/o Lelia Poore Spandou)

(1917 photo from Where Washington Worships)

Top: St. Columba's Episcopal second church at Murdock Mill Rd and Albemarle St (now 42nd and Albemarle).

Bottom: St. George's Mission Chapel on Fort Reno was established for blacks by members of St. Alban's and became a mission of St. Columba's. It was served by Father Edward Douse, a Jamaican. This frame church succeeded the mission's first meeting place, a row house at Fort Reno. Located on Howard Rd, it was adjacent to the Reno School.

ELDBROOKE METHODIST CHURCH AND PARSONAGE

(Photo c/o Dorothy Riley Federline)

Top: When this third sanctuary was dedicated in 1899, the name of Mt. Zion Methodist was changed to Eldbrooke Methodist, after Aquila Eld and Philip L. Brooke. Murdock Mill Road runs alongside the church and the cemetery behind it.

Right: The parsonage was to the right (north) of the church, facing River Road.

(Photo c/o Rebecca Parker)

sunfish or perch in the catch basin that carried reservoir overflow back into the Potomac.

Stafford Hawken recalls the "Two Dollar" swimming hole on Soapstone Creek. The creek then was so clean that picnickers not only waded in it, but also drank the clear spring water. Cyrus Perry dammed up the Murdock Mill Creek on his land in summer for swimming and in winter for ice-skating.

Winter Sports

The deep gravel pit (or mud puddle) behind "Dumblane" froze over during many cold winters— enough to skate on the surface. For those who did not have real ice skates, there were "snow skates" made of wood with a center runner and strapped onto the shoes. It was sometimes so icy the children could skate to school.

Sledding (people still call it sleigh-riding) was and is the number one winter sport in Tenleytown. But in the early days there seemed to be much more snow (sometimes to the tops of the fences); it lasted for weeks; and of course there was very little street traffic to ruin the snow on the best sledding hills.

Left: Remains of Murdock Mill, 1914. The Murdock Mill dam was badly washed out by a flood in June 1889 and was never repaired. The road leading from Tenleytown to the mill was called Murdock Mill Road. Remains of the stone mill race can still be discovered in the wooded area west of Massachusetts Avenue and 49th Street.

Below: The Mt. Tabor Baptist Church, 4620 Wisconsin Ave., changed its name to Wisconsin Avenue Baptist Church, but then moved first to 42nd and Fessenden and much later to Nebraska Avenue and Alton Place.

(1914 "The Rambler"; glass plate photo c/o Columbia Historical Society)

(1923 photo c/o Wisconsin Ave Baptist)

Left: The Rev. and Mrs. George McCullough, who lived in the Baptist parsonage at Belt Road and Davenport Street. Rev. McCullough was at Wisconsin Avenue Baptist from 1892 until 1916.

(Photo c/o Edith Grove)

133

River Road was the very steepest and longest hill, from Gloria Point down past the Harrys' at the bottom of the hill. As Dorothea Thompson told it, she'd go sleigh-riding by moonlight after choir practice at Eldbrooke: "I loved to go belly-whopping, and I'd go real fast down the ice frozen in the wide gutters on the side of the road—so fast I'd fly right over the hole at the bottom." (If you went too slowly, you'd crash into that hole!)

Bud Riley described a sled that held 10 or 12 people; it was called the "Tenleytown Truck." "Lick" Harry put together two Flexible Flyers to make a toboggan that was guided by whoever was at the rear.[272] It could go down River Road almost all the way to the Burrows' gate (Ellicott Street). But sometimes Mr. Burrows would salt the hill so his wagons could get up River Road—and that ended the sledding there.

Murdock Mill Road was the second best hill—not as steep, but it went downhill gradually for blocks and blocks—almost all the way to 46th Street. The boys would build a bonfire on sledding nights at the top of River and Murdock Mill Roads.

Children east of Wisconsin Avenue preferred Barney's Hill, the Graveyard Hill east of Fort Reno, Fessenden Street, Grant Road going down toward Rock Creek, or Albemarle Street east of Grant Road, even to Soapstone Hill. The Albemarle Street run was nearly half a mile long, and forming long sled-trains was great fun—they could coast to a stop just before Connecticut Avenue.

(Nowadays the best sledding is found at "Deal Hill" or Fort Reno—the east or west slopes of the Reno Reservoir near Fessenden Street. The streets that used to be favorites are now salted or sanded for road traffic, much to the displeasure of sledders young and old.)

A few families had sleighs with runners that were pulled by horses. Bells on the sleighs made a pleasant jingle and warned others of the approach of a sleigh across the silent, snow-filled streets.

Ray Johnson has written his early memories of December, the Christmas month:

"We always had programs at the school and church. Our mother would take us to Georgetown for shopping. Our father would take me with him to get the tree, over near Grant Road. We set it up in the rear parlor . . . . We had snow, as a rule, and all the boys and girls had sleds and snow skates . . . . In the rear of our home the field sloped down to River Road, so we had a good place to slide."[273]

Seventy-five years later, these traditions of Christmas and winter have not changed much in Tenleytown.

Sports and Other Entertainments

When spring came, the Tenleytown baseball team got into full swing. Home games were played on a diamond in the open field across from St. Ann's (now Nebraska Avenue and Alton Place), or on Heurich's field opposite Sidwell's School. The older youths and young men in their 20s are pictured circa 1912 in a variety of uniforms, but most with the T for Tenleytown cap.

The Tenleytown team played the Chevy Chase Grays as well as teams from Mount Pleasant and other neighborhoods. Hy Gorman, who became a star athlete at the University of Maryland, was later one of the Tenleytown baseball team's best assets.

This semi-outfitted team was a sight better than the 1880s team with whom Fred Heider played third

base—"his batting average might not have been so bad had he not made the bats himself."[274]

Doc Scholl, Dolsie Poore, Laurie Barr, Pop Richards, and "Pocky" George Burdette were early sponsors of the Tenleytown boys baseball club, which played on Sunday afternoons. Occasionally the games would be interrupted when Will Stanton, remembering that he had to ring the St. Ann's bells at 6 p.m., would leave—even if he was on third base—and zip over to the church!

The blacks also had a baseball team—they played on a diamond near the top of Fort Reno hill.

The first time Tenleytown children saw a movie was in 1902, when the Episcopal parish house in Tenleytown presented The Coronation of King Edward VII and Cinderella. Early movies were also shown in the open air, on a sheet in the Shoemakers' lot near Wisconsin and Davenport Street.

The first movie house was opened in Georgetown about 1914. Cost of the movie was five cents, and an ice cream soda at Stohlman's after the movie was another five cents. Tenleytown did not have its own movie theatre until the 1970s.

Horseback riding was another natural entertainment for the young people in the early 1900s—many families owned their own horses, and the children were allowed to ride them around town or perhaps along the many bridle paths in Rock Creek Park on Sundays.

Tenleytown men were dependent on horses for transportation and daily work—and they loved to compete in occasional races and to place bets on others' races. There were at different times race tracks at Brightwood, Georgetown, Mount Pleasant, Kenilworth, and Ivy City.

"The Tennallytown men lack spirit except where there is

1912 TENLEYTOWN BASEBALL TEAM

(Photo and identifications c/o James Melvin "Bud" Riley)

a lawn party or a church fair, a big day in the market, a special sale at the horse bazaar or the races. Ah, the races! Not to know good horseflesh when he sees it goes against the grain of your genuine Tennallytown man. He's a sport and he knows it, in spite of fifteen brand new policemen. You don't catch him being hang-head when it comes to betting on your new two-year-old; no sir, not he."[275]

Not only horses, but also dogs were the companions of Tenleytown men; many owned and trained hounds for bird and rabbit hunting. Dr. Anthony Ray's sister wrote about him,

"When the hunting season began in the fall, he would go for a few days with his dogs and gun out into the forests of Maryland or 'ole Virginny,' to shoot quail and other wild game."

Fred Heider was said to have had "the best bird and hound dogs in the entire country" and also had the reputation of being a crack shot with both rifle and shotgun.[276] (Note his dogs in the Heider photo, Chapter IV.)

Occasionally a dance would be sponsored by the Masonic Lodge or a church group, or even held in someone's home. (The Eldbrooke Methodist Church board minutes of 1911 "deplored," however, that young people had taken part in a dance held at St. Columba's Episcopal Church.) Most acceptable were square dances for young and

Some of the team players have the T for Tenleytown on their uniform.

Back row, left to right: Dr. Robert W. Scholl, sponsor; Randolph (Dolsie) Poore, sponsor; "Bud" Riley; Vic Rountree (Bureau of Engraving uniform); Wesley Beach; Joe Blinkhorn; Dick Volkman; Laurie Barr, sponsor.

Middle row: Joe Oldfield, Cleveland Dennison, Bus Hager, George Beck, Eddie Rabbitt.

Front row: Ernie Stephens, Duke Oldfield, John Stadtler, Nick Stephens, Mark Stadtler, Ray Sheaffer.

old. It was said that James "Pop" Richards played his fiddle for three hours straight at a square dance held at his place. Mame Burdette Colburn remembers that when her sister Lula and her husband Tom Nicholson were living in the old "Dumblane" house, they used the large rooms to have friends in for a dance.

Family get-togethers might include pitching horseshoes, playing croquet in the front yard, or just swinging on the porch swing, singing by the piano, or, for the kids, running through the attic or in the barn loft. Young people also went on church-sponsored hayrides and picnic outings up the C&O Canal. A favorite trip was by streetcar to Great Falls or to Glen Echo for an evening of roller coaster rides, hot dogs, and eventually, dancing in the Crystal Room Dance Pavilion.

Living in a rural village made it possible for the children to enjoy the simplest games, from sliding down a mud bank to having foot races as far as anyone could run. The existence of Civil War earthworks and ditches at Fort Reno made for all kinds of games of war, cowboys and Indians, cops and robbers, and athletic contests such as jumping from bank to bank.

The soapstone quarry at 35th and Alton was a great place to hunt for tomahawks and play Indians. Walton Shipley says they sometimes built fireplaces of soapstone, to "gleefully see them explode when heated."[277]

Children's pastimes were often centered around work that had to be done. The children accompanied their mothers when they went berry picking, or rode around with their fathers or local businessmen in their wagons.

As Ray Johnson (who was born in 1891) reminisces,

"Tennallytown was a vast enchanted place to spend those early years which I now know had much to do with my outlook and way of life in the future years. Looking back, it seems only yesterday, but I know it was long, long ago! I am very grateful I was privileged to be a part of it. The days never came too soon or brought a day too long.

"Spring with its uncertain weather and much winds was kite time, and all the boys had one. We made our own. May was real spring and the fields were full of daisies, with wild flowers everywhere . . . . The meadow larks built their nests in the tall grass and if you would watch when they came to them, soon there would be little speckled eggs.

"June brought summer and real warm weather, and school would soon close. We could now get rid of our shoes and feel that good warm earth on our feet. Our thunderstorms seemed to come from the hills to the northwest. We never had to worry if caught in a storm, as all we had on was pants and shirt. Soon as the sun came out, we were soon dry. How I loved the hot summer days with all the village to roam in."[278]

Tenleytown summers did not seem to be as hot then, long before the days of air conditioning. More grass and trees, less traffic and movement, and fewer people might be the reasons.

"The last of October was real fall, with warm Indian summer days and cold nights. The leaves were all colors and the frosty nights would ripen the persimmons. It was beautiful.

With our winter's fuel in and the rugs all down, we were ready for Thanksgiving."[279]

In a letter from Dorothea Thompson to her friend Lula Johnson, after Lula had moved away in 1908, Dorothea recalled the happy days of childhood spent in Tenleytown:

"Remember the walks down the River Road, over in Burrows' field, down in University Park, the hunts for blackberries, or the tea parties in the woods by the church, or the sleigh-rides in winter, on Vernie's [Vernon Chappell's] sleigh, down the back hill? Remember the games of 'Run Thief Run' after dark, or the swings on the old tree down by the River Road, or the see-saws we had on Mr. Gerhard's lumber, or the sand houses we made from his sand?"

Some of our readers will remember.

Professor Ireland

All was not play for the children of Tenleytown. For those who attended the Tenley School on Wisconsin Avenue, there were the twin disciplines of teacher/principal W.B. Ireland and teacher Maggie Callahan.

A 1903 newspaper article indicated that Mr. Ireland was previously a journalist and former literary critic of the New York Tribune. He was also a veteran teacher and principal in the public schools of Long Branch and Asbury Park, New Jersey.[280]

When "Pap" Ireland, as he was called, arrived in 1890 as a teacher of the 5th through the 8th grades, the Tenley School had been in its large, new brick building for eight years. The first four grades were on the first floor, the upper four grades on the second floor. But the school had only 80 pupils and was struggling to gain a reputation as a good school.

Because Mr. Ireland was an excellent teacher, with high standards, the Tenley School and its students quickly became a source of pride to the village. By 1903, there were 350 students and nine teachers, and Mr. Ireland had become the principal. The school building had been doubled in size in 1896.

William B. Ireland was also called "Professor" Ireland by his students and their parents. His cultured speaking voice and impatience with indolent students gained the respect of the people of Tenleytown. Many of the younger children were quite frightened of him because of his reputation for strictness, but his discipline was supposedly a good influence on the Tenleytown boys. As the 1903 journalist reports,

> "Years ago the juvenile male population of Tenleytown, before its surplus energy was diverted in these more useful channels, used to spend its time, week day and Sabbath, in playing marbles on the streets, and thus gradually acquiring habits of loafing, and even more pernicious ones. To counteract this tendency a boys' club was organized six years ago by Principal Ireland, and never choosing a more pretentious title than 'The Boys,' has grown to an active membership of 100."[281]

Ireland was a tall, slender man with a bald pate. His rimless glasses sat on a large nose, and if he ever smiled, it was not discernible under his large, drooping mustache; only his twinkling eyes gave him away.

As his obituary writer said,

> "Prof. Ireland was responsible for many of the more modern, up-to-date methods now in vogue in the public school system in Washington, and his influence and efforts, particularly in regard to the Tenleytown

PROFESSOR W.B. IRELAND

(Photo from 1909 Masonic program, c/o Edna Riley Snoots)

"Pap" Ireland, as he was called, served as teacher and principal in the Tenley School from 1890 until 1910. He died in 1912, at about 65 years of age.

school in recent years, were largely responsible for its growth and development along broader educational lines."[282]

"Pap" Ireland lived for many years with Mr. and Mrs. Eli Riley in their large house just across the Pike from the school. Later he roomed and boarded with Mrs. Alice Hunt at the house on Gloria Point, 4509 Wisconsin Avenue. He retired from Tenley in 1910 and was succeeded as principal by Miss Helen Walsh. He lived at the Gloria Point house until his death of pneumonia on February 22, 1912. He lay in state at the Singleton Lodge before his body was returned to Long Branch, New Jersey, for burial. Professor Ireland, who was about 65 at the time of his death, had never married.

The Reno Elementary School for black children in Tenleytown was built in 1903, replacing a frame schoolhouse on Grant Road. This building still stands behind the Alice Deal Junior High School. This view is of the east side of the school, facing Howard Road.

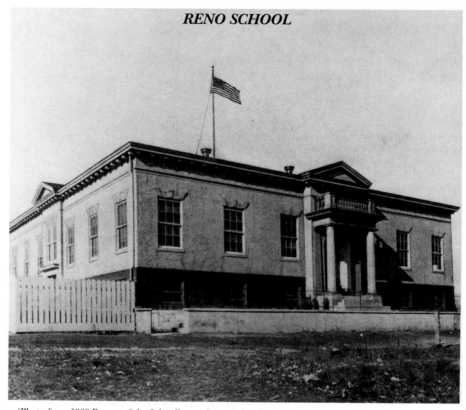

RENO SCHOOL

(Photo from 1908 <u>Report of the Schoolhouse Commission</u>, in the Washingtoniana Collection, Martin Luther King Memorial Library)

Maggie Callahan

Margaret G. (Miss Maggie) Callahan taught various grades at Tenley School, beginning in 1895. Maggie was the daughter of Mike Callahan, an Irish immigrant who had "made good money hauling gravel from Rock Creek in the old days."[283]

It was legend that Maggie Callahan had walked to school from her country home on Brookeville Road in Maryland, first to Dr. Chappell's early school, then all the way to Western High School—this was before there were streetcars on Connecticut Avenue—and then to teachers' college at Wilson Normal.

She was a heavy-set woman, about six feet tall, and always wore a white shirtwaist and long black skirt. Her eyes were blue and her grey hair was pulled up in a knot on top of her head. (See St. Ann's photo, Chapter IV.)

Maggie's large hands and feet were part of the legend. One story goes that Buzz Curran once drew two great big feet on the sidewalk at Grant Road and Wisconsin—and next to the picture he wrote the words "Sluefoot Mag." Miss Callahan came upon Buzz just as he was finishing his work of art—and "she knocked him clean across Grant Road." From then on her reputation was such that she had only to ask, "See this hand?" and she got immediate obedience.

There were some children, however, who had been raised by more delicate women and were so frightened of the stern, rough ways of Miss

THE IMMACULATA SEMINARY, 1930

(Photo from <u>The Book of Washington</u>, 1930)

Callahan that they hated going to school. Louise Voigt Moreland recalls that her sister refused to go back to school after the day Maggie Callahan picked up a rock off her desk and said, "I'm going to throw this at you cabbage-heads!" Mrs. Voigt soon transferred her daughters to the Chevy Chase School.

But Miss Maggie was appreciated and even loved by most of her students. She believed strongly in fairness, and would not let one child take advantage of another. She went out of her way to help the backward child, and knew how to inspire the best students to high achievements. As Flora Brown said, "The children of Tenleytown were generally not very knowledgeable. She educated them."

Maggie Callahan moved in with Dr. Chappell's family on Grant Road and lived there until her death of a heart attack in 1916, at age 50. A Catholic, she attended St. Ann's Church and was buried at St. John's Cemetery, Forest Glen.[284]

Jesse Lee Reno School

The old yellow-painted Grant Road school was abandoned by black students in 1903, but was occupied at least as late as the 1920s by Mr. Withers, an elderly white man who was superintendent of the county roads. Mr. William Myers, a janitor at the Tenley School, also lived there with his family for a while before it was torn down for construction of the Ben Murch School and playground in 1929-30.

The new Jesse Lee Reno School for black children was constructed on Howard Road in 1903. The school accommodated a kindergarten and grades 1-8; upon graduation, students went downtown, mostly to Armstrong High School, from 9th grade on.

The stucco-faced Reno School, which still stands as of this writing, originally had three or four large classrooms on the main floor, and at least four large rooms on the lower level—used for home economics and shop classes, assemblies, activities or

The Immaculata Preparatory School and College still stands on the west side of Tenley Circle. It was built in 1905.

139

WILLIAM TYLER PAGE

(Photo from Myrtle Cheney Murdock, <u>The American's Creed and William Tyler Page</u>, Washington, 1958)

William Tyler Page, author of "The American's Creed," was a vestryman and choir director at St. Columba's Church. He lived in nearby Friendship Heights, where Wisconsin Avenue crosses the District line into Maryland.

games, and storage. Because there were not enough class-rooms, teachers, or children to have a separate room for each grade, as many as two or three classes might be held in one room.

An early principal of the Reno School was Mr. Shippen, of Anacostia. The principal after 1908 was Miss Violet Tibbs; she also taught grades 5 through 8. She stayed on at Reno until she retired. Miss Gertrude Tibbs, Miss McEady, Miss Bates, Miss Donnell, Miss Fortune, Miss Hawkins, and Miss Martha Crumwell were other teachers. [285]

Private and Parochial Schools Reopened

In 1905 James Cardinal Gibbons of Baltimore asked the Sisters of Providence of St. Mary of the Woods, Indiana, to set up a school in Tenleytown. The hill on the west side of Wisconsin Avenue on which the school was built was called Mount Marian, and the school was named the Immaculata Preparatory School.

The first students enrolled were Gloria Hunt, who lived in the big house at Gloria Point, and Bessie Freeman, of 2319 Wisconsin Avenue. It was a "select and high priced school."

A St. Ann's School had existed from 1870 to 1896; it was re-established in 1905 by the Sisters of Providence, especially for boys and girls of the local Roman Catholic parish.

The old Dumblane house behind Immaculata eventually came to be the Dunblane Elementary School. The Immaculata Preparatory School and Immaculata College still stand at Tenley Circle.

William Tyler Page

William Tyler Page was a very highly respected and popular figure from Capitol Hill. He had started his career at the age of 13 as a page in the House of Representatives, and eventually became, in 1919, Clerk of the House.

During his 61 years on Capitol Hill, Page served under 11 Presidents—from Chester A. Arthur to Franklin D. Roosevelt. He never attended a university, but read avidly and took many correspondence courses over the years. He was respected as a man of learning, especially about the organization and functions of the federal legislative bodies. [286]

William Tyler Page and his wife, Mary Anna, moved to a large house in Friendship Heights in 1905, and began their association with St. Alban's Episcopal Mission in Tenleytown, now called St. Columba's. Page became choir director in 1907 and his wife was the organist; they had five children, all of whom attended St. Columba's. Page was elected first Senior Warden of the vestry of the church in 1924.

It was in 1918 that William Tyler Page became nationally famous. He had learned of a contest to write an American's creed; and, one May day in 1917, walking home from church along Wisconsin Avenue, he thought of fashioning such a creed along the lines of the Apostles Creed he had just recited. Basing the text on the American historical documents that he had studied for years, Page eventually formulated a 100-word

American's Creed and submitted it as an entry in the national contest.

He was informed in March 1918 that he was the winner; and his was from then on a name recognized nationally, and especially known to every person on Capitol Hill, in Friendship Heights, and in Tenleytown.

The American's Creed

I believe in the United States of America as a government of the people, by the people, for the people, whose just powers are derived from the consent of the governed; a democracy in a Republic; a sovereign Nation of many sovereign States; a perfect Union, one and inseparable; established upon those principles of freedom, equality, justice, and humanity, for which American patriots sacrificed their lives and fortunes.

I therefore believe it is my duty to my Country to love it; to support its Constitution; to obey its laws; to respect its flag, and to defend it against all enemies.

—William Tyler Page

Father Mallon

Father Joseph C. Mallon was rector of St. Ann's Roman Catholic Church from 1902 until 1910. Under his pastorate a lovely stone church was built for the congregation of 200; the parochial school grew in size and reputation; and the influence of this church was felt throughout Tenleytown in the person of Father Mallon.

He lived across the street from St. Ann's in the frame house on the southeast corner of Wisconsin and Grant Road. When a new rectory was built at the northwest corner of Wisconsin and Yuma, Father Mallon and his mother moved into it.

Father Mallon cared for the poor in person—he'd take Mr. O'Day's unsold vegetables around to people who had little to eat. He'd ask Dr. Chappell or Dr. Ray to go with him to make sick calls. And he'd accompany Miss Ada Poore of Grant Road on visits to poor blacks at Fort Reno.

A young man from Rhode Island, Will Stanton, lived with Father Mallon for many years while attending the Georgetown College School of Medicine. Father Mallon, who was a cousin of the Stantons, was as proud as any father when young Will became a prominent physician in Washington.

In 1910, Father Mallon moved to Baltimore and was succeeded by the Reverend Thomas Smyth.

Miss Ada Poore

When her mother died in 1900, Ada Poore was 20 years old. There were four older brothers and sisters who were already married. But, in addition to Ada, there were seven younger ones at home to care for. So she helped her father raise the rest of the family.

Over the years Miss Ada Poore became a legend, not only at St. Ann's, where she was a devout worshiper and choir member, but also throughout Tenleytown. She was tireless in service to others, active in civic affairs, charitable in her personal relations, and a model for many in the neighborhood. As soon as she heard that a family needed something in the way of food, clothing, or household items, she or her fellow parishioners at St. Ann's would provide them.

Miss Ada never married, but continued to live in the Poore home on Grant Road until her death in 1962.

(Photos c/o Clara Poore Broderick)

Top: Father Joseph C. Mallon in 1897. The rector of St. Ann's Catholic Church from 1902 until 1910, he was a very popular figure in the neighborhood.

Bottom: Miss Ada Poore in 1959. Miss Ada lived all her life on Grant Road, and devoted it to her family, her church, and her neighbors.

John Bernard Harry built this house on River Road about 1906, for his family of two boys and four girls.

(1975 photos by Judith Helm)

The Pernas, stonemasons from Italy, built these houses in the 4100 block of Chesapeake Street about 1910.

J. Bernard Harry

John Bernard Harry, one of Tenleytown's most successful businessmen, was a member of the fifth generation in the Tenleytown area through the Nevitt branch of his family tree. He was born in 1867 in a house on the east side of the Rockville Pike, where Albemarle Street now intersects Wisconsin.

Although he was eventually an active Methodist, Bernard was baptized by and named after Father Bernard Maguire, Jesuit president of Georgetown College and a friend of his mother's family. Bernard Harry was able to attend the Grant Road school only until he was 12, when he went to work on a nearby farm, pitching hay 10 hours a day for $5 a week. Bernard also worked as a custodian at St. Ann's for 25¢ a week until he had earned enough to buy his first suit of clothes. Another story goes that he used to whitewash inside plaster walls for 50¢ a day.

Whatever Bernard Harry's early work experience, he eventually became one of Tenleytown's most prosperous and legendary sons. He worked at Edward Brooke's grocery stall at the old Center Market as a teenager; and in 1887, when he was 20, he and Mr. Brooke opened Brooke & Harry's grocery store on 20th Street between G and H, N.W. The Brooke & Harry Manufacturing Co. (ice house and bakery) became the Tenley Ice Company, which delivered to Tenleytown area customers. It was located behind the Masonic Temple in Tenleytown.

In the early years of the 20th century Brooke & Harry's grocery was well known for selling the very finest meats and vegetables. Personalized service and home delivery made Brooke & Harry's the favorite of many Washingtonians, including some of the most prominent of their day.

J. Bernard Harry was 105 when he died in 1972.

Old Families Die Out

By the turn of the century, many members of the old original Tenleytown families had passed on. The Lightfoot, Nourse, Murdock, and Lyles families still had a few members living in their old Tenley area homes.

Barbara Lightfoot and her widowed sister Mary Ann Britt continued to live in the very old Tennally house on the east side of the Rockville Pike. In 1899 the roof of the house had been raised and dormers installed. The new police sub-station had been built just next door.

The Tennally family graves were located in the spacious back yard; but as the years passed, grass and dirt covered the flat gravestones, so that they became obscured.[287] Cedar trees grew in a line near the graves; there was a large flower garden and a lily pond stocked with goldfish.[288] The elderly sisters welcomed the local children inside for tea and cookies, to play the player piano, to visit with their little black dog, and to talk to the pet parrot, who had a shameless vocabulary.

The Nourses were still at home at "The Highlands," 3825 Wisconsin Avenue, into the 20th century. Three of the unmarried children of Charles and Rebecca Nourse stayed in the house, and lived to be quite elderly. Rosa died in 1902, at age 79; Mary died in 1908, at age 91; and "Mr. Jim," as he was called, lived until 1917, the year of his 89th birthday. He was the last member of his generation of a family known throughout the area—and especially at St. Alban's—for its devotion to Christian service of others.

The Nourse property was no longer an active farm after about 1910, and large portions were sold off. The old mansion house, begun in 1817, fell into disrepair. In about

1911 Mr. Jim moved out and the house was rented for many years. It was sold in the 1920s to Admiral Cary T. Grayson and was later bought by the Sidwell Friends School.

By 1916, "The Highlands" was obscured from the road by a stone wall and many trees, bushes, and vines. And Wisconsin Avenue, once a quiet country road, had become a busy thoroughfare.[289]

In 1869 the old Jesuit College Villa had been discontinued and the property on the west side of the pike was rented to a variety of tenants. The house and 64 acres were sold for $60,000 in 1887.[290] The buyer, Anastasia Patten, resold it for $110,000 to a "group of Virginians."

In 1898 millionaire John R. McLean bought the Villa, with 43 acres of land, and named the estate "Friendship." The house itself was actually on the land grant "Terra Firma," not on "Friendship."

When Massachusetts Avenue was extended beyond American University in 1913, the old "Friendship" house west of

(Photo from "The Rambler," The Star, January 3, 1915; glass plate c/o The Columbia Historical Society)

THE TENNALLY-LIGHTFOOT HOUSE

Porches had been added to the Tennally-Lightfoot house on Wisconsin Avenue by the time this photo was taken in 1913. Note the unpaved street and streetcar tracks in front of the house; the sidewalk seems to have been paved, however. In later years, stucco was applied to the outside of the house. It was torn down in the 1950s and Hechinger's expanded its lumberyard onto the site.

AREA POINTS OF INTEREST IN 1901

(Photos from "Suburban Washington As a Place of Residence," Citizens Northwest Suburban Association, 1901)

1. W.K. Ryan's house, "Dumbarton," which later became part of the Academy of the Holy Cross, east of Connecticut Ave. House was torn down.

2. Residence of John B. Nourse, "The Highlands." Now Sidwell Friends School.

3. Pierce Shoemaker house on Pierce Mill Rd (now Tilden St). Still standing.

4. Pierce's Mill, still standing at Rock Creek.

5. "Clifton Manor," the home of Charles C. Lancaster, formerly the home of James Wormley. It was on Pierce Mill Rd, east of Wisconsin.

Loughborough Road was torn down. The house had been sold by Murdock descendants in 1887 to James Davis; his daughter Achsah Davis in turn had sold the property to the American University founders in 1890.

Miss Mariamne Murdock died in 1914; and her married sister, Mrs. Louisa Childs, had no children, so the Murdock name—at least in this branch—died with them. The old Murdock Mill had long since fallen into ruin, and only the name Murdock Mill Road has lasted into the 1980s.

Also gone from Tenleytown was the Lyles-Magruder family. Mrs. Arianna Lyles had died in 1888 at "The Rest." The house was willed to a granddaughter, Eleanor Marshall Magruder, who raised her four children in the house. In 1902 an arti-

cle[291] appeared in a local newspaper, which described the history of "The Rest," the family that had lived in it for many years, and the valuable heirlooms on display in the house. The writer based much of his story on a personal visit to the house and an interview with Mrs. Magruder.

George Corbin Washington Magruder, her husband, was a surveyor with the Nicaraguan Canal Commission. Their oldest son, Bruce Magruder, was an officer of the D.C. National Guard, and owned the Guard mascot, a monkey named Meeko. Meeko could often be seen climbing out the window of the tower of the Magruder house and onto a rope strung between the branches of the tall old trees in the south yard.

In 1905 Mrs. Magruder died, at the age of 52. Her husband was at the time working in Oklahoma and her children had moved away. Unfortunately, the untended house was stripped of most of its valuable furnishings. Some were eventually reclaimed by the family, but most were lost forever.

Widower George C.W. Magruder moved to Oklahoma, and the old house was deeded to his daughter, Eleanor. In 1914 it was rented to Pinkney Cross of the D.C. Fire Department. Lt. Cross bought the house in 1920.

The Appeal of Tenleytown

A 1901 booklet, "Suburban Washington as a Place of Residence," was published under the auspices of a committee of the "Citizens Northwest Suburban Association," founded in 1892. The committee consisted of a group of prominent businessmen who wanted to encourage the purchase of year-round homes in this "magnificent region of rolling hills rising some 400 feet above the Potomac and diversified with numerous charming valleys, fields, woods, and ravines."

Here is a description of this area as viewed by The Rambler in the early 1900s:

"At this place [River Road and Murdock Mill Road] the panorama of the valley is unfolded to you. The view to the west is bounded by the range of hills close up under the base of which runs Little Falls Branch . . . . Looking down the valley, the eye passes the hills where shines the receiving reservoir and on to the hills that rise across the Potomac in Virginia. It is a pleasing prospect . . . ."[292]

The flowery promotional booklet quoted Dr. W. W. Johnston, "a physician of national reputation," who said that there was no more healthful region in the neighborhood of Washington than the northwest part of Washington county; it is "an elevated tableland overlooking the city with a rapid fall south and east" that insures perfect drainage, as well as pure air and "all the other necessary adjuncts to healthful country residences." Dr. Johnston also pointed out the remarkable longevity of the Pierces, Shoemakers, Greens, Nourses, and others in the "northwest suburbs" as being indicative of the healthful climate.

But the greatest appeal to the prospective home builder was the "fact that land in this beautiful suburb may yet be purchased by the acre at prices no greater than must be paid for single building lots" of 25 x 100 feet in a good location in the city—and here one can find "a well-lighted suburban street within 25 minutes ride of the White House," where one can "erect thereon a handsome and commodious home."

THE FOUNDERS OF ROBEYVILLE

(Photo c/o Allan Robey)

Robeyville

One group of new arrivals was the James Robey family from Merrifield, Virginia (Fairfax County). James Robey came about 1893 at the suggestion of his friend Edward W. Parks, a blacksmith, who told him about the new construction work and the large amount of land available.

A cabinetmaker, Jim Robey had two daughters and seven sons, all nearing maturity and most of the boys entering the construction trades also—carpenters, builders, contractors, plasterers, painters. Six of the nine children married local Tenleytown young people; the oldest, Fred Robey, married a Walther girl in 1893.

The Robey brothers of Tenleytown were all in the construction trades. Here three of the brothers pose with their father (and an unidentified man) in front of a house they were building. L to R: Harvey Robey, unknown man, James Robey (father), Elmer Robey, and Fred Robey.

Not pictured were Albert, Lonnie, Millard, Bernard, and sisters Virgie and Effie.

(Photo c/o Lelia Poore Spandou)

James Robey on front porch of his house in 4400 block of Alton Place, known as "Robeyville."

DEVELOPMENT OF AREA AROUND TENLEYTOWN CIRCA 1916

Robeyville is delineated as the second of two east-west blocks south of Murdock Mill Rd. Today the 4400 block of Alton Place (Robeyville) is surrounded by American University Park brick homes built after World War II.

Widowsville was the name given to the area along Wisconsin Avenue around Pierce Mill Road and Loughborough Road (Van Ness St.) intersections.

Reno was the highly populated area northeast of Tenleytown. On the site of the former Civil War fort, it was an integrated community.

In about 1905, the Robeys acquired land just east of the Walther house, off Murdock Mill Road. They proceeded to lay out a street—called Asbury Place (no doubt after Methodist Bishop Francis Asbury)—and to build, in conjunction with realtor Tom Giles, modest Victorian-style houses for themselves and for others on both sides of that street. The houses were frame or pebbledash over frame.

The Robeys anticipated a housing boom in the area around the new Methodist American University, believing that new streets and developments were on the way—and in the spirit of anticipated prosperity, named their little development Asbury Park. [The new Methodist University also influenced the naming of (John) Wesley Heights on the other side of Massachusetts Avenue.]

The Robeys' expectations eventually did come true. "Asbury Park"—now the 4400 block of Alton Place—is completely surrounded by streets and houses; but because of a depression in the financial and building business, they were 20 years ahead of the other developers of American University Park.

For two decades, the little one-block unpaved street remained isolated from the rest of Tenleytown—and it came to be called not Asbury Park, but "Robeyville" or even "Robeytown."

Even as late as 1925, there were cornfields and cow pastures surrounding Robeyville. Only a few houses on Albemarle Street, built in the early '20s, some scattered homes on Murdock Mill Road, the Enders' old red house on Yuma, and a couple of farmhouses on 46th Street kept it company.

Widowsville

Another area near Tenleytown had a distinctive name of its own—"Widowsville." This was the name given to the little collection of houses and stores on both sides of Wisconsin Avenue and Loughborough Road where they intersected and where Pierce Mill Road came in from the east (now Wisconsin and Van Ness).

It is popularly assumed that Widowsville (really pronounced Widdesville) came to be named because a large number of widows

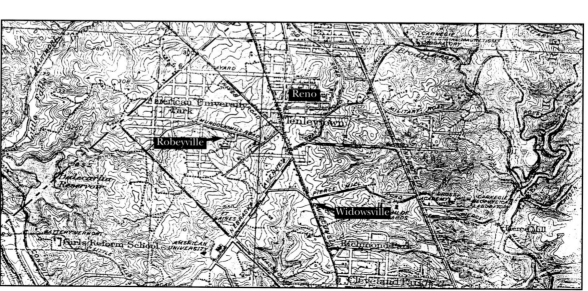

(Map from U.S. Geological Survey)

lived there. In any case, the name Widowsville was used by everyone to distinguish from Tenleytown that separate crossroads community, with its own store (Norris's) and blacksmith (Fitzgerald). Isaac Shoemaker even had a small inn there at one time, about where the new Tenley Mall office building has been built at 4200 Wisconsin Avenue.

The Widowsville community was also much closer than Tenleytown to the Nourses, the McLean estate, the old Loughborough place (which became a country club in the 20th century), and the few country estates along Pierce Mill Road.

One of the families in Widowsville was that of Alexander Yowell, a printer who worked downtown during the week but also was a photographer with a successful weekend business at an outdoor studio below the Cabin John Bridge—he took tintype photos of cyclists and others out for a day trip. The Yowells lived in part of Isaac Shoemaker's house and inn on Wisconsin Avenue after the latter moved up to Tenleytown.

Real Estate Developed Slowly

The construction of houses in and around Tenleytown was something that came in spurts and here and there. By 1905, there were a good many houses along Wisconsin Avenue, Grant Road, Belt Road, and on streets on Fort Reno—especially on Des Moines (later Davenport) Street. River Road still had scattered farmhouses, as did Murdock Mill Road, Loughborough Road, Pierce Mill Road, and the new Connecticut Avenue. In 1905 the population in and around Tenleytown was estimated at nearly 1,000 or a little over 200 households.

In the 1890s most of the dwellings at Fort Reno were small and cheaply constructed. Twenty

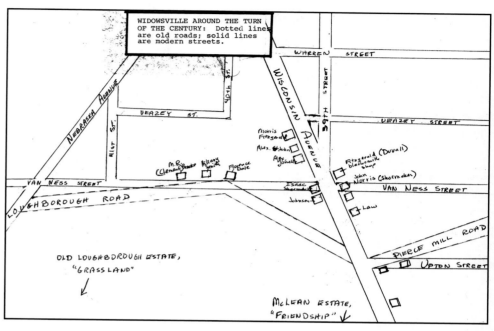

(Sketch by Judith Helm)

years later, these houses were aptly described as shacks. But larger and more substantial houses replaced and interspersed the shacks, until by the 1920s the Fort was quite changed in appearance.

Although a large number of Tenleytowners were in business for themselves—either in the village or in Georgetown or Washington— there were a growing number of men, often sons of immigrant craftsmen, who supplied labor and skills for the construction of new houses and buildings. Many were independent contractors; others were hired by local builders and developers.

Carpenters, plasterers, painters, tinners, and roofers were rarely short of work in the early 1900s. Most had come from rural Maryland and Virginia, where they had been unable to find work. Owners of horse teams and heavy equipment used in clearing land and for excavating foundations were also constantly employed after the building boom began.

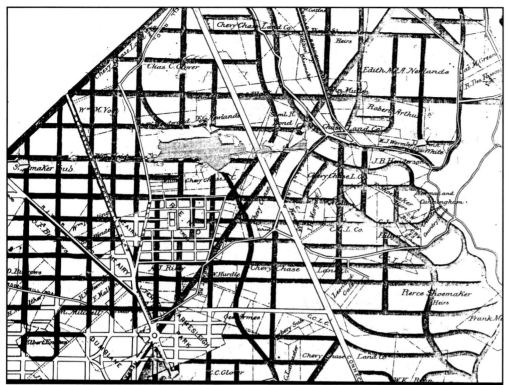

(Map of the District of Columbia, publ. by Thos. J. Fisher & Co., 1900; prepared by Andrew B. Graham)

Heavy lines show planned streets in 1900. Many were never cut in.

This was written in 1903 about Tenleytown:

> "The whole life of the town is marked by a spirit of municipal self-improvement which is displayed in every line of activity. There is no stagnation; no 'moss backism;' everything is making for progress and everyone is an enthusiastic factor in the development of the town's best interests."[293]

One of the most enthusiastic purveyors of progress in Tenleytown was Thomas J. Giles, brother of Police Lt. James Giles, and the first certified local realtor. In front of Tom Giles' little office on Wisconsin Avenue was a sign, "We Sell the Earth"; he also had an office downtown at 10th and F. Tom Giles kept busy—mostly west of Wisconsin Avenue—buying and selling properties, building and remodeling houses, and acting as broker for others' sales and rentals. George A. Armes and Hiliary Smith, later, were also two of the busiest real estate agents in Tenleytown.

As housing developments started nearby, before World War I, Tenleytown began to lose its identity. In addition to the large and affluent neighborhoods of Cleveland Park and Chevy Chase, there were University Park, Wisconsin Avenue Park, and Friendship Heights. New investors, ignorant of Tenleytown's historic past, referred to the neighborhood only as "Friendship."

University Park

At the same time as the Citizens Northwest Suburban Association was promoting the area for prospective buyers, the American University Park development was being initiated by James L. Tait and Augustus B. Omwake.

Tait and Omwake subdivided 170 acres of farmland south of River Road, from Brandywine to Fessenden and from 46th to 49th Streets—actually more than a mile from the American University site. There are still two stone fences at 46th and Davenport that marked the western entrance into the development known as University Park. The earliest accesses to the development were from either River Road or Murdock Mill Road; Massachusetts Avenue did not extend out to 46th Street until many years later. Croissant and Ferguson also developed a section called American University Heights.

Another couple of developers of American University Park were Charles P. Stone and Charles W. Fairfax, who were ingenious enough to provide Herdic bus service from the livery stable near the streetcar stop at Gloria Point down Murdock Mill Road or River Road to the new development—for not many prospective buyers traveled any way but by streetcar.

But the buyers did not come as fast and as eagerly as was hoped. Even as late as 1910, there was still only about one house per block in University Park. The streets in the development remained unpaved.

A 1910 <u>Star</u> article said that "the ruins of Fort Bayard were visible until last fall, when they were leveled by a purchaser of the fort site who intended building a fine house there, but which has not yet been built . . . . The fort site is now a part of American University Park." A Rambler article that same year mentioned a cluster of frame houses at the point where the District line crosses River Road.

The newly-cut road along the District line, replacing the old Shoemakers' lane, was called Boundary Avenue (now Western Avenue), and new streets were being built in every direction. Until this time the District line had been an indistinct border marked by boundary stones at one-mile intervals all around the city.

A wandering Brookeville Road (Belt Road) had been the only connection between Chevy Chase Circle and Wisconsin Avenue; and Willard Avenue and the Shoemakers' driveways had meandered from Friendship Heights westward to River Road.

But in 1907 Fred E. Woodward sounded the alarm in his "Ramble Along Boundary Stones":

"To this secluded spot have now come the surveyors with transit and steel tape and they, followed by the axe men, have carved a broad lane through the massive woods, and 'Boundary Avenue' with various intersecting streets will soon be its near neighbors, and houses and people will congregate, in its vicinity.

"Too soon, alas! will the change come for the true lover of nature, which ushers in the days of 'boom sub-divisions,' garish cottages and doubtful joys, and drives him still further afield if he wishes to commune with nature."[294]

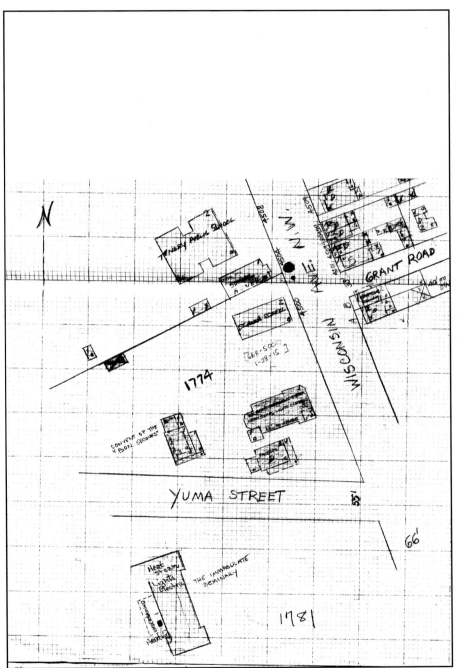

(Map copied by Priscilla McNeil)

Before Nebraska Avenue and Albemarle Street were cut in. Sanborn, Vol. I, Insurance Maps of D.C. 1903 (Tenleytown additions 1909 and 1913).

(Photo from "Suburban Washington As a Place of Residence," 1901)

(1974 photo by J. Russo)

AN EARLY HOME IN UNIVERSITY PARK

Top: Residence of developer James L. Tait.

Bottom: 4628 48th Street, the James Tait house in University Park.

Moving Houses

One common aspect of 1910 housing was the moving of houses from one place to another. Not only were new streets and developments being cut in that forced the moving of individual homes; but there were also an amazing number of houses that were moved great distances from their original sites.

The usual method of moving a house was to jack it up off its foundation, slide a large wheeled platform of girders underneath, and employ from 8 to 16 horses in the task of pulling it by cables, foot by foot, over fields, driveways, and roads. Not only did the ground traversed have to be reasonably level and free of holes, boulders, or stumps; the air space above also had to be free of trees, buildings, and power, telephone, and trolley lines.

Moving a house was accomplished in a day only if the distance was short and the barriers few. But moving a house a few blocks often took a few weeks. Sometimes the family would occupy the house at night while the horses rested midway. On other occasions, however, night-time might be the only time a large house could be moved—there would be no traffic to obstruct; and if necessary, the telephone, trolley, and power lines could be moved temporarily without disrupting customers.

Often when a new street was cut through, it meant moving or tearing down houses. Forty-first Street near the point of Wisconsin and Belt, for example, at one time began at Davenport Street and continued northward only. When Western (Boundary) Avenue was cut through, houses on the District-Maryland line were moved to one side or the other.

The cutting in of Nebraska Avenue from Van Ness Street north to Tenley Circle, on to Connecticut Avenue and beyond in the early 1930s, also caused the moving or destruction of many houses on Grant Road and other streets. And the building of Van Ness and Upton Streets east of Wisconsin obliterated Pierce Mill Road and most of its houses.

The Gloria Point House and Alice Hunt

Mrs. Alexander C. Hunt and her daughter Gloria lived on at "Gloria Point" after the death of the Governor (see Chapter IV). Gloria graduated from Immaculata Seminary in its first class in 1909, at age 18; she had been the first child enrolled, in 1905. Her mother, Alice Hunt, an educated woman, was described by many people as being "most peculiar," and the two women and their unusual "Gloria Point" house were viewed with much interest.

Mrs. Hunt continued to make structural changes and built additions to the large house. She took in some roomers, including Professor Ireland, principal of the Tenley School, and other teachers. Mrs. Hunt's friends included Mrs. E.D.E.N. Southworth, a noted writer who lived in Georgetown.

Gloria and her mother moved to Washington city in 1915. Gloria died of pneumonia in 1918, and her mother died in 1920. Four years after her death, photographs by Alice Underwood Hunt of black women at the Center Market were published in records of the Columbia Historical Society.[295]

The name Gloria Point continued, and is used even today by people who never knew about the Hunts. The beautiful old turreted, faded red frame house was used for years as a rooming and apartment house. It was called the Hilltop Hotel and Mount Airy as well as the Gloria

HOUSES THAT WERE MOVED

(1973 photo by Judith Helm)

(1979 photo by Judith Helm)

(1974 photo by John Russo)

Top: Samuel Burrows farmhouse moved from River Rd to 4624 Verplanck Place.

Middle: Wise/Walker house moved from Wisconsin Ave to 3908 Windom.

Bottom: Curran/Christian house moved from Naval Observatory site about 1890, to 3837 Albemarle (at Grant Road).

Point Hotel. Its front porch faced south, with the main entrance gate on the Wisconsin Avenue side of the triangle. An old water trough for horses was still in use on the River Road side of the point after the turn of the century.

The Gloria Point house, 4546 Wisconsin Avenue, was torn down about 1927, and a number of gas stations have occupied the site for the past 50 years.

Wisconsin Avenue Park

The second large-scale housing subdivision (after University Park) was advertised in 1909, on land that had been owned by Samuel Queen, Samuel Wendel, and William Heider. It was called Wisconsin Avenue Park, and was bounded by Wisconsin Avenue on the west, Harrison Street on the north, Belt Road on the east, and Davenport on the south.

Garrison and Harrison Streets were cut through to Wisconsin by 1912. In 1906 the new Reno Road had been built from Keokuk Street (Military Road) to Fessenden Street (Fort Reno). It was not continued south until some time later.

Wisconsin Avenue Park agents advertised in the 1909 Masonic dedication program as follows:

"City sewer, city water, city gas. Price 10¢ per square foot and up. Prices to be advanced when 50 lots are sold; only eleven left at these prices. Free certificates of title, no interest, easy terms."

By 1916 more than 100 houses had been built, ranging in cost from $4,000 for the most modest to $12,000 for the largest.[296]

Naming the Streets

As new streets were cut in the Tenley area, they were given names according to a system devised in the 1890s. American cities, bodies of water, and prominent men were the source of the alphabetical names. Cities included Warren, Yuma, Alton, Appleton, Davenport, and Keokuk.

Albemarle, Brandywine, Chesapeake, and Cumberland Streets were named after bodies of water. Other streets were named after Americans such as Andrew Ellicott, William P. (or Reginald A.) Fessenden, William L. Garrison, Benjamin (or William Henry) Harrison, and Daniel of St. Thomas Jenifer.

The old country roads kept their names, whether they were named after people—such as Grant Road and Loughborough Road—or destinations—such as Brookeville Road, Pierce Mill Road, and Murdock Mill Road. But eventually the northern part of Loughborough Road, often misspelled and mispronounced, became Nebraska Avenue.

Friendship Heights

The extension of the streetcar line beyond Tenleytown made possible the development of another new suburban community, Friendship Heights. This settlement of frame Victorian houses was begun by Henry W. Offutt, just northwest of the intersection of the Rockville Pike and Willard Avenue on the Maryland side of the District line.[297] The property had been owned mainly by the Shoemaker and Eld families.

Friendship Heights attracted affluent government employees and city businessmen, mostly newcomers to Washington. William Tyler Page was its most famous resident. A development within Friendship Heights was Albert E. Shoemaker's eastern section, The Hills; Somerset and Drummond were other large residential areas developed to the west and north.

Because of a lack of organized community planning, the village of Friendship Heights did not attain the growth, beauty, or cohesiveness of Chevy Chase, its suburban neighbor to the east. Although Friendship Heights eventually had an elementary school, now called Somerset Elementary, and a waiting station for the streetcar line, it had no stores in the early days, and no church or other community building, even though by 1915 there were about 50 homes.

Streetcars, Continued

In 1911 Dorothea Thompson wrote to her friend Lula Johnson:

"Tenleytown is still the same old place. The [street] cars still run where the sidewalks ought to be and the pedestrians still take the street, or rather, the clay road."

The electric streetcars that replaced the horse-drawn cars brought greater efficiency and many improvements in comfort, but the introduction of overhead wires as the means of conducting power brought a new eyesore to the main street of Tenleytown. The black trolley wires were strung over two parallel tracks, and then the new telephone poles were erected right between the two sets of tracks. Electricity poles and wires, in addition, were strung along the east side of the avenue—all in all, a great overhead network!

The electric power was conducted from the powerhouse through the overhead wires, and the metal bar, or trolley pole, sliding along those wires above the streetcar brought the current into the vehicle's motor. (Overhead wires were forbidden in Georgetown and Washington city, and so the streetcars were switched to an underground conductor rail.) The mischievous Tenleytown boys liked nothing better than jumping on the back of the streetcar when it stopped at Grant Road and pulling the trolley connection off so it would not move.

A new concrete, fireproof powerhouse and carbarn were built by 1903 on Wisconsin Avenue between Harrison and Jenifer, within two blocks of the District-Maryland line. This powerhouse generated electricity necessary for the car line extensions into Maryland, and housed the streetcars overnight and when they were in for repairs. A bus lot and terminal are now on the site of the original carbarn.

Some time after 1909, the frame "Tennallytown carbarn" on lower Wisconsin Avenue was closed and torn down. Calvert Street was eventually cut through (east to Observatory Circle) near where the old carbarn stood.

It took 25 minutes to travel from Tenleytown to the heart of the District by streetcar—30 minutes if you started at the District line, Friendship Heights. In 1901, six streetcar tickets sold for 15¢. Soon the fare was upped to 8¢ a ride.

Local drivers included Grover C. Daniels and Hartsell O. Bowman, who knew everybody on the Wisconsin Avenue route. Mr. and Mrs. Bowman had a tourist home and rooming house on Wisconsin Avenue near Harrison, where many unmarried motormen lived.

The streetcars usually ran every half hour in either direction. The morning newspapers were dropped off at Grant Road by one of the first cars out of Georgetown. The paper boy picked them up there and delivered them to the local subscribers. Young Ray Johnson delivered the afternoon Star to about 50 customers in 1906.

A freight streetcar left Georgetown daily about 11 a.m. and made deliveries to Tenleytown stops prior to the noontime meal. A similar freight car ran from the city along Connecticut Avenue to Chevy Chase.

STREETCAR BARN AND POWERHOUSE, WISCONSIN AVENUE AT INGOMAR STREET

(1909 photo c/o LeRoy O. King)

(Photo c/o Columbia Historical Society)

Top: Carbarn and powerhouse on Wisconsin Avenue, west side. Note overhead web of trolley wires, as well as tracks on west side of street.

Bottom: Interior view of Wisconsin Avenue carbarn, about 1914. Three of the cars have destinations "District Line."

(Photo c/o George Eiker)

The Tenleytown postman making his rounds. Charles Eiker poses on his horse "Billy." This photo was taken between 1910 and 1914 near Mr. Eiker's home on upper Wisconsin Avenue, just south of the District line.

Although the earliest electric cars on Wisconsin Avenue had their destinations painted on the sides, changeable signs eventually came into use, and "Tennallytown" was the first northern designation used. A 1914 photograph shows cars with the designation "District Line." But Mrs. John Sheiry wrote in her scrapbook[298] that her husband was instrumental in having the signs on the cars changed to "Friendship Heights."

This use of the name "Friendship Heights" on streetcars was one of the first steps in the disuse of the name Tenleytown. Newcomers to the area might well have assumed then, as some do now, that the high point where River Road leaves Wisconsin Avenue is the beginning of an area known as Friendship Heights.

Before the days when automobiles were popular, going for a ride on the streetcar was an entertainment in itself. A Saturday or Sunday afternoon, or a summer evening, was often spent riding a streetcar to the end of the line, seeing the sights along the way, and then riding back again. Some city folks would get off the streetcar at Tenleytown just to look around, perhaps pick the wild flowers, and get on the next car going back to D.C.

Post Office

From 1846 until 1900, the local post office was called the "Tennallytown Post Office." The name "Tenley" came into use in 1900 when Andrew Burga became postmaster; but within five years, the post office was again using the name "Tennallytown."

The controversy over the spelling of the name had become heated as early as 1886, when The Washington Star editorialized on the subject, urging the name "Tenley" because it was asserted that that was the spelling used by the original settlers of that name! The Star further urged the dropping of "the superfluous and awkward affix" of -town, although popular usage of the suffix was likely to continue:

"When Tenleytown attains the greatness for which destiny and the northwest march of improvement from Washington seem to intend it, it may, however, be confusing if the name of the post-office varies from the popular name of the place."[299]

Before 1901, Tenleytown people had to pick up their mail from the post office. But in that year, delivery service was begun to outlying parts. The newly cut Massachusetts and Western Avenues formed the western corner of the rural delivery service of the Tenleytown post office. The southern borders of service were Loughborough Road and Pierce Mill Road, and the eastern limit was Broad Branch Road up to Western Avenue.

These boundaries were also considered the overall area of

Tenleytown; but its center section was always Wisconsin Avenue from Grant Road to River Road.

In 1907 postmaster Andrew Burga, the first letter carrier on horseback, was joined by two more—Charlie Eiker, whose route included the roads east of Wisconsin Avenue, and Harry "Kitty" Barrett, whose route was the west side.

In inclement weather the mailmen used horse and buggy to deliver the mail twice a day. In 1914 Mr. Eiker bought himself a new Ford; the D.C. post office did not provide vehicles even for the "rural" letter carriers.

Horseless Carriages and Paved Streets

Gas engine cars had been around since the 1890s, but one of the first cars to be seen on Wisconsin Avenue was in 1906—and it got stuck in the mud!

The first Tenleytown man to own a car was Web Chappell, a builder who lived on Yuma Street behind St. Ann's. In 1910 he bought a new Maxwell one-seater. Neighbors came out to see it pass by whenever they heard the chug-chug-chug of its engine.

Wisconsin Avenue in Tenleytown was paved from time to time with tar and sand (macadamized); but it had all the characteristics of a hard-packed dirt road—in dry weather, that is. There were many holes in the street. It was also barely wide enough at one time for two streetcars and two horse-drawn carts to pass each other.

Wisconsin Avenue was twice widened and all the trees cut down. A 1928 article about Tenleytown and Wisconsin Avenue[300] recalls that Barbara Lightfoot [1838-1927]

"saw the highway in front of the house develop from an ungraded dirt road, with high hills bounded by woods, to a stone turnpike and, later, to the Avenue

—in its present form...—and never, from the very first to the present day, was it completed."

Anyone who has walked or driven on Wisconsin Avenue through the recent Metro subway construction can appreciate the timelessness of that quote of 50 years ago.

The first sidewalk in Tenleytown, built before 1900, was made of wooden planks, on the east side of the pike only. The mud oozed up around it, and the rusty streetcar tracks ran alongside it. Eventually a flagstone sidewalk was substituted, which extended from O'Day's at Grant Road up to the Lightfoots' house. The boardwalk resumed on up to Brandywine Street.

The Rambler in the early 1900s described the bad condition of River Road, especially after crossing the line into Maryland:

"The roadbed had been worn down by long use and washing, and the banks between which it passes are grown with brambles and some trees. The wheel track does not go straight, but sways from side to side of the right of way. Where repairs to the roadbed have been made the work has been done by laying down large pieces of gneiss and quartz, and these, washed by rain, make rough going."[301]

This describes the long downhill on River Road going west to Little Falls Branch and Willard Avenue. The 1905 Boyd's Directory refers to the River Road as the "Upper falls rd. fr. Tenleytown to District line."

Raymond Johnson, who left Tenleytown in 1907, remembers that all the horses and horse-drawn vehicles going to and coming from Georgetown had to meet where the River and Rockville Roads met. "I still remember how crowded it was when the traffic met at Gloria Point."

Grant Road was always a narrow, winding, dirt alley-type road—but an important link to Connecticut Avenue, Broad Branch Road, and Brightwood from Tenleytown. It was paved eventually, but it has never been widened.

A little cinder road called Chappell Lane (on the original Chappell property) was one of the few turns off of Grant Road—this is where Fletcher had his row of houses built, now visible on the west side of the 4800 block of Nebraska Avenue. This lane turned off by Luther Derrick's house (another pretty Victorian, still standing at 3701 Grant Road).

Connecticut Avenue remained a country road used solely by street-cars and horse-drawn vehicles until 1907, when the "million dollar" Taft Bridge across Rock Creek was built and the Avenue began to take shape. The road was surfaced, automobiles became more frequent, and houses and stores were built along the street.

Albemarle Street was first built about 1890 from Connecticut Avenue west to where Reno Road is now, then eventually to 38th Street, later to Grant Road, and finally all the way to Wisconsin Avenue. There it connected with the Albemarle Street coming east from 45th Street.

Albemarle had been opened west of Wisconsin Avenue in 1906, at the request of St. Columba's Episcopal Church, whose members wanted easier access to the church from the Avenue. Brewer Christian Heurich, owner of the property, lost a battle to prevent the opening of that street.[302]

For many years, there were no road markers in Tenleytown—a stranger had to ask for a particular house or road. When new streets began to be cut through, three-foot high obelisk-shaped street markers

Sketch of early concrete corner street marker

were used with the street name painted on them.

The old gravelled Loughborough Road (begun to be called Nebraska Avenue in 1905) was still "just a cow-path." It left Wisconsin Avenue opposite the Pierce Mill Road, angled northwest along what is now Van Ness Street, and then southwest, and went past the old Loughborough/Whitney estate, "Grassland." It passed the American University, under construction for so many years, and branched off into Tunlaw, Ridge (Foxhall), and Chain Bridge Roads, before becoming the Little Falls Road, and going between the government reservation surrounding Dalecarlia Reservoir and the Girls Reform School; it ended at Conduit Road.

In 1905 Yuma Street was opened just one block to the west of Wisconsin Avenue, providing a muddy driveway between the new Immaculata School and St. Ann's; the alley allowing rear access to the St. Ann's and Tenley schools was called 41st Street. In 1905, when the Convent of Bon Secours was established, and in 1910, when Web Chappell built a new house at 4131 Yuma, Yuma was still a dirt street.[303]

The names Brookeville Road and Belt Road used to be interchangeable just northeast of Tenleytown. This road was the only direct route from Tenleytown to Chevy Chase Circle until the 1920s, when Reno Road and other new streets changed its direction. But even though it was much traveled, Brookeville Road was nothing but ditches and mud when it rained.

John Jay Daly, in his history of Blessed Sacrament Parish, Chevy Chase, tells us of the difficulties Father Thomas Smyth had in traveling from St. Ann's to the new mission parish, during the years 1910-1922:

"Washington in those days . . . was known as The City of Magnificent Distances. The most Magnificent of all these Distances was that stretch of roadway which unfolded itself between Tenleytown and Chevy Chase. On foot it amounted to a mild marathon. In a horse-drawn buggy it took up the best part of a morning, and the rest of the afternoon was spent going home . . . .

"At first [Father Smyth] had been driven in a buckboard, behind a spirited horse that promised to be a runaway on the slightest provocation—the raising of an umbrella, for instance, or the dropping of a handkerchief as someone crossed a thoroughfare.

"Later there was the exhilarating experience of driving back and forth from Tenleytown in a two-cylinder Maxwell . . . . In his memoirs, Monsignor Smyth wrote, 'This machine . . . was equipped with a rather raucous horn, sounded so frequently that it soon became one of the outstanding characteristics of life as it was lived in Tenleytown.'

"In a day when Washington City has an automobile for every third person [1961] it is difficult to imagine Father Smyth and his lone charger that came rollicking up Wisconsin Avenue, from Tenleytown . . . . Chickens, cows, horses and other animals were frightened by the coughing of the engine, a two-cylinder cough that sounded like the echo from a B&O freight engine."[304]

The difficulty of commuting back and forth along Belt Road was given as a main factor in Father

Smyth's transfer to the young Blessed Sacrament parish in 1922.

One of the lanes leading off Belt Road up to Fort Reno later became Fessenden Street. But before Fessenden was cut all the way through to Connecticut Avenue, it went only as far as 39th Street, which also ran south alongside the first reservoir at Fort Reno to Davenport Street. Fort Reno streets were never paved, and the cars easily got stuck on its steep, muddy lanes.

Before Indoor Plumbing

Underground sewers were not installed in Tenleytown and Reno until 1914—and not in Robeyville until 1928. Before that time, very few houses had indoor plumbing. Outhouses and outdoor water pumps were used by nearly every family. Ray Johnson remembers the house he grew up in at 4626 Wisconsin Avenue, built in 1893:

"Our water was carried in from a wood pump at the foot of the rear porch stairs. At times in the hot weather the water had to be boiled and cooled in quart jars, then put in the ice-chest to get real cold. There was no inside plumbing . . . . Near the rear gate on the alley was a privy. Under was a tarred wooden box; a box of lime was inside and used for sanitary conditions. A call was made to the Health Department when cleaning was needed. We called the cleaners the 'honey men.'" [305]

All Tenleytowners were not so lucky as to have a water pump near the back door. Irene Houser Cottingham said that when they moved into a house on Wisconsin Avenue in 1909, they had to cross the street to fetch water from the closest hydrant.

In the early days at Fort Reno, all water was obtained from an outdoor well—actually a hydrant-type affair with a spigot or push-pump. Mary Daniel recalls one up on Ellicott Street, behind her grandmother's house, perhaps as late as 1919. Other hydrants were shared by families in two or more houses. Water around the hydrant kept the spot always muddy or icy.

By 1921 most residences had indoor bathrooms, especially all of the newer houses. But as late as the 1930s there was still little provision for sewage disposal at Fort Reno.

Turn of the century houses lacked not only plumbing, but also central heat. A latrobe cast-iron stove in the living or dining room was the latest heating apparatus. It was a "half round" stove with an isinglass window in the front.

Ray Johnson continues:

"Our fuel was hard coal with wood for kindling. It was delivered in a two-wheel cart, which backed through the carriage house to a rear basement window." [The Washington Gaslight Company sold coal, or coke, at 15¢ for a large bag or 25 bushels delivered for $2.50.] [306]

National Bureau of Standards and Environs

A gravelled, winding Pierce Mill Road led up to the new National Bureau of Standards from Connecticut Avenue. The government had acquired part of the old Adlum property on the south side of Pierce Mill Road from the Chevy Chase Land Company and from the Sterrett family, beginning in 1901. One of the frame Sterrett houses stood until 1976 southeast of Reno Road and Van Ness Street.

On this land, just west of Connecticut Avenue, were erected

(1942 photo c/o Ray Johnson)

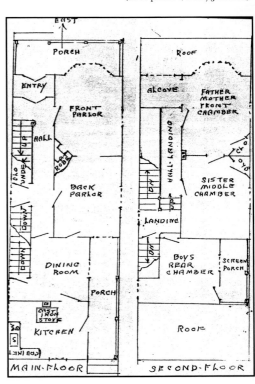

Top: 4626 Wisconsin Avenue, Ray Johnson's boyhood home.

Bottom: Johnson's sketch (1950) from memory of the house he lived in 1891-1907 (since torn down). The house was built by Fred Parks.

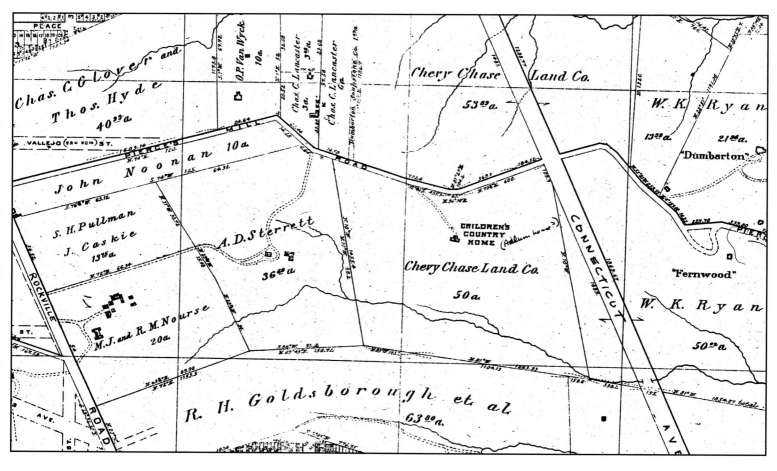

(1894 G.M. Hopkins map of Washington, Vol. 3)

Pierce Mill Road and its houses before the Bureau of Standards bought land, and before Van Ness and other streets were cut through. Old parts of Pierce Mill Road have become parts of today's Van Ness, Upton, and Tilden Streets.

the first brick buildings of the newly-established government bureau "to provide standards of measurement for commerce and industry, the public, and the Government."[307]

Its research and testing functions also brought an increasing number of scientists and technicians into the residential neighborhood as the Bureau grew year by year. In addition, it provided employment for long-time residents of the area. From 14 employees in 1903, the Bureau grew to 135 in 1910 and 1,150 in 1918, during World War I. By the end of World War II there were over 2,000 employees. At its largest, the National Bureau embraced 28 buildings on a campus of nearly 70 acres.

The Adlum house, "The Vineyard," remained standing for a few years after the Bureau of Standards was begun. "The Vineyard" house, surrounded by Adlum's numerous unusual trees

and plants, was east of the Bureau's buildings, on a hill southwest of the newly-cut intersection of Connecticut Avenue and Van Ness Street.

The old frame house had been occupied for a few years by the Children's Country Home and subsequently by a woman who ran a home for Civil War veterans. It fell into a state of decay and was torn down in 1911.[308]

On the north side of Pierce Mill Road (Van Ness Street), once opposite the entrance to "Springland," was the old home that Charles C. Lancaster had bought from the Wormley family in 1894 and renamed "Clifton Manor." In 1904 Lancaster sold the house and property to Scott Welker, who was in the distilling business.

Scott Welker hired architect Jay Dow to design a new stone country house, which he called "Woodlands." Mr. and Mrs. Welker lived in the new house for many years, surrounded by large trees, beautifully landscaped grounds, flowers and shrubs and even, for a time, blue peacocks.

In 1920 Welker sold the stone house, by then with the address of 3535 Van Ness Street, to Alfred Pembroke Thom. Thom renamed the house "Pembroke Park" and made some structural additions. His son, Alfred P. Thom, Jr., occupied the house in 1935.

In 1929, when Van Ness Street had replaced much of Pierce Mill Road, Reno Road was cut through only north of the Bureau of Standards, going toward Chevy Chase. Van Ness Street maintained the curve of the old road east of Reno Road in order to avoid cutting down the large old beech and oak trees that had been so precious to the Wormleys, Lancasters, Welkers, and Thoms.

During the early years of World War II, the Bureau of Standards bought the stone Welker-Thom house and 12 acres of land from Mrs. Gertrude Thom for about $125,000. The stone house, which is now abandoned, was referred to as The Manse, and was surrounded by buildings of the Harry Diamond Laboratories, a defense-oriented affiliate of the National Bureau of Standards.

Some of the first red buildings of the National Bureau of Standards still stand, ivy-covered, on what is now the campus of the University of the District of Columbia. In the early 1960s the NBS moved most of its staff to new headquarters near Gaithersburg, Maryland.

Another old Wormley house, also on the north side of Pierce Mill Road but closer to Wisconsin Avenue, was owned for a time by O.P. VanWyck. A large, flat-roofed frame box of a house, it contained more than 12 rooms, and was eventually put to use as a boarding house by Mrs. Everard Todd before its destruction when Van Ness Street was cut through.

NATIONAL BUREAU OF STANDARDS

(1973 photo by Jerry Yurow)

(1981 photo by Petra Schultze)

Top: These brick buildings of the Bureau of Standards were begun in about 1903, near Pierce Mill Road (Van Ness Street).

Bottom: "The Manse" at the Bureau of Standards—originally "Woodlands," then "Pembroke Park." The 1910 country house now stands vacant at 3535 Van Ness Street.

PIERCE MILL ROAD AREA CIRCA 1916

(Map from U.S. Geological Survey)

Samuel Hazen Bond's "Dumblane"

On the west side of Wisconsin Avenue, another new country estate was under construction—the "Dumblane" house of Mr. and Mrs. Samuel Hazen Bond. Built just south of the old "Dumblane" (or "Dunblane"), the new mansion was constructed in the summer of 1911, and is still standing today behind stone and iron gates at 4120 Warren Street.

Hazen Bond was a wealthy lawyer, active in local amateur theatricals. He build his dreamhouse at an elevation of over 400 feet, facing an uninterrupted view to the west of Maryland, across the Potomac Valley to Virginia and, on a clear day, the Blue Ridge Mountains 50 miles away in West Virginia. The tremendous old Dumblane Oak, most prominent in this region, was on the south side of Bond's new home.

The new "Dumblane" was a Craftsman house, designed and con-structed by architect and designer Gustav Stickney of New York. Use of 10-pound vari-colored, 12-inch "Tapestry" bricks, and mortar mixed with gravel, combined with wide-overhang green tile roofs, made the new house look like an old one trans-ported from Germany.

The interior of Bond's "Dumblane" was modern for 1911 in that it was simple, uncluttered and in many places unadorned. Much of the wood furniture—seats, bookcases, desk, sideboard, china closets—was built in. There was a full basement, with nine rooms, including wine cellar, laundry, valet's quarters, and space for storing 30 tons of coal. The other three floors comprised 17 rooms and four bathrooms.

Bond's "Dumblane" was the first house in Tenleytown (not counting the McLeans') to have a tennis court, a central vacuum cleaner system, a coal elevator, an electric washer, a clothes dryer, a billiard room, an

(Photos from The Craftsman, 1913, c/o Mrs. S.H. Bond)

electric victrola, and an intercommunicating system of seven telephone lines![309]

The Bonds did not, however, participate in the community life of Tenleytown; they remained relatively unknown, and the interior of their house was not seen by the local folk.

Mr. Bond remarried in 1927, after his first wife had died. He continued on at "Dumblane" until his death in 1962, at age 91.

Telephones

The first telephones had been installed in the city of Washington and Georgetown in 1878. But it was not until the mid-1890s and the Chevy Chase development that a few phones were installed in the suburban areas. The two exchanges in the Tenleytown neighborhood were CLeveland and CHevy Chase, followed by one, two, or three digits. There was no clear geographic division for the exchanges, for there

were CLeveland numbers in Friendship Heights and Bethesda, and CHevy Chase numbers on Grant Road and Pierce Mill Road.

Telephone switchboards were first installed by the Chesapeake and Potomac Telephone Company in the home of the operator. In Tenleytown the first operator was a Mrs. Davis, who had the switchboard in her home on Grant Road. Then Mrs. Katherine Easley, the policeman's wife, had the exchange in her house on Wisconsin Avenue at Belt Road. There was another exchange for Friendship Heights in an operator's home.

The first Tenleytown building for the CLeveland exchange was built in 1908 on Wisconsin Avenue, just south of the fire station. It was a small frame building, set back from the street.

In 1929 a new telephone building on the same site replaced the old, and two new exchanges, EMerson and WOodley, replaced CLeveland. And

SAMUEL HAZEN BOND'S "DUMBLANE"

Top: Approaching from the east along Warren Street, 1913.

Bottom: Original western facade of the house. The Dumblane Oak is to the right (south side of the house).

(Photo c/o Greta Achterkirchen Pillsbury)

Mr. and Mrs. William Achterkirchen and their daughter Greta.

Mr. and Mrs. Achterkirchen and their daughter Margarethe (Greta) lived upstairs in the large house. Greta Achterkirchen recalls that her father's stationery read The Irvington House, 4500 Wisconsin Avenue, Tenallytown, D.C. They took in occasional roomers, but no longer was the place used as a weekend stopover for farmers or other travelers.

Achterkirchen's Irvington House Inn had 13 rooms in addition to the business downstairs. In 1904 Heurich had the ground level porch enclosed to enlarge the saloon. A large white stairway on the north side of the building led to the second-story porch and living quarters. Another porch was above it, across the third story. Large white round pillars ran all the way to the roof of the third floor porch.[310]

The downstairs was the saloon— for many years the only saloon in Tenleytown, and therefore a very well known one. Achterkirchen's dominated the landscape, because it was one of the largest and tallest buildings in Tenleytown. And it dominated the lives of many local families because of the time—and money— spent there by the men. Women and children did not go into Achterkirchen's. The more adventurous children would lie down on their stomachs in front of the open bar doors and spy on the men inside. In the darkness they could see a huge mirror over the long bar.

Achterkirchen's was known variously as the tavern, the saloon, the barroom, and the whiskey store. And it had a bad reputation among many—no doubt promoted by active members of the Anti-Saloon League, who wrote in 1904 that Mr. Achterkirchen was "given the privilege of dispensing liquors to the young men of Tenleytown, whom the church and temperance people of the village are endeavoring to elevate."[311]

with the dial system came a standardized four digits after the exchange. Not until 1960 were five digits, and the first move to seven digits, instituted. This coincided with the latest addition to the WOodley exchange building, which is still operating at 4268 Wisconsin Avenue.

An example of the development of local phone numbers is that of the Willows Hotel owner, Mrs. Karl Heurich. Her original number was CLeveland 7. In 1929 it became WOodley 0007; and in 1960 it was WO 6-0007, then 966-0007 (later the number of the A&P Tea Company).

Achterkirchen's

While Christian Heurich owned the old Tenleytown Inn, he had a series of innkeepers working for him. In 1903 innkeeper Ernst Loeffler moved to Georgetown and William Achterkirchen became the keeper of the old Tenleytown Inn. For the next twelve years it was known as Achterkirchen's, although the property was still owned by Heurich.

The location of a horse trough and the freight scales in front of Achterkirchen's was a stroke of good fortune for the business—the wagon drivers' desire for efficiency was easily satisfied by stopping for a beer while the wagon load was weighed. Ray Johnson recalls "there was much activity at the saloon—many horses and wagons and drunks. We always walked on the other side of the road at those times."

Beer was sold by the glass or by the "growler"—a tin bucket with a lid and handle—that was filled from the tapped keg. Many men carried their own growlers to Achterkirchen's to get them filled. In 1906 Achterkirchen hired George Henry F. Kolb as bartender; he remained for eight years.[312]

In 1914 the Anti-Saloon League was successful in having a local ordinance passed that prohibited the locating of a saloon within a certain distance of either a school or a church. Since one of Achterkirchen's closest neighbors on Wisconsin Avenue was the Tenley School—on the other side of Heinrich's blacksmith shop—not to mention the proximity of the Methodist, Episcopal, and Catholic churches—the saloon quickly lost its license to sell liquor.

The Achterkirchens ran the business as a restaurant only, for about a year, but it was no longer a money-making undertaking, and they soon moved to Baltimore.

John E. Nichol tried to run the restaurant for a short time, selling "near-beer" with the food; soon Howard G. Crandall took it over. By 1918 Crandall's hotel had become a hardware store, and eventually specialized in auto accessories—still in the first floor of what had been the old Tenleytown Inn.

President Roosevelt Visits

President Theodore Roosevelt, while he was in office from 1901 to 1909, was a well-known figure to Tenleytowners. He often walked or rode horseback with his daughter Alice or with friends from the White House, north through Rock Creek Park bridle paths, then westward up to Tenleytown and along its dirt roads and streets.

Word passed quickly when the President was riding by, and everyone would come to the porch or to the road and wave. President Roosevelt never failed to wave back, and often stopped to have a few words with the children. The oldest Harry children recall taking turns feeding apples to the President's horse in exchange for a greeting and flashing smile from the President.[313]

President Roosevelt was seen riding his horse in all weather—he greeted the children who were sledding on River Road, and the appearance of snow or wind did not keep him indoors.

Sunday afternoon was the most likely time for the President's visits. One old-timer on River Road got so used to Roosevelt's appearance that he missed it when it stopped:

"Kinder lonesome around here since Mr. Roosevelt left. I used to put my chair in the road and watch for him to pass. Nothing doing of a Sunday now."[314]

How times have changed! Not only is the President now surrounded by Secret Service men in an enclosed car, but no one would dare put his chair in River Road of a Sunday now!

President William Howard Taft also occasionally rode horseback near the Bureau of Standards during his term of office (1909-13), but he was never so visible in Tenleytown as President Theodore Roosevelt.

First Reservoir and Water Tower

In 1899 a water reservoir was built at Fort Reno to serve the growing population in the far northwest section of the city. The last vestiges of the Civil War fort were removed, for the highest level of elevation in the city had been chosen for the reservoir. A few homes were displaced by the decision to locate at Reno. Banker Charles C. Glover was at the time given much credit "for securing for the city" the site for this reservoir.[315]

The water capacity for the original reservoir was 5.5 million gallons. It was open to the elements, and had a fence around it. To prevent anyone from going near the water, a guard was on duty day and night. The Sub-T policemen found that the Reno pumphouse was the only place to get warm on a cold winter's night.

In 1903 a cylindrical red brick water tank was built, 60 feet high. The storage of water at this higher elevation provided pressure needed to serve water to the homes and buildings in the highest elevated sections of the city. This tower was a landmark in all directions, visible from as far away as northern Virginia.

A residence for the supervising engineer of the Reno plant was also built at the base of the brick tower. Walter Krobisch and his wife were the first residents. The house had an address on Donaldson Place, which came uphill from Belt Road, crossed the top of the hill, and continued downhill to Howard Street on the east (now toward Alice Deal Junior High).

(Photo c/o National Park Service)

The first water tower at Reno Reservoir was built in 1903, with the engineer's house attached to it. Photo is dated 1926.

In 1916 a second reservoir was built, to the south of Donaldson Place. This displaced the Bangerter family, who moved down to 41st Street, after having lived on their home place since 1869. This reservoir, paved over with cement and then covered with sod, had a 5.4 million gallon capacity. At that time the pumphouse was also enlarged.

The reservoir area became a favorite place to go on a sunny day to enjoy the view. You could see to Soldiers Home, to the new Cathedral under construction, or even to Sugar Loaf Mountain in Frederick County, or the Shenandoah Mountains in Virginia or West Virginia. And on the 4th of July, you could see some of the fireworks from the Washington Monument grounds—this was before

there were so many tall trees and buildings to interfere with the view.

*   *   *   *

Flora Brown's aunt left Tenleytown soon after the Civil War and did not return until 1907, when she remarked that, to her amazement, Tenleytown hadn't changed at all! And her hearers were very pleased to see that it was so. True, Tenleytown had successfully retained its rural character, despite the addition of new people, new houses, new businesses, new problems.

But it was no longer isolated from the city; its people could no longer be concerned only with themselves. Although their memories had grown dim of the intrusions of the world during the Civil War 50 years earlier, Tenleytowners were apprehensive that the peaceful existence they still had in 1914 was about to end. No doubt this made them savor even more the pleasures of life in Tenleytown.

"I used to love this wild country," recalled Dorothea Thompson.

"It was a lovely life we had," said Mary Chappell Robey.

253 "A Real Little Thrums," op. cit.

254 Mame Burdette Colburn, interviews February 11 and 27, 1975, by the author

255 Interview with Hattie Burrows Porter, March 8, 1975, by Priscilla McNeil and the author

256 "Tenleytown: A Seven-Hilled Citadel of Health," op. cit.

257 "Tenleytown: A Seven-Hilled Citadel of Health," op. cit.

258 Interview with Margaret Achterkirchen Pillsbury, August 11, 1976, by the author

259 "Police Lieut. Giles, Veteran, Expires," The Evening Star, August 29, 1925

260 D.C. Fire Department, 100 Years of Glory, 1871-1971, D.C. Fire Fighters Association Committee on Glory. Washington: Mount Vernon Publishing Company, 1971

261 Raymond Johnson, "Boyhood Days," 1974, unpublished manuscript

262 John Daly, Landmark in Chevy Chase: Story of the Shrine of the Most Blessed Sacrament 1911-1961

263 "A Real Little Thrums," op. cit.

264 D.C. Medical Society 1938 obituary of John W. Chappell and other materials provided by Flora Brown, 1973

265 Annie Ray Thomson, "Characteristics and Background of Dr. Anthony M. Ray," unpublished manuscript, c/o Edith Ray Saul

266 Records of Immaculata College

267 Reports of the President's Homes Commission, Washington: The President's Homes Commission, 1908

268 Terrence Downs, "Sunset on the Palisades," Potomac, The Washington Post Magazine, February 5, 1978

269 50th Anniversary booklet, Wm. R. Singleton Lodge, F.A.A.M., 1951, Carl E. Schoenhals, historian

270 Official Program of 1909 Housewarming, c/o Edna Riley Snoots

271 The Rambler, The Star, December 22, 1912

272 Interview with Berenice Parks Bergling, December 1, 1977, by the author

273 Johnson, "Boyhood Days," op. cit.

274 1948 Biography of Fred Heider, Singleton Lodge

275 "A Real Little Thrums," op. cit.

276 Heider Biography, op. cit.

277 Walton Shipley, "I Remember," Origins, 1975

278 Johnson, "Boyhood Days," op. cit.

279 Ibid.

280 "Tenleytown: A Seven-Hilled Citadel of Health," op. cit., and "Prof. W.B. Ireland Dead at Age 65," The Evening Star, February 23, 1912

281 "Tenleytown: A Seven-Hilled Citadel of Health," op. cit.

282 Ireland obituary, 1912, op. cit.

283 Samuel J. Henry, The Old Days With Horse and Hound, 1916

284 "Margaret G. Callahan Drops Dead on Street," The Evening Star, September 27, 1916

285 Interviews with Howard N. Davis, 1976

286 Myrtle C. Murdock, The American's Creed and William Tyler Page, Washington, 1958

287 "With the Rambler" (J. Harry Shannon), The Sunday Star, January 3, 1915

288 Lillian Cutlip, "Old Tenley House . . . to be Opened to the Public," The Washington Herald, June 19, 1932, p. F-4

289 Margaret B. Downing, "Literary Landmarks," RCHS, Vol. 19, 1916

290 Interview with Father Joseph I. Durkin, S.J., April 25, 1975, and Barnum, "The Old Georgetown Villa," op. cit.

291 "Old Colonial Manor," 1902, op. cit.

292 The Rambler, "When Water from Little Falls Branch Flowed Into the Aqueduct," Evening Star, no date (Scrapbook 6, CHS)

293 "Tenleytown: A Seven-Hilled Citadel of Health," op. cit.

294 Fred E. Woodward, "A Ramble Along Boundary Stones," RCHS, Vol. 10, 1907, p. 72

295 Sarah M. Huddleson, "Mrs. E.D.E.N. Southworth and Her Cottage," RCHS, Vol. 23, 1919, p. 75, and Washington Topham, "Centre Market and Vicinity," RCHS, Vol. 26, 1924

296 Wisconsin Avenue Baptist Church records

297 Scrapbook of Annie F. Sheiry, Montgomery County Historical Society

298 Sheiry, op. cit.

299 Editorial, The Washington Star, December 12, 1887, p. 2

300 "May D. Lightfoot Recalls Olden Days," Top Notch, November 1928

301 "When Water from Little Falls Branch Flowed Into the Aqueduct," op. cit.

302 The battle is described in A Short History of St. Columba's Church in Washington, D.C., by Mathilde D. Williams, published 1960 by the parish.

303 Immaculata archives

304 Daly, op. cit.

305 Raymond Johnson, "Our Home," 1973, unpublished manuscript

306 Johnson, "Our Home," ibid.

307 Rexmond C. Cochrane, Measures for Progress: A History of the National Bureau of Standards, Washington: U.S. Department of Commerce, 1966

308 Peter and Southwick, Cleveland Park, op. cit.

309 "Dumblane: A Southern Craftsman Home," The Craftsman, February 1913

310 Letter to the author from Margaret Achterkirchen Pillsbury, September 19, 1973

311 The Protest, D.C. Anti-Saloon League, May 1904, pp. 117 and 119, as referred to in Milton Rubincam, "Christian Heurich and His Mansion," RCHS, 1960-61, p. 181

312 Interview with Marie Kolb Reed, May 26, 1975, by the author

313 Jessie Fant Evans, "Mrs. Parker's Family Is Linked to History of Washington," The Evening Star, June 16, 1950

314 1915 newspaper clipping (unsourced) calls River Road the "Road of the Presidents"

315 American Biographical Directory 1908-09, Washington, D.C., listing for Charles C. Glover

THE AMERICAN UNIVERSITY

(Photo from "Suburban Washington as a Place of Residence," 1901)

VI

CHANGES:

1914–1939

Hurst Hall was the first building of the American University, completed in 1897. It was also called the College of History.

The Beginnings of the American University

Educators desiring to build a Methodist university in the nation's capital had purchased, in 1890, land on Loughborough Road southwest of Tenleytown. The high ground chosen was part of Addison's and Murdock's original "Friendship," near the Civil War Fort Gaines. Nearly 100 acres were bought up from seven or eight landowners, including Miss Achsah Davis, who owned the Murdock house.

In 1893 a charter for the American University was granted by Congress, and ground was broken in 1896. The first structure was completed a year later. Of classic Greek design, it was named Hurst Hall, after the college's foremost founder, Bishop John F. Hurst of the Methodist Episcopal Church. In 1902 President Theodore Roosevelt laid the cornerstone for a second building, the McKinley Hall of Government—named after the assassinated President who had been a trustee of the University.

Despite its ambitious beginnings, the University suffered serious financial setbacks, and McKinley Hall was not finished for more than twelve years. Finally, in May 1914, President Woodrow Wilson addressed a gathering of dignitaries and residents on the occasion of the formal opening of the American University. And the first students of the Graduate School of Arts and Sciences occupied Hurst Hall in October 1914.

The Rambler, describing the view in 1915 from the churchyard in Lewinsville, Virginia, across the Potomac, wrote, "The buildings of the American University and other landmarks in the Tenleytown neighborhood stand out against the sky."[316] The other landmarks included the Immaculata School and the Reno brick water tower.

Massachusetts Avenue had been extended west only as far as Loughborough Road by 1912. Banker Charles C.

THE AMERICAN UNIVERSITY

(Photo from <u>Book of Washington</u>, 1930)

Aerial view of the campus of American University as seen in 1930. Nebraska Avenue (old Loughborough Road) runs along the right side of the photo. The Metropolitan Memorial Methodist Church had not yet been built, at the corner of Nebraska and New Mexico Avenues.

Glover, Sr., had built a beautiful country house, "Westover," facing Massachusetts Avenue. The old Loughborough Road had been straightened, paved, and renamed Nebraska Avenue by 1917. Most Tenleytowners called it, appropriately, New-Braska Avenue.

Future prospects for higher education in far northwest Washington inspired Louis Shoemaker, who wrote about the neighborhood west of Rock Creek Park:

". . . the following educational institutions have been established: the Carnegie Geophysical Laboratory, American Methodist University, Old Georgetown College, Washington Select School for Boys, Naval Observatory, National Cathedral School for Girls, Catholic Young Ladies Seminary, [and] Dunbarton, the new home of the Sisters of the Holy Cross . . . .

"As Egyptian civilization followed the Nile, to the shores of the Mediterranean, thence over Europe and subsequently gave to the world Athens, Carthage, Troy and old Rome, let us hope that our educational institutions, which could be planted in no better place than on the beautiful territory west of Rock Creek, may eventually afford the best evidence of our civilization and that it may follow the Potomac rather than the Nile, thence over the shores of the Chesapeake, rather than the Mediterranean, broadcast, not over one country, but over the civilized world."[317]

Shoemaker's theory on the possible impact of our local educational institutions on the whole world may seem a bit over-blown; but the impact of the people who have studied and worked in these institutions cannot be overestimated. Shoemaker correctly recognized the trend of the spread of educational institutions beginning in the area around old Tenleytown.

Mount Vernon Seminary

The Mount Vernon Seminary for young ladies had been founded as a private residential school in 1875 in downtown Washington by Mrs. Elizabeth J. Somers. In 1914 she purchased 15 acres of the old "Grassland" estate, on the east side of Loughborough Road, for her school. In 1916 the first building was begun at the new site.

The Seminary was opened in 1917 at 3801 Nebraska Avenue, as the road was called by then. It was a large brick building of classic Colonial architecture with many classrooms and capacity for 130 residential students. There were also tennis courts, extensive playing fields, and landscaped grounds.

In 1922, a brick house, "Gatesley," was built for the headmistress of Mount Vernon, at 3701 Nebraska. In 1925 a large Colonial brick chapel was dedicated on the north side of the campus, between Nebraska Avenue and "Grassland." (The Loughborough mansion was used through the 1930s as The Country Club.)

In the late 1920s Mount Vernon Seminary acquired 16 acres more, and a large fieldhouse was erected. The school remained on this campus until 1942, when it was taken over by the Navy Department for use during World War II.

Soldiers in Tenleytown Again

After the entry of the United States into the first World War in April 1917, the American University offered its two buildings, Hurst Hall and the still unfinished McKinley Hall, to the War Department. Those few students who were enrolled at the American University began to attend classes in professors' homes.

The War Department finished the McKinley Building in 1918 and initiated its chemical warfare

(Photo c/o American University Archives)

(Photo c/o Mount Vernon College)

research unit there. Army scientists here experimented with gases and explosives.

The area of the campus south and west of the two buildings was named Camp American University, and the area to the north was called Camp Leach. During the year and a half that the American University was

Top: Massachusetts Avenue was paved this far in 1912, as seen looking east from Nebraska Avenue—now the site of Ward Circle. The Charles C. Glover estate, "Westover," is at far right.

Bottom: Mount Vernon Seminary as it appeared on Nebraska Avenue, early 1920s. Nathan Loughborough's old "Grassland" estate and barn are still visible just north and east of the Seminary. The Navy took over the campus at the beginning of WW II.

WORLD WAR I IN TENLEYTOWN

(Photo c/o American University Archives)

(Photo c/o Clara Poore Broderick)

Top: Soldiers at Camp Leach, American University, 1917-1918. In this view taken from Hurst Hall, looking toward Tenleytown (Immaculata is visible in the distance), soldiers and horses line up along Nebraska Avenue, right.

Bottom: Soldiers from Camp Leach have breakfast at St. Ann's Church hall after Sunday Mass.

occupied by the War Department, hundreds of barracks and training buildings sprouted on what had been peaceful countryside.

The Army Corps of Engineers brought in thousands of soldiers for training before shipping them overseas to fight in Europe. The December 1917 issue of Roll Call, the newspaper of the Mount Vernon Seminary across the road, described some of the engineering regiments: "The 30th is the Gas and Flame Section; the 6th is Bridge Builders and Trench Diggers; the 24th is Camouflage; the 20th is Foresters."

Each of these regiments practiced its functions in the open fields around the camp. Local residents were fascinated watching the soldiers digging trenches and transforming the area into practice battlefields. Pits for chemicals and explosives were dug on the campus. Mortar shells blew up plaster of Paris horses and men.

"War game" maneuvers were held and tents erected in a field southwest of Immaculata and Dumblane. Horses and soldiers trained for cavalry duty, and platoons executed marching drills on open fields north of the McLean estate and across Wisconsin Avenue from Immaculata Seminary. Five bungalows in the 4300 block of 44th Street were built at this time for use by Army officers and their families.

The citizens of Tenleytown were generous in their personal welcomes to the soldiers in the encampment at American University. No doubt some recalled their grandparents' hospitality when thousands of young Union soldiers were stationed at Fort Reno and Fort Bayard just 55 years earlier. As in the Civil War, Tenleytown was again the site of the largest military encampment within the borders of the District of Columbia.

The local churches and pastors led the movement to serve the young servicemen. The Rev. William W. Shearer of St. Columba's Episcopal Church started a Bible class for soldiers. It met every Sunday morning and had a large attendance. St. Columba's and St. Alban's took turns having Monday night socials for the soldiers and the local population, and these were very popular. It was reported that on one such occasion, "500 of the regiment" turned out.

An "exemplary case of Christian unity" was also demonstrated when the local Episcopal, Catholic, Methodist, and Baptist clergy cooperated in providing a service of worship and preaching at the camp every Sunday.[318]

The influenza epidemic in 1918-19, however, forced the curtailment of all church services and school classes for a time. Tenleytown, as well as the rest of the East Coast, suffered from the sickness, and a few residents died. The Ned McLean family of the "Friendship" estate on Wisconsin Avenue made their grand house available as a hospital for convalescent soldiers during the epidemic.

Many Tenleytown families invited soldiers for dinner on a regular basis, and they continued correspondence and friendships with the young men after the war was ended. Some families also made rooms available to the soldiers' wives, parents, or sweethearts, so that they could visit before their soldier boy was shipped off to France. At least one Tenleytown girl, Lelia Poore, met and married a soldier stationed at Camp American University.

During and after the war, the Singleton Masonic Lodge drew such large attendance from among the soldiers at its Grand Visitations that they were held in the Hall of History at the University. In October 1920,

the chancellor of American University, Bishop John W. Hamilton, and General John J. Pershing were elected to honorary membership in Singleton Lodge,[319] as a result of their encouragement of Tenleytown Masonry during the war years.

World War I brought hostility to Germans—even in Tenleytown, with its many German immigrants. And so, because of the suspicions of a few, Mr. Krobisch, a German immigrant, was removed from his post at the Reno reservoir, for fear he might seek reprisals against the American people by poisoning the water. Mr. Krobisch was replaced by Mr. Parker, whose wife and three children moved into the house at the reservoir and were there for many years.

The original reservoir was finally covered over, and, to the delight of the area residents, paved concrete tennis courts were constructed on top of the reservoir; they were open to everyone all week long. This was the first community sports center in Tenleytown.

Tenleytown had its young men in the war, too. St. Alban's recorded that 126 of its young men had served in the armed forces, four of them dying in France. Three of the Riley brothers—Ed, Howard, and Dr. Harry B. Riley—served during the war, but were not sent overseas. Young Hart Sonnemann of Grant Road was killed in Europe; he was a grandson of the Walthers of Murdock Mill Road.

Back to Normalcy

After November 11, 1918, and the signing of the Armistice, the military encampments at American University were gradually vacated and razed. The intersection of Nebraska and Massachusetts Avenues became once again a corner of a university campus.

The American University began to grow at a much greater pace than before the war. The McKinley Building continued to house the Fixed Nitrogen Laboratory of the Department of Agriculture until about 1940. The government had started a new building for chemical research in 1918, but it stood unused after the war until 1925, when it was completed as a women's residence.

The undergraduate College of Liberal Arts opened in 1925 at the Nebraska Avenue site. That same year a Colonial-style chancellor's house replaced the old historic Murdock house, which had been allowed to fall into ruin and then was torn down. The remains of Fort Gaines, however, were still visible in 1930 just north of the newly-cut Massachusetts Avenue extension. By 1930 a library, gymnasium, and men's dormitory had been constructed.

The original plans for American University, calling for "26 magnificent white marble structures," had to be abandoned as overly ambitious.[320]

The McLeans of "Friendship"

Although they were by no stretch of the imagination ever Tenleytowners, there was one family whose influence was felt very strongly in the village: the McLeans.

John R. McLean, owner of The Cincinnati Enquirer and The Washington Post, had bought for more than $250,000 the old Georgetown Villa retreat house and 75 acres in 1898.[321] Because part of his purchase was within Thomas Addison's original land grant, McLean had renamed the College Villa estate "Friendship." Since the old Murdock house "Friendship" also remained standing for another 20 years, the histories of these two "Friendship" houses have often been confused.

REMAINS OF "FRIENDSHIP" TORN DOWN

(1910 photo c/o Columbia Historical Society)

(Photo by Priscilla McNeil, 1973)

Top: The old Murdock house, "Friendship," (above) was replaced by the new American University chancellor's house (below) in 1925.

McLean was a man of great wealth, ability, and ambition, who had been nominated for President (in vain) at the Democratic convention in 1896. He also served as president of the Washington Gas Company for 19 years.

Mr. and Mrs. John R. McLean used "Friendship" as their summer and weekend house; their main residence was an impressive contemporary brick structure at 1500 Eye Street, N.W.

In writing of the country house, Grace Dunlop Peter said, "After extreme remodeling and additions there was little left to suggest the old house of former owners except the substantial brick center."[322] After remodeling, the house did resemble a French villa rather than an American country house. A 1909 writer, perhaps exaggerating only a little, described "Friendship" as "An American Versailles." The main entrance was on the north side of the house, but it was usually photographed from the south side.

The grounds of the McLean estate were meticulously landscaped with boxwood hedges, trees, flowers, and grass, into a park-like atmosphere. The "monks' walk" was retained from Georgetown Villa days. A reflecting pool, fountains, and statuary added to its formality. McLean built a long stone wall that still stands today, with a water trough below a lion's head—horses stopped here to drink.

John R. McLean and his wife welcomed the people of Tenleytown into their grounds, and had an amicable relationship with local tradesmen and residents. In 1911 Mr. McLean presented to St. Columba's Episcopal Church a 700-pound bell, for which the congregation built a tower.

A favorite attraction was the McLeans' water and clock tower,

THE McLEAN ESTATE, WISCONSIN AVENUE

facing on Wisconsin Avenue, just inside the main gate (where Porter Street is now). A yellow frame structure about 30 feet high, it stored water for the McLean estate and featured a huge clock that could be seen by all. To re-wind the clock, a McLean employee climbed up a narrow staircase that encircled the tower.

The McLeans' son Edward Beale McLean, called Ned, lacked John R.'s ambition and drive, his ability and strength. Ned was married to Evalyn Walsh, daughter of Thomas F. Walsh, who had made millions in mining silver and gold in Colorado. The marriage united two of the wealthiest families in Washington, and the young couple had a honeymoon trip of many months, cruising around the world. It was on a 1911 trip to Europe that they bought the world-famous Hope Diamond, a 44.5-carat cut blue diamond whose legend of misfortune they chose to ignore.[323]

John R. McLean died in June 1916 at "Friendship," and Ned inherited the country house, as well as his father's newspaper publishing empire. In the spring of 1919, after the convalescing soldiers who had been residing there moved out, Ned, Evalyn, and their sons Vinson, Jock, and Ned, Jr., moved in; the McLeans lived there on and off for the next 20 years. Their moving in was of immense interest to the Tenleytowners. The horse stables were transformed into garages for Ned's many cars—Fiats, Lancias, Mercedes, and Isotta-Fraschinis.[324]

The McLeans had some 30 employees; some of them, like Arthur Buckman and Benjamin F. Pyles, were hired from Tenleytown. Harry Breeden, who was a bodyguard for the boys for 11 years, recalled that the household also included about 40 dogs, two donkeys, and a monkey. Others remember bright blue peacocks, goats, and

(Photo from <u>Washington Daily News</u>)

Top: 1936 photo of the McLeans' water tower, clock, and observatory that was a landmark along Wisconsin Avenue for about 40 years.

Bottom: The McLeans' "Friendship."

(Photo c/o Robert Truax)

(Harris & Ewing photo c/o Harry Breeden)

(Photo c/o Columbia Historical Society)

*Top: Evalyn Walsh McLean, baby
Vinson, and Ned McLean.*

*Bottom: The interior of
"Friendship" as decorated by
Evalyn Walsh McLean.*

geese, as well as horses and cattle. Evalyn McLean described her own menagerie:

"A mad place, truly!—with a monkey in my bathroom, a llama on the lawn, and our corridors shrill with the curses of our parrot . . . . In the stables . . . midget horses and the coach . . . that had once belonged to General Tom Thumb . . . ."[325]

When their first child, Vinson, was born in 1909, he was easily the most famous American baby. He was given everything—not only Tom Thumb's coach and miniature horses, but also two goats, a snow-white burro, and 56 sheep. Instead of taking little Vinson to the circus, the McLeans had Ringling Brothers bring the circus to "Friendship."

Because of their fear of kidnapping and robbery, Ned and Evalyn McLean had many guards around their estate, and did not welcome the local people into the grounds. These younger McLeans took very little interest in the affairs of the neighborhood.

The first of a series of misfortunes (often blamed on the Hope Diamond) was the death of Vinson McLean at age nine. As Mrs. McLean told it in her autobiography, she and her husband were in Louisville for the May 1919 Kentucky Derby, and her sons were at "Friendship" under the care of their grandmother, Mrs. Walsh, and the staff of servants.

On Friday morning, May 9 (she said it was Sunday), Vinson and the old valet Meggett were out on Wisconsin Avenue: "Across the street they saw an old friend driving a wagon loaded with ferns. The driver was a gardener who had worked for us, a man named Goebel." Vinson and Mr. Goebel chatted merrily, and then Vinson playfully snatched a few ferns and ran in fun, back across the road while Goebel yelled. The boy did not see a "Tin Lizzie" Ford approaching slowly; it struck him, but not hard.

He did not seem to be badly hurt. He walked back to the house with Meggett, but Grandma called doctors. Internal bleeding might have started, for later in the afternoon Vinson became paralyzed. At 6 o'clock that night he died, apparently of a fractured skull.[326] The death of "America's richest baby" saddened the nation, as well as the neighborhood.

In 1921 the McLeans had a daughter, Emily, who later changed her name to Evalyn. That same year, Ned McLean was chairman of the inaugural committee for President Warren G. Harding. "A private dance for some 600 GOP merrymakers" was held by the McLeans.[327] Thus began an era when "Friendship" was increasingly famous as the scene of the fantastic extravaganzas of Evalyn and Ned McLean. As their social prominence grew, so did their involvement with nationally known figures, most notably President Harding.

"Because of our wealth, the rich scenes in which my husband and I moved were peopled with the great and the powerful of our generation. When any one of these might wish to meet his kind at play around Washington, a likely place to make the contact was our country estate . . . .

"Some of our acres had been remolded into a golf course where the grass was far more costly than any kind of Oriental rugs; and partially, that is why our country house became the playground of President Harding and all those who wished to win from him some inch or two of official stature."[328]

A nine-hole golf course and a tremendous swimming pool were centers for Mrs. McLean's parties. She entertained lavishly and constantly; occasionally 300 would be invited for dinner.

The malevolence of the Hope Diamond may not have had any force over President Harding and his administration. Nevertheless, some of Harding's cabinet appointees and cronies, including Ned McLean, were involved in disreputable business deals that brought shame to Harding's administration. Most notable was the Teapot Dome scandal, involving bribes to Cabinet members for exclusive oil rights to private interests. Harding died suddenly on a trip to California in 1923, when the specter of impeachment was beginning to loom.

Back at "Friendship," the McLeans' marriage was disintegrating. Ned's drinking habits were known to all the local residents, for he had frequented Achterkirchen's saloon, and more than once succeeded in disturbing the peace along Wisconsin Avenue.

Eventually Evalyn McLean had her husband committed to a hospital for the mentally ill. After a few years, she divorced him—but not until she was assured possession of the "Friendship" estate. The Washington Post was sold to ex-banker Eugene Meyer in 1933; ownership of The Cincinnati Enquirer was also transferred.

The difficult times curtailed her entertaining activities, but Evalyn McLean did continue her annual Easter and Thanksgiving luncheons to benefit charity. And on December 31, 1936, on the occasion of son Jock's 21st birthday, she gave her first New Year's Eve ball in ten years. She had another wing built onto the house to accommodate the 600 guests. Meyer Davis' orchestra played

for the old folks, and Benny Goodman entertained the younger set.[329]

Ned McLean died in Shepherd-Pratt Institute in Baltimore in 1941. After her children had moved away, Evalyn Walsh McLean decided she could no longer maintain the large estate at 3600 Wisconsin Avenue. And so, in 1942, after she had given her last party there, she sold "Friendship" to the United States government for a reported $1 million and moved into a house at 3308 R Street, Georgetown—which she promptly renamed "Friendship."

The government razed the beautiful and historic old mansion south of Tenleytown and destroyed the golf course, pool, clock tower, and landscaped lawns, in order to build McLean Gardens, a housing development for the war workers who were pouring into Washington.

Evalyn Walsh McLean died in the spring of 1947 of pneumonia.[330] Much of her personal estate was sold at auction one year later. The Hope Diamond was turned over to the Smithsonian in 1958 by Harry Winston, New York gem dealer.

New Streets, New Houses, and Disappearing Farms

In 1916 Margaret B. Downing wrote, referring to Wisconsin Avenue, that the Nourse house, across from the McLeans, was "only a stone's throw from what is now a very busy thoroughfare leading out of Washington city, but what was [in the 1820s] a quiet country road."[331]

Downing's concept of Wisconsin Avenue as a busy thoroughfare was just a hint of the growth in local auto traffic and the need for greater development of Tenley area streets in the years to come.

The new development around Tenleytown was identical to the residential and commercial

LONG BEFORE TENLEY CIRCLE: 1917

(Photos c/o Della Lewis Beasley)

Top: Looking north to Grant Road from the 4300 block of Wisconsin Avenue, or about where Tenley Circle is now: a "very busy thoroughfare."

Bottom: Looking south from the same place: 1917.

development of other areas of the District. And as post-World War I Washington expanded north and west, Tenleytown and its old roads and buildings were swallowed up.

C. Harold Gray, writing in 1937, after the transformation had taken place, recalled the old roads that were obliterated:

"Tenleytown was the nucleus of an extensive country road net which has since largely disappeared. Murdock Mill rd. and Pierce Mill rd. led from the village to the mills which gave these arteries their names. Belt rd. extended to Brookeville, Md., and Grant rd. reached Brightwood, D.C.

"The Georgetown-Rockville rd. (now called Wisconsin avenue) and River rd. are the only old routes entering Tenleytown that have retained any importance today. The other trails have disappeared or become mere alleys as Washington has grown out to and completely surrounded the old town.

"In extending Washington's wide, straight streets through the community, many of the buildings were removed and its appearance changed almost beyond recognition."[332]

Curbs, sidewalks, grass boulevards, and the planting of trees made the new streets very attractive, and the pain from the loss of open spaces was easier to bear. Street maps of the 1920s indicate many planned new streets that were never cut through, however.

In 1919 had come one of the many widenings and repavings of Wisconsin Avenue, prompted by the new need for auto lanes in addition to the two streetcar tracks. Despite the widening, the street was not paved for autos north of Brandywine

Street, and large holes were still a problem. The west side of Wisconsin Avenue was widened so much that the Baptist Church's frame building, north of Brandywine, had to be moved back about 30 feet.

World War I had brought local construction to a halt. But in 1918 builders Harry A. Kite and Samuel E. Kite, Jr., led the resurgence of home building in the area. They bought many acres of Curran and Magruder property east of Wisconsin Avenue—some of which George Armes had acquired between 1891 and 1905 and subdivided as "Armesleigh Park." The Kite brothers liked this name and used it for their new subdivision.

Armesleigh Park contained detached frame two-story houses with stone foundations, in the 3800 blocks of Albemarle (which was then not connected to Grant Road or Wisconsin Avenue), Alton, and Yuma, and on 39th Street. After 1922 the Kites acquired a little more land and built houses on Windom Place and 38th Street.

Also in the early '20s Fred Heider began to develop what had once been his father's farm on upper Wisconsin Avenue. He sold the old farmhouse to Ward W. Griffith, owner of Griffith Consumers (the address was then 4200 Harrison Street). Heider built large new houses at 5101 Wisconsin (in 1923 the Marcerons occupied it) and at 4215 Harrison for his family. Then, as Harrison, Ingomar, and 42nd Streets were paved, Heider built houses on those blocks, one by one, and sold them off.

The area known as Chevy Chase, D.C., was very successfully developed by the Chevy Chase Land Company; prices of lots in this area doubled and sometimes tripled.[333] Most lots were sold individually and so there was a great variety in the styles of houses.

A VARIETY OF HOUSING

(1974 photo by John Russo)

(Photo c/o Louis Perna)

Top: The 3800 block of Windom Place, built 1920s

Bottom: Stone house at 39th and Harrison, built in the 1920s by the Pernas.

CHURCHES EXPAND IN 1920s

(Photo c/o Wisconsin Avenue Baptist Church)

(Photo c/o Rebecca Harry Parker)

Top: The Wisconsin Avenue Baptist congregation kept its name even when it built this below-ground-level sanctuary at 42nd and Fessenden, in 1924. A second level was not built until the Armenian Apostolic congregation bought the property in 1953. Wisconsin Avenue Baptist Church is now at Tenley Circle.

Bottom: The new Eldbrooke Methodist Church, begun 1926, and the parsonage next door, both facing onto River Road. The parsonage has since been replaced by a parking lot. Photo dated 1936.

The result was a very beautiful neighborhood. Streets that were developed west of Connecticut Avenue at this time were Harrison, Huntington, Ingomar, Jenifer, Jocelyn, Kanawha, Keokuk, and on north; and 38th Street, Reno Road, and 39th Street. Most of the houses were substantial in size, whether of brick, stone, frame, or pebbledash.

The new residents were generally well-to-do, and many were well known. Ossie Bluege, third baseman for the Washington Senators, lived at 39th and Garrison. Prominent lawyers, writers, educators, businessmen, and government employees were attracted to this neighborhood in large numbers for the first time.

On the west side of Wisconsin Avenue, builder Morris Cafritz revived the moribund development of American University Park after World War I. Although, like Wesley Heights, it had been designed as a community appealing to and limited to retired Methodist clergymen or other Protestants, its growth was disappointingly slow. Cafritz, who was not a Methodist, acquired 30 to 40 acres of the Shoemaker and Perry land just east of the District line and along River Road; he developed modest housing, mostly bungalows, south of Fort Bayard and north of Murdock Mill Road, which was not yet obliterated.

The late "Reds" Kirby, who was a police officer in the 8th Precinct, remembered one day in 1925 when he was walking down a country lane off Murdock Mill Road. He heard the sound of hammering and found a local landowner putting up a LAND FOR SALE sign. When Officer Kirby found the man wanted $1,000 for a lot (now 46th and Albemarle), he thought that was a pretty high price!

Church and School Expansion

The constant growth of the population increased attendance at the local churches and forced them to take steps to accommodate their enlarged congregations.

In the early '20s, Ida Gore recalled "the little [Baptist] church was pitiful . . . . Fifty was a big crowd."[334] But within four years, the Baptist Church on Wisconsin Avenue north of Brandywine was so crowded that the congregation had to move into a new, larger church. They began a new building at 42nd and Fessenden in 1924.

In 1922 the members of Eldbrooke Methodist Church had also decided that a new and larger church building was in order. The properties at Gloria Point, between River Road, Wisconsin Avenue, and Brandywine Street, were for sale at that time, and so the church bought them, with an eye to possibly building a new sanctuary there.

By 1925, however, the decision had been made to rebuild the new church on the old site. So the Gloria Point properties were sold, and the Methodist congregation began building a large, Spanish style sanctuary and Sunday school wing in 1926. In the last service in the old church (1925), the printed program explained the decision to erect a new, modern building:

> "This section of the city is developing rapidly. New streets are being laid out, and many new houses are being built, and the population is increasing. Our Sunday School has outgrown its present quarters . . . ."

Also in 1926, St. Columba's Episcopal Church, just behind Eldbrooke, began construction of a new stone church.

St. Ann's Catholic Church did not increase the size of its sanctuary at that time, but its parish school

THE ELDBROOKE MEN'S BIBLE CLASS, ABOUT 1935

(Photo c/o Louis Pyles)

(Photo c/o Louis Perna)

(Photo c/o River Road Presbyterian)

Top: St. Columba's Episcopal Church, 42nd and Murdock Mill Road, built 1926. Granite used in exterior was from Perna quarry in Guilford, Md.

Bottom: The River Road Presbyterian Church, dedicated in 1937, at 4420 River Road. It was built of North Carolina granite in a Gothic design. An educational unit was added in 1950.

attendance grew to 150 pupils—partly because of overcrowding at the Tenley School, and partly because of the church's campaign to enroll all of its children in the parochial school.

In 1937 the Presbyterian Church bought part of the old Burrows farm on River Road. A stone church was built on River Road where the Burrows' front yard had been.

The new public elementary school, named after former regional superintendent Bernard T. Janney, was completed on the newly-extended Albemarle Street in 1925. At first older children (through 8th grade) moved over to Janney Elementary School and the younger ones remained at the old Tenley School. When a second wing was finished at Janney in 1932, and the 7th and 8th grade pupils were attending the new Alice Deal Junior High (which was opened in 1931), the old Tenley School was finally vacated. It had been described by residents as a "very old building condemned many years ago as unsafe."

As the citizens' plea for greater school facilities in 1930 went on to say,

"There has been greater building activity here than in any other part of the city, and there is assurance that it will continue . . . . [For example] several large apartments, development of Fort Bayard Park, and erection of a laundry [Tolman's] with 125 employees and their families to live in this section. The Ben Murch School does not offer relief—[not] even transfer of pupils to the proposed Reno Junior High School in the event that one is built."[335]

The old Grant Road School was torn down in the spring of 1929 to make way for the Ben W. Murch

Elementary School, which opened in 1930 at 36th and Ellicott Streets.[336] This new school took children north of Albemarle and east of 39th Street away from Janney, and also relieved overcrowding at the E.V. Brown Elementary School in Chevy Chase.

St. Ann's, after much difficulty, was able to purchase the old Tenley School, and after refurbishing it, moved its parochial school in, in the fall of 1933. The old St. Ann's parish school was eventually torn down.

New Building

After recovering from a temporary depression in the early 1920s, builders had their heyday in Northwest Washington in the late 1920s. The Devonshire Apartments appeared at Wisconsin and Van Ness. The Home for Incurables was begun on Upton Street (which was no longer Pierce Mill Road). The Methodist Home was built on Connecticut Avenue at Ellicott (George Armes' house had long ago been torn down).

The old rural landscape was hardly visible anywhere in the area. The Voigt pastures and stables, however, still remained in 1928, north of Albemarle and 38th Streets. A part of Enders' dairy farm behind Dumblane was one of the last holdouts; there were still some open fields and two or three small farms between Wisconsin Avenue and 46th Street. The building boom went on; as each new street was cut in, houses were erected in block after block.

Western Avenue was extended to Massachusetts Avenue—which reached to the District line in the 1920s. The east-west streets such as Brandywine, Butterworth, and Chesapeake were then opened onto Western in about 1928.

Bus service was introduced to American University Park residents in the 1930s. One of the earliest

THE JANNEY SCHOOL

(Photo c/o Janney School)

(Photo c/o Janney School)

(Photo c/o Alice Kunk)

Top: The Bernard T. Janney Elementary School on Albemarle Street, built 1925. This photo was taken before 1932, when a second wing was built on the west side (right of photo).

Bottom left: Blanche Pulizzi, principal 1925–1941.

Bottom right: Nell Hiscox, principal 1942–1970.

181

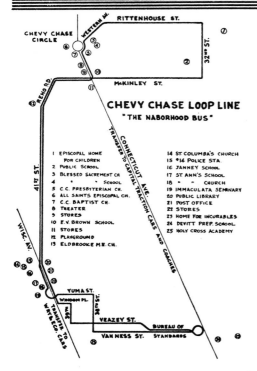

Extended Route
Of the
Chevy Chase Loop Bus Line

"The Naborhood Bus"

Extension of route now provides two direct connections from Connecticut Avenue Street Cars or "De Luxe" Coaches, also to Street Cars on Wisconsin Avenue.

———o———

Free transfers issued to cars on cash fare and 2 cent transfers on token fare. Free transfers to Chevy Chase Coach Line on coach fare. Commutation fare 5 cents with no transfer privileges, are sold in books of 20. No change in schedule.

THE CAPITAL TRACTION CO.

routes was west from Wisconsin along Fessenden to 49th, then south to Massachusetts Avenue.

Harry Wardman, builder of the Wardman Park Hotel, built semi-detached brick houses west of Wisconsin on Ingomar and Jenifer. The Pernas and Gaspar Segreti built stone houses on Brandywine and 42nd Street. And the stone and stucco Volkman house on Wisconsin Avenue across from Immaculata was a real showplace. It was built in 1922.

The Top Notch newspaper, the official organ of the Friendship Citizens Association, reported local new construction and the names of purchasers of the many new homes. An editorial in October 1930 cheered that

"[Washington's] great good fortune is its position as the center of activities of the greatest and richest country in the world.

"Washington is certain to

grow. It may not have a spectacular growth, but in the very nature of things it is destined to become one of the great cities of our land. We could not help it if we tried—and fortunately very few Washingtonians are trying to check its progress. Those few are doing so indirectly—by their opposition to improvements, by standing in the way of the city's good and that of its people.

"This is an excellent time to buy real estate in Washington. It will be worth more later on."[337]

Albemarle Street was finally cut through west from Grant Road to Wisconsin Avenue around 1931. This continuation had been postponed for a long time because it meant tearing down or moving houses on both Grant Road and Wisconsin Avenue. On Grant Road, the Christian and Chappell houses were moved a few

feet to the north, but the Sonnemann house was torn down. Many houses on the south side of Grant Road were also removed for the eventual opening of 39th Street to Albemarle and the new Nebraska Avenue.

In 1925 the streetcar tracks were moved from the east side of Wisconsin Avenue to the center, south of Gloria Point, and a new string of poles ran alongside the tracks.

In 1928, when the east and west sides of Wisconsin Avenue were paved for autos, there was an unpaved center strip that came to be used for parking cars. The local citizens associations were instrumental in having this and other local streets paved in the middle, to prevent the increasing number of accidents caused by this arrangement.

In 1929 and 1930 new sewers were laid, Wisconsin Avenue was widened again, and many of the unsightly poles and wires that cluttered the Avenue were removed. It was resurfaced from Massachusetts Avenue to the District line. By the mid-'30s there were rarely any horse-drawn wagons on Wisconsin Avenue; the automobiles and trucks had taken over completely.

This widening of Wisconsin Avenue also shortened the front yards between the stores or houses and the street. Living in the houses that faced on the Avenue became less desirable, and most houses were turned into stores or torn down and replaced by stores.

Good-bye to Old Sub-T

The police Substation-Tenleytown, always called Sub-T, also grew out of the small quarters it had occupied for 20 years on Wisconsin Avenue. Some of the officers in the 1920s were still mounted on horses, even though patrol cars were available. Arthur C. Belt was the captain for many years.[338] Belt was from Ohio, but his extended family of relatives in Maryland indicates he may have been descended from Joseph Belt of "Cheivy Chace." In any case, Arthur Belt and his family moved from the old Chappell house near Broad Branch Road to Belt Road in 1924.

In 1926 a new Tenleytown police station was begun on an empty field on Albemarle Street, across from the new Janney School and behind the old Achterkirchen place. The police vacated the old Sub-T and occupied their new Georgian brick building, 4125 Albemarle, in October 1927.

It was no longer a sub-station of Number 7 in Georgetown; it was its own Precinct Number 14. By 1932 the Metropolitan Police Department had renumbered it Precinct 8, and "Numbah 8" it remained through the 1960s.

The new brick police headquarters "looks for all the world like a

(1977 photo by Judith Helm)

(1930s photo c/o National Park Service)

Top: William A. Volkman and his wife (Lillian Riley) built this house in 1922, before Tenley Circle was cut through. It is now on the Circle, at Wisconsin Avenue and Yuma Street.

Bottom: When Albemarle Street was cut through to Wisconsin Avenue in 1931, the three houses at left, facing Grant Road, had their back yards cut off. In this view from Nebraska Ave., Mostow's is the large brick building at Albemarle and Wisconsin; this picture was taken 10 years before Sears was built.

TENLEYTOWN POLICE STATIONS

(1924 photo by Capitol Photo Service, c/o Mrs. James L. Giles, Jr.)

(Photo by Petra Schultze)

Top: Capt. Thaddeus Bean of Georgetown (front, center) poses with the men of Sub-T in front of the pebbledash Tenleytown police building. Lt. James L. Giles, in charge of Sub-T, is in the front row, 4th from left. Four

officers standing at right are in motorcycle uniform.

Bottom: This building at 4125 Albemarle Street served as the Tenleytown police station (Precinct Number 8) from 1927 until 1974.

wayside church in a New England village." Before Christmas 1927 the <u>Star</u> carried an article about the police pursuit of an elusive house burglar nicknamed "The Cat":

"The reign of fear extends from Woodley road to Chevy Chase Circle and from Connecticut Avenue to Wesley Heights . . . .

"There are six fine cells in this churchlike police station and the 'Cat' is welcome to a free run of all six of them if any of the 14th precinct men can lay their hands on him. He has afforded these officers the most baffling problem they have been called upon to solve since the precinct was organized."[339]

Prohibition

One of the most difficult chores of the Tenleytown police during the 1920s was enforcing Prohibition. The 18th Amendment, prohibiting the manufacture and sale of alcoholic beverages, was in effect from 1920 until 1933.

Achterkirchen's saloon had gone out of business long before 1920. The beautiful old Willows, run by Karl and Mamie Heurich, continued for a while to function as a restaurant, although it could no longer serve beer and mixed drinks. For a time it was even rented out as a residence; but then it enjoyed a revival as an evening spot after Prohibition was repealed. A 1934 ad indicated:

"music by Quill Wylie, featuring Alice Edwards, vocalist . . . . Tasty sandwiches and drinks that are properly prepared from liquors of the finest vintage served inside or on the Open Air Terrace . . . . No cover charge . . . . Ample parking facilities . . . . Open till 2."

The grand old Willows Hotel on Wisconsin near Western, however, gradually fell into a state of dilapidation in the late '30s. It was torn down after the death of its owner, W.H. Voigt, in 1938.

Thanks to local bootleggers, drinking went on pretty much uninterrupted in Tenleytown during Prohibition. Everyone in town eventually knew who the bootleggers were. The children even knew how to recognize the light blue color on a car's wheel or tire that identified the "secret" supplier of whiskey. One irony was that the leader of the local Anti-Saloon League had a brother-in-law who was one of the Tenleytown bootleggers.

And of course the policemen knew. As described by realtor Harold E. Doyle in a letter in July 1938, regarding Fort Reno: "During Prohibition this area housed about a dozen bootleggers, a list of whom was given me by a police officer."[340]

But the buyers, as well as the sellers, were their own friends and neighbors—their Masonic brothers, their church brothers, and often their police brothers. And so there was nothing to do but to look the other way. The one regulation that the police did try to enforce, however, was transporting whiskey over the state line. Since the District-Maryland line was crossed by many streets in the Tenleytown district, this work kept the officers busy.

A New Library

The new Bernard T. Janney School had been in session for a year when, in September 1926, a sub-branch of the D.C. public library was opened in one room on the first floor of the school. The growing population, especially through the Friendship Citizens Association, had voiced a need for a local library branch, and this was the first step.

TENLEY LIBRARY AND MASONIC LODGE

(1958 photo c/o Tenley-Friendship Library)

(Sketch from Singleton Lodge 50th Anniversary Book)

Top: When the police vacated Sub-T in 1926, the Tenley Branch Library was moved from Janney School to this building, and remained until 1960. The address was 4539 Wisconsin Avenue (east side), just south of the Lightfoot house.

Bottom: The three-story Singleton Masonic Temple, built in 1926, had the Friendship post office in the first floor until 1941. It's at 4441 Wisconsin.

GAULEY'S TENLEYTOWN PHARMACY

(Photo c/o Ruth Gauley Perna)

(Photo c/o Gladys Morders)

Top: Exterior view of Gauley's Tenleytown Pharmacy at Wisconsin Avenue and Grant Road, and the drug store's delivery truck—1931.

Bottom: Interior of Gauley's, 1939, showing soda fountain and lunch tables. Dr. Gauley is at far right; young man in center is Ralph Morders.

When the police department vacated its Sub-T building at 4539 Wisconsin Avenue, the prisoners' cells were removed and the place was completely remodeled for library use in 1927. Two small rooms on the left were for children's books. On the right was the large librarian's desk and counter. In the room beyond was the general library, furnished in 1930 with chairs, a settee, and a lamp.[341] A second floor apartment over the library was occupied by caretaker David Carroll and his wife for nearly 20 years.

The Tenley library remained at this site for 32 years. Within eight years of the acquisition of the old police station, however, the local citizens were agitating for a larger and better equipped library. The cramped quarters at the Tenley branch proved frustrating for many years.

Masonic Lodge Enlarged

"Because of the increase in our membership and larger attendances created congestion at our meetings, sentiment crystalized for enlargement" of the Masonic Temple in 1925.[342] Under the leadership of Worshipful Master A. Clifford Wilkins, an enlarged Temple was constructed. The first meeting in the new quarters was held February 8, 1926—the 25th year of the Singleton Lodge. The Tenleytown station post office continued to be located in the first floor of the Masonic Temple until 1940.

Dr. Gauley Becomes Pharmacist

Dr. Winslow W. Gauley came to Tenleytown as a pharmacist in 1922, when Dr. Robert Scholl retired. Scholl's Pharmacy, at the northeast corner of Wisconsin Avenue and Grant Road, became the Tenleytown Pharmacy.

(Photo c/o Angelina Bredice Neam)

(Photo c/o Marvin Tievsky)

Doc Gauley re-introduced the soda fountain to Tenleytown. As not-so-oldtimers recall, the "Tenleytown Special" was the deluxe sundae—vanilla ice cream with chocolate sauce, walnuts, whipped cream, and a maraschino cherry on top. Gauley's was a very popular place with the young people.

Another pharmacist, Dr. Morgan, opened Morgan Brothers drugstore in the early '30s at 4231 Wisconsin Avenue, at Veazey Street. As McLean Drugs, it remained at that address until the 1970s.

New Businesses

Each year brought new stores and businesses to Wisconsin Avenue. Some took over existing stores, some turned houses into stores, and others built entirely new buildings.

After the livery stable closed on the west side of River Road at Wisconsin Avenue, a small building on the site was used for a shoe and boot repair shop. Gaetano (Tony) Bredice, beginning about 1915, had the tiny shop just north of Achterkirchen's. Bredice later

(1927 photo c/o Rosalie Miller)

Top left: 1926 photo of Wisconsin Market at 4909 Wisconsin Avenue. Pictured left to right are David Tievsky, David's brother Abe Stein and David's wife Fannie Tievsky.

Top right: 1939 photo of Bredice shoe repair, 4629-41st Street. Errigo's Tenleytown Shoe Repair was two doors to right.

Bottom: Harry Rinis, prop., in Friendship Cleaners & Dyers

187

(Photo from <u>Top Notch</u>, April 1930)

(Photo from <u>Top Notch</u>, January 1930, c/o Edith Grove)

Top: Isaac C. Sykes, barber, with William Trigger and the bootblack, Edmund Stewart. Sykes shared space at 4507 Wisconsin with Harry B. Randall, dyer, cleaner, and presser.

Bottom: Bottle filling room in Loudoun Farms Dairy store (4515 Wisconsin), which became Chevy Chase Dairy.

moved to the 4600 block of 41st Street.

Another shoemaker in Tenleytown, also an Italian immigrant, was Giovanni Errigo. About 1911 Errigo set up his shoe shop on the east side of the Avenue right where Albemarle Street now cuts through. He also served for a while as lamplighter for the old gas street lights; he carried a ladder and a five-gallon gas can, lighting the street lamps in the evening, turning them off in the morning. Street lights were soon changed to electric and tungsten.

The Capital Ice Cream Company had occupied for a time the old French-Harry house north of the Masonic Temple and in front of the American Ice Company. When the ice cream store went out of business, Gus "Bean" Lucas opened in its place the "Tenleytown Lunch," the first modern restaurant in Tenleytown.

Eventually the old house in which Lucas' restaurant was located was torn down, for the extension of Albemarle Street; but the Chevy Chase Dairy continued its milk processing and bottling operations just south of it, at 4515 Wisconsin.

Local dairyman Francis Enders supplied much of the milk to the first local bottler, Loudoun Farms Dairy. In 1930 Loudoun Farms had been replaced by Wise Brothers' Chevy Chase Dairy, who named this bottling outlet on Wisconsin Avenue "Branch 6." (The Chevy Chase Dairy was sold to Chestnut Farms, which later sold to Sealtest Dairy.) Wise Brothers continued to run a "dairy store" in Tenleytown until about 1939, when Peoples Drug moved in.

In about 1927 Wenzel Nikl, an Austrian who had worked for years for a caterer, opened the Highland Bakery at 4525 Wisconsin. He baked over 100 loaves of bread a day, according to a 1930 interview in

(Photo c/o Johnson's Flower Center)

Top Notch, and made his own ice cream. Mrs. Nikl and their daughter continued the bakery into the '40s after Mr. Nikl died.

A new row of shops was built in "downtown Tenleytown" in the late '30s, between the public library and Mostow's. These new businesses included the American Trailer Company, Freemans' (later Frank Burrows') market, Frank Poch's Hardware (1918 to 1958), Nikl's bakery, and the Beau Brummel Cleaners.

Will Trigger, the barber, moved down to the Albemarle Street side of Mostow's liquor store with Isaac C. Sykes, who specialized in cutting both men's and women's hair in the new, short styles. Harry Randall's cleaners and dyers was in the same building as Sykes.

South of Albemarle Street, these stores remained on the east side of Wisconsin during the '30s: the post office and J.C. "Dick" Burrows' meat market and grocery (both beneath the Masonic Temple); the Chevy Chase Dairy; Slattery's appliances and records (which replaced the Eli Riley house after 1935); Layton & Smith's grocery (Paul Layton's son John became Metropolitan Police chief in the 1950s); and Winslow Gauley's Tenleytown Pharmacy on the corner of Wisconsin Avenue and Grant Road.

By 1937, High's Dairy had opened a store just south of the Masonic Lodge, in the former Chevy Chase Dairy store. High's remained in that block until the 1970s.

Down Wisconsin Avenue, in what used to be called Widowsville, the last blacksmith, Morris Fitzgerald, went out of business, and Henry Harper opened one of the first auto service stations on Wisconsin Avenue—on the northwest corner of Wisconsin and Loughborough; this was just before Van Ness Street was cut through.

On the north side of that intersection, Raymond T. Johnson opened a general roadside produce market in 1933. Gradually he added flowers and bedding plants to his

Old Loughborough Road as it went west from Wisconsin Avenue; as seen in 1928 from the top floor of the then-new Devonshire Apartments. In foreground is Harper's filling station (later Hamm's), selling Penn Straight Gas. Along Loughborough Road are three houses that still stand on what is now Van Ness Street. Along the top of the hill, L to R, are the Hillcrest Children's Center; house at 4200 42nd Street; the Dumblane Oak tree; Samuel Hazen Bond's "Dumblane" house; the Dumblane School; and three houses on Yuma near 42nd St.

GOULDS' STORE, WISCONSIN AVENUE AT GRANT ROAD

(Photo c/o Donna Burrows Rose)

Originally built as a home by Andrew J. Riley, Jr., and occupied by Father Mallon before a rectory was built for St. Ann's. A Chinese laundry for many years, and a general store run by the Burdettes in the 1920s. The Goulds owned the store when this photo was taken in the 1930s. Grant Road is to the left, and the house at 4415 39th Street is visible, far right, at the corner of 39th and Alton Place.

stock, until the flower and grocery stores were side by side. In 1952 the market was discontinued, and Johnson concentrated on flowers only. Today Johnson's Flowers is one of the few old businesses that have prospered into the 1980s, although at a different site, still in the Tenley area.

In 1929 the Friendship Building was constructed on the northeast corner of Wisconsin and Windom. Gus Haris' restaurant occupied the first floor, facing Wisconsin, and a beauty shop faced Windom. Upstairs was a large hall rented by realtor Joseph Wise and used by the Junior Order of United American Mechanics (Reno-Esther Council 26), and by two dancing teachers, Susan Hall and Mary Day, founder of the Washington School of Ballet. A dentist, F. Noel Marceron, and a doctor, Karl Dortzbach, had offices there. The Reno-Esther Building, as it was popularly called, was the first office building in Tenleytown.

The Edward F. Goebel family, having long lived in Tenleytown, had after World War I a very successful florist, nursery, and landscaping

business at 5021 Belt Road. In the early 1930s, when the city cut a street through their property, the Goebels moved to a new site in Wheaton, Md.

In the 1920s there were a number of Jewish merchant families in Tenleytown. The best known were the Mostows, Goulds, Rinises, Freemans, Tievskys, and Gormans. Abraham and Rose Mostow had moved their general store from 41st Street to the corner of Wisconsin and Albemarle—until the mid-'20s they were still selling feed for horses and farm animals. In about 1933 the Mostows turned the business into a liquor store.

Joseph Gould, his wife, and children Anna and Joe had a store across Grant Road from Gauley's on Wisconsin Avenue—in the same large house previously occupied by the Chinese laundry and the Burdettes. The Goulds specialized in nickel pickles, a tantalizing offering of penny candy, and notions. When the National Park Service took their house to make parkland around Tenley Circle, the Goulds moved up to the other side of Doc Gauley's,

(Photos c/o George Eiker)

replacing Layton and Smith. Anna Gould Luber retains her gift shop, Joanne's, in that building today.

In 1920 Harry Rinis, an immigrant from Poland, opened a clothes cleaning and tailoring establishment on the southeast corner of Chesapeake and 41st Street. Mr. Rinis kept the Friendship Cleaners & Dyers until he retired in 1965, a few months before he died.

Israel Freeman took over the J.C. Burrows market on Belt Road for a time, then used the building (formerly the Templars Hall) for a warehouse and in 1930 moved to 4523 Wisconsin Avenue, where he ran a grocery store for many years.

Joseph B. Gorman's grocery store on Grant Road at Brandywine Street continued to operate as part of the District Grocery Stores (DGS) chain into the 1950s, even after Nebraska Avenue had cut off Grant Road.

Upper Wisconsin Avenue

The family grocery stores in Tenleytown were threatened by the arrival of the first chain markets in about 1925. An A&P store arrived on the east side of upper Wisconsin Avenue, south of Fessenden Street; and a Sanitary store appeared on the northeast corner of Wisconsin and Fessenden. The need was greatest in that neighborhood, for the new residents there on both sides of Wisconsin Avenue had no grocery store within walking distance. The new chain stores were not large, but they carried a greater variety of modern foods than the old "Mom and Pop" stores. Soon the A&P moved to the west side of Wisconsin south of Fessenden, and an Acme opened on the east side.

The west side of upper Wisconsin Avenue had been owned by the Shoemaker family for a century prior to this time, and it was for the most part Shoemaker heirs who sold this property for business and residential development. In the early '30s, 42nd Street was extended north from Albemarle Street across River Road and up to Wisconsin Avenue. Safeway Stores now lease part of that site from the Harry family.

The east side of upper Wisconsin Avenue was developed from land once owned by the Heiders (from Chesapeake to Ingomar) and the Voigts (from Ingomar nearly to the District line).

Two Voigt houses on the east side of upper Wisconsin Avenue. (Left:) 5239 Wisconsin, built by William Voigt and occupied by his daughter, Louise Eiker, in the early 1930s, when this photo was taken. (Right:) Walter Eiker stands north of Frederick Voigt's house, set back from Wisconsin Ave. This house has been moved to 4232 Ingomar Street. Notice the chickens in the yard in this rural Tenleytown photo, circa 1915.

191

UPPER WISCONSIN AVENUE STORES IN THE '30s

(Sketch from October 1930 Top Notch, c/o Edith Grove)

Top: Robert Veitch's Friendship Pharmacy, Wisconsin at Ingomar, replaced the Fred Voigt house. It has since housed various restaurants.

Right: The Tolman Laundry, newly opened in 1930 on the west side of Wisconsin, across from Voigts. It closed in 1974 when the Jenifer Theatre building was built next to it.

(Photo c/o George Eiker)

The row of small brick shops built in the late '20s on the west side of Wisconsin south of Fessenden still stands today. William Dumbell was the owner of the "Toggery Department Store" at 4934 Wisconsin (selling dry goods, toys, clothing, and household items).

Another dry goods store, two grocery stores, a shoemaker, a bakery, a barber, a cleaners, and the American Stove Company were all accommodated in that block—in addition to the A&P, Bert Allison's cafe, and, eventually, Van Sant's pharmacy on the corner.

Pharmacist Van Sant was very successful with his drugstore at Wisconsin and Fessenden. For teenagers in the '30s it was "the place to go." Geralis Florist and now York Florist have succeeded the drugstore.

The Tolman Laundry opened a modern plant in 1930 at 5248 Wisconsin. The public opening featured a huge cake of Ivory soap; customers entered a contest to guess its weight, which turned out to be about 300 pounds.[343]

Grocery Stores

When James "Pop" Richards' Belt Road Market was torn down, he moved to 4853 Wisconsin. This was also a "rustic" old store with open cookie, candy, and pickle barrels, which reflected Pop Richards' casual attitude toward sanitary measures. He "was generally out of most everything but the bare essentials," but was very popular nevertheless, since he extended credit to lots of people in the area, especially during the Depression.[344]

John Sheaffer's grocery store had been on the west side of Wisconsin at Chesapeake since soon after the turn of the century. Sheaffer's daughter, Anna Dougherty, eventually turned it into a variety store, since so many competing grocers had come into the area. In more recent years, the building has housed a record store, a Chinese tailor, and a Chinese restaurant.

A small family grocery store, George Claggett's Market, was opened in the 1930s at 4233 Wisconsin (later Maggie's Restaurant). A modest-sized Sanitary grocery opened first in a small store north of Brandywine on 41st Street. It soon closed and reopened south of Albemarle Street, where it remained until about 1935.

In 1939 the Giant supermarket opened at 4555 Wisconsin Avenue, just north of the Lightfoots' house. The Cohen brothers founded their Giant supermarket chain in the

District with great success, because of their innovations in self-service, pricing, and efficient checking-out. The Giant replaced two old double houses that had been built and rented out by the Lightfoots. But the old Tennally-Lightfoot house remained next to the Giant until the 1950s.

When Brandywine Street was cut through east of Wisconsin in the '30s, the old Willett house and store, occupied by Simpson's hardware and bought by the Pernas, was moved back onto Brandywine, where it remains.

In the late '30s one newspaper reporter[345] counted 21 grocery stores and five drugstores on Wisconsin Avenue between Woodley Road and Western Avenue.

The ultra-modern Giant Food Store, which opened in Tenleytown in 1939, featured parking on the roof. The old Tennally-Lightfoot house is barely seen to the right in this picture. Hechinger's Lumberyard, at Wisconsin Avenue and Brandywine, now occupies the store and the property that once was Lightfoot's.

(1942 photo by Marjorie Collins; Library of Congress)

193

THE METHODIST CEMETERY, TENLEYTOWN

(1979 photos by Judith Helm)

Top: Located on old Murdock Mill Road, behind Eldbrooke Methodist Church, this cemetery has existed since 1855.

Bottom: In foreground are markers for Queen, Riley, Harry, and Walther. In background is St. Columba's Episcopal Church.

Cemetery Changes

When the St. Columba's Church members built their new, larger church sanctuary in 1926, they knew that the D.C. Department of Highways was planning to cut 42nd Street through from Albemarle to River Road and Wisconsin Avenue, and to pave the badly-rutted Albemarle Street. The old frame church that was torn down would have stood right in the way of the 42nd Street extension.

In addition, the St. Columba's congregation used part of the adjacent "St. Alban's burying ground," as it was originally called, for the new church. The Episcopal burying ground had been used from 1855 through the 1890s by members of both St. Alban's and its Tenleytown mission, St. Columba's. Most of the graves were poorly marked or not marked at all, however. The Methodist Cemetery adjoined the Episcopal burying ground—both were along the north side of Murdock Mill Road, just behind the new police station.

In 1927, then, when the District was ready to cut 42nd Street through, it was necessary for most of the St. Columba's graves to be disinterred, and a corner of the Methodist cemetery was also removed. A few families claimed the graves of their ancestors and made arrangements for them to be reinterred elsewhere. But most graves were unclaimed and were dug up by steam shovel.[346]

The Methodist Cemetery actually added some of the Episcopal graves to the west side of its property. Ever since then, the burying ground has been under the administration of the survivors, called the Methodist Cemetery Association. In the early 1940s the entire cemetery was resurveyed and a complete list made of those buried there.

TENLEY CIRCLE, 1936

(Photo c/o Emelie Wisch)

Nebraska Avenue and Tenley Circle

The opening of Alice Deal Junior High School in 1931 and the subsequent construction of Woodrow Wilson High School in 1934-35 coincided with the extension of Nebraska Avenue northeast of Wisconsin Avenue.

"New-Braska Avenue" had initially followed the route of the old Loughborough Road, including a jog eastward to Widowsville, where it met up with the west end of Pierce Mill Road. But soon Nebraska was continued in a straight northeasterly direction to Wisconsin Avenue, where a traffic circle (Tenley Circle) was formed out of part of Immaculata's land—and continued on to cross Grant Road and Albemarle, past the Wilson and Deal schools, towards Reno Road and Connecticut Avenue. More houses were torn down or moved to accommodate the new avenue.

The circle at Nebraska, Wisconsin, and Yuma, initially called "The Wisconsin Avenue Circle," was

paved in 1936 to coordinate the traffic from these three intersecting streets. May B. Lightfoot, wife of the heir to the Tennally property, reportedly pressed for naming the new circle Tenley Circle. Mrs. Lightfoot was one of the few residents who saw any value in retaining the old name. Most of the local citizens associations' efforts were geared toward destruction of the old and unattractive (including the name Tenleytown) to allow for construction of the new and modern (including the name Friendship).

In 1930 the Devonshire Downs Citizens Association received a response from the D.C. Commissioners to their request that the circle at Wisconsin and Nebraska be named Friendship Circle. The Commissioners said that about three years earlier they had directed that it be named Tenley Circle, and saw no reason for changing it.

In this connection, there have been various efforts over the years to change the names of the old roads, for practical and esthetic reasons. The Records of the Columbia

Nebraska Avenue was newly paved around Tenley Circle and across Wisconsin Avenue in this 1936 picture. Immaculata Seminary, the Catholic rectory, and St. Ann's second church are on the west side of Wisconsin.

EXISTING AND PLANNED STREETS, 1924

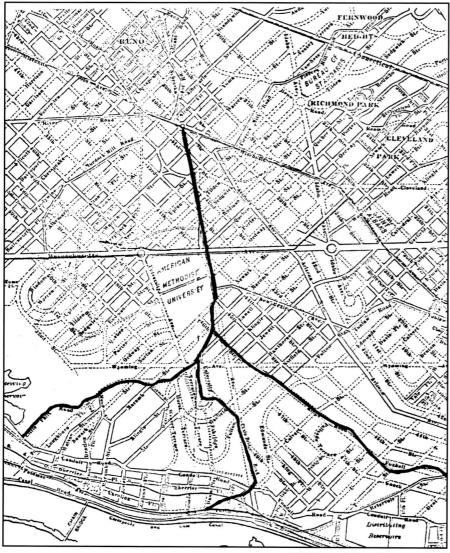

(1924 Foster & Reynolds map, revised)

The tracing of Loughborough Road (Nebraska Avenue) shows the three routes from Tenleytown to the Potomac—Ridge (Foxhall) Road, Chain Bridge Road, and Little Falls Road (Loughborough extended).

Historical Society[347] reported Alexander B. Hagner's recommendation that the name of Grant Road be changed to Randolph Street; there were at least four other streets named Grant around the city, and not yet one named Randolph.

In 1936 ex-Senator Thomas Gore, who lived on a large estate at Broad Branch Road and Albemarle Street, proposed changing Reno Road to Oklahoma Avenue. (Gore had represented Oklahoma in the Senate.) As late as 1959 the District Surveyor urged changing Reno Road to Washington Avenue. Both suggestions were hotly debated and finally rejected.

A traffic circle was also planned at the intersection of Nebraska and Massachusetts Avenues in 1934. Some people were against another circle because it slowed down traffic. The traffic circle was built, however, as a site for a statue that Harvard University presented to the city. The statue, unveiled in 1938, is of Major General Artemas Ward, first commander of American Revolutionary forces at Boston. The landmark has been known ever since as Ward Circle, adjacent to the American University campus.

Nebraska Avenue was also extended in a southwesterly direction along the line of the old Loughborough Road, but with a new direct connection to Conduit Road (MacArthur Boulevard). Before this new construction, Loughborough Road had linked Tenleytown to the Potomac River by three routes—Ridge Road (Foxhall), Chain Bridge Road, and Little Falls Road (see 1924 map).

Four New Plans for Fort Reno

The early roads had come into being one by one, to fill a need to get from one place to another. Water and sewer facilities were likewise originally constructed as needed, without planning for future growth. Park areas were completely unknown in this area as long as its character was mainly rural. But, in the 20th century, increasingly decisions on the building of new streets and water and sewer facilities were made by city bureau heads after long sessions with planning committees, engineers, and citizens' groups.

Four inter-related decisions were made by city departments in the late 1920s that resulted in a complete change in the character of Fort Reno and much of Tenleytown east of Wisconsin Avenue: 1) the Water Department decided to build a new, larger reservoir and water tower; 2) the Board of Education planned a junior high school and a high school; 3) Congress passed a bill to allow the National Capital Parks to acquire the entire Fort Reno area and to develop a landscaped public park; and 4) the National Capital Park and Planning Commission designed a scenic Fort Drive to connect the city's Civil War forts.

New Reservoir and Stone Tower

An urgent need for increased water services prompted the excavation in 1928 of a new underground reservoir with a 20-million-gallon water capacity. This reservoir, south of the crest of the Reno hill and the earlier reservoir, took land from a few Reno residents.

A second water storage tower was also completed in 1929. This tower, designed to resemble a French Norman castle tower, provided additional resources for serving those highest elevated sections of Washington.[348] Surface of the water in this tower was 60 feet above ground level, or 485 feet elevation, and its capacity 160,000 gallons. A Dutch water boy weathervane

THE STONE WATER TOWER AT FORT RENO, BUILT 1929

(Photos c/o National Park Service)

Top: View of the new tower as taken from the old tower, 1935. To the east and south are seen the Methodist Home and apartment houses on Connecticut Avenue and, in the foreground, houses on Fort Reno that were soon to be torn down.

Bottom: Road construction before the days of heavy machinery. These black laborers wielded shovels near the old Reno reservoir and the newly-built water tower.

JUNIOR AND SENIOR HIGH SCHOOLS

(Photo c/o National Park Service)

(Photo c/o Harvey Davison)

Top: The brand-new Alice Deal Junior High School, with Fort Drive under construction, about 1931. Many houses had been removed for construction of the school and Fort Drive.

Bottom: Woodrow Wilson High School was built to serve the Tenley area in 1935. In the foreground, high school cadets drilling on the playing field south of the Reno reservoir. Note houses still standing on Chesapeake Street, later demolished.

revolves on the top of the tower. A Tudor-style house for the chief engineer, with an address on DeRussey Street, adjoined the newer tower. Municipal Architect Arthur L. Harris received for his architectural design of the stone tower an award from the Washington Board of Trade in 1929.

Mr. Parker and Mr. Scherer were resident engineers whose families lived with them after World War I at the Reno "reservoy," as it was called.

Junior and Senior High Schools

In 1928 the school board had authorized the District Commissioners to purchase land at Fort Reno for a junior high school. When the property owners declined to sell, condemnation proceedings were initiated in order to acquire the land. Building began in August 1930, and Alice Deal Junior High School opened for students one year later, September 1931. Purchase of the site and construction of the school had cost something over $49,000.[349]

In 1930 land along Chesapeake and south nearly to Albemarle—still called "French's Woods" by Tenleytowners who recalled when the French sisters owned it—was acquired for the construction of the new high school. This land was referred to in the newspapers as the Reno section, and it was proposed that it be called the Reno High School.

But the presidential name Woodrow Wilson High School was chosen when the all-white school opened in 1935. A ball field at 39th and Donaldson was readied by 1939—formerly Bangerter's pasture and the site of a number of substantial houses on the north side of Chesapeake. Before Wilson High School opened, students had to travel into the city to attend Western, McKinley Tech, Central, or Business High Schools.

(Photo c/o National Park Service)

By 1945 the last of the Reno blacks' houses were removed, across the street from Alice Deal Junior High. And although there were black children who continued to live on 41st Street near Ellicott, and scattered blacks lived elsewhere west of Rock Creek Park, the Jesse Lee Reno Elementary School had only 16 children enrolled in 1947,[350] and so it was finally closed in the early 1950s, and the children had to go east of Rock Creek Park to black schools. Integration did not come to D.C. schools until 1954.

A Park at Reno

The federal government had decided in the late '20s to reclaim every Civil War fort around Washington that could be reclaimed, to turn each fort site into parkland, to commemorate each as a national historic landmark, and ultimately to link the chain of forts around the city by a Fort Drive.

Cuno H. Rudolph, president of the Board of D.C. Commissioners, had written to a Congressman in 1926 urging the passage of a bill to provide for the purchase or condemnation of property in the Reno subdivision: "This irregular, ill-devised subdivision constitutes a blight upon this part of D.C." He urged the condemnation of the entire area of 52 acres, noting that the "territory surrounding is being developed by high class residences."[351]

Senator Roscoe Patterson of Missouri had introduced a bill "to establish a national military park at Fort Reno, D.C."[352] Senator Patterson's original idea was to include land all the way east to 36th Street (there was no Nebraska Avenue or Reno Road there then). A modified bill called the Cramton Bill was passed in 1930. City officials acted promptly when the bill was passed and moved to establish a new park in Tenleytown.

Fort Bayard property between River Road, Western Avenue, Fessenden Street, and 46th Street was also acquired by the National Park Service at this time.

These proceedings prompted much public debate over the government's right to "condemn" private lands for public use. Residents of Fort Reno protested; they talked to

The view from the stone water tower at Fort Reno shows tennis courts (left) above the reservoir, and houses where the Alice Deal Junior High playing fields would later be. Fessenden Street, Reno Road, and Connecticut Avenue are in the distance. Beyond is Rock Creek Park.

DECAYING HOUSES AT FORT RENO, 1930s

(Photo c/o Donna Burrows Rose)

(Photo c/o National Park Service)

Top: Fort Reno street scene, 1937.

*Bottom: Address unknown. Taken
by Park Service photographer
prior to demolition.*

lawyers; they held meetings—but they did not obtain the support of any body of influential people, and their protests were ultimately in vain. Government purchases of land in the Reno area continued through the '30s. The 1930 census indicates that blacks constituted between 10% and 20% of the population of Census Tract 11, which includes Reno.

The Friendship and Chevy Chase Citizens Associations had been instrumental in obtaining the new Alice Deal Junior High and, in 1935, the Woodrow Wilson High School. But there is no indication that they used their considerable influence to protect the interests of the black or the white people who had lived at Reno for two or three generations.

In fact, the citizens associations were very eager to rid the area of all unsightly old buildings, including those on Grant Road, to increase the park facilities as well as the school facilities for their children, to get a swimming pool and a stadium for Wilson High School, and accordingly to raise the property values of their increasingly affluent neighborhoods.[353]

Announcement of the event was soft-pedaled in the Friendship Citizens Association's Top Notch newspaper, October 1930:

Fort Reno Being Acquired

Inquiry at the office of the Park and Planning Commission reveals what will be interesting and somewhat startling news to many of our readers; that the Commission, following of necessity what may be termed the absorption process, has already acquired something like three fourths of the Reno tract area. This is good news, welcome to practically every reader of this paper. The Commission plans to acquire the entire tract for park, school and other public uses, and is attaining its aim as expeditiously as its limited powers warrant.

In a related article on the construction of the Alice Deal Junior High School is the editorial statement, "Friendship congratulates itself and longs for the dawn of the jubilee year when the entire Reno tract can celebrate its complete redemption." An earlier edition of Top Notch had referred to Reno as "the rendezvous of bootleggers."[354]

As Kenesaw M. Landis wrote,

". . . the old Negro settlements around the Civil War fort sites have been gradually whittled down. The white population, once indifferent to these hilly regions because they were too far out of town, has come to consider them highly desirable residential sections."[355]

The government paid each landowner for the property that was taken. The financial settlements, however, were less than generous. And Reno was not a dilapidated neighborhood, on the whole. Although the removal of buildings extended over a decade, no resident was given the option of remaining; all had to go.

Many Reno residents had just built new homes or made improvements to existing homes, stores, or churches when word came of the government takeover. Lawyers recommended that the residents take what they were offered, that they were too few in number to wield any defensive power. Many residents openly resented the removal; others accepted it "for the common good." Any active resistance was overcome by a feeling of impotence or unimportance in the government's scheme of things.

MORE FORT RENO HOUSES: STURDY HOMES ON DIRT STREETS AS THEY LOOKED IN THE 1930s

(Photos c/o National Park Service)

Top: Three houses on the north side of Ellicott Street, uphill from Belt Road.

Bottom: The Brooks house on Davenport Street, on the east side of Fort Reno.

DAVENPORT STREET, FORT RENO

(1930s photos c/o National Park Service)

Top: The 3900 block of Davenport Street, going uphill toward the reservoir. It was formerly known as Prospect Street, and was informally called "Magruder Row," having been built by a Magruder.

Bottom: Houses in the 4000 block of Davenport.

As in many projects to remove "blight" from a neighborhood, the residents at Fort Reno were obliged to seek housing elsewhere, on their own. A few, mostly whites, found other homes in Tenleytown; but others, mostly blacks, moved to areas of the city where rentals were not so expensive as the new Tenleytown houses—to Brookland, to Georgetown, to Mount Pleasant, to Benning, to Southeast.

Harold E. Doyle, of Thomas J. Fisher & Co. real estate, wrote in July 1938 to the director of planning, National Capital Park and Planning Commission:

"I and a number of my friends many years ago took over between 200 and 300 lots in the section for the purpose of preventing further building for colored occupancy . . . .

"My interest [is] in eliminating the subdivision of 25 foot lots on 30-foot streets . . . . The colored folks would, I am sure, scatter. Three or four who have worked for me have gone N.E. to about 45th and Benning Road, where there is quite a large settlement.

"There would seem to be no good reason to retain this comparatively small area for the use of colored, especially on such narrow streets and occupied by small poor frame houses, some of which are . . . tumbling down."[356]

By 1939 most of the Reno residents had gone; their houses had been razed, some of the area was landscaped, and a ball-playing and drill field for Wilson High School appeared north of Chesapeake Street.

The three Negro churches at Reno were also displaced by this plan. St. George's Episcopal records indicate that the congregation was discontinued in 1929 "because of the change in the character of the neighborhood."[357] Members of the St. George's Mission followed Father Edward Douse to St. John's, Georgetown.

St. Mark's Methodist folded, and its members attended Sligo and other city and suburban AME churches.

The projected parkland also embraced the site of Rock Creek Baptist. This church, situated at the far southeast corner of Fort Reno, at Chesapeake and Nebraska, was not forced to move until 1945. Rock Creek Baptist's property was purchased for $15,000, and the congregation moved to 24th and H Streets, N.W.

The forced removal of the residents cut off the very strong roots they had in the Reno settlement—in some cases, roots that went back two generations, or 65 years. The social order at Fort Reno had been long-established; these feelings of community and status were lost when the residents moved, family by family, to other neighborhoods—most often to neighborhoods that had no long-standing sense of community, family ties, or traditions. There they became strangers, newcomers, displaced people.

Fort Drive

The Reno parkway improvement plan was one part of the citywide plan to provide an elevated scenic automobile road, Fort Drive, connecting the major Civil War forts in the city. Fort Reno would thus have been connected to Battery Kemble, east of Chain Bridge Road, and to Battery Terrill, north of 30th and Garrison Streets. Fort Bayard would not have been connected with the Drive.

The Northwest Suburban (Friendship) Citizens Association had long supported this plan, which called for the northern extension of

BEFORE AND AFTER WILSON HIGH WAS BUILT

(Photo c/o National Park Service)

(Photo c/o Donna Burrows Rose)

Top: Looking south from the Reno reservoir in the early 1930s. Chesapeake Street, which marks the southern boundary of Fort Reno, has only a couple of houses and empty fields on the south side. Beyond the trees are blocks of houses in North Cleveland Park, and in the distance, the Cathedral, as yet towerless.

Bottom: Looking north toward Chesapeake Street and the towers at Reno, in 1937. Wilson High School (built 1936) is partly visible to the left.

(Photo c/o Spencer W. Scott)

(1947 photo by Paul Hochman, c/o Washingtoniana Collection, Martin Luther King Memorial Library)

Top: The Scott children standing in their Sunday clothes on the Wilson HS grounds, across the street from their home on Chesapeake Street. Standing, L to R: Marjorie, Elizabeth, Francis T., Jr. Front, L to R: Patricia and Spencer. Photo taken about 1940.

Bottom: Old houses in the 3900 block of Chesapeake contrast with new ones across Nebraska Ave— the "Wakefield" development.

Nebraska Avenue across Wisconsin Avenue and a curving link (never completed) with the old Military Road across Rock Creek Park.

An extension of parkland south of the new Woodrow Wilson High School and across Albemarle Street to Tenley Circle necessitated the removal in the late 1930s of another nine houses on Grant Road, all owned by whites, and the Goulds' store, at Grant Road and Wisconsin, across from St. Ann's. These houses lay in the path of the projected Fort Drive, which was expected to be more extensive than it came to be.

The master federal plan for recreation areas and parklands around the old forts, and a scenic Park Drive to link them, was a commendable idea. It was supported by all groups that were interested in the beautification of the city. It was also supported by traffic engineers who thought that these new in-the-city throughways would take commuter traffic away from residential and commercial streets.

As early as 1924 Charles C. Glover had donated to the District 80 acres of land on either side of the Foundry Branch south of Massachusetts Avenue.[358] For 20 years it was planned that a wide road known as Arizona Avenue would connect Tenley Circle and Fort Drive with Battery Kemble and an approach to the Canal Road freeway. This link in the proposed Fort Drive along the Foundry Branch was never built; instead, the Glover-Archbold Park was developed as a nature trail and public parkland.

Completion of the Fort Drive plan was shelved indefinitely in the late 1930s and was finally scrapped in 1948 as being too expensive.

*   *   *   *

It is pleasant to walk around the large area of land that was once the Reno community, to be above and away from the traffic of Nebraska or Wisconsin Avenues, to walk across the hilly fields of grass and hear the wind blow through the trees; it is exhilarating to be able to see for miles during the day, or to be able to see all the stars at night. The Fort Reno Park is enjoyed by a great variety of people. But it must be remembered at what price this enjoyment was bought.

Citizens Associations

Citizens associations came into existence long before the days when Washington residents could vote for representatives to Advisory Neighborhood Commissions, for School Board members, or for D.C. Council members.

Residents formed themselves into citizens associations as soon as they saw the need for group action to acquire new sewage lines, streets and street repairs, bus lines, schools, post offices, libraries, and other local services to keep up with local growth.

The Northwest Suburban Citizens Association was formed in 1892. In 1928 its name was changed to the Friendship Citizens Association, for by then there were many other citizens' groups in the "Northwest suburbs." The name Tenleytown Citizens Association was not chosen.

The Chevy Chase Citizens Association had been formed in 1909, and the Connecticut Avenue Citizens Association merged with it in 1920. The American University Park Citizens Association had come into being by 1927, and the Devonshire Downs (North Cleveland Park) Citizens, in 1926. They belonged to the Federation of Citizens Associations, which required an association to have 50 paid-up white members.

The Northwest Suburban (Friendship) Citizens Association's

GRANT ROAD HOUSES RAZED

(Photos c/o National Park Service)

Top: Four semi-detached houses on the south side of Grant Road; Donaldsons, Burdettes, and Weavers lived there in the 1930s.

Bottom: Five houses on the north side of Grant Road; Earps, Voigts, Morders, Baileys, and Skinners lived there in the 1930s.

THE DUMBLANE OAK TODAY

(1979 photos by Judith Helm)

Left: The centuries-old Dumblane Oak and the southeast garden side of Wiley Buchanan's house, at 4220 Nebraska Avenue.

Right: Front (north) entrance to Buchanan home.

early campaigns were for schools (Janney Elementary, Alice Deal Junior High, and Woodrow Wilson High); for increased police and fire protection and library service; for recreation areas and playgrounds; and against "commercial encroachment." An early campaign for a hospital in the Friendship area did not succeed.[359]

An additional function of the Friendship Citizens Association in the '30s was the promotion of neighborliness and the communication of information to residents. Before the extensive new residential development, such deliberate efforts had never been necessary, for neighborliness was a thing to be taken for granted; local information and gossip was easily acquired through relatives, neighbors, storekeepers, and churches.

But now there were so many new people that one could not possibly know them all. So in 1923 the Northwest Suburban Citizens Association began to publish a monthly newspaper, Top Notch, edited by Albert P. Seiler. The association also sponsored a community Christmas tree, a contest for the best Christmas decorations, and an annual spring banquet where residents could "get to know each other."

A look at the list of officers and committee chairmen of the Friendship Citizens Association in 1940 shows that by then only one was from an old Tenleytown family, and perhaps three were newcomers who married girls from pre-World War I Tenleytown families. Although the older families may have been members of the Association, it is understandable that those elected to leadership positions were the ones who wanted to effect improvements—and therefore change—in the neighborhood. The natives had difficulty seeing any need for changing conditions they had always lived with.

More New Homes

The building of new houses continued at a good pace during the late 1930s, despite the terrible economic depression elsewhere in the country. Throughout the city, there were only 2,000 residential building permits issued from 1931 to 1935; but the number tripled to more than 6,000 in the years 1936 to 1940.

In the two-and-a-half year period from January 1937 to July 1939, 1,274 homes were built in the area bounded by Western and Massachusetts Avenues, Rock Creek Park and the District line. The average price of the homes was $8,000 to $10,000 in 1939.[360]

West of Wisconsin Avenue, Boss and Phelps developed Brandywine Street near 43rd in 1930, and called the area Fort Bayard Park. Morris Cafritz continued to build on Davenport Street in American University Park. Baker built on Butterworth, and Brown Brothers built on Albemarle, Alton, and Yuma.[361] Further south there arose new houses on Warren Street, near 44th, some by Cooley Brothers, some by Albert Walker. Most of the other houses built at that time were individual, custom-built homes.

There were only three large houses on Yuma Street at 42nd before 1930. Monroe Warren then built some of the first Colonial brick two-story homes that typify American University Park. He called his section, at 44th and Yuma, Grasslands after the historic Loughborough estate that was still standing at that time on Nebraska Avenue.

A few spectacular individual residences were built in the area. David Lawrence, newspaperman and syndicated columnist, built a beautiful "villa" at 3900 Nebraska Avenue, opposite "Grassland," in the 1920s. It has since 1950 been occupied by the Swedish ambassador.

Next door was a large home on 7½ acres purchased from the Glover estate, and occupied by Mrs. Andrew Parker, whose husband had been president of Woodward & Lothrop. In 1972 the property was sold to the government of Japan for $2 million. A new, modern embassy has been constructed at the site, 4000 Nebraska Avenue.

In 1924 Scott E. Welker, builder of the stone mansion on the Bureau of Standards land, had a large new house built for himself and his wife on Nebraska Avenue, south of Samuel H. Bond's "Dumblane" house. Focal point of the new three-acre estate was the centuries-old Dumblane Oak, and the house, named "UnderOak," was built around "Washington's most magnificent huge oak" tree.

"UnderOak," at 4220 Nebraska, was featured in the May 1924 issue of <u>American Architect</u>. Victor Mindeleff was the architect.

In 1941 Mr. and Mrs. Wiley Buchanan moved into "UnderOak"; they added a large wing on the northeast side of the house in 1951,

THE WASHINGTON HOME

(Photo by Judith Helm)

The Washington Home for Incurables was built at 3720 Upton Street in 1927.

before leaving for Luxembourg, where Buchanan was U.S. Ambassador. He was Chief of Protocol under President Eisenhower from 1957 to 1961. The Buchanans still own the house, which they rented to Marjorie Merriweather Post (in the 1950s) and to Henry Kissinger and his bride Nancy (in the 1970s).

A large seven-bedroom stone house with a beautiful garden was built at 4110 Warren Street in the 1940s, next to Bond's "Dumblane" house. The first occupant was Senator Homer Capehart; the second, Charles P. Maloney, owner of Maloney Concrete; and the third, His Eminence Patrick Cardinal O'Boyle, who still resides there, near St. Ann's rectory.

North Cleveland Park

What is now called North Cleveland Park, east of Wisconsin Avenue, was developed extensively in the late 1920s and early 1930s.

First, the Sterretts developed a section appropriately called Springland, since it surrounded their old brick family home

"Springland," which still stands on Tilden Street; 34th Street was at first extended only from Rodman north to Springland Lane.

Then an enormous construction of semi-detached brick homes took place on Van Ness, Veazey, Warren, Windom, Yuma, and Albemarle Streets, and on Reno Road, 37th, 38th, and 39th. By 1940 there were almost no lots undeveloped in the North Cleveland Park area.

The Tudor, the Italianate, the Spanish stucco, and a functional mid-'30s American style brick predominated. Much of this construction was done by Harry Wardman, who in a period of 20 years built about 5,000 homes and 400 apartment buildings in the District of Columbia.

Other builders in the area included W.C. Miller, J.S. Williams, C.H. Small, and B.F. Saul.[362]

(Photo by Judith Helm)

The Devonshire Apartments, the first apartment houses in Tenleytown, were built in the early 1920s at 4105 and 4115 Wisconsin Avenue.

The Washington Home for Incurables had moved from Georgetown to 3720 Upton Street in 1927. Two wings were added to the large nursing facility in the 1930s. In the 1970s the name of the institution was changed to The Washington Home.

Wakefield and Chevy Chase, D.C.

North of Albemarle Street, R.B. Warren developed 100 brick homes between Nebraska Avenue and Connecticut Avenue, and gave his section the name Wakefield. A 1947 photo by Paul Hochman (see p. 204) contrasts the Wakefield brick homes across Nebraska Avenue with the old wooden Reno homes on Chesapeake Street, still occupied by black families when the photo was taken.

The 1930s developments of houses and apartments on either side of the Connecticut Avenue corridor drew the focus of these residents away from Tenleytown and towards Chevy Chase and Connecticut Avenue. A big step in that direction was the opening in 1938 of the first shopping center in the area—the Chevy Chase Park 'n' Shop, in the 4400 block of Connecticut, east side. This modern center had not only a large A&P, Peoples, Woolworth's, and Best's; but it boasted the area's first sports center—an ice skating rink and bowling alleys.

There were also two movie theaters on Connecticut Avenue—the Chevy Chase (now Avalon) near McKinley Street, which opened in 1922, and the Uptown, south of Ordway Street.

The Hilltop

In 1918 Howard G. Crandall took over the old Tenleytown Inn (still owned by Christian Heurich); but Crandall completely changed its nature to cater to what was expected

The necessity for another elementary school prompted the construction in 1932 of the Phoebe Hearst School on 37th Street, behind Sidwell's Friends School.

A large playground, extending to 37th Street and Idaho Avenue, was constructed along with the Hearst elementary school; it was designed to serve Cleveland Park, Richmond Park, and Devonshire Downs. Richmond Park was the area south of the Bureau of Standards, around 34th and Porter Streets, and Devonshire Downs was the name given to the new development between the Bureau of Standards and Wisconsin Avenue. The Devonshire Apartments, built in the '20s, faced Wisconsin at what had once been Widowsville.

The Devonshire Downs Citizens Association was formed in 1926, and met in the lobby of the new Home for Incurables. In 1930 the Association changed its name to the North Cleveland Park Citizens Association. In the late '30s and early '40s, the North Cleveland Park Citizens Association met in the second-floor hall at 3923 Windom Place, the Reno-Esther Building.

to be the source of revenue in the future—automobiles. Crandall sold Standard brand oil, gas, and automotive supplies very successfully for a few years. His became the first filling station in Tenleytown, under the name of the Hilltop gas station.

In 1924 George W. Bryan took over the auto accessories and service business and carried it for another 14 years. In 1930 a "fully equipped" multi-brand gas station was constructed on the northwest corner of Wisconsin and Albemarle, south of the old inn. It was "conducted under the auspices of the Hilltop Service Station" and supplied Amoco, Sinclair, Standard, and Esso brands of gas.[363] Before its completion, the October 1930 Top Notch announced that "According to reports this is to be one of the finest [service stations] in the eastern part of the U.S."

But in 1939 the large building which had served as inn, hospital, saloon, home, restaurant, and auto service station was razed, along with the blacksmith shop and other small buildings. An empty lot sat there for nearly two years while debates ensued about the use of the property. The small frame gas station, never really one of the finest in the east, continued there for a short time; a miniature golf course even appeared for a while. The southern part of the vacant lot, near Albemarle, was convenient for parking. A used car lot occupied part of the space.

In 1940 Christian Heurich sold the Hilltop property to Sears, Roebuck and Co. for a department store.

Gasoline Alley

With the amazing increase in automobiles (159,000 registered in D.C. in 1930) came an increase in filling stations on Wisconsin Avenue. From Van Ness Street to the District line, there were at least 16 gas stations during the 1930s. Sometimes

(Photo from The Washington Times)

there were four stations at an intersection—one on each corner.

The best known station owners, the ones who maintained their businesses for years, included (starting at Van Ness and going north) Hamm, Harper, Willoughby, Raines, Barron, Bradshaw, Wrenn, Clark, Phelps, Markham, Wolfe, Bartemeier, McDowell, Bohrer, Johnson, and Lapidus. Of the old-timers, only the Phelps family is still in the business, with Tenleytown Amoco at Wisconsin and Ellicott.

A modern phenomenon appeared in the late 1930s next to Paul Hamm's service station at Van Ness Street. It was the first drive-in restaurant on Wisconsin Avenue, Stouffer's Park 'n' Drive, at 4110 Wisconsin, featuring "Dining room or car service on our large parking area." Stouffer's was soon taken over by J. Willard Marriott, who added it to his chain of Hot Shoppes Drive-In Restaurants.

Post Office

From 1909 until 1940, the Tennallytown post office was located beneath the Masonic Lodge hall at 4441 Wisconsin. In October 1920,

THE HILLTOP

The old Tenleytown Inn, as it looked about 1935, occupied as an automobile accessory place and filling station. This historic three-story inn and saloon was built in the early 1860s, and was bought by Christian Heurich in 1889 and run by William Achterkirchen. About 1939 it was torn down for the construction of Sears, Roebuck on the west side of Wisconsin Avenue.

when "Tenleytown" was decreed to be the proper spelling, the first superintendent was Charles Hurley, who had grown up on Davenport Street.

Since 1916 the three letter carriers—Charlie Hurley, Kitty Barrett, and Charlie Eiker—had worn uniforms. Frank Law and George Riffle Payne, both local boys, were two other popular mailmen for many years. By the late '20s, the letter carriers were making two deliveries a day, and this continued until World War II.

In the early '20s, only these five mailmen were working out of the Tenleytown post office. But 20 years later, after the move to the new, larger station south of Upton Street in 1940, there were dozens of employees.[364] The many new federal and Navy installations west of Rock Creek Park, as well as many close-in parts of Bethesda, Maryland, were covered by the new "Friendship" post office, as it was renamed in 1940.

Disappearance of "Tenleytown"

The commercial growth along Wisconsin Avenue was accompanied by an abrupt decline in the use of the old name Tennallytown or Tenleytown. The first issue of Community News in 1937, for example, contained an ad for Bell's Hairdresser at 4013 Albemarle: "Tennleytown's newest beauty salon." But in the very next issue, the ad read, "Friendship's newest beauty salon."

The Community News was "published in the interest of Cleveland Park, Glover Park, Wesley Heights, University Heights, Friendship Heights, and Friendship."[365] There it was—or wasn't—in black and white.

Minutes from a 1924 meeting at Eldbrooke Methodist Church indicate the intensity of feeling about the loss of the name "Tenleytown":

"The name of Tenleytown was ushered in feelingly by Dr. Chappell and ruthlessly handled by [postal superintendent] Charlie Hurley who rashly asked where Tenleytown's boundaries now existed with North Cleveland Park, West Chevy Chase, American University Park, Derrickville, Robeyville, etc. squeezing out the life blood of dear old Tenleytown and endeavoring to replace it with Friendship."

C.W. Shoemaker
Acting Secretary
June 10, 1924

John Clagett Proctor reported in The Star (November 10, 1929) that the name Tenleytown—or Tennally-town—was being crowded out by the name Friendship,

"there having been considerable contention over the spelling of the former name. Incidentally, this is the passing of a very beautiful old name, which might well be regretted. Some argue that the word had too many Ls. The post office, however, did not feel that way about it, and for years used the old spelling Tennallytown until the controversy grew so warm that it dropped the name entirely and used the word Friendship."

In the minds of official Washington, Tennallytown, or Tenleytown, no longer existed.

Youth Problems

In the days when all the Tenleytown families knew each other, there was no real fear of crime from anyone but strangers. One of the biggest deterrents of crime was familiarity or at least acquaintance-ship. If you knew your neighbor's name, it was less likely he would infringe on your rights or property.

Every neighborhood had boys—and girls—who were mischievous, and some had honest-to-goodness bullies. But they could usually be kept in control by firmly-speaking adults who could call them by name. And in a village like Tenleytown, these adults were most likely their neighbors and often their relatives.

But then new developments were built in Tenleytown. The new residents did not know the young people or their families. The new children were not known to the old-timers. To complicate matters further, the new residents were very often, though not always, in a higher

income bracket than the third-generation Tenleytowners, and class distinctions were made by some. Racial incidents were prompted by actions of whites who had no appreciation for the sense of belonging of the blacks at Fort Reno.

Writer Carolyn Hughes, in "A Nostalgic Look at Alton Place," recalled that her street in the Armesleigh Park development was

"somewhere in limbo between Cleveland Park and Chevy Chase. In Tenleytown really, a name, incidentally, our parents never liked, probably because of the 'Grant Road gang' that made it so known."[366]

As in other localities across the United States, there were gangs of tough-looking local teen-age boys from time to time in the 1930s, who were inspired by movies starring John Garfield, Humphrey Bogart, and Jimmy Cagney.

The coming of movies, news-reels, and sensational magazines ended the days of innocence of young people in Tenleytown. Toughness had become a virtue, and the boys' nicknames reflected it: "Snake," "Gook," "Scruff," "Screechie," "Biffy," and "Moose" were known to everyone—but of course their mothers still called them Charles, Everett, John, etc.

The local football team was the epitome of this image of toughness—witness the Tenleytown "Bonecrushers" of the '20s and '30s! Charles "Sharkey" Burdette was a star fullback. Some of the Bonecrushers' opponents were teams from Alexandria, Brentwood, and other localities.

The Janney Athletic Club (football) and The Athletic Club of Friendship, also known as the Skinker Brothers Eagles (baseball), thrived in the late '20s and early '30s. In the summer of 1930 the tough

THE TENLEYTOWN BONECRUSHERS FOOTBALL TEAM, 1920s

(Photo c/o Emma and Allen Weaver)

(Front row, L to R:) (unknown); Robert "Bump" McCray; Robert "Bob" Burdette; Charlie Poore; Allen "Scruff" Weaver; George Harper; William "Buck" Barbee.

(Back row, L to R:) William "Gus" Moxley; William "Bits" Hopkins; John Stadtler; and Woodrow "Woody" Weaver.

"THE BOYS" OF WILSON HIGH SCHOOL, 1939

(Photo c/o Harvey Davison)

(L to R:) John "Gook" Guthrie and his Model A Ford; George "Moose" Janios and his '35 Ford; George Harper and his '35 Ford; and John "Bootie" Hopkins and his '38 Ford.

(Photo c/o Robert Truax)

(Photo c/o Edith Grove)

Top: The Tennally-Lightfoot house, 4551 Wisconsin Avenue, as it looked in the late 1930s. The Lightfoot sisters had died, and their nephew Jerome Lightfoot and his wife May occupied the house until her death in 1935.

Bottom: May and Jerome Lightfoot on a Sunday motor outing.

baseball Eagles of Tenleytown completed a successful 42-12 season.[367]

The Tenleytown Athletic Club, made up of Negro players from Fort Reno, played teams from Sandy Spring, Lyttonsville, and "Monkey Hollow."

Most of the so-called "youngbloods," after soldiering in World War II, turned out to be stable family men with good jobs; some were very successful businessmen. Gus Moxley, known in some circles as "the mayor of Tenleytown," is the owner of a roofing business; Vinton Dove, once upon a time of Grant Road, is a general contractor; and Hy Gorman, who played baseball for the University of Maryland, owns Gourmet Beverages on Macarthur Boulevard. Today, you will find most of the former "Tenleytown boys" enjoying retirement at their beach homes, or babysitting with their grandchildren.

There were successful efforts in organizing the young people into youth groups. Boy Scout and Girl Scout troops sprang up in the churches: Troop 100 at Wisconsin Avenue Baptist (founded 1918); Troop 19 at Eldbrooke Methodist (founded before 1931); and Troop 4 at St. Ann's (founded 1936). The new Presbyterian Church on River Road formed a Boy Scout troop in 1937. Troop 100, the oldest Boy Scout troop in continuous operation in D.C., now meets at River Road United Presbyterian Church.

Girl Scout troops were organized at St. Alban's and Eldbrooke. Carolyn Hughes has a happy memory of roller skating down the middle of Wisconsin Avenue to Girl Scout meetings at St. Alban's—there was so little traffic, the girls were in no danger.[368]

The Lightfoots

Members of the Lightfoot family did what they could to educate the newcomers about the history of the area.

First of all, they kept the old Tennally house in good repair. Although a house had possibly been built on the site by the Tennallys in about 1795, 1800 was the usually accepted date for the construction of the oldest part of the Tennally-Lightfoot house at 4551 (later 4541) Wisconsin. Daniel Lightfoot's addition was made in 1845. A local DAR chapter mounted a plaque on the front porch of the house attesting to its historicity. The old frame house was stuccoed over during the 1920s.

Mrs. Mary Ann Britt, the elder of the Lightfoot sisters, died in 1918 at the age of 83 at the home. Her sister, Barbara Lightfoot, died in April 1927. Her obituary in The Star pointed out that she had passed her entire 91 years in the historic Tennally house, which had been given to her mother in 1822.[369]

John Jerome Lightfoot, Jr., was a member of the third generation of Lightfoots in Tenleytown to live in the house, beginning in 1927, when his maiden aunt Barbara died. Mr. Lightfoot, an attorney with the Veterans Bureau, and his first wife, May, were a very handsome couple and soon became well known to the residents. Jerome was a notary public, and helped many neighbors with their taxes and other financial matters. May was a flamboyant woman who smoked cigarets, drove a Model T Ford, and took a lively interest in the neighborhood.

An active clubwoman, May Lightfoot opened the Tennally house to the public for one time only, in 1932, to benefit the American Legion, Henry Spengler Unit. Her husband's version of the history of the house was published in the newspapers.[370] Mention was made of the Tennally (Tenley) graves that lay unmarked and mostly buried in their backyard.

May Lightfoot died in 1935, and the same year Jerome was remarried, to Mrs. Kathleen Graham. They continued to live in the house even after they sold land on their north to the new Giant supermarket; the library on the south side separated the Lightfoots from the row of new stores.

Nourses Leave "The Highlands"

One historic house in the area that was not torn down is "The Highlands" (now Sidwell Friends School), built of stone in the 1820s by Charles Nourse. The Nourse heirs lived in the house until about 1910. It was occupied from 1911 to 1923 by Interstate Commerce Commissioner Balthasar Meyer and his family. Their daughter, Sylvia, became well known as a harpist with the National Symphony Orchestra.

In 1916 Margaret B. Downing wrote,

"A glimpse of this interesting old house with its white pillars supporting the overhanging roof, can today be seen from the road, behind a stone wall and through the branches of the old trees."[371]

The front of the Nourse house is now clearly visible from Wisconsin Avenue, but then it was hidden by wistaria vines, large box hedges, and trees.

From 1900 until about 1910, the Washington School for Boys had occupied a site just north of "The Highlands." It was described as a "preparatory school of the very highest order," receiving "pupils of any age, whether as boarders or day pupils." It was "located in the country" and had extensive athletic grounds around its white frame buildings. The main building, Dunster Hall, was located at 3901 Wisconsin.

In 1913, Thomas W. Sidwell, who had founded Sidwell's Friends School, bought the old Washington School for Boys buildings and campus for his elementary school students. The older students remained at 1809 Eye Street, where the Friends School had been since 1883.[372]

In 1924 the Nourse heirs sold "The Highlands," including 25 acres, to Rear Admiral and Mrs. Cary T. Grayson, who called the house "Eagles Nest." They modernized the mansion, raising the roof to give a higher third story. The Grayson family lived next door to the Sidwell Friends School for nearly 20 years.

Admiral Grayson was a Virginian who had been the White House physician to President Wilson (1913-21). He was well known in the East as a leading huntsman who belonged to one of the most exclusive clubs in America—New York's Jockey Club.[373] When he first moved to Wisconsin Avenue, Grayson used the old stone tenant house as a clubhouse, entertaining his poker-playing friends, many of them also President Wilson's official advisers and friends.

In 1931, Grayson turned over the little stone building and a large parcel of land for development of an elementary school and a large playground. The school and playground were named after Phoebe Apperson Hearst, a founder of the PTA and an early promoter of kindergartens in Washington.

Mrs. Herbert Hoover attended the laying of the cornerstone of Hearst Elementary School, on 37th Street south of Tilden. When the school opened in October 1932, a flag was presented by Mrs. John Jerome Lightfoot on behalf of the American Legion.

WHEN THE GRAYSONS WERE AT "HIGHLANDS"

(Photo from Tebbs Collection, Library of Congress)

(Photos by Priscilla McNeil)

Top: The back (east) side of "The Highlands" as it looked when occupied by the Graysons in the 1930s. It is now Sidwell Friends School.

Bottom left: Tree near Quebec Street, on Hearst playground, bears plaque of appreciation to Admiral Grayson.

Bottom right: Stone house built by Nourses, occupied into 20th century. Part of Hearst Playground now.

A plaque on a large tree at Hearst playground reads,

"When this land, once a part of the property known as Highlands, became a playground, Admiral Cary T. Grayson requested that this tree be saved. It now records its gratitude to him, 1938."

Cary Grayson died in 1938, and his widow moved out in 1940. "The Highlands" was rented to a French attache, then to newlyweds Betsey Cushing Roosevelt and John Hay (Jock) Whitney—grandson of William Whitney, who had lived at "Grassland" 60 years earlier.

In the 1950s, Mr. and Mrs. Allen Dulles rented "The Highlands"; he was at that time director of the Central Intelligence Agency. The Sidwell Friends School bought the old house in 1955 and it is still maintained as their administration building. "The Highlands" was renamed "Zartman House," after Helen Zartman Jones, associated with the school for 36 years.

Thomas Sidwell had died in 1936, prior to the completion of the move in 1938 of all departments of the Friends School to 3901 Wisconsin Avenue.

The field across Wisconsin Avenue, owned by Christian Heurich, was used as a playing field by Sidwell School and its rivals, as well as by the local Tenleytown teams in the '20s, before the Hearst and Reno playing fields were completed.

Institutions for Children

The Hillcrest Children's Center opened at 4119 Nebraska Avenue, south of Van Ness Street, in 1927. Originally founded as the Washington City Orphan Asylum in 1815, it had been located at various sites in the city for over a century. Appleton P. Clark was the architect for the new Tudor-style stone buildings arranged as a village on 14 acres of landscaped grounds. Mrs. Calvin Coolidge laid the cornerstone for the new city orphanage, which housed many children in three large "cottages." There were also a laundry, infirmary, and houses for residential staff.

In 1967, because of a fewer number of unadopted orphans and the expense of maintaining the large campus, Hillcrest Children's Center moved to 1325 W Street, N.W., and changed its orientation to day care for retarded and deprived children. The Nebraska Avenue land was purchased by the National Presbyterian Church, and some of the original Hillcrest buildings are still used as a school by the church.

In 1929, the Washington Home for Foundlings was opened in a new large stone building at 4610 42nd Street, at Brandywine. This was a private nonsectarian institution, for white infants only. It had previously been located on 15th Street.[374] At its busiest, there was a staff of 12 nurses caring for 24 babies at a time at the 42nd Street facility.

In 1954, after 25 years on 42nd Street, the Home for Foundlings was in financial difficulty and was threatened with closing.[375] By 1957 the building was up for sale. The Home closed its facilities, moved to Connecticut Avenue, and became the Peirce-Warwick Adoption Service, which still exists 24 years later.

The abandoned stone building over the years was vandalized beyond recovery. The Episcopal Diocese bought the property, tore down the old orphanage, and built the Friendship Terrace Apartments for the elderly, which opened in 1970. Changing times had called for changed facilities; infants now found homes much more readily than the aged.

TWO ORPHANAGES

(1979 photo by Judith Helm)

(Photo c/o Peirce-Warwick Adoption Agency)

Top: Formerly the Hillcrest Children's Center on Nebraska Avenue; now National Presbyterian School.

Bottom: Washington Home for Foundlings, built 1929 at 4510 42nd St., near Brandywine. Torn down 1968.

*   *   *   *

Great changes occurred in Tenleytown between the two World Wars. In these 25 years the suburban village became part of the city. Horses gave way to motorcars. Old lanes were obliterated by new streets. New housing developments meant that neighbors no longer knew each other, and the new "community spirit" felt by the newcomers was lost to the old-timers.

Schools and churches expanded their rolls and their structures. The saloon closed down. Stores replaced houses on Wisconsin Avenue. Chain stores replaced small shops.

The community of Fort Reno was completely eradicated in these years. Blacks were no longer a significant part of the community. But what discrimination there was, was transferred to the working class residents of three generations in Tenleytown.

Tenleytown, the village, had been replaced by Friendship, the neighborhood.

(Photo c/o George Eiker)

Cornerstone laying at St. Columba's Episcopal Church, 42nd and Murdock Mill Road, June 1926.

[316] J. Harry Shannon, The Star, January 3, 1915

[317] Shoemaker, "Historic Rock Creek," RCHS, op. cit.

[318] Wilson, The Story of St. Albans Parish, op. cit.

[319] 50th Anniversary Booklet, Singleton Lodge, op. cit.

[320] Washington, City and Capital, op. cit.

[321] The Washington Post, August 12, 1898, p. 10

[322] Peter, Cleveland Park, op. cit.

[323] Evalyn Walsh McLean, Father Struck It Rich, Boston: Little, Brown & Co., 1936

[324] George Kennedy (The Rambler), The Evening Star, March 12, 1951

[325] McLean, Father Struck It Rich, op. cit.

[326] Ibid. and Washington Herald, May 10, 1919

[327] Constance M. Green, Washington: Capital City, Vol. II, p. 276. Princeton University Press, 1962

[328] McLean, Father Struck It Rich, op. cit.

[329] Washington Daily News, December 31, 1936, p. 18, and Kennedy (The Rambler), The Evening Star, op. cit.

[330] "Nannie Chase Recalls: Glimpses of Fabulous Hope Diamond Days," The Sunday Star, October 9, 1955

[331] Downing, "Literary Landmarks," RCHS, op. cit.

[332] C. Harold Gray, "Washington, The Planned City, Is Really a Collection of Old Villages; Small Towns Swallowed as D.C. Grew," The Washington Post, May 30, 1937

[333] Atwood, Francis G. Newlands, op. cit., p. 39

[334] Mrs. Ida C. Gore [at age 81], personal interview with Jerry N. Hess, February 7, 1969. Tape courtesy of Wisconsin Avenue Baptist Church.

[335] Records of the North Cleveland Park Citizens Association, 1930

[336] "Old School House To Be Destroyed," Top Notch, May 1929

[337] Albert G. Seiler, editorial, "Northwest Section Growing Faster Than All Others," Top Notch, October 1930

[338] James W. Peters, interview with the author, February 1973

[339] "The Cat," The Star, December 4, 1927, p. 5

[340] National Archives RG 79, file 55480/683, Fort Reno

[341] D.C. Public Library News, 1949 issue on file at Tenley-Friendship Library

[342] 50th Anniversary booklet, Singleton Lodge, 1951, op. cit.

[343] George Eiker, interview by the author, June 10, 1975

[344] Harvey D. Davison, interview by the author, December 5, 1974

[345] The Washington Post, August 27, 1939

[346] "Steam Shovel Turns Ghoul in Graveyard," Washington Daily News, undated

[347] "Street Nomenclature of Washington City," RCHS, Vol. 7, 1903, p. 237

[348] Roy Orndorff, interview by the author, January 6, 1976

[349] 1937 Report of D.C. Commissioners

[350] Lillian G. Dabney, The History of Schools for Negroes in the District of Columbia, 1806-1947. Washington: Catholic University of America Press, 1949

[351] Letter dated February 3, 1926, in National Archives file RG 79, 55480/683, Fort Reno Land Acquisition Papers

[352] Undated clipping in vertical files, Washingtoniana Collection, Martin Luther King Memorial Library

[353] The Evening Star, July 12, 1936

[354] Top Notch, June 1930

[355] Kenesaw M. Landis, Segregation in Washington, Chicago: National Committee on Segregation in the Nation's Capital, 1948

[356] Letter from Harold Doyle, op. cit.

[357] Records of the Episcopal Diocese

[358] Allen C. Clark, "Charles Carroll Glover," RCHS, Vol. 39, 1936-37

[359] "Friendship Citizens Pitched In to End 'Good Old Days,'" The Evening Star, March 15, 1955

[360] "Northwest Area Activity Sets Progressive Record," The Washington Post, August 27, 1939

[361] James Henderson, interview by the author, July 15, 1975

[362] Records of the North Cleveland Park Citizens Association

[363] "New Hill Top Gas Station," Top Notch, July 1930

[364] Charlie Hurley, interview by the author, May 13, 1972

[365] The Community News, December 9, 1937, Vol. 1, No. 1

[366] Carolyn Bell Hughes, "A Nostalgic Look at Alton Place," National Capital Area Realtor October 1970

[367] "Janney Athletes Reorganize Team," Top Notch, October 1929, and "Janney Athletic Club Finishes Big Season," January 1930

[368] Hughes, op. cit.

[369] "Miss B.E. Lightfoot Dies at Homestead," The Washington Star, April 11, 1927

[370] Cutlip, "Old Tenley House...To be Opened to the Public," Washington Herald, op. cit.

[371] Downing, "Literary Landmarks," RCHS, op. cit.

[372] Peter, Cleveland Park, op. cit.

[373] Wecter, Saga of American Society, op. cit.

[374] Washington, City and Capital, op. cit.

[375] 1954 newspaper article, Washingtoniana Collection, Martin Luther King Memorial Library

(<u>Evening Star</u> photo c/o Washingtoniana Collection, Martin Luther King Memorial Library)

VII

MODERN TIMES:

1940–1981

Sears, Roebuck: Big Business Arrives

Sears, Roebuck parking roof on opening day, October 1, 1941. The view shows many large trees behind the stores on Wisconsin Avenue. Mostow's and the Masonic building near the corner of Albemarle Street are also visible.

When Christian Heurich announced in 1940 that he was selling the old Tenleytown Hotel property to Sears, Roebuck & Co. for a department store, local businessmen and residents protested. Their protests were based on two assumptions: that the new business would ruin the old—the small store owners would not be able to compete; and that the auto traffic generated by the store would prove dangerous to pedestrians, especially to students at Janney and St. Ann's schools.

The first assumption was partly true. When Sears opened its new store in October 1941, small businesses whose goods were duplicated by Sears did suffer and eventually fold. But other stores soon recognized that a boon to prosperity had arrived in their midst. New shoppers from all over Washington and nearby Maryland were brought to the Tenley-Friendship area.[376]

There was a definite upsurge in traffic to and from the store, and a traffic light was installed at Wisconsin and Albemarle. One exit from the rooftop parking lot, however, led to Albemarle near 42nd, and the other to River Road at Murdock Mill Road.

Arrival of a department store in Tenleytown abruptly affected the shopping habits of many local women who had for years taken the streetcar downtown to Woodward and Lothrop, Hecht's, Kann's, and Lansburgh's to buy their clothes, their children's clothes, and household purchases. Now it was just a quick walk or ride to Sears.

A large platoon of area women also found employment at the new department store, in clerical or sales positions. Area men were also employed in the sales, engineering, stocking, and loading areas.

(Photo c/o Harriet Beane Kerins)

(Photo c/o Gladys and Ralph Morders)

Top: No longer a drugstore, the building at Grant Road and Wisconsin became the Tenleytown Delicatessen. Pete and Nick Zaimes were the owners in 1942.

Bottom: Home for the holidays, 1942: friends pose in front of the Devonshire Grill, on Wisconsin Ave. between Veazey and Warren. (L to R:) Ralph Morders, Al Weaver, Roy Weaver,_____ Neci, John "Bootie" Hopkins, and Jack Thompson.

From the time Sears' automotive center first opened, at the River Road entrance, Sears' garage was crowded with cars from all over northwest Washington.

Because of its attraction for many shoppers, Sears supplemented one function of the local churches and taverns—that of a place to meet neighbors and catch up on the news.

But the most significant aspect of the arrival of the Sears store in Tenleytown was as a harbinger of things to come—the growth of commercial development along Wisconsin Avenue, and the resulting disappearance of the peaceful "Main Street." The trend to commercial development has continued relentlessly.

A Peoples Drug Store had opened next to the Masonic Lodge in 1939. Three years later Doc Gauley, unable to compete with the large chain store, closed the Tenleytown Pharmacy at the corner of Wisconsin and Grant Road. Pete and Nick Zaimes opened the Tenleytown Delicatessen where Gauley's pharmacy had been.

In 1941 four old houses south of the library were torn down and replaced by Kresge's 5 and 10¢ store. This followed shortly after the opening of Sears across the street.

The Navy Takes Over Mount Vernon Seminary

On October 12, 1942, the U.S. Navy notified the Mount Vernon Seminary on Nebraska Avenue that the school property was to be taken over for "essential war activities." War was again making changes on the face of Washington, and the Mount Vernon campus was one local site chosen by the Navy. MVS moved out and the Navy moved in, in December 1942.[377]

The Mount Vernon staff decided not to close their school. They rented

(Marjorie Collins photo c/o Library of Congress)

GAS SHORTAGE, JUNE 1942

Service station at corner of Wisconsin and Western Avenues (the District line) displays timely sign at beginning of gas rationing. The Hot Shoppes drive-in at left burned down and was replaced years later by the Chevy Chase Woodward & Lothrop store. The Howard Johnson's Restaurant across the street remained until 1977, when it was torn down for Metro subway construction. The Chevy Chase Shopping Center had not been built, but the bus terminal was behind Howard Johnson's. Mazza Gallerie Mall was constructed on this site in 1977.

rooms above Garfinckel's store in Spring Valley for classrooms, and houses in the Wesley Heights neighborhood for dormitories for the students. Three years later, the school bought 16 acres of land on Foxhall Road, and opened again at a new campus in 1946.

The Navy established a communications center on the Nebraska Avenue site, and fenced off the area for security. Large new "tempos" sprang up around the colonial brick Mount Vernon Seminary buildings, and a row of frame office and dormitory buildings arose along Nebraska and Massachusetts Avenues.

Most of the workers at the Naval Communications Center or Annex, as it was called, were women in the Naval Reserve—WAVES. Local veterans were amazed on returning to Tenleytown in 1944 to see 5,000 young women housed on both sides of Massachusetts Avenue from Ward Circle to 46th Street.

There were also male workers at the Navy site, including Marines back from overseas duty. A bomb disposal unit, camouflage developers,

and searchlight testers were active in the neighborhood. As in World War I, residents again became used to seeing men (and this time, women) in uniform, military vehicles, and rows of camp housing where once there were fields.

After the war the Navy remained at the Nebraska Avenue site, which has become known as the Naval Security Station. The National Security Agency had many employees there in the 1960s, before moving to Fort Meade, Maryland.

The many temporary buildings along Massachusetts Avenue were eventually removed, except for the one housing an indoor swimming pool; this was acquired by the American University. In 1975 some of the frame buildings along the east side of Nebraska Avenue were removed, and for the first time in three decades, the front of the lovely brick colonial main building of the old Mount Vernon Seminary was visible from the street. The Naval Security Station is still behind fences, however.

Wartime Measures

The effect of the war in Europe and the Pacific was soon felt at home, mainly in the form of shortages. Rationing was instituted in 1942—first rubber tires, then sugar, coffee, canned goods, shoes, meat, and butter. Every Tenleytown family was issued ration books with stamps to be turned in when rationed goods were bought.

Salvage efforts were widely publicized and hugely successful in the Washington area. Collecting newspapers, rubber, and tin cans was something everyone could do, and local school children devoted much effort to these drives.

Members of churches, clubs, and schools became active in first aid and home sewing courses, sales of war stamps and victory bonds, blood banks, and bandage rolling. Gas rationing came to D.C. in June 1942.

Local citizens volunteered for special duties during the World War II years. Volunteer air-raid wardens patrolled each neighborhood during city-wide blackouts and air-raid drills. Teams of citizens watched night and day for enemy aircraft from high towers such as the one at Alice Deal Junior High School.

Victory gardens were very successful in this neighborhood of big backyards. Some public space was also set aside for growing vegetables. The 40-year-old gardens still remain actively tilled on Fort Reno land off Belt Road near Chesapeake. Until 1977, a very large garden area was also maintained next to the Washington Home on Upton Street.

Although Fort Reno had been confiscated for use as a park, the government established a military station and installed communications equipment at this highest point in the city when World War II broke out.

The water reservoir at Fort Reno was again very precious to the com-munity, and defense officials deemed it necessary to enclose the entire reservoir with a high fence, to keep out saboteurs and nosy neighbors alike. Thus ended the time when residents could drive past the water towers and reservoirs, and climb up into the towers for a long view of the city. This also curtailed the availability of the cement tennis courts that had been on top of the reservoir since it was covered over during World War I.

The local impact of World War II was greatest in the enlistment of all able-bodied young men of Tenleytown, who joined up as readily as boys from elsewhere in America. The Tenleytown Bonecrushers of yesteryear became the fighting men of the U.S. Army and Navy.

McLean Gardens

Evalyn Walsh McLean sold her "Friendship" estate to the government, and in the winter of 1942-43, demolition of the beautiful old buildings and grounds began. The stone wall on Wisconsin Avenue, with its lion's-head water trough, was retained; a circle of elaborate statuary was saved, along with some landscaping and trees. New, winding streets were cut in, providing an attractive setting for the approximately 100 buildings of garden apartments, efficiencies, and hotel-like residences for men and women.

The McLean Gardens apartment development opened in 1943. It housed about 3,500 people, mostly civilians (and mostly women) who had come to Washington to work for the war effort. Because of its size, McLean Gardens became a little new town within the city, with its own community newspaper, restaurants, social centers, and common-interest groups. It remained a unique apartment development for middle income residents, a well-kept village, for nearly three decades.

In 1947 the government sold the popular housing development to the Fairmac Corporation, a division of the Hartford Insurance Co. CBI-Fairmac, now a division of ITT, owned the development into the 1970s, and succeeded in removing most of the residents, tearing down most of the buildings, and dismaying most of the Tenley-Friendship community with its proposals for luxury apartment towers, more office buildings, and another shopping center.

In 1979 a coalition of residents and developers formed the McLean Gardens Limited Partnership and negotiated the purchase of McLean Gardens, including 43 acres of grounds. Apartments were rebuilt and sold as condominiums, beginning in 1980. New buildings are also planned for a community of eventually 3,000 persons.

Postwar Housing Boom

After the slow period between 1931 and 1935, residential building permits tripled in the next five-year period, 1936-40, to 6,178. And during the half decade that included wartime, residences were constructed at an even greater rate of 6,315.[378]

What with the development of McLean Gardens and the building of blocks of new homes in American University Park, the population of Census Tract 10 (bordered by Wisconsin, Western, Massachusetts, and Macomb) doubled from 1940 to 1950, while adjoining areas remained relatively constant.[379]

Whereas houses built in the 1920s and 1930s had been frame or stucco, the new houses in American University Park were nearly all brick. They sold for an average of $10,000 to $12,000.

The newer houses were no longer built with front porches. This small change in residential architecture dictated a major difference in social patterns of the new residents—it made each family a little more isolated from the one next door and reduced residents' access to the street and to passers-by.

Postwar local housing developed on either side of Reno Road, east of Wilson High School, and west of Nebraska and Wisconsin.

In 1951, Leon Shainis exhibited the first air-conditioned houses in American University Park. These brick homes, called Freedom Manor, sold for 50% more than the $10,000-12,000 that new American University Park homes had brought in the '40s.

Because of the large number of children in the area, the Friendship Playground was developed nearby, at Van Ness and 45th Street, in 1954. This recreation center has been a focal point for American University Park children for over 25 years.

In the 1940s and 1950s, housewives rolled their folding carts to the local grocery stores on Wisconsin Avenue or in Spring Valley (Massachusetts Avenue) nearly every day. The small size of the family refrigerator, the rationing of foods, and the housewife's devotion to fresh vegetables, fruit, and meat made this customary. The regular home delivery of milk, eggs, and bread made the trips lighter. A sign in the housewife's window told the "Holmes to Homes" bread man when she wanted him to stop.

Home delivery of dairy products gradually diminished until by the 1960s very few homes were served. Fewer women were home during the day to receive the deliveries, people shopped by car in area supermarkets, and they brought their groceries home to large refrigerators that could hold enough food for at least a week.

FRIENDSHIP LIONS

(Del Ankers photo c/o John VanLandingham)

Friendship Lions

In 1946 the most active local businessmen and professionals formed the Friendship (not Tenleytown) Lions Club. A few of the charter members, such as Dick Burrows, Charlie Hurley, Joe Gould, and Frank Volkman, had been raised in Tenleytown. Some, like Lynn deLashmutt, Roland "Reds" Kirby, and Bill Parker, had married local girls. Most had come to the Tenley area to open a business, and were successful and popular in the neighborhood—such as Ray Bradshaw, Glenn Cox, Charlie Gregory, James Henderson, Al Peake, Arthur Rinker, John VanLandingham, Tom Wheeler, Stanton C. Willoughby, and Bill Wohlfarth.

The Friendship Lions Club had in its charter membership also the local Methodist, Episcopal, and Catholic clergymen, and medical professionals—a doctor, a dentist, a veterinarian, a pharmacist, and an optometrist. The managers of Sears, Peoples, Kresge's, Riggs, and other businesses, plus a variety of

The Friendship Lions Club poses in 1962, with boutonnieres indicating charter members.
(Standing, L to R:) Roland Kirby, Bob Freeman (visitor), Arthur Rinker, unknown visitor, Ray Johnson, Ray Bradshaw, Charles Hurley, Bill Wohlfarth. (Sitting, L to R:) John VanLandingham, Dr. Eugene Higgins, Msgr. Russell Phelan, Rev. C.R. Mengers, Joe Gould, Stanton Willoughby.

other civic-minded men, completed the charter membership of the 1946 Friendship Lions Club. They first met at the Masonic Hall, and then for many years at the Westchester Apartment Hotel on Cathedral Avenue.

Thirty-five years later, the group is still in existence, though very few of the original members are still around, and they now meet at Kenwood Country Club. It has long been, however, a strong link in the Tenley-Friendship community.

(1973 photo by Jerry Yurow)

(1981 photo by Bob Gerber)

Top: Statuary and fountains from the former McLean estate were retained in the McLean Gardens housing development.

Bottom: Detached brick houses at 4312 and 4316 Yuma St. typify American University Park development.

The Uptown Citizen

A neighborhood newspaper, The Uptown Citizen, was founded in the late '40s by Jerry David Britt in the Mount Pleasant area. Britt moved the editorial offices in 1964 to an old house built by Mary Ellen French at River Road and Brandywine; this therefore moved the focus of his newspaper to the area west of Rock Creek Park.

As a neighborhood newspaper— "delivered biweekly to homes in northwest Washington and Chevy Chase"—Britt's paper was filled with news of civic, fraternal, social, religious, literary, and patriotic organizations. It reported the awards received by children and adults, announced the musical and dramatic offerings to which the public was invited, published photos of brides, and devoted a large amount of space to ads from local businesses and support for them.

The Uptown Citizen still includes most of these on its pages, and has long been known especially for its back pages of classified ads—selling or seeking goods and services for the residents of Washington west of Rock Creek.

J. David Britt died in 1972, and his wife M.T. Britt took over as editor. This was about the time that the project was undertaken to extend the Metro subway from downtown, out Connecticut Avenue and then west under and into the Tenley area. The Uptown Citizen quickly became a more useful instrument in keeping citizens informed on government, political, and local agency plans and activities that would affect them.

As the residents themselves have become more aware, more informed, more politicized, and more active, The Uptown Citizen has also become all of these things. Mrs. Britt has also led the community in the re-use of the name Tenley rather

---

than Friendship. <u>The Uptown Citizen</u>, like the old <u>Top Notch</u> newspaper, usually promotes development and change in the Tenley area, in the name of progress.

Civil Defense at Reno

The 1950s brought the United States' entrance into the Korean conflict and a resumption of anxiety about protecting the target area of Washington, D.C., and its residents in case of bombing attack.

In 1954 an underground defense communications establishment was begun at Fort Reno, always the focus of attention during wartime. Radar and other sound-sensitive antennas, dishes, and horns were installed atop a new brick tower at Reno—the one that does not hold water. The underground communications center reportedly links the White House with other larger centers in the Middle Atlantic states.

Army anti-aircraft units occupied the five frame houses remaining on Chesapeake Street during the Korean War. Civil Defense employees took over the old Reno School building on Howard Street.[380]

The rolling fields of Fort Reno, now empty of houses, became again an armed camp when uniformed National Guard reserve troops set up tents and camped for two-week or week-end periods of duty.

Citizens were asked to volunteer to help the authorities protect vital spots from attack—including the Reno reservoir, the Western Union transmitter on 41st Street, and eventually the three television stations whose offices and antennas were moved into this high-elevation neighborhood.

School children and adults again participated in Civil Defense drills, and homeowners fixed up bomb shelters in their basements—stocked with enough food, water, and first aid

BROADCAST HOUSE

(Photo by Bob Gerber)

Broadcast House, CBS's television station (WTOP) in Washington, was built in 1953 on Brandywine Street at 40th.

materials to keep their families alive for a few days or weeks. The local newspapers published suggested auto routes for evacuation of city residents and workers to the country in case of an aerial attack.

Although these activities diminished somewhat after the Korean War ended in 1953, and the Civil Defense employees left the Howard Street building in the 1960s, the defense communications equipment is still maintained; a Civil Defense warning siren is still blown from Reno on Wednesday mornings at 11 a.m.

In the early 1950s the houses on the north side of Chesapeake Street were finally pulled down. But lack of funds, on the one hand, and eventual lack of unified community support, on the other, postponed indefinitely the construction of a planned swimming pool at Fort Reno. Forty years after it was first proposed, the pool was finally built as a south annex to Wilson High School.

Another large underground water reservoir (20 million gallons) at Fort Reno was completed in 1957 to increase the water supply to northwest Washington, where residential population growth was slowing down but commercial growth was zooming.

Broadcasting Stations

In October 1953 television station WTOP (CBS) moved its offices from the Warner Building downtown to a small building on Brandywine Street one block east of Wisconsin. This site was chosen for its high altitude and therefore better broadcasting ability. Few members of the WTOP staff knew that the Riley slaughterhouse had once been on that site.

The large building that houses the modern studios of WTOP-TV, called Broadcast House, took a year and a half to build. In January 1954 a 373-foot WTOP antenna was completed. At 410 feet altitude, this reached 783 feet above sea level.

NBC STUDIOS

(1979 photo by Judith Helm)

NBC Studios in Washington (WRC radio and TV) have been since 1958 at 4001 Nebraska Avenue, on the former site of "Grassland," the Loughborough-Whitney estate.

Broadcast House was formally opened February 3, 1954, and a "time capsule" filled with contemporary documents was sealed in the large sphere at the entrance—to be opened not in 100 years, but in 1,000 years—in 2954 A.D.!

In 1973 a new, taller antenna (639 feet) was completed—this one WTOP shares with WJLA-TV (formerly WMAL-TV), whose studios remain at Connecticut and Albemarle. Built at an altitude of 410 feet, the tower reaches to 1049 feet above sea level.

In 1956 the NBC network bought the old "Grassland" house and grounds on Nebraska Avenue just north of the Naval Security Station. The Georgetown Day School had occupied the Loughborough house from 1947 until about 1956.

NBC had the old house and gardens razed and built a modern building for its network and local (WRC) studios. The new studio building was completed and occupied in 1958.

The third television station to come to the heights of Tenleytown was WTTG-TV, Channel 5 (Metromedia). WTTG built its studios facing Wisconsin at Harrison, on property rented from the Heider heirs, and the Heider-Griffith house was torn down in 1959 and replaced by the Channel 5 antenna, 700 feet high. The new Metromedia offices, as they are now called, were dedicated in 1963. WASH-FM radio also has its broadcast studio in that building.

Commercial Development, Upper Wisconsin Avenue

In 1945 the Heider-Marceron home at 5101 Wisconsin was sold and transformed into the Chevy Chase Funeral Home. This was the first such changing of a house into a commercial establishment on upper Wisconsin Avenue. The old house was torn down in 1975 and a new office building was constructed on the site.

Ernest Adams opened a funeral home at 4748 Wisconsin in 1955, putting a brick front on an old house. It was followed in the same building by the Timothy Hanlon Funeral Home in 1960; Hanlon was joined by the Warren Taltavull Funeral Home in 1968.

In 1960 the old farmhouses on the west side of the 5100 block of Wisconsin were torn down; they had been owned successively by the Shoemaker, Offutt, Markham, and Riley families. By 1962 the new red brick Georgian colonial Gawler's Funeral Home was completed on that site at the southeast corner of Wisconsin and Harrison. Gawler's, which moved from Pennsylvania Avenue, has extensive landscaping in front and a large parking lot in the back.

Louise Voigt Eiker sold the old Voigt farmhouse in 1940. Offices were built in front of it, across the street from Tolman Laundry, in the 5200 block of Wisconsin Avenue.

By 1952 electric streetcar service north of the District line was curtailed. At the Wisconsin and Western terminal, riders now transferred from streetcars to buses going north through Bethesda.

After the opening of Woodward & Lothrop's Chevy Chase branch at the District line in 1950, the next great leap in commercial development in the Friendship Heights area was the Chevy Chase Center.

THE FIRST UPPER WISCONSIN AVENUE HOME TO BE TURNED INTO A BUSINESS

(1960 photo from Vanishing Americana, by Everett Wilson)

Located northeast of Wisconsin and Western, behind a Howard Johnson's and the streetcar terminal, the semi-circular row of shops was approximately on the site of the original road from Georgetown to Rockville before the Brookeville Road spur was by-passed for a straighter Wisconsin Avenue.

The naming of Woodie's first branch as "Chevy Chase" and the nearby shopping center as the "Chevy Chase Center" rankled the sensibilities of those who felt firmly that Chevy Chase was along Connecticut Avenue and not along Wisconsin Avenue. However, it was the Chevy Chase Land Company that developed the new shopping center at Wisconsin and Western—and who could quarrel with their right to use the name "Chevy Chase"?

When it was completed in September 1954, the Chevy Chase Center contained space for 22 stores and an office building—much larger in size than the previous shopping centers at Connecticut and Albemarle or Massachusetts and 49th.

There was no shortage of people to shop in these new stores at Friendship Heights, for the Bethesda suburbs were growing at a fast pace. Residential development within the District was slowing down, only because there were fewer lots available.

Commercial Development, Tenleytown

The vanguard Giant supermarket at Wisconsin and Brandywine was closed by 1954. An auto sales store and a sport shop succeeded Giant, each for a short time. In 1959 Hechinger's opened its lumberyard in the same large building, with the parking lot on the roof. The first

A house built by the Heider family was transformed into The Chevy Chase Funeral Home, at 5101 Wisconsin Avenue, in 1945. It was torn down in 1975 and replaced by an office building.

(Washington Post photo c/o Ben and Maureen Gilbert)

Looking east across Wisconsin Avenue: Sears rooftop and parking lot across the street (right side of photo) dominate the landscape in the early 1950s. The St. Ann's-Tenley School was still standing, and the Tenley-Friendship new library had not been built, at Wisconsin and Albemarle, far right. Wilson High School, Reno reservoir, Alice Deal Junior High, and playing fields are visible, as is the new Broadcast House, 40th and Brandywine.

lumberyard in the area, Hechinger's also sold hardware, household goods, and every conceivable building and repair item for the handyman. It became second only to Sears in drawing customers to the Wisconsin-River Road intersection.

Sears, Roebuck's rooftop parking lot, meanwhile, was inadequate for its large amount of business. East of Wisconsin and behind the row of stores opposite Sears, there was for a time an additional graded ground-level parking lot for Sears customers, with bluestone gravel and a retaining wall. But then in 1959 a four-level open-air parking building was constructed for Sears customers, with entrances from both the western alley and 40th Street on the east.

Jerome Lightfoot and his second wife had rented out the historic Tennally-Lightfoot house and moved to Chevy Chase. Before he died in 1955, Mr. Lightfoot decided to sell the house and property to Hechinger's.

And so, in 1959, the 160-year-old Tennally-Lightfoot house was torn down, and Hechinger's lumberyard expanded onto the site. The large yard behind the house was made part of Sears parking garage. Tradition says that when bulldozers began digging up the yard, the bones of the forgotten Tennally graves were discovered—and excavation was halted until they were disposed of.

Victor Adding Machine shop was built at 4543 Wisconsin Avenue. Mike Sklar's Mitchel's Sport Shop took that over in 1961. Mitchel's is especially popular with school athletes and tennis players.

Joe's Variety Store at 4011 Albemarle Street was a small, chaotic, dimly-lit store that opened in 1937, catering to the children in the community. Joe Gould (son of Mr. and Mrs. Joseph Gould, grocers, and brother of Anna Luber) sold toys, games, costumes, models, candy, and gum. "A child's garden of toys, Joe's is the favorite haunt of the

(Winged Camera Service photo c/o Louis Burman)

after-hours set from nearby St. Ann's and Janney schools."[381]

When Joe died in 1965, his widow Cecile continued running Joe's Variety for a few more years. When she at last closed the store, the old neighborhood mourned the loss of yet one more old-fashioned family business in Tenleytown. Antosh's Radio and TV rented the store until 1974, when the Metro construction plans indicated a move was again in order for them; the small row of stores on Albemarle Street was torn down for the subway construction.

Abraham and Rose Mostow gave up their liquor business at Wisconsin and Albemarle in 1963. Nathan Gildenhorn acquired the Tenley Liquors, but the Mostows continued to own the building. The "Tenley" brands of gin, scotch, and bourbon are bottled for the sole distribution of Tenley Liquors. The early Tenley labels, according to Mr. Gildenhorn, included a brief history of the name

Tenley. And since John Tennally was a tavernkeeper, it is an appropriate naming.

Kresge's 5 and 10¢ store on Wisconsin Avenue eventually became a Drug Fair pharmacy. In the 1960s the Top Value Stamp store rented that space from the owners, the heirs of Frank Burrows. Since 1974-75 the District of Columbia National Bank and the new Tenley Wine and Liquors have occupied the site.

The first office building in "downtown" Tenleytown was opened in July 1955 by Louis Burman. Called the Wisconsin Building, its address is 4000 Albemarle Street. The first floor of the building now has a Hudson Bay Outfitters store facing onto Wisconsin, between the Masonic Lodge and Baker's Photo Supply.

The large stone Frank Perna house at 4101 Brandywine Street, between Wisconsin and River Road, gave place in 1959 to the modern brick building of the Friendship

Aerial view of Tenley area in early 1950s shows nearly all land is developed. This view is looking north, with Wisconsin Avenue running from bottom right to upper left, and Nebraska Avenue from lower left to upper right. New are the Hot Shoppes drive-in at Van Ness Street, the Wisconsin Avenue Baptist Church at Tenley Circle, and the Wisconsin Building on Albemarle Street. Still standing are the Tenley-St. Ann's School, the old St. Columba's Church, and many houses on Brandywine and Chesapeake Streets, near Broadcast House.

229

RIGGS—THE FIRST BANK IN TENLEYTOWN

(Photo c/o 1930 <u>Book of Washington</u>)

(1979 photo by Judith Helm)

Top: The Farmers & Marchants Bank of Georgetown opened a branch at Wisconsin and Warren Street in 1927. A year later the Riggs Bank took over the F&M Bank, and this branch, called the Friendship Branch, has always been one of Riggs' busiest branches.

Bottom: A remodeling of the Friendship Branch of Riggs occurred in 1959.

Animal Hospital. The veterinary hospital was previously located at 4615 41st Street; Homer Dennewitz had been the veterinarian there.

Other New Construction in the 1950s

The jump in the birthrate in the 1940s led to overcrowding in the schools and churches in the 1950s. In the expectation that this growth would continue, many schools and churches added to their facilities at that time.

Ground was broken in 1954 for the new Wisconsin Avenue Baptist Church on the east side of Tenley Circle. This level site had been used for years as a ball field and occasionally even as a fairground. The new red brick Baptist sanctuary building was occupied by the end of 1955, and a southern wing was completed in 1960.

Also in 1955 the Immaculata Seminary and Dumblane Hall, as the elementary school was called then, tore down a little "summer-house" gazebo-type structure between the two schools. In its place were constructed three much-needed buildings—a gymnasium-auditorium, a dormitory, and a building for classrooms and a dining hall for Immaculata students.

Another local playing field was lost when in 1958 the huge Equitable Life Insurance Building was constructed at 3900 Wisconsin Avenue. This remarkable Williamsburg colonial style red brick office building, with its landscaped grounds and circular driveway, replaced the old Sidwell Friends sports field and tennis courts just north of McLean Gardens on what had been Christian Heurich property. In 1975 Equitable announced the sale of the building to "Fannie Mae"—the Federal National Mortgage Association—for $13 million. FNMA began renovation in 1976 and moved in two years later.

The Heurich heirs have retained much of the Tenleytown acreage acquired by Christian Heurich before and after the turn of the century. North of the Equitable Life building is Heurich property—now occupied by Johnson's Flowers, Roy Rogers, and the new Tenley Mall office building at 4200 Wisconsin. Heurich heirs also still own the Gloria Point property on which the Sunoco service station stands.

The Riggs Bank (Friendship Branch) at Wisconsin and Warren opened a large, new building in February 1959, remodeling the earlier bank building that had been on that site since 1927.

New Tenley-Friendship Library

After years of complaint, argument, and delay, a new library for Tenleytown was begun in 1959. The site on the southwest corner of Wisconsin and Albemarle had been chosen in 1955 by the D.C. Public Library for the new branch. The old branch, in the small building once occupied by Tenleytown police, had been inadequate for two decades.

But the land chosen for the new library was on one corner of the Janney Elementary School's playground, and many residents, led by the Janney PTA, fought long and hard to keep the site for a playground and to have the new library built elsewhere—perhaps closer to Wilson High and Deal Junior High Schools. It was expected that the new library would generate more auto traffic and need for parking space, which were even then problems. But the D.C. Library administrators insisted that the library should be on Wisconsin Avenue, close to public transportation and shopping.

TWO TENLEY LIBRARIES

(Photo c/o Ellen Wright)

(1979 photo by Judith Helm)

Top: Former police station, occupied by the Tenley Library from the mid-1920s until 1960.

Bottom: View of new Tenley-Friendship Library at the corner of Albemarle and Wisconsin. Sears store is across the street to the right.

Ground was finally broken in July 1959, just north of the old Tenley School, which had become St. Ann's School. The new Tenley-Friendship Branch Library, as it is called, was dedicated in October 1960.

The old police-library building was eventually torn down; the site is now occupied by the Waffle Shop.

Police Report Describes Neighborhood

A 1958 article on Tenley's 8th Police Precinct, with headquarters on Albemarle Street, described its wide area of responsibility, north of Glover Park and west of Rock Creek Park.[382] It was the largest D.C. precinct in territory.

Within the precinct there were 16 public and parochial schools, and eight other educational institutions, including Sidwell Friends, American University, and Dumbarton College of the Holy Cross, east of Connecticut Avenue. And there were 12 banks, where there had been only three in 1948.

The 8th Precinct always had an enviably low crime rate, mostly attributed to the middle- and upper-class makeup of its 70,000 residents (in 1958). Housebreaking and store thefts were its biggest crime problems. "Number 8" policemen were also assisted by the security forces of the Park Service, the Cathedral, the Naval Security Station, the Sheraton and Shoreham Hotels, the American University, the Bureau of Standards, and McLean Gardens.

In 1974 the Police Department was reorganized so that Precincts 7 and 8 became the Second District. The red brick police station on Albemarle Street was vacated, and the police moved into modern new facilities on Idaho Avenue and Newark Street, south of McLean Gardens.

End of Streetcars

Throughout the 1950s, Capital Transit had experienced financial difficulties, and in 1956, O. Roy Chalk bought the bus and trolley system, renaming it D.C. Transit. Congress allowed Chalk's purchase on the condition that trolley service be eliminated. And so, on January 3, 1960, came the end of the Tennallytown-Pennsylvania Avenue streetcar line, No. 30, the last overhead trolley line in D.C.[383]

The Friendship Heights carbarn was torn down to make a parking lot for buses. Eventually the streetcar tracks, passenger platforms, and "plow pits" were ripped up and Wisconsin Avenue was repaved and widened to six lanes. Buses took over the routes of the streetcars, which had given 70 years of faithful service.

1960s: Drastic Changes in Old Vistas

The National Presbyterian Church Center was built on the Nebraska Avenue campus of the Hillcrest Children's Center in 1969. Its outstanding features are a bell tower, huge sanctuary, dramatic walks and gardens with lighted fountains, and meeting rooms for religious and community groups.

The Sisters of Bon Secours occupied the large Spanish-style building at 4101 Yuma Street, behind St. Ann's, for many years. In the early 1960s, however, the order moved away and the large building was sold to the French International School. The new occupants remodeled the building into classrooms, and used it until 1975, when overcrowding forced them to move to a larger site in Maryland. It is now occupied by the Oakcrest School.

The Sheridan School moved from Sheridan Circle to a new brick building at 36th Street and Alton Place in 1964.

A Safeway store near the intersection of Wisconsin, 42nd, and Ellicott was built in the early '60s on land once owned by the Shoemakers, then the Wendels, and now the Harrys. In 1977 Safeway management proposed expanding the store to double its size, to accommodate and attract more shoppers. Local residents protested, fearing increased traffic and gradual commercial encroachment into the residential neighborhood. But the new store construction was begun.

The Burrows market, in what had been the post office underneath the Masonic Temple, finally closed in 1966, and Peoples Drug Store expanded into the space. Because of its popularity with local teenagers and the disappearance of rival drugstores, Peoples enjoyed a period of prosperity throughout the '60s. In the late '70s Peoples was replaced by the American Security Bank.

The Avenue Becomes The Strip

Wisconsin Avenue began its recent career as an entertainment strip when its first movie theatre, the K-B Cinema, opened as a first-run movie house on Wisconsin Avenue near Harrison Street in 1965. Then the Outer Circle 1 and 2 opened at Wisconsin and Ellicott in 1969. This is a double theatre, showing two movies at once. Often featuring foreign films, it was built on the site of a liquor store and a used car lot, which had succeeded Pop Richards' second general store.

K-B Studio 1-2-3 (showing three movies at one time) opened in 1972 at Brandywine and Wisconsin. It was really the first neighborhood theatre attracting children to Saturday matinees. The Jenifer Cinema I and II, in a new office building at Jenifer Street, opened in 1975 with the block-buster "Jaws." In 1979 the

Tenley Circle Theatres opened at 4200 Wisconsin Avenue, in the Tenley Mall at Van Ness Street. These theatres are owned by the Tenley Theater Corporation.

As beer taverns have long existed on Wisconsin Avenue, it followed that drinking, dancing, and music places would be very popular. Mr. Henry's, a night spot on Capitol Hill, opened a "Tenley Circle" branch—at Wisconsin and Windom, in the Friendship Building. Mr. Henry's - Tenley Circle was replaced in 1980 by Winsor McKay. In warm weather customers sit at tables on the sidewalk under a large awning.

Up and down Wisconsin Avenue are many such businesses that do especially well on weekends and in the warm months. Young people from all over the Washington area have long congregated at Maggie's, which features pizza and beer. It was called Manny's for a few years, but has recently been reincarnated as Maggie's.

The presence of bars in a neighborhood has its negative effects, mostly noise and disorder caused by youthful drinkers. In early 1976 a patron of one of these businesses on upper Wisconsin Avenue was shot and killed by another, who was promptly captured by a police officer of the 2nd District. It was happening in the 1930s and it was still happening in the 1970s.

Among the many popular casual eating places have been the Hot Shoppes (later Phineas, now Charley's Place) and Roy Rogers (where balloon seller Mark Johnson used to chant "Make the children happy, make the ladies happy, make everyone happy, smile balloons!").

Other successful places include Armand's Chicago Pizzeria (formerly McLean Drugs); the Waffle Shop (spelled Wafle Shop, where the Police Sub-station and library once

TENLEY CIRCLE, THEN AND NOW

(Photo c/o Wisconsin Ave Baptist Church)

(Photo by Judith Helm)

Top: Late 1940s: People stand on islands in middle of Wisconsin Avenue, waiting for streetcars at Tenley Circle. In background is the empty lot on which the Wisconsin Avenue Baptist Church was built in 1954. Before Nebraska Avenue was cut through, this lot was a favorite ball field.

Bottom: 1973: The intersection of Wisconsin Avenue (looking south toward the Cathedral) and Nebraska Avenue as seen from the roof of the Wisconsin Building. St. Ann's Church is to the right.

233

4101 YUMA STREET

(1977 photos by Judith Helm)

Originally, the Convent of Bon Secours; then, the French International School; now, the Oakcrest School occupies the building on Yuma Street, behind St. Ann's Church. At top, the front view; at bottom, the back view.

were); Steak 'n' Eggs (formerly the Toddle House); and Hamburger Hamlet—a remarkable place where one can get a cocktail or a chocolate milkshake with dinner or lunch. Fred Norris, a Tenleytown native, owns the well-known Dancing Crab Restaurant on 41st Street.

The old building on the corner of Wisconsin and Grant Road has, since the turn of the century, been O'Day's grocery, Dr. Scholl's Pharmacy, Doc Gauley's Tenleytown Pharmacy, Zaimes' Tenleytown Delicatessen, the Clover Beef House, Broadcasters Beef House, Adriatico, and now, Grant's Tomb. At any rate, it has been popular with local residents in its many functions over the years.

The Tenley Inn, a small restaurant at 4606 Wisconsin Avenue, opened in 1975 north of Brandywine Street—very near the site of Tennally's original tavern. Many Tenleytown restaurants specialize in ethnic foods—the Serbian Crown (Serbo-Russian), the Round Table (Greek), the Mikado (Japanese), the Shanghai Delight (Chinese), and Il Nido (Italian).

Nearly as numerous as restaurants are financial institutions on Wisconsin Avenue. By 1978 there were ten savings and loan associations and seven banks—branches of downtown businesses. Five were called the Friendship or Friendship Heights branches, three were called Chevy Chase, five were identified by their Wisconsin Avenue addresses, and one was called Uptown. Only the D.C. National Bank, at 4537 Wisconsin, called itself the Tenley Circle office.

The National Permanent Federal Savings and Loan Association, with its Friendship Heights branch at 5001 Wisconsin, has as its chairman of the board and president John W. Stadtler, a third-generation Tenleytowner and a past president of the Washington Board of Trade.

WISCONSIN AVENUE AT ALBEMARLE

(1973 photo by Judith Helm)

(1981 photo by Petra Schultze)

Top: Peoples Drug Store occupied the corner from 1939 until the late 1970s.

Bottom: American Security Bank replaced Peoples at Wisconsin Avenue and Albemarle. The entrance to the Metro subway will be to the left, across the street from this site.

PIZZA, BEER, AND MUSIC

(1979 photo by Judith Helm)

(1981 photo by Petra Schultze)

(1979 photo by Judith Helm)

Top: Armand's Chicago Pizzeria.

Middle: Maggie's.

Bottom: Mr. Henry's - Tenley Circle.

BEFORE AND AFTER AT WISCONSIN AND VAN NESS STREET

(Photos by Judith Helm)

*Top: Johnson's Flowers had
vacated this building when the
picture was taken in 1973.*

*Bottom: The new Tenley Mall
had replaced it when this picture
was taken in 1979.*

Top: The Hot Shoppes Restaurant at 4110 Wisconsin Avenue, as seen in 1977, when it was closed. It had been opened as a drive-in restaurant in the late 1930s.

Bottom: The same building transformed by the Marriott Corporation into the Phineas Restaurant in 1979. In 1981 it became Charley's Place.

(Photos by Judith Helm)

ACROSS FROM SEARS

(1974 photo by John Russo)

(1973 photo by Judith Helm)

Top: The Wafle Shop (that's how it was spelled on the awning) was undergoing a renovation when this photo was taken. It is on the site of the old Tenleytown police station and library.

Bottom: Joe Corvelli's American Valet and the General Electronics store remain. The Wisconsin Restaurant, however, has been replaced by the Adriatico restaurant. It was Poch's Hardware until 1956.

THE OLDEST STORE IN TENLEYTOWN

(1973 photo by Judith Helm)

Broadcasters Beef House in 1973, this building on the northeast corner of Wisconsin and Grant Road was formerly known as: O'Day's store, Dr. Scholl's Pharmacy, Doc Gauley's Tenleytown Pharmacy, Zaimes' Tenleytown Delicatessen, and the Clover Beef House. In 1978 it became the Adriatico restaurant and, in 1980, Grant's Tomb. To the left are Joanne's Gift Shop, run by Anna Luber, and Baker Photo. Slattery's Appliances has been replaced by Hudson Bay Outfitters.

(1981 photo by Bob Gerber)

Friendship Heights Development

In the early 1960s, one of the Shoemaker heirs sold a few acres beyond Woodward & Lothrop, in Maryland, and the large GEICO offices and parking lots were constructed. So began one of the speediest changes in the character of a neighborhood. Other residents of Friendship Heights sold their modest-looking houses and lots for anything up to a half million dollars for one acre.

By the 1970s the price had doubled, and a newspaper reporter labeled Friendship Heights "the hottest piece of real estate in the United States." As commercial growth overtook residential growth, Friendship Heights became a neighborhood of high-rise apartments, office buildings, department stores, and parking lots.[384]

The Irene, the Elizabeth, Highland House, and the Trianon are the "sky-scraping" apartment buildings that grew up north of Willard Avenue and west of Wisconsin. The Barlow Building on Wisconsin Avenue houses 14 floors of offices.

A Montgomery County sewer moratorium and zoning restrictions prevented some development. A Friendship Heights Development Plan was put together to protect residential and commercial owners from further area changes or additions that might prove detrimental. Woodward & Lothrop was prevented from constructing an expanded retail and commercial center.

On the District side of Friendship Heights, the numerous gas stations were replaced by office or bank buildings—up to five stories high. McDowell's service station was replaced by a building containing Herman's Sporting Goods, a sandwich shop, a creperie, the Jenifer 1

1973: BEFORE SUBWAY CONSTRUCTION BEGAN

(1973 photos by Judith Helm)

Top: Albemarle and Wisconsin, looking north toward Friendship Heights.

Bottom: 41st and Wisconsin, looking south toward Hechinger's and Sears.

and 2 theatres, and a Riggs Bank branch. The Tolman Laundry next door was closed in 1973, after 43 years at that address.

On the southwest corner of Wisconsin and Western a huge shopping complex known as the Mazza Gallerie was completed in late 1977, after five years' construction. A Neiman Marcus department store is located in this mall, which contains nearly 50 stores and five levels of underground parking.

The construction of these and many other buildings along Wisconsin Avenue has brought hundreds of shoppers and office workers and their cars to the area daily. Non-resident parking bans have gone into effect from Friendship Heights to Tenleytown. The eventual extension of the subway to Friendship Heights, planned for 1983, may bring some relief to the automobile problem in the area.

Traffic and the Subway

The installation of traffic light signals on Wisconsin Avenue began in the mid-'40s and grew at an increasing number of intersections, until traffic is now stopped by a light every three or four blocks. The River Road bottleneck, the widening to six lanes, crosswalks for pedestrians, safety for school children, the streetcar and then the bus routes and schedules, noise and pollution—all of these have been factors in the Wisconsin Avenue traffic situation.

Although it is no longer a trolley route, Wisconsin Avenue remains a bus route as well as a truck, commuter, and tourist route. Old U.S. Route 240 takes Wisconsin Avenue from Massachusetts Avenue north into Maryland, where it becomes Maryland Route 355 (Rockville Pike) through Rockville to Frederick.

According to an early 1970s article in the American Motorist, Wisconsin Avenue was one of the busiest city streets in the United States. A Metro tabulation of 1973 indicated that there were 35,000 cars daily on that stretch of Wisconsin Avenue between River Road and Tenley Circle, and 23,000 cars daily on the adjacent portion of the Avenue.

On November 18, 1972, citizens marched up and down Wisconsin Avenue in an organized protest against high-rise developments planned in Georgetown, on the McLean Gardens site, and at Friendship Heights.[385] The basis of their protest was the anticipated increase in people, traffic, pollution, and crime, and the ruining of pretty streets and neighborhoods with high-rise buildings and cement parking lots. Epitomizing the protest was a bicyclist dressed in Revolutionary War garb and displaying a sign, "The Developers are Coming! The Developers Are Coming!"

The rally was a demonstration that concerned citizens were actively seeking a moratorium on the development of Wisconsin Avenue, urging the "down-zoning of current permissive densities," a study of the corridor, preservation of the McLean Gardens low- and moderate-income housing, and a rechanneling of developers' money into the inner city.

A 1974 Washington Post article pointed out that Wisconsin Avenue had been spared the "urban blight" that had attacked other Washington streets that had originally developed and flourished because of their trolley line service.

The reasons for Wisconsin Avenue's continued good health, it said, were that parking spaces have generally been available for shoppers; Sears and Hechinger's are unique, large in-town stores that attract thousands weekly; occupants of office buildings between shopping areas provide day-time vitality to stores and restaurants; and there are many unique and good restaurants, stores, and other businesses all along the Avenue.[386]

In 1968 a plan was first announced to extend the projected Washington subway from downtown, north out Connecticut Avenue to the Van Ness Center, then west under Yuma Street to beyond 39th Street, under the Baptist Church lot and the Wisconsin Building to a "Tenley Circle" station under the row of stores opposite Sears, Roebuck. Then the subway was planned to continue north, with the next station at Friendship Heights, through Bethesda to Rockville—all under the east side of Wisconsin Avenue or adjacent to the Rockville Pike.

The Metro subway construction was to have begun in late 1971, and to have been finished by 1976. But delays (holding back of funds, labor strikes, lawsuits, environmental studies, neighborhood hearings, changes in plans) all added to the increased cost and time schedule for the subway. Underground digging and blasting began in 1975 in the Tenley area. Houses on Yuma Street and Bradshaw's Exxon station at 41st and Brandywine were torn down to provide space for above-ground vent and fan shafts.

A large opening was made at Wisconsin and Albemarle in June 1975, cutting off Albemarle Street's through traffic east of the Avenue until it reopened in 1981. The grey brick building at Wisconsin and Albemarle—the old liquor store—and the small row of stores and apartments on Albemarle were razed in 1977 to prepare for the station.

The construction phase in the Tenley area consisted of boring a tunnel 100-200 feet under Yuma Street, Nebraska Avenue, and the east side of Wisconsin Avenue going north. Blasting was necessary to progress through the rock.

A Washington Metro Area Transit Authority (WMATA) geological report of the area, prepared in 1973, shows that the first five geological strata in the area are fill dirt, clay, silt, sand, and gravel, and the sixth stratum down is rock. It is this layer of rock that the subway tunnel penetrates.[387]

In 1979 Harold Gray, a past president of the Federation of Citizens Associations, headed a citizens movement that resulted in the Metro Board's changing the name of the planned "Tenley Circle" subway stop to "Tenleytown." The board approved the change in 1980.

In 1981 it is expected that the Tenleytown station will open in 1983. The projection by the WMATA Office of Planning was that ten years after area operations were to begin, the Tenleytown subway station would be handling nearly 26,000 passengers a day, either boarding or alighting, with a morning rush hour peak of 4,000 persons.

Although the subway construction has forced some businesses to fold, it makes further Wisconsin Avenue development more attractive. Prices of houses and commercial real estate in the area have increased at a higher rate than in most other areas of the city, and the opening of the Tenleytown subway stop is expected further to increase the value of local property.

Smaller businesses are more and more being replaced by medium-rise office buildings, three to five stories high; so far there are no new apartments along Wisconsin Avenue.

The future development of the corridor depends on decisions made by the D.C. government, zoning commissioners, planners, developers, businesses, and residents—acting individually or corporately.

SUBWAY PLAN FOR TENLEYTOWN (TENLEY CIRCLE) STATION AND ALTERNATE ROUTES THAT WERE PROPOSED

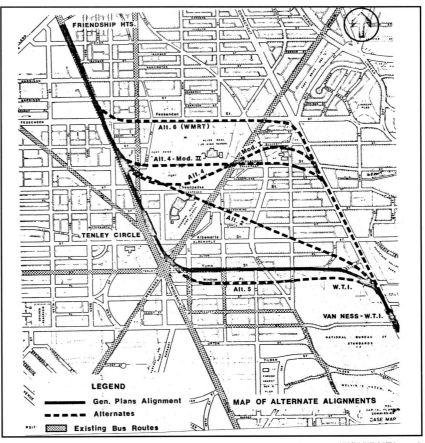

(1974 WMATA map)

The heavy black line indicates the route of the Metro subway under construction through Tenleytown. The dotted lines were alternates that were proposed and discarded. It is expected that the Tenleytown station, as it will be called, will open in late 1983.

TENLEYTOWN CENSUS TRACTS 1970

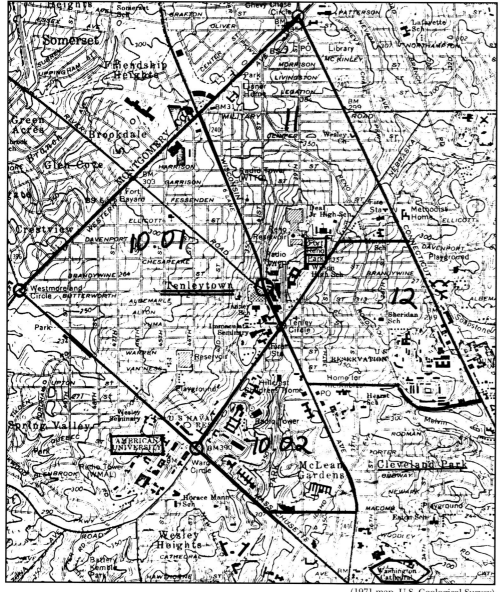

(1971 map, U.S. Geological Survey)

Census tracts 10.01, 10.02, 11, and 12 make up the Tenleytown area today, encompassing areas known as American University Park, McLean Gardens, North Cleveland Park, Chevy Chase (D.C.), and Friendship Heights (D.C.).

Residential Change and Real Estate Growth

The area around upper Wisconsin Avenue continues to grow and change, prosper commercially, and attract affluent residents.

As of 1970, 20,000 people lived in the four census tracts 10.01, 10.02, 11, and 12—bounded by Massachusetts and Western Avenues on the southwest and northwest, Connecticut Avenue on the northeast, and a southern boundary marked by Tilden, Reno, Upton, Wisconsin, and Macomb. These 20,000 people lived in 8,000 housing units—an average of 2.5 persons per household in an area of large homes but also many apartments.

Of the 19,500 area residents in these four census tracts who were identified by race in 1970, 482 were blacks—or 2 1/2% of the total population. Compare this with the 1930 census for tract 11 (which includes Fort Reno) when about 15% of the population were Negroes.

The 1970 census showed an average income of $16,000 per local household. The mean income in CT 10.01 was $21,000. The average "assessed" value of private homes was $34,000; that "average" house sold in 1976 for $79,500 and in 1980 for $130,000.

As house prices escalated, fewer working class people could afford to live in Tenleytown. In 1973 came the final blow to that black remnant that occupied a row of 1890s houses in the 4700 block of 41st Street. The realty company that owned the houses, which had become quite dilapidated, decided that the time had come to renovate them.

And so the last 16 blacks (in five houses) were told they had to seek residence elsewhere—and they left in December 1973 the houses they had lived in all their lives—a repeat performance of the 1930s disruption.

They scattered to apartments or rented homes around the city.

The row houses were then gutted and completely rebuilt into brick-façade, fully-equipped two bedroom "town houses" with no basement, no garage, no dining room, and postage stamp size front yards and back patios. Each sold for about $50,000 in December 1974.

Most working class residents remaining in Tenleytown—or middle class residents with modest means—are the long-time owners whose mortgages have been paid off. And as the inevitability of death and higher taxes removes them from these homes, they are replaced by buyers or renters whose monthly payments are so large that they must have very adequate incomes.

Beginning in the 1960s, the number of young families with children decreased in the area. More houses were being kept or bought by older couples and childless adults. As the local school population dwindled, children—most of them black—from overcrowded schools elsewhere in the District were transferred to the relatively uncrowded elementary, junior high, and senior high schools in the Tenley area.

By the 1970s whites were in the minority in the junior and senior high schools in the area, although elementary schools generally maintained white majorities. By 1977, the student population at Wilson High School was 60% black, 20% white, and 20% other—mostly Oriental and Hispanic. Private and parochial schools in the area were full.

Tenleytown has not yet lost its class heterogeneity, although the trend is in the direction of an ever more affluent neighborhood. There are still many older retired people on fixed incomes; and often their houses are inherited by their working class sons and daughters. Many houses are rented by groups of singles.

BEFORE AND AFTER: THE 4800 BLOCK OF 41ST STREET

Top: Blacks lived in these five 1890s row houses on 41st Street until they were evicted in 1973. The residents were related to Fort Reno blacks who were evicted in the 1930s.

Bottom: After thorough renovation, the like-new townhouses, as they are now called, sold for $50,000 each in 1974.

JOSEPH CURRAN FAMILY HOME, 39TH AND ALTON PLACE, BEFORE AND AFTER REMODELING

What was it that made a modest frame bungalow sell for $75,000 in 1978? <u>Location:</u> To live on a quiet, tree-lined street in a relatively crime-free neighborhood, but within walking distance of schools, Wisconsin Avenue stores, buses—and soon, the subway—is to many people the best of all possible urban worlds. And many are willing to pay what might be considered outrageously high prices for the chance to live there.

One effect of the new construction in the Tenley era, both subway and commercial, has been the unification of residents in protests against or in working for change.

(Photos c/o Dr. George Ellis)

Top: 1959 photo by DuFief of Curran house before remodeling.

Right: After roofline and porches were altered, 1960.

The Tenley Citizens Advisory Board, organized in 1974, comprises delegates from nearly a dozen citizens groups, including the Wisconsin Avenue Corridor Committee; the Friendship Citizens Coalition; the Chevy Chase, American University Park, Friendship, North Cleveland Park, and Forest Hills Citizens associations; St. Ann's Church; McLean Gardens; and Citizens for City Living. The Tenley CAB concerns itself with National Capital Planning Commission plans for the area, land use, zoning, traffic, the Metro, the environment, development, and historic preservation.

In the early 1970s the D.C. Recreation Department inaugurated a very popular Summer in the Parks program, bringing various musical programs—including the National Symphony Orchestra—to the Reno recreation area as well as to other parks around the city.

The National Capital Parks also began a series of free outdoor rock music concerts whose popularity was widespread. Unfortunately, the loudness of the electronically-amplified music disturbed neighbors for blocks around, and the sight of hundreds of long-haired teenage rock fans, many drinking wine and beer and smoking marijuana, was not pleasing to many of these same neighbors. The rock concerts have continued regularly, however, for nine summers.

On Sunday afternoons those same fields at Reno are used by local international teams for soccer games. Again, large groups of people—very different from the Saturday night crowd—congregate to enjoy the recreation facilities at Fort Reno.

The one recreational facility missing at Reno was a public swimming pool, planned since 1935. In 1979 a southern wing to Wilson High School was completed that housed an indoor pool for use by the public as well as by students.

TWO TENLEYTOWN LANDMARKS

(1965 photo c/o Rosalie Rinis Miller)

Tenleytown Lives Again

Interest in Tenleytown as a place, and the revival of the name Tenleytown—instead of Friendship or "the upper Wisconsin Avenue area"—was very apparent in the 1970s. The Uptown Citizen, The Washington Post, and (the late) Washington Star have increasingly used the old name. The Tenley-Friendship Library council, formed in 1972, has consistently favored the name Tenley over Friendship.

The year 1974 brought a flurry of student research activity in the area. A University of Maryland graduate class in architecture undertook a study of the projected impact of the subway on Tenleytown, which included a survey of the residential and commercial architecture of the area.

Oral history students at George Washington University interviewed elderly blacks in Washington, including descendants of the Fort Reno community. Classes in urban history at American University and in urban studies at George Washington University concentrated attention on the urban development of the Tenley area.

(1973 photo by Priscilla McNeil)

Top: Frank the Barber—Frank Errigo, whose shop on 41st Street closed in the late 1970s, was one of the most popular businessmen in the area.

Bottom: A committee to Save The Old Red Barn formed in 1976 to repair and preserve this relic on Belt Road near Brandywine. It was built about 1907 by the Grove family.

247

OLD AND NEW POST OFFICES

(1977 photo by Judith Helm)

(1980 photo by Judith Helm)

Top: The above Friendship Post Office branch stood on Wisconsin Avenue near Upton Street from 1940 until 1977. When it opened in 1940, it was called the Tenleytown station; but the name was soon changed to Friendship.

The abandoned Safeway store and parking lot are visible in 1977.

Bottom: The new Friendship Post Office opened in 1980 on the same site.

A group of high school students in Chevy Chase and Tenleytown participated in a 1973 summer work project of local history research and interviews, sponsored by Neighborhood Plannings Councils 2 and 3, the D.C. Bicentennial Commission, and the Mayor's office of Youth Opportunity Services.

The result of that summer's work was a walking tour of Tenleytown (published in The Sentry Post and The Potomac Current), one of Chevy Chase, and one of Cleveland Park. After their 1974 summer research, members of the student group published a booklet called Origins, a collection of essays on various aspects of Chevy Chase history, including the Tenleytown schools.

The 1975-76 version, Origins II, had student-written articles on a variety of Chevy Chase memories and landmarks, and one on "The Civil War in Northwest Washington." Their very visible publications did much to interest local residents—especially the young ones—in the history of the area.

In the summer of 1977 the local NPCs sponsored research by young people into the history of Fort Reno and the Reno community, and presented a Historic Reno Day for the public.

The Tenleytown Bonecrushers football team and the Tenleytown baseball teams are not now in existence; but residents remember seeing in 1972 the T-shirts of the Tenleytown Wineheads, a bowling team of local young men.

The Friendship name has remained popular, too, along Wisconsin Avenue from Newark Street (the Friendship Flower, Barber, Camera, and Jewelers shops) to Upton (Friendship Post Office), to Brandywine (Friendship Animal Hospital), to Fessenden (Friendship Delicatessen), to Ingomar

"THE REST," BUILT EARLY 1800s: 4343 39TH STREET

(1974 photo by John Russo)

(Friendship Dental Laboratory), to beyond the District Line (Friendship Savings and Loan). The Friendship Terrace apartment house for the elderly is at 4201 Butterworth Place.

The radio and TV stations, located as they are in Tenleytown, joined in the local history activities in their own way. WRC radio, on Nebraska Avenue, had a morning disc jockey named Jack Harris who talked about his students from the "Tenleytown Time Tone Training Institute" who would announce the time to rush-hour commuters in the spring of 1975. WASH-FM and WMAL-TV have featured short programs on the history of Tenleytown.

Anticipating the American Bicentennial heightened awareness of the history of the area, and produced large, new National Park Service signs at Fort Reno and Fort Bayard. St. Columba's Episcopal Church erected a sign commemorating its centennial in 1974. And St. Ann's Roman Catholic parish, which had its 100th anniversary 'way back in 1969, erected a new, modern sign in 1975.

"The Highlands" (Sidwell Friends), Pierce Mill, and "Rosedale" (3501 Newark Street) are listed on the National Register of Historic Places. In addition to these three, the Cathedral, Forts Reno and Bayard, and "The Rest" (4343 39th Street) are listed as landmarks of the National Capital.

But, as it has been 50 years since Tenleytown was a place name recognized by most Washingtonians, it will be a long time until it is again universally known as Tenleytown. As Evelyn Kengla recalled in 1974, "I heard a friend on the phone the other day— she was asking the [information] operator for a number, and said, 'It's out in Tenleytown.' I had to laugh—of course the operator wouldn't have any idea what she meant!"

Begun about 1801 by Charles Jones for his sister, Sarah Love. Arianna Jones Bruce Lyles acquired the house in 1835 and lived there until her death in 1888. The 3 1/2-story tower on the east side of the house was a late 19th century addition by the Magruder family. The Cross and Willett families have lovingly cared for "The Rest" in the 20th century. It is the oldest house in Tenleytown.

The blacks of Tenleytown have long had an annual reunion picnic on the first Sunday in August, and that tradition is carried on at a picnic site in Rock Creek Park, even though none of them still lives in Tenleytown. At the picnic the 100 or more people who come play baseball, play cards, enjoy their lunches, take pictures, and reminisce, sometimes fondly, sometimes sadly, about the old days in Tenleytown, the Fort, or at Reno.

As Della Washington recalls, the Tenleytown people "were nice and friendly—everybody was kin, and they helped each other." But, she added, perhaps with a touch of irony, "It's good to see that people are doing better nowadays."

[376] The Evening Star, October 1, 1941, p. A-13

[377] Mount Vernon College Centennial Year Calendar 1975

[378] Roger W. Allen, "A Summary of Twentieth Century Economic Development," RCHS, Vol. 49 (1973-74), p. 541

[379] Tenley-Friendship Library, vertical file "Tenleytown"

[380] Washington Daily News, June 24, 1953

[381] "The Peppermint Set Decides to Stick with Joe's Place," Potomac Magazine, The Washington Post, November 25, 1962, pp. 10-11

[382] Vertical file, "Police," Washingtoniana Room, Martin Luther King Memorial Library

[383] King, 100 Years of Capital Traction, op. cit., p. 81

[384] Information about Friendship Heights acquired mainly from Mark Shoemaker and Dorothy Sheiry Holland

[385] "Citizens Rally Protests Development," Uptown Citizen, November 1972

[386] The Washington Post, September 15, 1974

[387] Geological report prepared for WMATA by Mueser, Rutledge, Wentworth & Johnson consulting engineers, New York, 1973

Epilogue

Because the city of Washington swallowed up Tenleytown, we have to make an effort to remember it, to see it, to celebrate its existence. As Sigmund Freud wrote, "when a village grows into a town . . . the village becomes lost in the town. Memory alone can trace the old features in the new picture, and in fact the old materials or forms have been got rid of and replaced by new ones."

We have to make a special effort, as did the granddaughter in The Little House, to preserve what is precious, to protect the small and old, and occasionally to move again to the country in order to gain a perspective on the city.

We have so far been fortunate that there are still quiet spots and pretty places here in Tenleytown where it is not so difficult to imagine what it was like 100, or even 200, years ago. Will those places still be here in another century or two? Perhaps not. Let us take pictures of them now, and let us record something of our daily lives, so that our great-grandchildren will be able to "remember" Tenleytown in 1981.

BIBLIOGRAPHY

CHS = Columbia Historical Society

GPO = Government Printing Office

GUA = Georgetown University Archives

LC = Library of Congress

MCHS = Montgomery County Historical Society

NA = National Archives

RCHS = Records of the Columbia Historical Society

RG = Record Group

Washingtoniana = Washingtoniana Collection, Martin Luther King
     Memorial Library

Articles, Manuscripts, and Books

"A Real Little Thrums," The Washington Post, February 12, 1899

Albertson, B., Rambling Through Georgetown. 1975

Allen, Roger W., "A Summary of 20th Century Economic Development,"
    RCHS, Vol. 49, 1973-74

American Biographical Directory. Washington: 1908-09

American University Courier, April 1908

Armes, George, Ups and Downs of an Army Officer. Published privately
    in Washington: 1900

Atwood, Albert W., Francis G. Newlands: A Builder of the Nation. The
    Newlands Co.: 1969

Barnard, J.G., A Report on the Defenses of Washington. Washington:
    GPO, 1871

Barnum, Father Francis A., S.J., "The Old Georgetown Villa," 1955.
    Unpublished manuscript in Friendship-Villa Property file, GUA

Bates, Samuel P., History of Pennsylvania Volunteers, Vol. III. Harrisburg:
    B. Singerly, State Printer, 1870

Bathon, Mrs., Column in Washington Times-Herald, May 15, 1938

Benjamin, Marcus, editor, Washington During Wartime. Thirty-Sixth
    Annual Encampment of the Grand Army of the Republic, 1902

The Book of Washington. Sponsored by the Washington Board of Trade, 1930

Boyd, T. H. S., History of Montgomery County, Md., From Its Earliest Settlement in 1650 to 1879. Reprinted Baltimore: Regional Publishing Co., 1968

Boyd's Directory. 1905

Bradley, Gertrude S., Bethesda Not So Old. Gaithersburg: Franklin Press (n.d.)

Brown, Letitia Woods, Free Negroes in the District of Columbia 1790–1846. New York: Oxford University Press, 1972

Bryan, Wilhelmus Bogart, History of the National Capital Vol. I 1790–1814. New York: The MacMillan Co., 1914

Busey, Samuel C., Dr., Pictures of the City of Washington in the Past. Washington: Wm. Ballantyne & Sons, 1898

Catton, Bruce, Mr. Lincoln's Army. Garden City: Doubleday & Co. Inc., 1951

Clark, Eugene and Edythe, The Spirit of Captain John. New York: Carlton Press, Inc., 1970

Cochrane, Rexford C., Measures for Progress: A History of the National Bureau of Standards. U.S. Department of Commerce, 1966

Collins, Bridget M.A., "The Vanishing Breed," Origins, 1975

Cooling, Benjamin Franklin, Symbol, Sword & Shield: Defending Washington During the Civil War. Hamden, Conn.: Archon Books, 1975

Crew, Harvey W., Centennial History of the City of Washington, D.C. Dayton: The United Brethren Publishing House, 1892

Cutlip, Lillian, "Old Tenley House, Built in 1770, to be Opened to the Public," The Washington Herald, June 19, 1932

Dabney, Lillian G., The History of Schools for Negroes in the District of Columbia, 1806–1947. Washington: Catholic University of America Press, 1949

Daly, John, Landmark in Chevy Chase: Story of the Shrine of the Most Blessed Sacrament 1911–1961

D.C. Fire Department, 100 Years of Glory, 1871–1971. D.C. Fire Fighters Assn. Committee on Glory. Washington: Mount Vernon Publishing Co., 1971

D.C. Public Library News, 1949 issue at Tenley-Friendship Library

DeGraffenried, Baron Christophle, Relation du voyage d'Amerique, 1716. In Burgerbibliothek, Bern

deTrobriand, Regis, Four Years With the Army of the Potomac. Translated by George K. Dauchy. Boston: 1889

"Diary of Mrs. Wm. Thornton," August 1814, RCHS, Vol. 19, 1916

Dickson's National Capital Directory. 1888

Downing, Margaret B., "Literary Landmarks," RCHS, Vol. 19, 1916

Downs, Terrence, "Sunset on the Palisades," Potomac: The Washington Post Magazine, February 5, 1978

Downtown Urban Renewal Landmarks, National Capital Planning Commission. Washington: 1970

"Dumblane: A Southern Craftsman Home," The Craftsman, February 1913

Dunbar, Janet, J.M. Barrie: The Man Behind the Image. Boston: Houghton Mifflin Co., 1970

Early, Lt. Gen. Jubal, A Memoir of the Last Year of the War for Independence in the Confederate States of America. Lynchburg: Chas. W. Button, 1867

Evans, Jessie Fant, "Mrs. Parker's Family Is Linked to History of Washington," The Evening Star, June 16, 1950

Fleete, Henry, "A Brief Journal of a Voyage made in the Bark Virginia and Other Parts of the Continent of America," in J. Thomas Scharf, History of Maryland. Baltimore: 1879

French, Roderick S., "Chevy Chase Village in the Context of the National Suburban Movement, 1870-1900," RCHS, Vol. 49, 1973-74

Fry, Gladys Marie, "The Activities of the Freedmen's Aid Societies in the District of Columbia, 1860-1870." M.A. thesis, Howard University, 1954

Gahn, Bessie Wilmarth, Washington's Headquarters at Georgetown. Silver Spring: 1940

Gatchel, Theodore D., Rambling Through Washington. Washington: printed by The Washington Journal, 1932

George Washington Colonial Traveller 1732–1775, edited by John C. Fitzpatrick. One volume in a series of The Complete Diaries of George Washington. Indianapolis: Bobbs-Merrill Co., 1927

Grant, Bruce, American Forts Yesterday and Today. New York: E.P. Dutton & Co., 1965

Gray, C. Harold, "Washington, the Planned City, Is Really a Collection of Old Villages; Small Towns Swallowed as D.C. Grew," The Washington Post, May 30, 1937

Green, Constance M., Washington, Village and Capital 1800–1878, Vol. I, and Washington, Capital City 1879–1950, Vol. II. Princeton University Press, 1962

Guide to and Maps of the National Capital and Vicinity, Including the Fortifications. Engineering Platoon of the Engineer Corps, D.C. National Guard, 1892

Gutheim, Frederick J., The Potomac. New York: Holt, Reinhart & Winston, 1949

Hagner, Alexander B., "Street Nomenclature of Washington City," RCHS, Vol. 7, 1903

Haycock, Robert L., "60 Years of Public Schools of the Dist. of Col., 1885 to 1945," RCHS, Vol. 48-49, 1946-47

Henry, Samuel J., The Old Days with Horse and Hound: Being the Story of the Chevy Chase Hunt, 1892–1916. 1916

Hobbs, Horace, Jr., Pioneers of the Potowmack. Ann Arbor: University Microfilms, Inc., 1961 & 1964

Holland, James G., "A Unique Trip from Tenleytown," Washington Times, July 19, 1903

Holman, Doree Germain, Old Bethesda. 1956

Holmes, Oliver W., "Stagecoach Days in the District of Columbia," RCHS, Vol. 50, 1948-50

Holmes, Oliver W., "Suter's Tavern," RCHS, Vol. 49, 1973-74

Holmes, Wm. Henry, "Stone Implements of the Potomac-Chesapeake Tidewater Province," 15th Annual Report of [Smithsonian] Bureau of Ethnology, 1893–94. Washington: 1897

Howe, Mark DeWolfe, editor, Touched With Fire: Civil War Letters and Diary of Oliver Wendell Holmes, Jr. Cambridge: Harvard University Press, 1946

Huddleson, Sarah M., "Mrs. E.D.E.N. Southworth and Her Cottage," RCHS, Vol. 23, 1919

Hughes, Carolyn Bell, "Homespun: A Nostalgic Look at Alton Place," National Capital Area Realtor, October 1970

Jarvis, Edith Claude, "Old Chevy Chase Village," Montgomery County Story, November 1969

Kennedy, George, "The Rambler," The Evening Star, March 12, 1951

King, LeRoy O., Jr., 100 Years of Capital Traction. Dallas: Taylor Publishing Co., 1972

Landis, Kenesaw M., Segregation in Washington. Chicago: National Committee on Segregation in the Nation's Capital, 1948

"Laying of a Cornerstone of a new Catholic Church at Tennallytown," Georgetown News [1868], Tenleytown file, GUA

Leech, Margaret, Reveille in Washington, 1860–1865. New York: Grosset & Dunlap, 1941

Longyear, John M., "Georgetown [University] During the Civil War," Georgetown Today, 1975

Lowdermilk, Will H., History of Cumberland. 1878. Appendix: "Maj. Gen. Edward Braddock's Orderly Books"

Lukens, Maude D., "Rock Creek Trees, a Civil War Story," American Motorist, January 1931

Lyle, Maria Catherine Nourse, <u>James Nourse and His Descendants</u>. 1897

Lynham, John A., <u>The Chevy Chase Club—A History</u>. 1958

Magruder, C.C., Jr., <u>Colonel Joseph Belt</u>. Washington: Society of Colonial Wars in the District of Columbia (No. 5), 1909

Manakee, Harold R., <u>Maryland in the Civil War</u>. Baltimore: Maryland Historical Society, 1961

Marine, William H., <u>The British Invasion of Maryland, 1812–15</u>. Hatboro, Pa.: Tradition Press, 1965

<u>Maryland Geological Survey</u>, Vol. III. Baltimore: Johns Hopkins Press, 1899

Maryland State Roads Commission, Charles T. LeViness, <u>A History of Roadbuilding in Maryland</u>. Baltimore: 1958

<u>Mayflower's Log</u>, Washington, 1928

McLean, Evalyn Walsh, <u>Father Struck It Rich</u>. Boston: Little, Brown & Co., 1936

Miers, Earl Schenck, editor in chief, <u>Lincoln Day by Day: A Chronology</u>, Vol. III 1861–65. Washington: Lincoln Sesquicentennial Commission, 1960

Miller, Francis Trevelyan, editor in chief, <u>The Photographic History of the Civil War</u>, 1911, Vols. 9 and 10. Reprinted New York: T. Yoseloff, 1957

Mitchell, Mary, <u>Divided Town</u>. Barre, Mass.: Barre Publishers, 1968

Moore, Charles, editor, <u>The Improvement of the Park System of D.C.</u>, Senate Report No. 166, 1902

Mueser, Rutledge, Wentworth & Johnson consulting engineers, geological report prepared for WMATA. New York: 1973

Murdock, Myrtle C., <u>The American's Creed and William Tyler Page</u>. Washington: 1958

"Nannie Chase Recalls: Glimpses of Fabulous Hope Diamond Days," <u>The Sunday Star</u>, October 9, 1955

<u>Nevada: The American Guide Series</u>. Portland: Binfords & Mort, 1957

<u>The Night Side of Washington: An Illustrated Guide Book</u>. 1894 (CHS)

Peter, Grace Dunlop and Joyce D. Southwick, <u>Cleveland Park</u>. Washington: 1958

Peter, Grace Dunlop, "Unpublished Letters of Dolly Madison to Anthony Morris Relating to the Nourse Family of the Highlands," <u>RCHS</u>, Vol. 44–45, 1944

Presbytery of Baltimore, Minutes of the, 1786–1822 (LC)

Presbytery of the District of Columbia, Minutes of the, 1823–1858 (LC)

Proctor, John Clagett, "Joseph Lancaster and the Lancaster Schools," <u>RCHS</u>, Vol. 25, 1923

Proctor, John Clagett, "Tales of Tenleytown," <u>Sunday Star</u>, January 18, 1948

Proctor, John Clagett, <u>Washington and Environs</u>. Written for <u>The Washington Sunday Star</u>, 1928-1949

Proctor, John Clagett, article on "Tenleytown" spelling, <u>The Star</u>, November 10, 1929

<u>The Protest</u> (D.C. Anti-Saloon League), May 1904 (CHS)

"The Rambler," <u>The Star</u>, April 2, 1916

"The Rambler," <u>The Star</u>, December 22, 1912

"The Rambler" (J. Harry Shannon), <u>The Star</u>, January 3, 1915

"The Rambler," "When Water from Little Falls Branch Flowed Into the Aqueduct," <u>The Star</u>, n.d.

"The Rambler" (George Kennedy), <u>The Star</u>, March 12, 1951

Repetti, W.C., "Georgetown University and McLean Gardens," <u>Woodstock Letters</u>, Vol. 84, No. 1, 1955 (GUA)

<u>Report of the D.C. Commissioners</u>. 1937

<u>Reports of the President's Homes Commission</u>. Washington: The President's Homes Commission, 1908

Rinehart, Christie, "Friendship Citizens Pitched In to End 'Good Old Days,'" <u>The Evening Star</u>, March 15, 1955

Rock Creek Church (St. Paul's Parish), <u>Index to Register 1711–1845</u>

Rounds, Elizabeth and Neil Judd, <u>Lost Arrows: The Story of Indians in the District of Columbia</u>. Washington: Cleveland Park Community Library Committee, 1948

Rubincam, Milton, "Christian Heurich and His Mansion," <u>RCHS</u>, 1960-62

<u>Saint Ann's Church</u>, Centennial Book. Hackensack, N.J.: Custombook, Inc., 1969

Saul, John, "Nurseries in the District of Columbia," <u>RCHS</u>, Vol. 10, 1906

Scharf, J. Thomas, <u>History of Maryland</u>. Baltimore: 1879

Scharf, J. Thomas, <u>History of Western Maryland</u>, Vol. I. Baltimore: 1882

Searight, Thomas B., <u>The Old Pike: An Illustrated Narrative of the National Road</u>. Originally published 1894; reprinted by Greentree Press, 1971

"The Sessford Annals," <u>RCHS</u>, Vol. 11, 1908

Shannon, J. Harry, "The Rambler," <u>The Sunday Star</u>, January 3, 1915; see also "Rambler" articles

Shipley, Walton, "I Remember," 1973, published in <u>Origins</u>. Washington: 1975

Shoemaker, Louis P., "Historic Rock Creek," <u>RCHS</u>, Vol. 12, 1908-09

Simmons, George, "Roadside Sketches: Up Near Tenleytown," The Star, August 8, 1891

Simmons, George, "Roadside Sketches: Picturesque Regions North of Georgetown: Tenleytown and Bethesda," The Star, August 15, 1891

Smith, C.B., "Historical Sketch of County Schools," First Report of the Board of Trustees of Public Schools of D.C. 1874–75. Washington: McGill & Witherow, 1876

Smith, Margaret Bayard, The First Forty Years of Washington Society. Originally published 1906; reissue edited by Gaillard Hunt. New York: Frederick Ungar Publishing Co., 1965

Spicer, William A., History of the Ninth and Tenth Regiments, Rhode Island Volunteers. Providence: Snow & Farnham, 1892

Spratt, Zack, "Rock Creek's Bridges," RCHS, 1953–56

"Suburban Washington as a Place of Residence," an illustrated brochure published by Citizens Northwest Suburban Association, 1901

Sylvester, Richard, District of Columbia Police. Washington: Gibson Brothers, 1894

Taggart, Hugh T., "Old Georgetown," RCHS, Vol. 11, 1908

Taggart, Hugh T., "The Presidential Journey in 1800," RCHS, Vol. 3, 1900

"Tenleytown: A Seven-Hilled Citadel of Health," Washington Times, May 26, 1903

Thompson, Noma, Western Gateway to the National Capital [Rockville, Md.]. Washington: Stewart Printing Co., 1949

The Times and Patowmac Packet, GeorgeTown, August 4, 1790

Topham, Washington, "Centre Market and Vicinity," RCHS, Vol. 26, 1924

Townsend, George Alfred, "Houses of Bricks Imported from England," RCHS, Vol. 8, 1904

Townsend, George Alfred, Washington, Outside and Inside. Hartford: Jas. Betts & Co., 1873

Trollope, Frances, Domestic Manners of the Americans. Republished, ed. by Donald Smalley. New York: Alfred A. Knopf, 1949

Vandiver, Frank, Jubal's Raid. New York: McGraw-Hill, 1960

War of the Rebellion: A Compilation of the Official Records of the Union and Confederate Armies. Washington: GPO, 1880–1901, Series I, Vol. 37, Part 2

Washington, City and Capital, American Guide Series. New York: Hastings House, 1937

"Washington in 1890," The Star, January 1, 1891

Wecter, Dixon, The Saga of American Society: A Record of Social Aspiration 1607–1937. New York: Scribner's Sons, 1937

Weller, Michael I., "Comm. Joshua Barney: The Hero of the Battle of Bladensburg," <u>RCHS</u>, Vol. 14, 1911

Whyte, James H., <u>The Uncivil War: Washington During the Reconstruction 1865–78</u>. New York: Twayne Publishers, 1958

<u>The Works of Walt Whitman—Vol. II, The Collected Prose</u>. New York: Funk & Wagnalls, 1948

Williams, William Hazaiah, <u>The Negro in the District of Columbia During Reconstruction</u>. Unpublished M.A. thesis, Howard University, 1924

Williams, Mathilde, <u>A Short History of St. Columba's Church in Washington, D.C.</u> Published by the parish, 1960

Wilson, Mary B., editor, <u>The Story of St. Albans Parish 1854–1929</u>. Washington: St. Albans Parish, 1929

Woodward, Fred E., "A Ramble Along Boundary Stones," <u>RCHS</u>, Vol. 10, 1907

Wyckoff, J. Bernard, <u>Georgetown's Bicentenary</u>. 1951

Unpublished Letters

Harold E. Doyle to D.C. Park and Planning Commission (?), July 1938; in NA, RG 79, Fort Reno acquisition file 55480/683

Alexander W. Heron to Walton E. Shipley, June 16, 1974

Nathan Loughborough to Senate Commission on Roads & Canals, 1829; vertical file, Washingtoniana

Thomas Munroe to George Corbin Washington, 1828; vertical file, Washingtoniana

Margaret Achterkirchen Pillsbury to Judy Helm, September 19, 1973

Cuno H. Rudolph to Congressman (?), February 3, 1926; in NA, RG 79, Fort Reno acquisition file 55480/683

Chris Tenley to Judith Helm, November 20, 1974

Dorothea Thompson to Lula Johnson, undated (circa 1910)

Unsourced Newspaper Articles

"Old Colonial Manor," 1902

Obituary of John E. Chappell, September 1907

"Road of the Presidents," 1915

Article on Senator Patterson's bill "to establish a national military park at Fort Reno, D.C.," undated, in vertical files, Washingtoniana

Unpublished Manuscripts

Thomas Beall of George's Account Book (1802-1811) of John Murdock's estate. LC Manuscript Division

Burrows, Grover G., "Mrs. Harriet America Burrows 1828-1923"

D.C. Medical Society obituary of John W. Chappell, 1938

Johnson, Raymond, "Boyhood Days," 1974; and "Our Home," 1973

Sheiry, Annie F., Friendship Heights scrapbook (MCHS)

Thomson, Annie Ray, "Characteristics and Background of Dr. Anthony M. Ray"

Underwood, Norman, "Some Memories of Old Tenleytown, the Rockville Pike (now Wisconsin) Going Into Georgetown and Having a Branch Going Into Washington, D.C."

Repositories of Documents and Sources

American University Archives: photos

Colorado Historical Society, Denver: Vertical file on Alexander Hunt

Columbia Historical Society: Records; D.C. Masonic Records; numerous photos and glass plates

Daughters of the American Revolution Library

D.C. Recorder of Deeds: Land transfers from 1795 to the present

Eldbrooke United Methodist Church: Early records of West Georgetown Methodist Circuit; church records beginning 1873; official board minutes

Episcopal Diocese of Washington: early records of parishes in District of Columbia

Georgetown University Archives: Tenleytown, McLean Estate, and St. Ann's files

Immaculata Seminary/College: early records, archives

Janney School: records and photos

Library of Congress: photos, newspapers, manuscripts

Maryland Hall of Records, Annapolis: Acts of Assembly; patents for land grants; Chancery Court proceedings

Montgomery County Historical Society: scrapbooks, documents

Montgomery County Records: deeds, Minute Books

Mount Vernon College: photos and historic calendar

National Archives: Records of D.C. Post Office; Fort Reno Acquisition; U.S. Signal Corps; D.C. Censuses, 1790-1880; Civil War records; photos and maps

National Park Service: Fort Reno photos

North Cleveland Park Citizens Association: records

Office of Military History, Reference Branch

Singleton Masonic Lodge, F.A.A.M.: photos, centennial booklet, programs

Smithsonian Collection: D.C. catalog of artifacts

Tenley-Friendship Library: vertical files

Washingtoniana Collection, Martin Luther King Memorial Library: vertical files, photos, maps, newspapers, bound records

Wisconsin Avenue Baptist Church: records, photos, tapes

INDEX

geology, elevation, 2, 3, 22, 29, 41, 62, 97, 242, 243
Georgetown, 1, 9-11, 14, 15, 20, 22-25, 27-30, 35, 38, 39
Georgetown (College) Villa, 36, 57, 74, 78, 143, 171
Gerhard, 136
Gerhardt, 128
Giant grocery, 193, 213
Gildenhorn, 229
Giles, Lt. James, 120-122, 129, 184
Giles, Thomas J., 148
Gilpin, Dr. George, 106, 125
Gloria Point, 13, 80, 86, 120, 150, 152, 179, 182
Glover, Charles C., 101, 163, 167, 168, 204
Goebel, 72, 173, 174, 190
Gore, 179, 196
Gorman, 116, 134, 190, 191, 212
Gott, 129
Gould, 118, 128, 190, 204, 223, 228, 229
Grant Road, 22, 40, 50-51, 78, 79, 118, 125, 155, 182, 183, 204, 205, 210, 240
Grant Road School, 93, 94, 180
"Grassland," 25-27, 78, 87, 95, 169, 207, 226
Graves, 126
"Graveyard Hill," 127, 134
Gray, 176, 243
Grayson, 213, 214
Gregory, 223
grocery stores, supermarkets, 41, 81, 105, 114-116, 187, 191-193, 232
Guthrie, 211

H
Hager, 135
Hamm, 209
Haris, 190
Harper, 189, 209, 211
Harry, 37, 51, 54, 75, 84-86, 109, 110, 115, 117, 134, 191, 194
Harry, J. Bernard, 142
Hawken, Samuel McComas, 129
Hawken, Stafford, 100, 121, 125, 132
Hawkins, 140
Hearst, 208, 213, 214
Hechinger's, 21, 143, 193, 227, 228
Heider, 35, 71, 72, 113, 129, 134, 135, 152, 177, 191, 226
Heinrich, 117, 163
Henderson, 223
Heurich, Christian, 87, 95, 155, 208, 209, 214, 219, 230, 231
Heurich, Karl, 162
Higgins, 223
"Highlands, The," 31, 32, 78, 143-145, 213, 214, 249
Hillcrest Children's Center, 189, 214, 215
Hilltop, The, 208, 209
Hiscox, 181
Hoemiller, 72, 84
Holmes, Oliver Wendell, Jr., 56, 57
Hopkins, 211, 220
horses, 73-75, 82, 95, 96, 101, 117, 120, 134, 135, 183
hospitality, 54, 55, 170, 171
hospitals, military, 53, 57, 59, 63
hotel–see Tennallytown Inn
Houser, 112, 115, 116, 126
houses
    developments, 181, 182, 204, 206-208, 222-224
    estates, 78, 83, 84, 207

farm houses, 71, 81
Fort Reno, 67-70, 147, 200, 202
moving, 150, 151
Tennallytown houses, 75-79, 112, 142, 148, 157, 177, 244-246
Howard Street, 66, 69, 90
Howland, 94
Hughes, 210, 212
Huhn, 72
Hunt, 12, 18, 86, 105, 137, 150
hunting, 135
Hurdle, 12, 13, 62, 71, 109, 117
Hurley, 117, 129, 209, 210, 223

I
ice, 119
Immaculata, 139, 140, 150, 167, 170, 195, 230
Indians, 1-8
    Piscataways, 1, 7
    quarries, 1, 2
    settlements, 1, 9
    trails, 2, 3, 6, 9, 11-14, 25
Ireland, William B., 94, 136, 137
Irvington House, The, 162

J
Jack the Slasher, 86, 104, 105
Janios, 211
Janney School, 180, 181, 185
Jews, 190
Johnson, 77, 110, 123, 134, 136, 152, 153, 155, 157, 163, 189, 209, 223
Johnson's Flowers, 189, 190, 237
Jones, 12, 13, 25, 38, 126, 249
jurisdictions, 6, 7, 10, 15, 86, 98, 102, 106

K
Kengla, 72, 84, 249
Kirby, 178, 223
Kite, Harry and Sam, 101, 177
Kolb, 163
Krobisch, 163, 171

L
Lancaster, Charles C., 110, 144, 158
land grants, 5-9, 13
Lapidus, 209
Larrabee, 128
Law, 104, 120, 209
Lee, 117
Lenhart, 81, 127, 129
Lester, 118
library, 120, 185, 186, 231, 232
Lightfoot, 20, 21, 36, 57, 67, 143, 195, 212, 213
Lincoln, Abraham, 45-47, 53, 61, 63
Lindner, 117
Loeffler, Ernst, 72, 87, 162
Loughborough, 25-27, 33, 39, 40, 169
Loughborough Road, 25-27, 146, 147, 156, 167, 168, 189, 195, 196
Love, 12,
Love, Sarah, 24, 25, 249
Luber, 240
Lugenbeel, 93
Lyles, 24, 35, 39, 55, 78, 144, 249